THE ZONDERVAN 2025 PASTOR'S ANNUAL

An Idea and Resource Book

T. T. Crabtree

For a *FREE* downloadable copy of the book, please visit Zondervan.com/p/zpa2025/.

ZONDERVAN

The Zondervan 2025 Pastor's Annual
Copyright © 1984, 2004, 2024 by Zondervan

Published in Grand Rapids, Michigan, by Zondervan. Zondervan is a registered trademark of The Zondervan Corporation, L.L.C., a wholly owned subsidiary of HarperCollins Christian Publishing, Inc.

Much of the contents of this book was previously published in *The Zondervan 2005 Pastor's Annual.*

Requests for information should be addressed to customercare@harpercollins.com.

Zondervan titles may be purchased in bulk for educational, business, fundraising, or sales promotional use. For information, please email SpecialMarkets@Zondervan.com.

ISBN 978-0-310-15603-1 (softcover)
ISBN 978-0-310-15607-9 (ebook)

Unless otherwise noted, Scripture quotations are taken from the King James Version. Additional translations used are the following: Scripture quotations marked ASV are taken from the American Standard Version. Public domain. • Scripture quotations marked MLB are taken from *The Modern Language Bible—The New Berkeley Version in Modern English,* Revised Version (MLB). Copyright © 1945, 1959, 1969 by Hendrickson Publishers, Inc. • Scripture quotations marked MSG are taken from *THE MESSAGE.* Copyright © 1993, 2002, 2018 by Eugene H. Peterson. Used by permission of NavPress. All rights reserved. Represented by Tyndale House Publishers, Inc. • Scripture quotations marked NASB are taken from the New American Standard Bible®. Copyright © 1960, 1971, 1977, 1995 by The Lockman Foundation. Used by permission. www.Lockman.org. • Scripture quotations marked NIV are taken from The Holy Bible, New International Version®, NIV®. Copyright © 1973, 1978, 1984, 2011 by Biblica, Inc.® Used by permission of Zondervan. All rights reserved worldwide. www.Zondervan.com. The "NIV" and "New International Version" are trademarks registered in the United States Patent and Trademark Office by Biblica, Inc.® • Scripture quotations marked NKJV are taken from the New King James Version®. Copyright © 1982 by Thomas Nelson. Used by permission. All rights reserved. • Scripture quotations marked RSV are taken from the Revised Standard Version of the Bible. Copyright © 1946, 1952, and 1971 by the Division of Christian Education of the National Council of the Churches of Christ in the United States of America. Used by permission. All rights reserved. • Scripture quotations marked TLB are taken from The Living Bible. Copyright © 1971. Used by permission of Tyndale House Publishers, Inc., Carol Stream, Illinois 60188. All rights reserved.

Any internet addresses (websites, blogs, etc.) and telephone numbers in this book are offered as a resource. They are not intended in any way to be or imply an endorsement by Zondervan, nor does Zondervan vouch for the content of these sites and numbers for the life of this book.

All rights reserved. No part of this publication may be reproduced, stored in a retrieval system, or transmitted in any form or by any means—electronic, mechanical, photocopy, recording, or any other—except for brief quotations in printed reviews, without the prior permission of the publisher.

Cover design: Angela Grit
Cover photography: © Goinyk Production / Shutterstock

Printed in the United States of America

24 25 26 27 28 LBC 5 4 3 2 1

CONTENTS

MISCELLANEOUS HELPS

PREFACE

Favorable comments from ministers who serve in many different types of churches suggest that the *Pastor's Annual* provides valuable assistance to many busy pastors as they seek to improve the quality, freshness, and variety of their pulpit ministry. To be of service to fellow pastors in their continuing quest to obey our Lord's command to Peter, "Feed my sheep," is a calling to which I respond with gratitude.

I pray that this issue of the *Pastor's Annual* will be blessed by our Lord in helping each pastor to plan and produce a preaching program that will better meet the spiritual needs of his or her congregation.

This issue contains series of sermons by several contributing authors who have been effective contemporary preachers and successful pastors. Each author is listed with his sermons by date in the section titled "Contributing Authors." I accept responsibility for those sermons not listed there.

This issue of the *Pastor's Annual* is dedicated to the Lord with a prayer that he will bless these efforts to let the Holy Spirit lead pastors in preparing a planned preaching program for the year.

Contributing Authors

Tom S. Brandon	AM	January 5, 12, 19, 26
		February 2
		Messages on the Lord's Supper
		Messages for Children and Young People
		Funeral Meditations
		Weddings
Paul Branstetter	PM	December 3, 10, 17, 24
Mark Brister	PM	October 1, 8, 15, 22, 29
		November 5, 12, 19, 26, 30
		December 7, 14, 21, 28
Harold T. Bryson	PM	April 2, 9, 16, 23, 30
		May 7, 14, 21, 28
		June 4, 11, 18
James E. Carter	AM	March 9, 16, 23, 30
		April 6, 13, 20, 27
		November 2, 9, 16
H. C. Chiles	AM	August 31
Bennie Cole Crabtree		Sentence Sermonettes
T. T. Crabtree	AM	June 8, 15, 22
		July 6, 13, 20, 27
		August 3, 10, 17
		November 30
	PM	December 31
James G. Harris	AM	November 23
W. T. Holland	PM	July 6, 13, 20, 27
		August 3, 10, 17, 24, 31
		September 7, 14, 21, 28
David L. Jenkins	PM	January 1, 8, 15, 22, 29
		February 5, 12, 19, 26
		March 5, 12, 19, 26
		April 6, 13, 20, 27
		May 4, 11, 18, 25
		June 1, 8, 15, 22, 29
J. Estill Jones	PM	October 5, 12, 19, 26
		November 2, 9, 16, 23
Howard S. Kolb	PM	March 9, 16, 23, 30
D. L. Lowrie	AM	September 7, 14, 21, 28
		October 5, 12, 29, 26
Jerold R. McBride	PM	January 5, 12, 19, 26

		February 2, 9, 16, 23
Dale A. McConnell	AM	February 9, 16, 23
		March 2
		December 7, 14, 21, 28
Alton H. McEachern	AM	May 4, 11, 18, 25
		June 1
	PM	March 2
		June 25
R. Trevis Otey	AM	August 24
Chester L. Smith	AM	June 29
Fred M. Wood	PM	July 2, 9, 16, 23, 30
		August 6, 13, 20, 27
		September 3, 10, 17, 24

SUGGESTED PREACHING PROGRAM FOR THE MONTH OF JANUARY

■ Sunday Mornings

The church is the body of Christ through which he lives and continues his redemptive mission. "Let the Church Be the Church" is the suggested theme for five Sunday morning messages on the life and ministry of the church.

■ Sunday Evenings

A series of book studies, "Great Chapters from the Epistles of Paul," is the suggested theme for the evening messages in January.

■ Wednesday Evenings

The book of Psalms was the hymnbook of the Hebrew people. Through the Psalms, God spoke to his people and God's people gave testimony concerning him and often talked with him about their needs. "Let God Bless You through the Psalms" is the suggested theme for a study of thirteen choice psalms.

WEDNESDAY EVENING, JANUARY 1

Title: A Story of Two Men
Text: Psalm 1

Introduction

A study of any portion of God's Word is profitable, for inspired by the Holy Spirit, it is designed to communicate the love and instruction of God to humankind. The Psalms, however, are unique within the Holy Scriptures for a number of reasons, chiefly because of the tender and sensitive way in which many of them reveal the human soul in its quest for God.

Psalm 1 sets forth the character and lifestyle of a righteous person. This "good man" described here does not "freewheel"; that is, he has some rules, some standards by which he lives. He doesn't take his cues from what those about him are doing. Then, by contrast, the "unrighteous man" is also described in the psalm. Consequently, there are both light and darkness, good and evil, cast side by side in this introductory psalm.

I. The righteous man (vv. 1–3).

A. *The psalm opens with a benediction: "Blessed."* The original word translated "blessed" is plural in the Hebrew form: "O the blessedness of the man that walketh not . . ." The blessings of God upon the person who endeavors to follow in God's steps are many and continual.

B. *The righteous person determines to renounce the companionship of evildoers.* This does not mean that he becomes a snob or a Pharisee. He still reacts with godly concern and kindness toward *all* people. His actions are always evangelistic in intent, to the end that he might reflect *God's* goodness in his life.

   1. One's "walk" is the scriptural way of speaking of one's daily life and conduct. It entails *all* of one's relationships during any given day.
   2. The "ungodly" are those who ignore God and hold no respect for nor fear toward him. They claim no responsibility or duty toward him. Indeed, what worthwhile counsel or advice could such a person give?
   3. Note the progression here: Not only does the righteous individual refuse to "walk" in the counsel of the ungodly; neither will he "stand" in the way of sinners.
   4. The progression continues: The posture of sitting denotes decision and resolution. To "sit" with scorners means that one has identified with and cast his lot with them. "Scorners" are those who openly reject God and fling accusations at him.

C. *The positive character of the righteous person is set forth in verses 2–3.* He delights to "meditate" on the law of God, to read it by day and think on it by night.

II. The unrighteous man (vv. 4–6).

A. *The "ungodly" person is he who has consciously and deliberately made his choice to reject God.* As a result, he has become "like the chaff which the wind driveth away." Chaff, the weightless husks of grain, is useless. It is easily wafted in whatever direction the wind may be blowing, and the harvester determines to get rid of it completely.

B. *Because of his total moral irresponsibility, such an individual will not be able to "stand in the judgment."* That is, there will be no appeal for him, no defense on which he can stand. This would suggest that his choice of evil over good was conscious and premeditated.

C. *Furthermore, there will be no place for him "in the congregation of the righteous."* Before the day of judgment, like the "tares" Jesus describes in his parable of the wheat and the tares, this man may have congregated with God's people. He may have "looked" like them and he also may have "spoken their language." But in the judgment, the tares reveal their true nature; God makes the distinction between the righteous and unrighteous and passes judgment.

D. *"The Lord knoweth."* Only God can see into the innermost recesses of the heart and thus is the only one qualified to pass judgment. Because of this, "the way of the ungodly shall perish."

Conclusion

The pattern for the believer to follow is set forth in the lifestyle of the righteous man. "The law of the LORD" was his daily bread, even though, in David's day, the volume of spiritual inspiration was exceedingly small. Today we have God's full revelation in the Scriptures. Yet very few Christians are "Berean" searchers of the Scriptures. Fewer yet have committed very much of it to memory or even meditate on it sufficiently for the Holy Spirit to hide it in their hearts so that he can bring it to their remembrance in times of need. It is possible to claim a "negative Christianity" by not "walking in the counsel of the ungodly." But the positive side must be followed. We must "delight in the law of the LORD."

SUNDAY MORNING, JANUARY 5

Title: The Church's Thankfulness

Text: "Let the peace of God rule in your hearts, to the which also ye are called in one body; and be ye thankful" **(Col. 3:15)**.

Scripture Reading: Colossians 3:12–16

Hymns: "All Hail the Power of Jesus' Name," Perronet
"Great Is Thy Faithfulness," Chisholm
"Count Your Blessings," Oatman

Offertory Prayer: Our Father, we praise you for yourself and thank you for your deeds. We cheerfully give our offerings to you. In Jesus' name. Amen.

Introduction

The resurrected life of the Christian is described in Colossians 3. Hiding in all the wealth of this chapter is a precious nugget of gold. It is found in verse 15: ". . . and be ye thankful."

Of all people on earth, Christians have the most for which to be thankful. Thankfulness is to be a way of life for us.

When we are thankful, we will be especially thankful for three things.

I. We will be thankful for simple things.

What are simple things? The dictionary says that something "simple" is "uncompounded, elementary, plain, and unadorned." The simple things, then, are the things we tend to overlook or to which we grow accustomed. They are things we see every day, yet they truly count. They are the most apparent things, the everyday provisions of life. They are the "bread" kind of things. Jesus gave thanks for bread. Matthew 15:36 says, "And he took the seven loaves and the fishes, and gave thanks."

II. We will be thankful for suffering.

Suffering touches every life at some time. Even today as you read your newspaper, you will likely read of a death somewhere, a fire at someone's house, a death-dealing earthquake somewhere on earth, or a tragedy taking many lives. How do you respond to suffering?

Jesus set the example for us all: "And he took the cup, and gave thanks" (Matt. 26:27). He thanked his heavenly Father for "the cup" of his suffering, for the offering of his body in death and the pouring out of his blood in sacrifice. In other words, he thanked his Father for his suffering, crucifixion, and death. How courageous and heroic that was!

Our way is to complain about the hard things in life. And sometimes the will of God may lead to hardships. It takes love and surrender to say to him, "Thy will be done!" It takes drawing a bigger circle around life and its circumstances to give him thanks.

III. We will be thankful for spiritual things.

We are so rich, not necessarily in material things but in spiritual. Let us be thankful for these riches:

A. *Salvation.* We have experienced spiritual deliverance—past, present, and future. "I thank God through Jesus Christ our Lord. So then with the mind I myself serve the law of God; but with the flesh the law of sin" (Rom. 7:25).

B. *Christian fellowship.* "I thank my God upon every remembrance of you" (Phil. 1:3).

C. *Dynamic Christian faith.* "First, I thank my God through Jesus Christ for you all, that your faith is spoken of throughout the whole world" (Rom. 1:8). This is witnessing faith. This is a church with victorious faith.

D. *Answers to prayer.* "Father, I thank you that you have heard me. I knew that you always hear me" (John 11:41–42 NIV).

Conclusion

What a privilege we have to be thankful! Exercise that privilege daily and as often as needed. This is how God's peace can rule in your heart and how your Christian life can be fully lived. Be thankful!

Sunday Evening, January 5

Title: A Church That Behaves

Text: "Although I hope to come to you soon, I am writing you these instructions so that, if I am delayed, you will know how people ought to conduct themselves in God's household, which is the church of the living God, the pillar and foundation of the truth" **(1 Tim. 3:14–15 NIV)**.

Scripture Reading: 1 Timothy 3:14–15

Introduction

The Hickory Grove Baptist Church of Conway, South Carolina, once made national news. Judge O. A. Rankin ordered the church to reinstate sixteen former members who had been ousted. He said the congregation's vote to oust the sixteen people was "null and void and of no effect." The church, on the other hand, contended that the state had no authority to determine who could be members of it or of any other church. And so the matter was appealed to a higher court.

Apparently beneath it all there was a behavioral problem. A church that behaves does not find itself in such an embarrassing situation. But not all churches always behave. Because the church throughout the ages has been made up of ordinary human beings saved by the grace of God, behavior has always been a problem. For instance, behavior was a problem in the church at Ephesus where Timothy was ministering. In fact, it was such a problem that Paul spells this out in the main purpose of his letter. "I am writing you these instructions so that . . . you will know how people ought to conduct themselves in God's household" (1 Tim. 3:14–15).

In this letter, we discover three characteristics of a church that behaves.

I. A church that behaves provides teaching of sound doctrine for its members (1 Tim. 1:7; 4:1–6).

The Living Bible reads, "As I said when I left for Macedonia, please stay there in Ephesus and try to stop the men who are teaching such wrong doctrine. Put an end to their myths and fables, and their idea of being saved by finding favor with an endless chain of angels leading up to God—wild ideas that stir up questions and arguments instead of helping people accept God's plan of faith" (1:3–4). Paul "urged" (NIV) Timothy to remain in Ephesus for the express purpose of providing sound teaching for the church.

A. *Through confrontation with heresy.* "Try to stop the men who are teaching such wrong doctrine. Put an end to their myths" (v. 3 TLB). As distasteful as it is, sometimes the only way to counter bad theology is through open confrontation. Some people respond to no other approach.

B. *Through affirmation of truth (4:1–6).* Here Paul encourages Christians to affirm the truth. If confrontation is effective in countering heresy, affirmation is even more effective in establishing the truth. The negative may sometimes be necessary, but the positive is welcome at all times.

    Verse 1 asserts that man can become either an instrument of the supreme good or the supreme evil. As human beings, we are faced with the eternal choice—to whom are we going to give our lives, God or God's enemy?

The Christian affirmation is found in verse 4. This is a good pattern to follow. Rather than feeling obligated to confront and refute, point by point, every false doctrine, we will do better to affirm with joy and enthusiasm the truths of God.

A church that behaves provides sound teaching for its members. Such a church is aware that belief determines behavior.

II. A church that behaves follows scriptural qualifications for its leaders (3:1–13).

First Timothy 3:1–13 outlines scriptural qualifications for church leaders. A church that does not follow scriptural qualifications for its pastor, ministers, and deacons soon finds itself in trouble and with discord. It develops all kinds of behavioral problems. A church cannot be too careful in following scriptural qualifications for its leaders. For both pastors and deacons these qualifications are "ideal goals" given to bring out the best in us. No one has ever *perfectly* embodied these qualifications.

A. *In its choice of a pastor (vv. 1–7).* In verses 2–7 Paul lists no fewer than fifteen qualifications for a pastor. I think it noteworthy that one qualification not found on this list is that the pastor must be perfect. The same is true of deacons.

B. *In its ordination of its deacons (vv. 8–12).* Paul lists in 1 Timothy 3:8–12 the qualifications to be followed in selecting deacons. In some ways it is more important that a church be careful to follow scriptural qualifications in its ordination of deacons than in its choice of a pastor. Pastors are called from church to church, but deacons often spend a lifetime in the church that ordained them. A great deal of unchristian behavior in churches would be avoided if churches would be careful to follow scriptural qualifications for its leaders.

III. A church that behaves affords a practical demonstration of its concern (5:1–8, 17–20).

A church that behaves cares about people. No one has to ask if it cares for people. Its lifestyle and mission are in themselves a practical demonstration of its concern. Paul mentions four groups toward which the church demonstrates its concern.

A. *Older adults (vv. 1–2).* "Rebuke not an elder . . ." I think it significant that older adults are first on Paul's list of those for whom we are to show concern. It is a tragedy that some are prone to think that simply because a person is old, he is no longer in control of his senses, his opinion is of no value, and his feelings are not worth considering. We must show affection and respect to senior adults. An elderly man is to be treated like a father and an elderly woman like a mother.

B. *Young people (vv. 1–2).* Rather than criticizing youth, a church that behaves expresses its concern for youth by providing programs and personnel, buildings and budgets, time and effort.

C. *Widows (v. 3).* Paul mentions "widows who are really in need" (NIV)—that is, widows who are truly dependent, left all alone. But compassionate concern is not limited to them. Christian concern should be expressed to all who are left alone by death, be they widows or widowers.

D. *Pastors (ministers).* The Living Bible reads, "Pastors who do their work well should be paid well and should be highly appreciated, especially those who work hard at both preaching and teaching. For the Scriptures say, 'Never tie up the mouth of an ox when it is treading out the grain—let him eat as he goes along!' And in another place, 'Those who work deserve their pay!' Don't listen to complaints against the pastor unless there are two or three witnesses to accuse him. If he has really sinned, then he should be rebuked in front of the whole church so that no one else will follow his example" (vv. 17–20).

   All ministers have is their reputation. Their ability to function in their profession is dependent on their good name. Paul says that unless two or three witnesses are willing to be named, to go to court, and to run the risk of a libel suit, don't listen to their accusations against a person's character (v. 19). On the other hand, if the person is guilty of serious wrong, he or she should be dealt with firmly and yet redemptively (v. 20).

Conclusion

I'd rather see a sermon than hear one any day;
I'd rather one would walk with me than merely tell the way.
The eye's a better pupil and more willing than the ear;
Fine counsel is confusing, but example's always clear.
The best of all the preachers are the men who live their creeds,
For to see good put in action is what everybody needs.

—*Edgar Guest*

Wednesday Evening, January 8

Title: The Lord's Ultimate Victory
Text: Psalm 2

Introduction

Three types of messianic psalms can be found in the Psalter. There are the "directly messianic," which contain a total prophecy about Christ and relate to him alone (such as Psalms 22, 45, 72, and 110). There are the "typically messianic," which refer to some historical situation concerning an earthly king who is a type of Christ. And there are psalms that contain a mixture of the first two types.

I. Bitter opposition from the Lord's enemies (vv. 1–3)

A. *David expresses both wonder and amazement that the nations would dare to defy God.* "Rage" means to stir up riots; "imagine," to plot or calculate to discredit God and his people; "vain thing," that which is futile and empty of meaning.

B. *Satan is committed to opposing God, his servants, and his work in the earth.* He leads an organized opposition composed of rulers and kingdoms that are hostile to God and righteousness. They "counsel together," or take their stand against God.

C. *Historically, verse 3 reflects the attitude of David's enemies toward his subjection of them.* They rebelled in an attempt to shake off the unwelcome yoke of Israel from their necks, even though David had not dealt more harshly with his opponents than necessary. His wars were defensive, designed to protect the land God had promised Israel through Abraham. This is a picture of an unbeliever's resistance toward God, who desires to be "Lord" of his or her life.

II. Calm assurance in the face of opposition (vv. 4–6).

A. *David presents the Lord as being "amused" at the foolish actions of his enemies, but it is the amusement of contempt.* It is the picture of calm and majestic dignity. We must not forget another scene, however, in which Jesus "beheld the city [Jerusalem], and wept over it" (Luke 19:41).

B. *When God's hour comes (the Day of the Lord), he will blaze forth in righteous anger.* Ultimately he will "vex" or "terrify" his enemies when his patience is exhausted.

C. *In verse 6 David is restating poetically what the prophet Nathan had declared to him (2 Sam. 7:5–17) concerning his anointed kingship.* It symbolizes the eternal kingship of our Lord Jesus Christ.

III. The divine promise to the Lord's anointed (vv. 7–9).

A. *Verse 7 is a poetical restatement of 2 Samuel 7:14.* Through Nathan, God had "issued a decree" to David. David *was* God's son, who was begotten or raised up for his mission and anointed by Samuel. "This day have *I* begotten you." The "I" is emphatic, which means, "It is not you who inaugurated this very special relationship; *I* did." (See John 3:16.)

B. *Verse 8 projects historically God's promise to David that the heathen nations that surrounded Israel would be subservient to him.* John 17 is Jesus' prayer for his own. He "asked" for those who were to become his.

C. *In verse 9 we see the ease with which the Savior will shatter his opposition at the end of time.* Martin Luther made a spiritual application in regard to our "wills" at conversion: "For he slays our will in order to establish his own will in us. He puts to death the flesh and its lusts in order to make alive in us the Spirit and the things that he desires."

IV. An exhortation to submit to the Son of God as Lord (vv. 10–12).

A. *David now expresses his own feelings.* He has no desire to see people suffer; nor does he gloat over the destruction of his foes. He merely expresses in strong terms the certainty of God's victory. He addresses the leaders (kings and judges), for their attitudes will influence the attitudes of the people.

B. *"Serve the* LORD *with fear" (v. 11) suggests not fright, but reverence, awe, and humility.* "Rejoice with trembling" suggests the shouts of adoration that characterized the jubilation of the people when their King appeared.

C. *"Kiss the Son" (v. 12) depicts reconciliation.* The appeal of love has gone forth. The sinful heart has felt the impact of God's searching love.

Conclusion

"Blessed are all they that put their trust in him" (v. 12). One's faith may be as slender as a spider's thread; but if it is real, one is "blessed" of God. He honors any genuine faith expressed toward him.

SUNDAY MORNING, JANUARY 12

Title: The Church's Faith Life

Text: "Lord, . . . grant unto thy servants, that with all boldness they may speak thy word" **(Acts 4:29)**.

Scripture Reading: Acts 4:23–30

Hymns: "Blessed Be the Name," Wesley
"Faith Is the Victory," Yates
"My Faith Has Found a Resting Place," Edmunds

Offertory Prayer: Dear heavenly Father, thank you for the privilege of giving our gifts to you. May your name be honored as we give our tithes and offerings to your church for use in the world. In Jesus' name. Amen.

Introduction

One of the first prayers of the early church was to be granted confidence to speak God's Word. This is something we desperately need—confidence in God; and such confidence in him will produce confidence in ourselves.

Without confidence we are afraid—afraid to live, die, serve, pray, or witness. With confidence we are bold and fearless. We can do all things through Christ; we can live for Christ with authority! The church needs the kind of faith life that makes it powerful in the world.

There are four areas of confidence that will strengthen you to face whatever confronts you. There are four things you can trust God for.

I. You can trust God's grace.

A. *You can trust God's grace to save.* Salvation is by grace through faith (Eph. 2:8–10). God's grace provides salvation from self, sin, and Satan.

B. *You can trust God's grace to show you who you are.* You say, "Who am I?" The answer is wonderful! You are no longer under condemnation; you are a forgiven sinner; you are a child of God. According to Galatians 4:6–7, you are born of the Spirit and led by the Spirit. You are no longer a slave but a son. You are in God's family, an heir of God and a joint-heir with Christ. How glorious!

II. You can trust God's providence.

If this is not true, then life has little meaning.

A. *You can trust God's certainty of purpose.* Isaiah 46:8–11 teaches this. The Bible says that it is God who is working all things together (Rom. 8:28).

B. *You can trust his supply for every need.* Philippians 4:19–20 affirms that God is the source of our supply! The writer of these words, Paul, a prisoner of Rome, is trusting the Lord to supply his needs. And he rejoices and tells others to rejoice.

Matthew 6:30–33 emphasizes the truth that you can trust the heavenly Father to meet your needs.

George Mueller's life is a living testimony of God's provisions for him and the thousands of orphans he cared for during his lifetime. He fed the orphans out of God's hand. Mueller's faith was so dominant that he rested calmly in the divine assurance that God's hand would deliver a bountiful supply when the moment of need arrived, no matter how great that need. He and worry parted forever. Though he was concerned, he never fretted at delay in receiving answers to his requests.

We too can trust the Lord to supply our needs!

III. You can trust God's Word.

A. *You can trust God that he has revealed his Word.* Second Timothy 3:16–17 says: "All scripture is given by inspiration of God, and is profitable for doctrine, for reproof, for correction, for instruction in righteousness: that the man of God may be perfect, thoroughly furnished unto all good works." He who authored the Word is still making his Word personally known to us so that we may know his thoughts.

B. *You can trust God to prosper his Word.* Isaiah 55:11 says, "So is my word that goes out from my mouth: It will not return to me empty, but will accomplish what I desire and achieve the purpose for which I sent it"

(NIV). If God sent it, he will prosper it! This is true in your life, your family, his church, and among his people in his work.

C. *You can trust the power of God's Word.* Hebrews 4:12, "For the word of God is quick, and powerful, and sharper than any twoedged sword, piercing even to the dividing asunder of soul and spirit, and of the joints and marrow, and is a discerner of the thoughts and intents of the heart." God's Word is sure and fully dependable. God's Word has wisdom for every need.

IV. You can trust God's Spirit.

A. *You can trust God's Spirit to make certain the indwelling presence of God in your life.* He makes real the presence of Christ in us (Eph. 3:17).

B. *You can trust God's Spirit to renew you spiritually.* Isaiah 40:28–31 gloriously affirms this.

C. *You can trust God's Spirit to endue you with spiritual power to do God's will.* This is the teaching of Acts 1:8.

John 4:13–14 proclaims the Holy Spirit as the overflowing spring in a believer's life. His presence and power are available to all Christians and are never exhausted.

Conclusion

Four things build the church's faith life: God's grace, God's providence, God's Word, and God's Spirit. How rich is the church and how powerful, as he grants us his confidence.

Sunday Evening, January 12

Title: Be a Courageous Christian!

Text: "You then, my son, be strong in the grace that is in Christ Jesus. And the things you have heard me say in the presence of many witnesses entrust to reliable men who will also be qualified to teach others. Endure hardship with us like a good soldier of Christ Jesus" **(2 Tim. 2:1–3 NIV).**

Scripture Reading: 2 Timothy 2:1–7

Introduction

The last recorded words of Paul are found in 2 Timothy. Paul had been arrested. His trial had proceeded far enough that he knew there was no hope of escape. While waiting in the Roman prison for the "time of his departure," he wrote these words to Timothy, a trusted friend.

Those were not easy days in which to be a Christian. To dare to be a leader in a local church was to volunteer to be a martyr. So Paul wrote this letter to his "son" for the purpose of encouraging Timothy to be a courageous Christian in the most trying times the church had ever faced.

Today, North American Christians may not be nailed to crosses or thrown to wild animals or burned as torches, but the need is as great now as it was in Paul's day for us to be courageous.

I. A courageous Christian has a heritage to enjoy (2 Tim. 1:3–6).

Paul's purpose was to inspire and strengthen Timothy for his task at Ephesus. To keep his courage high and his effort strenuous, Paul reminded Timothy of the heritage that was his to enjoy.

A. *The belief of others in you (vv. 3–5).* Paul reminded Timothy of his own belief and confidence in him. No greater encouragement is ours than to know that someone believes in us. An appeal to honor is effective. The fear that we might let down those who believe in us is a constructive fear. The fact that others believe in us and look up to us is a heritage to enjoy.

B. *A Christian family that supports you (v. 1:5; 3:15).* Paul reminds Timothy of his family tradition. If Timothy failed, not only would he mar his own name, but he would lessen the honor of his family name as well. A Christian family is one of the greatest gifts a person can have.

C. *A calling that requires the best in you (v. 6).* Your calling to be a witness for Christ requires the best that is in you. Be courageous in witnessing.

II. A courageous Christian has a hope to share (1:12).

Verse 12 contains three key words.

A. *Ashamed.* The hope and faith we have in Christ are never a cause of shame but always a truth to share.

B. *Know.* The reason for this hope was Paul's personal knowledge of Jesus Christ. Merely to know Christ was all that Paul needed in order to trust him. The Greek word *oida* ("know") means "fullness of knowledge"—the kind of knowledge that comes from a personal experience with another.

C. *Committed. Paratheke* means "a deposit committed to someone's trust."

III. A courageous Christian has help to offer (2:2; 3:15–4:5).

A. *Winning and discipling others (2:2).* It is not only our privilege to receive the gospel, it is our duty to transmit it. All Christians must look on themselves as links between two generations. Barclay says that the reception of the faith is the privilege of Christians; transmission of the faith is the responsibility of Christians.

A church grows not by addition ("We had four additions last Sunday"), but by multiplication. You lead someone to the Lord and stay with that person until he or she begins to lead others to the Lord.

Ask yourself not "How many spiritual children do I have?" (that is, "How many have I led to Christ?"), but "How many spiritual grandchildren and great-grandchildren do I have?"

B. *Proclaiming Bible truths (3:16–4:5).*
   1. That are addressed to our own needs. "The whole Bible was given to us by inspiration from God and is useful to teach us what is true and to make us realize what is wrong in our lives; it straightens us out and helps us do what is right" (3:16 TLB).
   2. That will equip us to win others (3:17).
   3. That may not always be popular (4:1–5).

IV. A courageous Christian has hurts to avoid (2:14–16, 21–23; 3:1–7; 4:10).

For the courageous Christian to be effective in the service of Christ, he or she must avoid certain hurts. Paul mentions four of them in this letter.

A. *Theological arguments (2:14–16, 23).* There are times when too much talk can be positively dangerous (see vv. 14, 16, 23). The Christian alternative is found in verse 15.

B. *Moral compromise (2:22).* Doesn't it seem quite shocking that Paul would suggest that the young preacher Timothy could be tempted sexually? Some think there are three sexes—men, women, and preachers! Still others think the three sexes are boys, girls, and Christian youth. But Christian young people have the same physical urges as non-Christian young people. And when they fail to "flee youthful lusts," the same emotional and biological consequences are experienced by them as by any other young person.

C. *Social trends (3:1–5).* Paul warns Timothy to avoid the hurt of social trends. He says that as time passes on, social trends will not get better but worse.

D. *Spiritual unfaithfulness (4:10).* The spiritual pilgrimage of Demas is often repeated today.

V. A courageous Christian has a heaven to gain (4:6–8).

Paul wrote these words in the midst of persecution. This was the darkest hour in his life. He was about to be executed for a crime he did not commit. Friends were forsaking him. Yet there is no doubt that the church, though now apparently defeated, would eventually be triumphant. There is no doubt that the second Paul's head would be cut from his body, he would go directly to Christ, whom he loved and served so devotedly.

Conclusion

Across the ages Paul still challenges us to be courageous Christians. "Be strong in the grace that is in Christ Jesus. . . . Endure hardship with us like a good soldier of Christ Jesus" (2:1, 3 NIV). Be a courageous Christian!

Wednesday Evening, January 15

Title: The Glory of God's Law
Text: Psalm 19

Introduction

Psalm 19 is an eloquent song of praise to the glory of God's law, even though David begins his song of praise in adoration toward God solely in terms of his glory in nature. Yet the most prominent feature of this psalm is praise to God for his law (his Word). It can be divided into three sections: first, "the glory of the Lawgiver" (vv. 1–6); second, "the glory of the law and its applications" (vv. 7–10); and third, "the law in relation to man" (vv. 11–14).

I. The glory of the Lawgiver (vv. 1–6).

A. *The "heavens" are plural, describing their variety: the watery heavens with their clouds, the aerial heavens with their calms and storms, the solar heavens with the glories of the day, and the starry heavens with the marvels of the night.* "Are declaring" is the proper tense of the verb, indicating that every moment God's existence, power, and goodness are being sounded abroad by the heavenly heralds that shine upon us.

B. *"Day and night" pour forth their information.* Each day is poetically envisioned as informing the next day of God's glory; thus, the Good News has been uninterrupted through the ages. "Speech" and "language" indicate that in all languages, humans have recognized in some way the glory of God in nature (see Rom. 1:20).

C. *The bridegroom went forth to meet the bride in glorious apparel, and he was preceded by a blaze of torchlight (v. 5).* He scattered the darkness before him. The sun is also likened in this verse to a well-conditioned athlete preparing to run a race.

D. *In verse 6 David dwells on the vastness of the course traversed by the sun.* He was writing poetically and symbolically in light of the understanding of his day.

II. The glory of the law (vv. 7–10).

A. *Whatever proceeds from God is perfect in its kind (v. 7).* That salvation is not by the law is not the fault of the law, but of humans, who cannot keep the law. The law itself "is holy, and the commandment holy, and just, and good" (Rom. 7:12). "Converting the soul"—the law, by instructing people, restores them from moral blindness to the light that is theirs by nature (Rom. 1:19) and, as a further consequence, in many cases restores them from sin to righteousness as they repent of their sins and receive Christ as Savior.

B. *God's precepts "rejoice the heart" of the godly (v. 8).* They are not felt as stern commands, but as gracious revelations of what God wants people to do for their own good.

C. *Every law of God, every commandment, is designed for humankind's benefit, both physically and spiritually (v. 9).* There are no capricious laws of God that have no bearing for good on the person expected to keep them.

D. *God's law is of far greater good to humans and therefore far more to be desired than any amount of riches (v. 10).* The sweetness of honey indicates the satisfaction God's Word brings to the individual who takes it into himself.

III. The result of keeping God's law (vv. 11–14).

A. *David felt that God's law was a constant source from which he was taught and instructed ("warned" carries this idea more than that of a negative rebuke).* The reward that comes to one who endeavors to abide by God's commandments is incalculable (v. 11).

B. *"Know thyself" is an idealistic challenge, but who can do it?* David felt this exasperation (v. 12), which was made more acute as he studied God's law. He prayed that God would keep him from sins committed unconsciously and in ignorance.

C. *Furthermore, he feared that in times of weakness he would be guilty of committing "presumptuous sins" (v. 13), or willful, intentional, deliberate sins.*

D. *David was concerned that not only what he said, but also what he thought in the depths of his heart, meet with God's approval (v. 14).* And he knew that he could do this only as the Lord was his constant "strength and redeemer."

Conclusion

In summary, the cry of David's soul in this psalm was that he might always recognize the glory of God's law and, as God gave him strength and wisdom, have the determination to apply it daily to every part of his life.

SUNDAY MORNING, JANUARY 19

Title: The Church's Prayer Life

Text: "A prayer of Habakkuk the prophet. . . . LORD, I have heard of your fame; I stand in awe of your deeds, O LORD. Renew them in our day, in our time make them known; in wrath remember mercy" **(Hab. 3:1–2 NIV).**

Scripture Reading: Nehemiah 1:4–11; Acts 1:14; Ephesians 6:18

Hymns: "Revive Us Again," Mackay
"Send a Great Revival," McKinney
"Teach Me to Pray," Reitz

Offertory Prayer: O God, our Father, blessed be your name. We give our offering to you with praise for your provision. May it be used to honor your name. Amen.

Introduction

Prayer is the chain that binds all of today's Scripture passages together. Prayer precedes blessings. Prayer and power in the church go hand in hand.

Habakkuk was a man of prayer who appeared on the scene unannounced. Who he was and of what family or tribe he was born, we are not told. His name is said to mean "ardent embracing" or "wrestling." From his book we understand that he was a man who wrestled with God. He interceded in prayer and stretched out in faith as he sought to rend the heavens and bring down the power of God his people so desperately needed.

The question for us is, how do we pray for power in the church?

I. Pray directly.

Pray like all of those in the Bible prayed. Nehemiah just talked to God. So did Habakkuk. We must remember that if we need power in our lives, we need only ask God for it. If we need help in our family, we must ask him! Let the church simply ask the Lord for his power. James 4:2 says, "You do not have, because you do not ask God" (NIV). Jesus said, "Ask and you will receive" (John 16:24 NIV).

II. Pray submissively.

Pray with a yielded will to the Lord. James 4:6–7 gives the key to God's grace—humbling ourselves before him. Second Chronicles 7:14 clearly spells out the importance of brokenness before God in God's word to Solomon. King David humbled himself in such prayer when he said, "The sacrifices of God are a broken spirit: a broken and a contrite heart, O God, thou wilt not despise" (Ps. 51:17). We must deal with the pride in our lives.

III. Pray earnestly.

James 5:16 says, "The effectual fervent prayer of a righteous man availeth much." *Fervent* means "stretched out." A track star stretches out all he has to run his race. This picture can be applied to fervent prayer. Praying earnestly means hungering and thirsting after righteousness (Matt. 5:6). It is reflected in the cry of the psalmist, "O God, thou art my God; early will I seek thee" (Ps. 63:1).

God gives spiritual power when his church reaches the point of desperation in prayer. Stephen Olford says, "We will never have revival until God has brought the church of Jesus Christ to a point of desperation. As long as Christian people can trust in religious organizations, material wealth, popular preaching, and promotional drives, there will never be revival."

IV. Pray boldly.

Confident praying is found in 1 John 5:14–15. Bold praying is faith praying, and it is faith praying because it is according to God's will. Mark 11:24 says, "Whatever you ask for in prayer, believe that you have received it, and it will be yours" (NIV).

V. Pray unitedly.

Acts 1:14 says, "These all continued with one accord in prayer and supplication." God honors unity in prayer. "If two of you shall agree on earth as touching any thing that they shall ask, it shall be done for them of my Father which is in heaven" (Matt. 18:19). Division and dissension block revival.

VI. Pray militantly.

Ephesians 6:10–18 describes militant prayer. After all, prayer is spiritual warfare, because Satan fights the church. We are to wear our spiritual armor and pull down spiritual strongholds (2 Cor. 10:4–5).

VII. Pray continually.

Paul instructed his readers on how to pray: "Pray in the Spirit on all occasions with all kinds of prayers and requests. With this in mind, be alert and always keep on praying for all the saints" (Eph. 6:18 NIV). Furthermore, he admonished, "Pray without ceasing" (1 Thess. 5:17). Likewise, Jesus taught, "Men ought always to pray, and not to faint" (Luke 18:1).

VIII. Pray thankfully.

The spirit of the church is to be thanksgiving. Paul wrote, "Do not be anxious about anything, but in everything, by prayer and petition, with thanksgiving, present your requests to God. And the peace of God, which transcends all understanding, will guard your hearts and your minds in Christ Jesus" (Phil. 4:6–7 NIV).

IX. Pray responsively.

Jesus, speaking to the church in Revelation 3:20, said, "Behold, I stand at the door, and knock: if any man hear my voice, and open the door, I will come in to him, and will sup with him, and he with me." Jesus is standing outside the church waiting for someone—even one person—to respond.

Conclusion

A man visited Wales in 1904 to learn the secret of the Welsh revival. Evan Roberts, leaders of the revival, stood to speak and said, "There is no secret. 'Ask and ye shall receive.'"

That is the answer. Revival comes to God's church when his people prevail in prayer.

SUNDAY EVENING, JANUARY 19

Title: The Challenge of the Blessed Hope

Text: ". . . while we wait for the blessed hope—the glorious appearing of our great God and Savior, Jesus Christ" **(Titus 2:13 NIV)**.

Scripture Reading: Titus 2:11–13

Introduction

Believing that Christ was definitely returning in the immediate future, a group of sincere people sold all their earthly possessions, took their children out of school, and retreated to the mountains. As they waited in their white robes, they anticipated being the first to welcome the returning Lord.

You could write the rest of the story. After weeks and months of waiting, they finally came down the mountain disillusioned and in despair. They misinterpreted the challenge of the blessed hope. Christ's return is not a challenge to speculate, but to serve—not to retreat, but to advance. It is a call not to leisure, but to labor.

Through Paul's letter to Titus, the blessed hope of Christ's return confronts us with a threefold challenge. The challenge of the blessed hope is the challenge of:

I. A commission to be fulfilled.

"The reason I left you in Crete was that you might straighten out what was left unfinished and appoint elders in every town, as I directed you" (Titus 1:5 NIV). The blessed hope of Christ's return has always challenged Christians to fulfill his commission. "Left" implies that Titus was left behind intentionally in Crete to do a specific job. Before Paul's departure he told Titus what to do; now he puts it into writing.

A. *To organize.* "The reason I left you in Crete was that you might straighten out what was left unfinished and appoint elders in every town, as I directed you" (Titus 1:5 NIV). Titus's task was to straighten out what was left unfinished. "Straighten out" means that his task was to set things in order. He was to be personally involved in the process, not merely to give orders to others. "What was left unfinished" reveals that several serious defects still needed Titus's attention. The letter indicates a lack of organization.

Knowing that Titus also had the gift of administration, Paul challenged him in the light of the blessed hope to organize the churches for fulfilling their maximum ministry.

B. *To stabilize.* "For there are many rebellious people, mere talkers and deceivers, especially those of the circumcision group. They must be silenced, because they are ruining whole households by teaching things they ought not to teach—and that for the sake of dishonest gain" (vv. 10–11 NIV). The danger of the false teachers was that they were trying to persuade Christians that they needed more than Christ and more than grace in order to be saved. They were intellectuals for whom the gospel was too simple and too good to be true.

These people were unruly. They were like rebellious soldiers who refused to obey their commands. They refused to accept the guidance, doctrine, and control of the church. Their doctrine upset entire households. Truth often makes a person rethink his or her ideas. Christianity does not avoid doubts and questions. Rather, it faces them fairly and squarely. But teaching that ends only in doubts and questionings is bad teaching. Any teaching that disrupts the family is false teaching. The Christian church is always supportive of the family.

C. *To evangelize the world.* "Even one of their own prophets has said, 'Cretans are always liars, evil brutes, lazy gluttons'" (v. 12 NIV).

Now here is a wonderful fact. Knowing this to be true, Paul does not say to Titus, "Leave them alone. They are hopeless." Rather, he says, "They are sinners and everyone knows it. *You go and convert them.*" Few passages demonstrate more clearly the optimism of Paul, who refused to consider anyone hopeless.

II. A conduct to be followed (2:1–9; 3:1–2).

Verses 1 and 2 relate doctrine and deportment, creed and conduct, belief and behavior. The two are inseparable. The blessed hope of Christ's return binds them together.

Seven specific groups are listed.

A. *Senior men.* "Teach the older men to be temperate, worthy of respect, self-controlled, and sound in faith, in love and in endurance" (2:2 NIV).
   1. "Temperate." By this Paul meant that older men should have learned that the pleasures of self-indulgence cost far more than they are worth.
   2. "Worthy of respect." This speaks of the conduct of persons who know they live in the light of eternity.
   3. "Self-controlled." This describes the person who has everything under control.
   4. "Sound in faith." This speaks of the passing of time, making one's faith even stronger.
   5. "Sound in love." This means that love should increase with age.
   6. "Sound in endurance." The passing of time should impart more and more patience.

B. *Senior women.* "Likewise, teach the older women to be reverent in the way they live, not to be slanderers or addicted to much wine, but to teach what is good" (v. 3 NIV). Their behavior and conversation should be lessons for the younger men and women.

C. *Younger women.* "Then they can train the younger women to love their husbands and children, to be self-controlled and pure, to be busy at home, to be kind, and to be subject to their husbands, so that no one will malign the word of God" (vv. 4–5 NIV). The younger women should take seriously their homemaking duties.

D. *Younger men.* "Similarly, encourage the young men to be self-controlled" (v. 6 NIV). Younger men are to be aware of and avoid those things that would destroy their Christian witness.

E. *Christian leaders.* "In everything set them an example by doing what is good. In your teaching show integrity, seriousness and soundness of speech that cannot be condemned, so that those who oppose you may be ashamed because they have nothing bad to say about us" (vv. 7–8 NIV). If the teaching of Christian leaders is to be effective, it must be backed by the witness of their own lives. They must demonstrate all that they teach. Here Paul deals with leaders' motives, manners, and message.

F. *Christian workers.* Paul's instruction for slaves can be applied to all workers. "Teach slaves to be subject to their masters in everything, to try to please them, not to talk back to them, and not to steal from them, but to show that they can be fully trusted, so that in every way they will make the teaching about God our Savior attractive" (vv. 9–10 NIV). The Christian worker is to be obedient, efficient, respectful, honest, and faithful.

G. *Christian citizens.* "Remind the people to be subject to rulers and authorities, to be obedient, to be ready to do whatever is good, to slander no one, to be peaceable and considerate, and to show true humility toward all men" (3:1–2 NIV).

   This passage mentions six qualifications for the good citizen.

   1. He is to respect authority.
   2. He is to carry his own load.
   3. He is to guard his lips.
   4. He is to be gracious.
   5. He is to be kind.
   6. He is to be gentle.

III. A contrast to be finished (vv. 3–8).

In verses 3–4 Paul reminds us of the contrast between our lives before and after salvation. In verses 5–7 Paul tells us how we are saved. In verse 8 he challenges us to finish the work that was begun in us when we were saved.

Conclusion

Earlier Paul assured the Philippian Christians that "he who began a good work in you will carry it on to completion until the day of Christ Jesus"

(Phil. 1:6 NIV). There is a marked contrast between the "before and after" of salvation. Now we are challenged to carry the contrast that began at salvation to its logical conclusion—Christian maturity.

"And this is my prayer: that your love may abound more and more in knowledge and depth of insight, so that you may be able to discern what is best and may be pure and blameless until the day of Christ" (Phil. 1:9–10 NIV).

WEDNESDAY EVENING, JANUARY 22

Title: The Suffering Messiah
Text: Psalm 22

Introduction

Of all of the psalms dealing with the passion of the Messiah, this is undoubtedly the noblest. It is identified as a messianic psalm clearly because Christ used its opening words in the extremity of his agony on the cross. The psalm falls into two easily identifiable parts.

I. Forsaken by God (vv. 1–21).

A. *Verse 1 contains a pitiful cry for help.* Though persons may have such crushing experiences that they feel God has forsaken them, still none could experience what Jesus did, for no one has had the close relationship with the Father that Jesus had. Jesus' "why" was not so much an attempt to find the deepest reason for his suffering as it was a cry resulting from his ability to comprehend it with his sinless humanity. For Jesus, as the Son of God, knew that he would become sin for humankind (see 2 Cor. 5:21).

B. *After the despair of verses 1–2, there comes hope in the holiness of God (vv. 3–5).* Because of who he is, God could never abandon one who trusts in him.

C. *In verses 6–8 David describes the scornful treatment experienced at the hands of the enemy.* The figure of a "worm" is a reference to utter helplessness and frailty (see Job 25:6; Isa. 41:14). Ridicule from others produces a particular kind of hurt in a person. In verse 7 we see Calvary emerging. The laughing taunts were flung at Jesus first by the priests and leaders and then by the passersby. Verse 8 is vividly reminiscent of the taunts our Lord's crucifiers heaped upon him.

D. *A plea for help to the God who has always been a helper is the essence of verses 9–11.* The pendulum swings back to hope from the pit of despair. Here is an indirect reference to the virgin birth and God's protective care during Christ's infancy (the flight to Egypt).

E. *The enemies of our Lord are likened to the strong bulls from the grassy plains of Bashan, ready to dash this poor victim whom they have encircled (v. 12).*

Escape for him seemed impossible. In verse 13 the figure of speech moves from "bulls" to ravenous wild beasts who are anxious to devour him.

F. *Verses 14–18 provide a graphic picture of our Lord on the cross.* His heart was broken by the rejection of his people. He experienced excruciating physical thirst, and his hands and feet were pierced. Verses 17–18 depict the brutal beating at Pilate's court and the casting of lots for his garments.

G. *The last desperate cry for help comes in verses 19–21.* Even though people have totally rejected Christ, God will not be far off.

II. Delivered by God (vv. 22–31).

A. *Note the difference between the two halves of this psalm.* In the first half, the statements are short, like gasps of distress. Now they are longer, for the speaker is free and delivered from pain. All that is described now is but the fruit of the experience through which the sufferer has passed.

B. *Verses 22–25 express praise to God for this deliverance.* Verse 22 may point to Christ's appearance in his resurrected body to the disciples in the upper room. Only they could comprehend the import of what had happened. Jesus acknowledged the Father's help on the cross after all (v. 24).

C. *The various classes and kinds of people sharing in the blessings are alluded to in verses 26–31.* The "meek" are those who will most consciously respond to the blessings that come as a result of what has happened in this psalm. It is the meek, and those who earnestly seek the Lord, who are recognized. Then, in verse 27, the scope widens to include "all the families of the nations" (NIV). This is the missionary impact of the psalm, which continues through verse 31.

Conclusion

Though God turned away from Jesus momentarily while he was on the cross, the hiding of his face was only temporary. Jesus' cry was heard, and he was comforted. Likewise, God's ear is ever attuned to hear the cry of his people in their times of distress, and he never fails to respond.

SUNDAY MORNING, JANUARY 26

Title: The Church's Witnessing

Text: "He saith unto them, Follow me, and I will make you fishers of men" **(Matt. 4:19)**.

Scripture Reading: Matthew 4:17–22

Hymns: "The Church's One Foundation," Stone

"Rescue the Perishing," Crosby
"Send Me, O Lord, Send Me," Coggins

Offertory Prayer: O God, our Father, we have so much to give! Break open our hearts and remove our selfish, stingy spirits that we might become generous givers to you and to others. In Jesus' name. Amen.

Introduction

Jesus' ten-word command here is important to every Christian: "Follow me, and I will make you fishers of men" (v. 19). It is his constant command to his church. It follows his first command in his earthly ministry—the command to repent (v. 17). Repentance is the first step in the Christian life, but it does not end here. Next is the command to follow Christ and to witness to others.

The pronouns in our text are important: *me, I,* and *you.* Jesus was promising that his person and power in us will result in something different in our lives and in the lives of others.

The verbs are extremely important too. *Follow* is a plural verb. Christ is calling all of us to follow him. It is a decisive action. *Make* means that Christ in us does mighty things through us. Christ makes us soul-winners. Soul-winners are made, not born.

The key is to follow Christ! Following Christ precedes fishing for men. The exciting reality is that every one of us can see this fulfilled in our lives.

The church's witnessing involves four things.

I. A life vision.

Having a life vision means that we turn our life's direction over to Jesus Christ. It means that we think in terms of others, not ourselves. It means that life is more than time; it is eternity. It means following Christ and learning from him. As we do, we learn several things:

A. *We learn his vision (John 4:35; Mark 16:15).*
B. *We learn his wisdom and ways (Matthew 5–7).*
C. *We learn his spirit of compassion, faith, and obedience.*
D. *We learn his prayer power.*
E. *We learn his sacrifice.* He went to the cross in death. He is the grain of wheat that fell into the ground.
F. *We learn his victory in resurrection power!*
G. *We learn his power, the power of the Holy Spirit.*

II. Spiritual responsibility.

Every Christian senses a personal responsibility for winning souls. It is built-in and is prompted by the Holy Spirit. Dr. C. E. Matthews tells of the time he taught intermediate boys in Sunday school. At that time it had not occurred to him that he could win a lost soul. He didn't even know who the lost in his class were.

One day a class member, fourteen years of age, was killed by lightning. Dr. Matthews asked the boy's father, "Are you a Christian?" He replied, "Not a very good one." Then Matthews asked, "Was your son a Christian?" The question startled the father, and he answered, "I don't know. Do you know?" Matthews was startled too and answered, "No, I do not." There they stood, neither knowing whether or not the boy was a Christian. That experience brought C. E. Matthews to consider his spiritual responsibility.

There are six reasons why we know we are responsible.

A. *This is what the Old Testament says (Prov. 11:30; Ezek. 33:7–8).*

B. *We know we are responsible because Christ said so (Matt. 5:13; John 15:5).*

C. *We know we are responsible from Jesus' example (John 1:43; 4:1–54).*

D. *We know we are responsible from the example of New Testament Christians like Andrew, Philip, and Paul.*

E. *We know we are responsible because the cry from hell begs us to be (Luke 16:27–28).*

F. *We know we are responsible because the heavenly Father rewards those who do win souls (Dan. 12:3; Matt. 28:19–20; James 5:19–20).*

III. A dynamic spirit.

A. *A spirit of commitment, as expressed by Jesus in his commitment to baptism.* He identified himself with sinful humans, to die, be buried, and rise from the dead.

B. *A spirit of compassion.* In Matthew 9:36–38, Jesus saw the multitudes and was moved with compassion. This charged his life and controlled him. Compassion in us is God's love in us and through us.

C. *A spirit of cleansing.* Jesus spent his entire ministry teaching, training, and exemplifying how the disciples were to live. Then, on the last night before his crucifixion, he said to them, "You are clean . . ." (John 13:10 NIV). Our spiritual lives are to be clean, with no unconfessed sins. Our personal relationships are to be clean. Our attitudes and activities are to be clean from any negative spirit. We can have power when we are clean.

D. *A spirit of control.* This is not human control or mind control, but Holy Spirit control! Jesus promised the Holy Spirit to empower us to witness (Acts 1:8). We cannot be soul-winners without the work of the Holy Spirit, for he illumines the mind, stirs the heart, and moves the will of the unbeliever. The Holy Spirit indwells our spirits, fills our souls, and controls our bodies if we allow him to do so.

IV. A victorious personal witness.

Jesus Christ will make you a soul-winner! He has made me one and is continuing to do so. Being able to witness to the redeeming grace of God in Christ is a victory every Christian ought to know!

Conclusion

This is what the church needs today—to be witnessing by means of life and lips. The church needs to reach inward and outward at the same time. The words of Jesus are still real for us today. If we follow him, he will make us fishers of men. Will you commit yourself to him and to that goal?

SUNDAY EVENING, JANUARY 26

Title: Pleading the Cause of a Fallen Friend
Text: "I appeal to you for my son Onesimus, who became my son while I was in chains. Formerly he was useless to you, but now he has become useful both to you and to me" **(Philem. 10–11 NIV)**.
Scripture Reading: Philemon 10–21

Introduction

What do you do when a friend falls? Do you drop him? Do you join those who say, "I'm not surprised, because *now* I remember this or that"?

You should say, "Guilty or not, if ever he needed a friend, he does now. He needs not to be stepped on but lifted up and assured that someone cares." Have you ever found yourself pleading the cause of a fallen friend?

This is exactly what Paul was doing in the one-page letter he wrote to Philemon. He was pleading the cause of his fallen friend Onesimus. This seems to be the only Christian thing we can do when a friend falls.

I. The facts involved (Philem. 2, 11; 1 Cor. 10:12).

A. *Guilt is not to be denied.* "Formerly [Onesimus] was useless to you, but now he has become useful both to you and to me" (Philem. 11 NIV).

Pleading the cause of a fallen friend does not mean that we deny his guilt. Quite plainly, Onesimus was guilty! Onesimus was a runaway slave and probably a thief. Onesimus had found his way to Rome to lose himself in the crowds of that great city. Somehow he had come into contact with Paul, and Paul led him to become a Christian.

Neither Onesimus nor Paul denied the guilt. But once the guilty admitted his wrong and accepted Christ's forgiveness, Paul did not hesitate to plead his cause.

B. *As Christians we are to behave as such.* "I pray that you may be active in sharing your faith, so that you will have a full understanding of every good thing we have in Christ" (Philem. 6 NIV).

Christian generosity and charity must have been characteristics of Philemon. Now Paul is asking him to be even more generous.

Christ desires that we be magnanimous and generous toward others, even as he has loved us though we too have done wrong.

C. *We may be the next to fall.* "Wherefore let him that thinketh he standeth take heed lest he fall" (1 Cor. 10:12).

Again and again a fortress has fallen because its defenders thought it impregnable. The acropolis of Sardis was built on a jutting rock that was thought to be impregnable. When Cyrus was attacking the city, he offered a reward to anyone who could find an entrance. A soldier named Hyeroeades was watching one day and saw a soldier in the Sardian army drop his helmet over the wall. He watched him climb down after it and remembered the path. That night he led a group of men up the cliffs by that very path. When they reached the top, they found it unguarded. They entered and captured the city. Life is hazardous; we must be ever on guard lest we fall.

II. The forgiveness sought (Philem. 4–17).

A. *The basis for this forgiveness.* "Therefore, although in Christ I could be bold and order you to do what you ought to do, yet I appeal to you on the basis of love. I then, as Paul—an old man and now also a prisoner of Christ Jesus" (vv. 8–9 NIV).
   1. Their love for Christ (v. 5).
   2. Their Christian treatment of others. "Your love has given me great joy and encouragement, because you, brother, have refreshed the hearts of the saints" (v. 7 NIV).
   3. Their personal relation to you. "So if you consider me a partner, welcome him as you would welcome me. . . . not to mention that you owe me your very self" (vv. 17, 19 NIV).

B. *The kind of forgiveness sought.* "I appeal to you for my son Onesimus, who became my son while I was in chains" (v. 10 NIV).
   1. Forgiveness that forgets the past (v. 11).
   2. Forgiveness that restores in the present (vv. 12, 16).
   3. Forgiveness that builds for the future (vv. 11, 15). Paul makes a pun on Onesimus's name. Onesimus literally means "profitable." Once Onesimus was a useless fellow, but now he is useful. Now he is not only Onesimus by name; he is also Onesimus by nature.

III. The faith expressed (Philem. 18–25).

Wherever there is forgiveness there is faith, for faith is the foundation on which forgiveness is built.

A. *In the fallen (that he will not fall again) (vv. 18–19).*

B. *In those he has wronged (that they will forgive).* "Confident of your obedience, I write to you, knowing that you will do even more than I ask" (v. 21 NIV).

C. *In God (that he will grant grace to both) (v. 25).* There are times when, having done all that we can, we must place our faith in the goodness of God's grace. We must believe that his grace is sufficient and that he will grant his grace to both the offended and the offender. After we have pled the cause of a fallen friend, only the grace of God can so move in the human heart as to bring forgiveness and restoration.

Conclusion

Ignatius has written about the wonderful pastor at Ephesus. It may well be that Onesimus had become that pastor of Ephesus. If this is so, and I hope it is, then it shows what redemptive effect "pleading the cause of a fallen friend" can have.

Remember that Christians are not perfect, they are just forgiven. And as forgiven, they are to be forgiving.

Wednesday Evening, January 29

Title: The Good Shepherd
Text: Psalm 23

Introduction

In all of the Old Testament, there is probably not a portion of Scripture more familiar or more deeply loved than Psalm 23. Its simple and positive message has challenged, supported, and encouraged God's people throughout the ages.

I. The identity of the Shepherd (v. 1).

There is continuity in his role. "The Lord *is,*" without interruption, the Shepherd of his sheep. To his disciples, Jesus said, "Surely I am with you *always,* to the very end of the age" (Matt. 28:20 NIV). David adds the personal touch in his relationship with God with the pronoun "my," which was somewhat rare in the Old Testament.

II. The Shepherd's provision for his sheep (vv. 2–3).

We are not always sufficiently wise to stop long enough to recognize our innermost needs, so the Shepherd "makes" us lie down. And when we do, he always refreshes us with the supply of our needs. He then revives us.

III. The Shepherd's identity with his sheep (v. 4).

For many people this is the focal point of the psalm, for into their lives some great sorrow has come, and with the crushing experience there has come a new awareness of the continual presence of God with his own. The valleys are inevitable in human experience, and physical death is only *one* valley. Because of the awareness of God's nearness, we "walk through" the valley; we won't be there forever! Our comfort is in the presence of the

Shepherd's "rod," with which he fends off our enemies, and his "staff," which symbolizes support.

IV. The Shepherd's vindication of his sheep (v. 5).

Dealing with one's enemies is perhaps one of the most difficult challenges for anyone, and particularly with those who are members of God's family. The Old Testament concept of "an eye for an eye, and a tooth for a tooth" is often reflected in the Psalms (we call them "imprecatory psalms"). Yet Jesus introduced a new attitude God's people are to have toward their enemies. We are to love them, pray for them, and do good (actively) to them. The spiritual intimacy one has with the Lord is described in the Old Testament customs of anointing an honored guest with oil (an expensive perfume or ointment) and of filling one's cup to overflowing as an indication of unlimited hospitality.

V. The "rear guard" provided by the Shepherd (v. 6).

"Goodness and mercy" are God's "rear guards" who follow his people.

VI. Eternal fellowship with the Shepherd is promised (v. 6).

The doctrine of eternity is beautifully and simply revealed here: "And I will dwell in the house of the LORD for ever." Heaven and the afterlife were vague truths to the Old Testament saints. The New Testament provides marvelous clarity to this truth. Paul said that to be absent from the body is to be present with the Lord (2 Cor. 5:8). And our Lord Jesus assured his disciples that he was going away to prepare a place for them, that where he was, there they might be also (John 14:2–3).

Conclusion

Psalm 23 is not actually messianic—that is, it was not written to describe end-time events concerning the coming Messiah. Nonetheless, it *does* relate beautifully to the nature of our Lord Jesus. Jesus referred to himself as "the good shepherd." He often used the figure of the shepherd and the sheep in his teachings, highlighting this concept in his parable of the one lost sheep (Luke 15:4–7). So we can thank God for the preservation of this thrilling and delightful psalm.

SUGGESTED PREACHING PROGRAM FOR THE MONTH OF FEBRUARY

■ Sunday Mornings

Complete the series "Let the Church Be the Church" on the first Sunday of the month. Then begin a series with a strong evangelistic emphasis called "God's Provisions for Our Salvation."

■ Sunday Evenings

Use the theme "The Major Message of the Epistles" for Sunday evenings in February.

■ Wednesday Evenings

Continue the series "Let God Bless You through the Psalms," messages based on some of the choice hymns from the Hebrew hymnbook.

SUNDAY MORNING, FEBRUARY 2

Title: The Church's Motivation

Text: "He called ten of his servants and gave them ten minas. 'Put this money to work,' he said, 'until I come back.'" **(Luke 19:13 NIV)**.

Scripture Reading: Luke 19:11–27

Hymns: "Praise Him! Praise Him!" Crosby
"Glorious Is Thy Name," McKinney
"Stand Up, Stand Up for Jesus," Duffield

Offertory Prayer: Thank you, dear Father, for the commitment of your Son to redeeming lost humanity. Grant that we may truly commit ourselves to you and to all that you would have us be for your glory. In Jesus' name. Amen.

Introduction

Now is a good time to consider this question: What are we to do until Jesus comes?

The book of Revelation gives a prophetic vision of the church in heaven. It will be transported and assembled there at Jesus' coming for his people. There believers will worship Christ in his victory.

But what are we to do in the meantime? Jesus, in Luke 19:13 (KJV), says, "Occupy till I come." And in Matthew 24:14 he says, "This gospel of the kingdom shall be preached in all the world for a witness unto all nations; and then shall the end come." At his ascension, recorded in Acts 1:7–8, he adds, "It is not for you to know the times or the seasons, which the Father hath put in his own power. But ye shall receive power, after that the Holy Ghost is come upon you: and ye shall be witnesses unto me both in Jerusalem, and in all Judaea, and in Samaria, and unto the uttermost part of the earth."

"Occupy till I come." The word *occupy* means "to carry on a business." So Jesus is telling us to carry on his business until he comes. The verb tells us these things about his business: (1) It is an imperative business. The verb is a command. (2) It is a practical business. It deals with pragmatic matters. (3) It is personal business. It emphasizes personal responsibility. The command may be translated, "You occupy yourselves."

Three things in this parable motivate us to do Christ's business until he comes to take us to heaven.

I. Motivation of opportunity.

A nobleman gave ten minas to ten servants. They were to invest their money by using it for business purposes to gain more minas. They were doing his business, fulfilling their opportunity to invest.

Jesus is the nobleman; believers are his servants; and the minas represent what Christ has given us to invest. It is not money in this case; it is his gospel, his teachings, and his Spirit. We "occupy" with these until he comes.

To each one of us has been given Christ's "mina" as our opportunity for investment. It is the greatest "business" investment in all the world—telling others about Jesus Christ. The dividends returned are beyond computation. One bushel of wheat may yield thirty, forty, or fifty bushels. One life that is living and sharing Christ can experience a 30, 60, or 100 percent increase, plus know that these spiritual investments are forever!

Let us occupy! Do Christ's business! Tell the world! Tell our community! Train ourselves to do so! Occupy till he comes.

II. Motivation of accountability.

In Luke 19:15 the nobleman called for an accounting of each one. We too will have to answer: What have we done with what Christ has given us? One man made full use and gained ten minas. One man made partial use and gained five minas. One man made no use of his mina and had no gain. He did not spend it; he just kept it and wrapped it up in a piece of cloth.

We are like that in our Christian lives. Some make full use and multiply many times. Some make partial use and multiply less. Some make no use of their lives and nothing positive happens. They hide their "light" from others (Matt. 5:15–16), and God is not glorified.

We need to remember that there is an accounting time for us as Christians, when Jesus will judge us as to how we "occupied" ourselves. Just as in this parable there is a time of judgment and rewards, there is also the judgment seat of Christ. Second Corinthians 5:10 speaks of it. First Corinthians 3:13 identifies it as the judgment of our work, our occupying, our service, our witnessing, and how we lived the Christian life. Romans

14:10–12 teaches that we will give account of ourselves to God. This is powerful motivation!

III. Motivation of devotion.

The third servant had the wrong attitude and was not in fellowship with the king. He was self-centered and lacking in devotion. The first two were devoted, obedient, and loyal to their master. Nothing motivates us like response to Christ's love. His love constrains us! We occupy until he comes primarily because we are devoted to Jesus. We love him; we know him; we commit ourselves to him!

What about our devotion to Christ, our living Savior and coming Lord, who says, "Occupy till I come"? Can we sing:

> Am I a soldier of the cross,
> A foll'wer of the Lamb;
> And shall I fear to own his cause
> Or blush to speak his name?

Conclusion

A young American visited Valley Forge a few years ago when the wind-chill factor was sixty degrees below zero. He stood there recalling George Washington and the Colonial army in that bitter winter more than two hundred years ago. He thought of their devotion to their cause. With tears streaming down his face, knowing he could not show that kind of commitment to his country, he stood there in tender commitment to Christ. This is what it means to "occupy till I come." I call you to that kind of response.

SUNDAY EVENING, FEBRUARY 2

Title: The Superiority of Christ
Text: "So he became as much superior to the angels as the name he has inherited is superior to theirs" **(Heb. 1:4 NIV)**.
Scripture Reading: Hebrews 1:1–4

Introduction

Like a great concert organist, the writer of the epistle to the Hebrews reaches the climax of his theme. He pulls out the great stops of glory and honor, which reverberate with the unquestionable superiority of Christ. The writer announces that because Christ is supreme, it doesn't really matter whether Jerusalem remains or falls or whether the temple stands or is destroyed. The superiority of Christ assures the readers of the letter that their faith is not tied to a place or to a practice, but to a person—Jesus Christ, "the exact representation" of God himself.

Again and again the theme that recurs in this letter is "the superiority of Christ." Because of the superiority of Christ we have:

I. A Christ to exalt.

The thrust of the first ten chapters of Hebrews is that because of the superiority of Christ, we have a Christ to exalt. Two facts are given to support this:

A. *Christ is God's perfect revelation to humankind (Heb. 1:1–3).* Ever since that dark day when humans turned from God and chose to disobey him, God has been calling them back home. The psalmist tells us that "the heavens declare the glory of God; the skies proclaim the work of his hands" (Ps. 19:1 NIV). This is general revelation.

   The writer of Hebrews says the truth that came through the prophets was fragmentary. Each prophet had understood and expressed a fragment of God's truth. None had understood the whole. But with Jesus the situation was different. Jesus was not a fragment of the truth—he was the total truth. In Christ, God revealed himself to humans. This is what "exact representation of his being" means (Heb. 1:3 NIV).

B. *Christ is superior to all others.*
   1. The prophets (v. 1). Christ is superior to them because their revelation was partial; his was complete. Theirs was verbal; his was visual as well.
   2. The angels (vv. 4–8). Jesus is superior to all angelic beings. He is God's perfect revelation, and thus we have a *Christ* to exalt—not angels, not prophets, but Christ!
   3. Moses (3:3–6). To the Jews, no one occupied a higher place of distinction than Moses. But Christ is superior even to him.
   4. The priesthood (5:1). Under the old agreement the priests stood before the altar day after day offering sacrifices that could never take away sins. But Christ gave himself to God for our sins as one sacrifice for all time and then sat down in the place of highest honor at God's right hand.

      Only the superiority of Christ could bring about such a complete and final cleansing of sin. And because of the effectual sacrifice of Jesus, Paul affirms that "God also hath highly exalted him, and given him a name which is above every name" (Phil. 2:9).

II. A faith to exercise (Heb. 11:1).

Now that the author has established that because of Christ's superiority we have a Christ to exalt, he turns to the faith in Christ we are to exercise. Faith is trust that leads not simply to intellectual belief but to total commitment. The difference between life and death is faith or the absence of it. The writer does not define faith. He demonstrates faith in action through his roll call of the heroes of the faith (11:4–10, 17).

III. The heritage to honor (12:1–2).

The roll call of faith reminds us of the rich heritage that is ours. We dare not fail the past generations of the faithful who have handed the torch of truth to us. We have a heritage to honor.

A. *There are witnesses who watch us (v. 1).* The superiority of Christ reminds us that we have a heritage to honor—a heritage made possible by Christ.

B. *There are obstacles that would defeat us (v. 1).* If we are encircled by all the greatness of the past, we are also encircled by the obstacles of the present. No one can reach greatness when he or she is weighted down. Habits, pleasures, self-indulgences, or associations may hold us back and defeat us.

C. *There is a goal that challenges us (v. 1).* Jesus himself is our goal. We are to fix our eyes on the one who endured the cross for us and press on until we reach him (v. 2).

IV. A life to live (Hebrews 12–13)

A superior Christ demands a superior life.

A. *A life of divine discipleship (12:5–8).* There are many ways in which we may look at the disciplines God sends us. We must accept them as expressions of God's love.

B. *A life of Christian deportment.*

1. "Try to stay out of all quarrels and seek to live a clean and holy life, for one who is not holy will not see the Lord" (12:14 TLB).
2. "Watch out that no one becomes involved in sexual sin or becomes careless about God as Esau did: he traded his rights as the oldest son for a single meal. And afterwards, when he wanted those rights back again, it was too late, even though he wept bitter tears of repentance. So remember, and be careful" (12:16–17 TLB).
3. "Honor your marriage and its vows, and be pure; for God will surely punish all those who are immoral or commit adultery" (13:4 TLB).

Conclusion

Dr. S. D. Gordon tells of an elderly Christian woman whose age began to tell on her memory. She had once known much of the Bible by heart. Eventually only one precious bit stayed with her: "I know whom I have believed, and am persuaded that he is able to keep that which I have committed unto him against that day" (2 Tim. 1:12).

As time went on, part of that verse also slipped its hold, and she would quietly repeat, "That which I have committed unto him." At last, as she hovered on the borderline between this world and the spirit world, her loved ones noticed her lips moving. They bent down to see if she needed anything. She was repeating over and over again to herself the one word of the text, "Him, him, him." She had lost the whole Bible but one word. But she had the whole Bible in that one word.

Because Christ is superior, he is all we need.

WEDNESDAY EVENING, FEBRUARY 5

Title: My Light and My Salvation
Text: Psalm 27

Introduction

Probably no Old Testament character ran the gamut in variety of experiences as David did. From the placid, pastoral life of a shepherd over his father's flocks in Bethlehem to the tumultuous years spent as Israel's militant, conquering king, David experienced practically every emotion and anxiety known to man. Many of these he expressed in the beautiful psalms he wrote.

Psalm 27 is different from most of David's other psalms in that it reflects both confidence and anxiety. Two major sections constitute the psalm, with the last two verses serving as a conclusion.

I. Confidence in the midst of danger (vv. 1–6).

A. *The simple declaration in verse 1 is the most profound truth in the Bible. Light* means more than intellectual insight; it is spiritual perception. *Salvation* means deliverance from every form of evil, a daily deliverance from satanic harassment. "Light" also includes joy, life, and hope. When a person truly takes refuge in God, what can he or she fear?

B. *In verses 2–3 David reflects on past experiences to support his statement in verse 1.* He has found it true repeatedly that his enemies were the ones who experienced ultimate defeat, not he. "To eat up my flesh" is an Aramaic expression meaning "to slander." No matter how great the onslaught against him (a "host"), David would remain confident in God's care.

C. *Verse 4 reveals the roots of David's bold faith.* His one consuming desire was to bask continually in God's presence.

D. *David is confident of the security we have when we place our trust in God (vv. 5–6) and seek out God's close presence and fellowship.* The outcome of such close fellowship is that our enemies will be brought low, yet we will stand with heads uplifted and offer sacrifices to God out of appreciation and gratitude.

II. An anxious plea for help (vv. 7–12).

A. *In verses 7–8 we find the "mood change" in the psalm.* Suddenly the full confidence found in the first six verses is shaken. David seems to have temporarily lost his assurance of being heard and helped. But his faith is not gone; he knows that God can be called upon. We are reminded in verse 8 of the man who said to Jesus, "Lord, I believe; help thou mine unbelief" (Mark 9:24).

B. *David's faith grows timid and fearful; doubts begin to arise in his mind and soul.* Will God hear him when he prays? He pleads that God will not look away from him. Perhaps David's scarlet sin with Bathsheba had returned to haunt him. Satan is a master at dangling our past sins before our faces—sins that have already been confessed to God and forgiven by him.

C. *Because of the frustrations his enemies have caused within his own mind and soul, David feels that he cannot trust his own wisdom for guidance nor insure himself against the shrewdness and subtlety of his enemies.* The "plain path" he seeks and longs for can be provided only by God. He must be shown clearly *God's* way, the pathway of righteousness. Then he will go forward with confidence.

III. The reassurance of faith (vv. 13–14).

A. *The last two verses contain a kind of reminiscence of the first part of the psalm.* David said, "I had fainted, unless I had believed to see the goodness of the LORD" (v. 13). What are some causes of fainting?

1. A bad atmosphere. We often take on the spiritual coloring of those about us.
2. The sight of blood. Many Christians are not "in the fight" today because they are afraid of a little blood-letting.
3. Weakness. A lack of food (not consistently nourished by the Word) can cause it.
4. Chastisement. "My son, despise not thou the chastening of the Lord, nor faint when thou art rebuked of him" (Heb. 12:5).

B. *"Wait on the LORD" reminds us of the way in which God addressed Joshua (Josh. 1:6).* God does not always answer his people instantly. Sometimes the "waiting" is a spiritual therapy needed to strengthen our faith.

These last two verses constitute the conclusion of the psalm.

SUNDAY MORNING, FEBRUARY 9

Title: For Our Iniquities He Was Crushed

Text: "Surely he has borne our griefs and carried our sorrows; yet we esteemed him stricken, smitten by God, and afflicted. But he was wounded for our transgressions, he was bruised for our iniquities; upon him was the chastisement that made us whole, and with his stripes we are healed" **(Isa. 53:4–5 RSV)**.

Scripture Reading: Isaiah 52:13–53:12

Hymns: "Praise Him! Praise Him!" Crosby
"Alas! and Did My Savior Bleed," Watts
"When I Survey the Wondrous Cross," Watts

Offertory Prayer: Father in heaven, we are reminded vividly of the grace of your gift to us in the sacrifice of your Son, Jesus Christ. Help us to let your kind of love for a needy world fill our hearts as we bring tithes and offerings. Help us to give not only of our finances but to give ourselves in service to others. In Jesus Christ's name. Amen.

Introduction

Isaiah's song of "The Travail and Triumph of the Servant" is great preaching—but it is beyond preaching. No literary form can carry it. No oratory can match it. We could use the imagery of a drama. Observe who is on stage. The parts are being played by God, the people, the prophet, and the sufferer. There is magnificent drama as the man no one desires—who is disfigured and marred beyond recognition, who is despised and rejected, who is ugly and lowly—begins to take form as the one who would die for our iniquities and be exalted on the other side of the grave.

The poet can help us. He turns the phrases in such a way that we not only understand the message but also feel its significance. He writes of a highly exalted servant—a servant of Yahweh—who becomes so disfigured that people hide their faces from him. No one wants to even glance in his direction. Yet, even in his infirmity, through quiet strength and integrity, he becomes the ultimate conqueror.

No, neither the preacher nor the playwright, the painter nor the poet can capture it all. What happens in these sixteen sentences of Hebrew poetry cannot be fully analyzed or appreciated, but the experience of which they testify is essential to you and me.

I. There is an important recognition—it is our sin-sickness.

Hear the prophet again: He took up *our* infirmities; he carried *our* sorrows; he was pierced for *our* transgressions; he was crushed for *our* iniquities; it was *our* punishment he received; he was wounded for *us*. You have not heard this poem until to the very depths of your being you recognize that it was *your* sickness and *your* pain and *your* punishment and *your* transgressions and *your* iniquities that did him in. Put *your* life into this play of cursing; paint *your* face into this portrait of alienation; place *your* name in this poem of tragedy.

It is *we* who are ill; it is *we* who need a doctor; it is *we* who need medicine. It is *our* disease, *our* leprosy, *our* isolation, *our* rebellion, *our* alienation, and *our* estrangement that are the focus here. On center stage is *our* sin. At the middle of the painting is *our* sin. All through this poem it is *our* sin.

There is distance between God and us because *we* moved; there is alienation between God and us because *we* rebelled; there is apathy separating us from God because *we* don't care. God "has loved us with an everlasting love," but we have moved away from him; we have rebelled against him; we have been indifferent to him.

We are sick with sin, and often we want to ignore that fact. But to be healed, or delivered, we first have to recognize and acknowledge that we have a problem. We claim that we can control our problem—we can quit drinking anytime we want to; we can quit hitting our children, with either physical or emotional darts, anytime we want to. But until we recognize that we are sick (with such things as feelings of inferiority, dependency, impotence, alienation, or estrangement), we will not get well. We have to admit that the sin is ours. We have gone astray; we have turned from the right way—this is the reality of the situation, and this is what has to be dealt with.

II. There is an impressive redemption—it is his sacrifice.

The prophet's proclamation is clear: *He* took; *he* carried; *he* was crushed; *he* was punished; *he* was slaughtered; *he* was killed; *he* died. We were very sick patients indeed. In our transgressions we experienced infirmity, sorrow, punishment, and wounds. No doctor was capable of dealing with so many malfunctions. Only one doctor could help—the Great Physician.

He diagnosed our problem and called for radical surgery. He gave us a new heart, a new righteousness, and set our lives in a new direction. Now we are alive and well. Our sins have been forgiven.

Because of what this suffering servant did, many have repented of their sins and turned their allegiance to God. How did he do it? I don't know. Why did he do it? Because his love constrained him and so that his love would draw us. How could we see the suffering of such pure innocence and unadulterated love and not turn our hearts and minds and wills, yes, even our very lives to him? That is what Jesus' suffering does, and it is an impressive redemption indeed.

Conclusion

This redemption is offered to you. You can be delivered from your sin. You don't have to be sick anymore. If you remain ill, it is because you want to remain in your sin. The cure for this cancer of the soul is to return to the Creator. The medicine for your spiritually ill heart is the gospel of Jesus Christ. By faith accept God's acceptance of you even in your sin.

Sunday Evening, February 9

Title: The Characteristics and Conduct of a Religion That Works

Text: "Be ye doers of the word, and not hearers only, deceiving your own selves" **(James 1:22)**.

Scripture Reading: James 1:22–27

Introduction

Several couples had been invited to the home of some mutual friends for dinner. After the meal the host took his guests to the garage to show them his "pride and joy," a beautifully restored antique car. The owner had traveled across several states to find missing handles, lights, and other parts. The upholstery had been replaced with the same kind of material the car had when it was new. And a firm that specialized in restoring antique cars had painted it to match the original paintjob. Rebuilding the engine had been the greatest expense. The car was so old that replacement parts were no longer available, so parts had to be custom-made at a machine shop. After three years of labor and great expense, the car had been restored like new. For the entertainment of his guests, the host proudly cranked the engine. It started with the first turn, and the motor hummed smoothly, never missing a stroke.

Then one of the guests said, "We have known you for years, yet we never knew you owned this car, let alone that you had restored it! Why don't you use it—take it out and drive it?"

The host replied, "Oh, I don't want this car to use. I just like to hear the sound of a well-tuned engine."

Many people have a religion like that. It doesn't go anywhere! Their theology is sound enough; their orthodoxy is unquestionable. They have a "well-tuned" faith. But their religion makes no difference in how they act or what they say.

James addresses this problem, contending that ours is to be a religion that works!

I. The characteristics of a religion that works (James 1).

You can determine if a religion works not by analyzing it but by observing it. Certain characteristics easily identify a religion that works.

A. *Joy (v. 2).* If Christianity does not make you happy, it does not make you anything at all! A religion that works has joy even in the face of trials. Why such joy? The reasons are found in verses 3 and 4.

B. *Unwavering faith (vv. 5–8).* In verse 8 "double-minded" does not mean hypocritical; it means fickle—not being able to make up one's mind. Some are like a soldier who likes the uniform, the honor, and the parades. But when he gets on the battlefield and the enemy shoots back, he is not too sure about being a soldier after all. He becomes "double-minded."

C. *Humility (vv. 9–11).* Whether a person is rich or poor, if he has a religion that works, he is characterized by humility. Christianity brings to the poor person a new sense of his own value. Christianity brings to the rich person a new sense of his indebtedness to God. So the rich and the poor humbly rejoice together over the grace of God that has saved them both!

D. *Awareness.* There are two things of which we must be aware:
   1. The source of our temptations (vv. 13–15).
   2. The source of our blessings (vv. 16–17).

   As long as we do not get these confused, ours shall remain a religion that works.

E. *Freedom.*
   1. From petty conflicts (vv. 19–21). The naturalist John Burroughs says that when a hawk is attacked by crows or kingbirds, he does not make a counterattack but soars higher and higher in ever-widening circles until he is so far above them that his tormentors cannot reach him.
   2. From envy (4:1–3, 11). Envy springs from a love for things and hatred of those who have them.

F. *Involvement (1:22–27).* To James real religion lies in the practical involvement of a Christian in service to others. A religion that works visits people in need—in need of comfort, in need of provisions, and in need of Christ. A religion that works makes a person a participant rather than a spectator.

II. The conduct of a religion that works (2:1–5:6).

A religion that works conducts itself in a proper manner. James says six things about the conduct of a religion that works.

A. *It is impartial (2:1–13).* Snobbery is not a childhood disease. Neither is it a problem you will "outgrow." Adults as well as youth are plagued with this malady. James asserts that a religion that works is impartial.

B. *It maintains a balance between faith and works.* A religion that works does just that—it works! In 2:14–26 James is saying, "Practice what you profess."

C. *It controls the tongue (3:1–12).* When you go to see your doctor for a checkup, she immediately does two things. First, she checks your pulse, and then she looks in your mouth. She may ask, "May I see your tongue?" You stick it out as far as you can, and she can judge by looking at it whether you are healthy or ill.

   Christ says to you today, "May I see your tongue?" And as he examines it, he can learn what is in your heart, for "out of the overflow of the heart the mouth speaks" (Matt. 12:34 NIV). He can determine if yours is a religion that works.

D. *It is guided by wisdom (3:13–18).* What is wisdom and how do you determine it? Who is really wise?
   1. Pure. Real wisdom is characterized by purity of morals. People who "step over the line," who smirk at your high standard of

personal morality and your Christian interpretation of love, are not "wise." They will live to see the day when they will wish they had the wisdom that is yours.

2. Peaceable. Not much wisdom is required to create a "stink," for even a skunk can do this. But it takes a person of real wisdom to fill the air with the fragrance of peace.
3. Generous. "Gentle" wisdom is gracious in its interpretation of the actions and words of others. It makes allowances for others.
4. Agreeable. This does not mean that you are to give in on every point or that you are to be easily influenced. Rather, you can be reasoned with, granting to others the right to disagree.
5. Merciful. Wise persons are willing to overlook another's wrong done against them and to grant forgiveness to those who offend, while they themselves are performing every possible act of kindness.
6. Fair to all. Wisdom is no respecter of persons.
7. Unpretentious. Wise persons do not pretend to be what they are not. Rather, always act in your own character, never under a mask.

E. *It is submissive to God's will (4:13–17).*
F. *It treats others fairly (5:1–6).*

Conclusion

Is yours a religion that works—really works? At the end of each day, you should ask yourself, "What have I done today that nobody but a Christian would do?"

Robert Ingersoll, perhaps the most widely known atheist of recent years, had a godly aunt. His aunt Sarah was a devout Bible student and a radiant Christian. One day she received by mail a package from her nephew. It was Ingersoll's most recent book attacking the Bible. On the flyleaf in his own handwriting were these words: "If all Christians lived like Aunt Sarah, perhaps this book would never have been written. Robert G. Ingersoll."

What the world is looking for is not clever sermons or pious words but a religion that works!

Wednesday Evening, February 12

Title: Longing for God
Text: Psalm 42

Introduction

This psalm is marked by deep feeling and rare poetic beauty. All through the psalm there runs a plaintive cry—the deep thirst of the soul for God. The authorship of the psalm is ascribed to "the sons of Korah"; and it is a "maskil," or psalm of instruction. Individuals among the sons of Korah are never mentioned, though we know from the Old Testament references that they were of the tribe of Levi (Num. 16:1; 26:8–11; 1 Chron. 6:22). Apparently they were a guild of singers at the temple (2 Chron. 20:19) and obviously were composers of psalms.

I. The pain of separation from God (vv. 1–5).

A. *The psalmist feels himself separated from God, and it is an inner sense of separation.* God does not seem to answer when he prays; apparently there is some barrier between him and God. It is a feeling that is as strong as or stronger than physical thirst, and he compares the feeling with that of a deer going about in search of water in a dry, barren land.

B. *In verse 2 that which has brought upon the psalmist his wretched feeling becomes apparent.* Something (we do not know what) has happened to keep him from worshiping in the temple, the sanctuary of God, the place of God's presence. This is the feeling Christians have when their prayers seem to go unanswered; indeed, their prayers seem to "bounce back" from a closed-up heaven.

C. *He has completely lost his appetite (v. 3).* "Instead of eating, I weep." Added to this deep pain is the taunt of those who say, "Where is your God?" They are saying this "continually." That is, on every hand, at every turn of the way, somebody is mocking the psalmist's faith because of the inconsistency they see in his life. When a Christian is obviously out of fellowship with the Lord and the church, unbelievers around him or her often have mocking thoughts, whether expressed openly or not.

D. *Then comes memory (v. 4).* The psalmist reflects on some experience of the past. Perhaps he recalls the great festivals in the temple in Jerusalem when he congregated with the "multitude" and enjoyed the incomparable fellowship of the congregation. Corporate worship has rewards all its own. One cannot worship on the lake or on the golf course just as well as he or she can in the assembly of God's people!

E. *In verse 5 the psalmist's spirit addresses his soul, reminding him that God has not abandoned him and challenging him to "hope in God"—to build on him, rest in him, in spite of "feelings."*

II. Assurance begins to return through earnest prayer (vv. 6–11).

A. *The first part of the psalm is largely complaint, and there is still some undercurrent of it here, but the spirit of prayer pervades a bit more prominently.* As a result, a larger measure of assurance is evident (v. 6).

B. *The psalmist may have stood on the banks of the Jordan River, or perhaps some other river or stream, where cataracts are visible.* He watched one wave roll over another; one, as it were, calling to the one succeeding it. It was a vivid picture of his grief and troubles. In verse 8 he begins to sense the truth he knew all along, that God never forsakes his people.

C. *Verses 9–10 contain the prayer this psalmist resolves to make to God.* There is no question about it: God is and will forever remain his "rock"—the firm ground on which his whole life rests.

D. *In the closing statement of the psalm (v. 11), the writer repeats as a refrain the thought expressed in verse 5, and it becomes the emphatic keynote of the psalm.*

Conclusion

Though our human experiences often seem to thrust God far away from us, he never leaves us nor forsakes us.

SUNDAY MORNING, FEBRUARY 16

Title: Christ Receives Sinful People
Text: "For the Son of man came to seek and to save the lost" **(Luke 19:10 RSV)**.
Scripture Reading: Luke 19:1–10
Hymns: "Brethren, We Have Met to Worship," Atkins
"To God Be the Glory," Crosby
"Christ Receiveth Sinful Men," Neumeister
Offertory Prayer: Our heavenly Father, today we rejoice over the fact that our Savior came into this world to rescue us from the waste and ruin of sin. Today we give not only our tithes and offerings, but also we give ourselves in efforts to help others come to know Jesus as the Savior from sin and as the Friend they need for the living of life. Bless the gift of our substance. And bless us as we give ourselves to you. We pray in Jesus' name. Amen.

Introduction

Our God is obviously a big God. He created the world. He flung the stars into place, instructed the mountains to rise, filled the oceans with water and fish, and out of dirt formed man in his own image and breathed into him the breath of life. And still he is about the business of sustaining and redeeming the whole world. As the old song aptly puts it, "He's got the whole world in his hands."

I don't find it hard to believe in a big God. When I look at the majesty of creation I expect a big God. What I want to know is, Does he have time for me? Is he a *personal* God? I know he wants to redeem the whole world, but how about me? Does he have time for this little drop in the bucket?

I. The setting.

Jesus was passing through Jericho on his way to Jerusalem for his royal and triumphal entry into the city. On his mind was the redemption of the whole world, for which he had come. In the previous episode in the gospel of Luke, Jesus had healed blind Bartimaeus. As Jesus arrived in Jericho, Zacchaeus, a tax collector who was short in stature, wanted to see him. Zacchaeus's profession had alienated him from Jewish society in general and the Jewish religious community in particular. For Zacchaeus to collect taxes for Rome was to acknowledge Rome's right to do so, and that necessitated the tacit admission that Caesar was king and not Yahweh.

To make matters worse, the tax collector's profit came from the extra he could extract from citizens beyond what they legally owed. Thus the tax collector was seen not only as a conspirator and a traitor but also as a cheat and a thief.

But Zacchaeus's problems did not end with his social ostracism; he was at odds with himself as well. Life was lonely without friends. And mark these words: life without vital, intimate relationships is absurd and without meaning! Zacchaeus knew it. He knew that he was not who or what he was supposed to be. Luke rarely recorded names, but in this story he did so to make a point. The name *Zacchaeus* meant "pure, innocent, just, righteous"; yet this man had become a corrupt, manipulative, and despicable tax collector. Those with whom he lived did not see him as pure and just, but rather as a cutthroat, cheat, robber, informer, and traitor.

II. The encounter.

But this day someone different was coming to town. Zacchaeus had heard that Jesus was a friend of sinners and that he even ate with them. Just once this little man wanted to be treated like a human being. He wanted to feel love and care and respect and friendship coming to him from another person. Maybe this man could give him some warmth. In an act of desperation, the outcast went to see this friend of sinners—but he faced obstacles. Being a short man, he could not see over the crowds, and they certainly were not going to make room for him. He risked mingling with a crowd of persons who wanted a chance to get even: to taunt him, to push him out of the way, to kick and hit him. He was desperate.

Since Zacchaeus was too short to see over the crowds, he climbed a tree to catch a glimpse of Jesus.

What would happen now? Would Jesus walk by unaware of Zacchaeus's presence and thus unintentionally ignore him? After all, many had overlooked this little man. We know the feeling. What we think or want is often unimportant to everyone but ourselves. Or would Jesus be aware of Zacchaeus's presence in the tree and intentionally ignore him? After all, everybody else was ignoring him on purpose. Sometimes we know that feeling too.

Now was the moment of encounter. Jesus was probably walking with his head down, for on his shoulders was the weight of the world. He was going to Jerusalem to live out his last week. It was about time for him to be betrayed, arrested, deserted, denied, tried, insulted, beaten, sentenced, and executed—in short, it was about time for him to redeem the whole world.

Who would have expected what happened next? Jesus stopped under the tree, looked up, and said, "Zacchaeus." Jesus called him by name! Imagine that! This obviously significant person had called this little man by name as if they were friends—or at least could become friends. Next Jesus instructed Zacchaeus to come down. And then Jesus invited himself to dinner! The Son of God having dinner with this sinner? Preposterous! Crazy! Wonderful! Jesus felt he had to: "I *must* stay at your house today," he said (v. 5 RSV). Jesus couldn't redeem the whole world without saving one person. He knew that. Calling scoundrels such as Zacchaeus was essential to who he was and why he had come. And that is still true. He still calls us by name and has dinner with us sinners.

III. The salvation.

Jesus scandalized pious Jews by accepting the hospitality of a social and religious outcast. He showed that he had courage by boldly and publicly associating with all kinds of people. When it came to the welfare of people, Jesus knew nothing of taboos and protocol. He ate with tax collectors, prostitutes, even religious types.

Zacchaeus was beside himself. This unique man had spoken to him with acceptance and grace and had offered him warmth and worth. Jesus would become Zacchaeus's friend, companion, and savior. Zacchaeus's response was eager and joyous acceptance. But then he did something we don't dare do—he let the joy and excitement of Jesus' friendship get the best of him. Under the impact of unconditional acceptance, a transformation took place in the value of things. Zacchaeus stood up and said excitedly, "Look, Lord! Here and now I give half of my possessions to the poor, and those I have cheated I will pay back four times the amount!" Grace had caused Zacchaeus to far exceed the demands of the law.

Notice that it was after the commitment Zacchaeus made that Jesus said, "Today salvation has come to this house" (v. 9 RSV). Do not let this story end too early. Grace led to commitment. Jesus' openness to Zacchaeus had the effect of bringing Zacchaeus to a new awareness of himself, his possibilities, and his place in life. Salvation is committing yourself to the lordship of Jesus Christ in the best way you know how—no more and no less. Zacchaeus accepted God's acceptance of him.

Conclusion

As Augustine was fond of saying, "He loves each as if there were no other in all the world to love, and he loves all as he loves each." God loves us and calls us by name. He accepts us. We cannot get so despicable that God doesn't desire us. We cannot get so outcast that Jesus does not invite us in. We cannot be so lost that he cannot find us. We cannot be such traitors that he cannot forgive us. We cannot be such scoundrels that he cannot accept us. We cannot be such sinners that he will not come to dinner. That is good news!

Well, what are you waiting for? Come down out of that tree!

Sunday Evening, February 16

Title: Salvation for the Suffering
Text: "Beloved, think it not strange concerning the fiery trial which is to try you, as though some strange thing happened unto you: but rejoice, inasmuch as ye are partakers of Christ's sufferings; that, when his glory shall be revealed, ye may be glad also with exceeding joy" **(1 Peter 4:12–13)**.
Scripture Reading: 1 Peter 4

Introduction

When you are suffering, nothing is more welcome than good news. And the news that Jesus Christ provided salvation for the suffering was indeed good news for the persecuted Christians in Asia Minor. In fact, Peter uses the word *suffering* fifteen times in this letter.

Peter was writing to a young church suffering at the hands of local authorities. The church's trial was, in a real sense, a "fiery trial" (4:12), for every night Christians were being burned. The Devil, "as a roaring lion," was indeed walking about seeking whom he might devour (5:8). Peter encouraged his readers not to think it strange that they had to suffer. And he reminded them that they were not forgotten and that through suffering Christ purchased their salvation.

To encourage the church in a time of persecution, Peter underscored four basic truths about salvation for the suffering.

I. The certainty of salvation (1:3–5).

It isn't difficult to hold on to our assurance as long as all is well. But when the clouds of adversity seem to hide God, we may wonder if God has not forsaken us.

To these persecuted and mistreated believers, Peter says that especially in such trying times they should praise the name of their heavenly Father because of the certainty of salvation that will see them through. He describes this certainty in strong words.

A. *The source of this certainty*—"his abundant mercy." God's mercy is abundant, great, overflowing, immeasurable.
B. *The duration of this certainty*—"unto a lively hope." The New International Version translates this as "a living hope."
C. *The means of this certainty*—Christ's resurrection makes possible our resurrection.
D. *The content of this certainty*—"to an inheritance." An inheritance is a settled and secure possession.
E. *The quality of this certainty.*
    1. "Incorruptible." Incorruptible does mean "imperishable," but it also means "unravaged by any invading army."

2. "Undefiled." Our inheritance is incapable of being defiled.
3. "Fadeth not away"—unfading. The certainty of salvation does not fade with the passing of time.

F. *"Reserved"*—to guard, to keep, to preserve.
G. *"Kept by the power of God"* means that God enables us to face and experience problems, to bear them, to conquer them, and to move on.
H. *"Ready to be revealed."* Our salvation in all of its completeness is as though it were already ours. It is ready right now in heaven for us to claim.

II. The cause of salvation (1:18–19).

It is reassuring when we are suffering to know that we were saved and kept saved not by our own righteousness but by "the precious blood of Christ." There are some things, then, that silver and gold cannot do. There are some tragedies that silver and gold cannot mend. If a heart is aching, silver and gold cannot soothe it. It requires "love divine," the kind of love expressed in the "precious blood of Christ."

What can wash away my sin?
Nothing but the blood of Jesus;
What can make me whole again?
Nothing but the blood of Jesus.

III. The conduct of salvation (chaps. 2–4).

A little boy who had not been feeling well had been naughty all day. When his father came home from work, his mother said, "Jimmy has been a bad boy." Little Jimmy replied, "It's hard to be good when you feel bad!" Most of us who have felt bad know that it *is* hard to be good.

Peter, realizing this to be true, encourages suffering Christians to be good even though they may have every reason to feel bad. He contends that regardless of our suffering, salvation demands a certain kind of conduct. Saved people conduct themselves differently than unsaved people, and circumstances should not alter that conduct.

Some things must be stripped off. The words "laying aside" are descriptive. They describe stripping off one's clothes. Peter lists some of these soiled garments. They are malice, guile, hypocrisy, envy, and evil speaking (2:1). Then he mentions five areas of life in which we are to portray the conduct of salvation.

A. *As citizens (2:13–17).* The view of the New Testament is perfectly logical and just. It holds that a man cannot accept the privileges of the state without also accepting the responsibilities the state demands from him.
B. *As employees (2:18–25).* Peter is saying that even when we are treated unfairly by our "masters," we are to portray the conduct of salvation. Who knows? Through this we may lead a lost employer to Jesus.

C. *As wives (3:1–6).*
D. *As husbands (3:7).*
E. *As church members (3:8–9).* Peter writes that church members are to have unity, compassion, love, pity, and courtesy.

IV. The challenge of salvation (chap. 5).

Peter says, "I exhort," that is, "I challenge you" (v. 1).

A. *A challenge to the pastor (vv. 1–4).* The challenge to "feed the flock of God" includes preaching, teaching, and being an example in serving.
B. *A challenge to youth (vv. 5–8).*
   1. Learn to follow (v. 5).
   2. Practice humility (v. 6).
   3. Trust God (v. 7).
   4. Be on guard against Satan (v. 8).

Conclusion

Missionary Adoniram Judson experienced many hardships trying to reach the lost for Christ. For seven years he suffered hunger and privation. During this time he was put into Ava Prison and for seventeen months was subjected to incredible mistreatment. For the rest of his life he carried scars made by the chains and iron shackles that had cruelly bound him.

Unbroken in spirit, upon his release Judson asked for permission to enter another province where he might resume preaching the gospel. The ruler denied his request, saying, "My people are not fools enough to listen to anything a missionary might say, but I fear they might be impressed by your scars and turn to your religion!"

Suffering need never defeat us. Rather, it can become a platform from which we can better bear testimony of Jesus Christ.

Wednesday Evening, February 19

Title: God Our Refuge and Our Strength
Text: Psalm 46

Introduction

This is another psalm written by "the sons of Korah." Its inscription states, "A song upon Alamoth." *Alamoth* means "soprano," from the Hebrew word *almah,* "virgin." Some believe that *alamoth* signified a temple choir composed of women who sang antiphonally to the "Sheminith," or male choir.

The psalm appears historically to be a praise to God because of the great deliverance that took place in the days of King Hezekiah (701 BC), when Sennacherib's forces were disastrously destroyed after having threatened the city of Jerusalem, and when the omnipotence of the God of Israel was proved as it was on few other occasions.

Martin Luther's hymn "A Mighty Fortress Is Our God" was partly based on this psalm. Psalm 46 breathes the spirit of confidence in the Lord in the midst of grave danger that few other psalms do.

I. A testimony from those who trust in the Lord (vv. 1–3).

A. *Only God is our refuge in the face of calamities of every sort.* The fact that the psalmist says that God is "a very present help in trouble" suggests his presence has been proved. No testimony is as convicting as one that speaks out of the rich reservoir of experience.

B. *Regardless of the severity of the calamity, there will be no fear (v. 2), because the Lord is "our refuge and strength."* The psalmist undergirds his claim by mentioning awesome natural calamities—earthquakes, floods causing mudslides, etc. (vv. 2–3). Even these frightening demonstrations of nature's fury will not cause fear for the one who has confidence in God.

II. God's presence in the dangers of war (vv. 4–7).

A. *The psalmist's natural pride in the Holy City is obvious.* His inference is that the city had a quietness and confidence all its own. He may be comparing the turbulent river mentioned by Isaiah (8:6–8) with the quiet and insignificant streamlet that runs from the fountain of Siloam to the Euphrates or Tigris. It may symbolize the insignificant appearance of the kingdom of God in the eyes of the world (v. 4).

B. *The fact that God's presence is with the seemingly diminutive nation of Israel makes the difference between God's people and the mighty pagan nations that defy God (v. 5).*

C. *The reason God's people can remain unmoved in the midst of world-shaking calamities is because "the* Lord *of hosts is with us" (vv. 6–7).* This is not to be taken as a "good luck charm," however. God demands righteousness of a nation, regardless of who the people are, in order for him to be their "shield and buckler."

III. "Come and see" what the Lord has done (vv. 8–11).

A. *Whereas the psalmist has been speaking in generalities concerning the power of God on behalf of his people, he feels at this point that he must become specific.* Obviously he is referring to a particular occurrence, which serves as a tangible evidence of all that he has claimed for Jehovah.

B. *Verses 9–10 set forth the particulars promised in the preceding verse.* And surely, Sennacherib's humiliating setback furnished colorful evidence of the psalmist's previous claim. Also, a bit of well-taken instruction is included here for those who set themselves in opposition to the Lord of Hosts.

C. *Verse 11 serves almost as a refrain and certainly as a recapitulation of all that has been said before.* The Lord of Hosts *is* with us (note the present tense). He isn't there just in times of crisis; he is there continually.

Conclusion

There are times, of course, when God requires human involvement and instrumentality. But there are other times when we must simply stand back and let God work. It is then that we begin to appreciate a God who is indeed "our refuge and strength."

SUNDAY MORNING, FEBRUARY 23

Title: Birth from Above
Text: "Jesus answered him, 'Truly, truly, I say to you, unless one is born anew, he cannot see the kingdom of God'" **(John 3:3 RSV)**.
Scripture Reading: John 3:1–15
Hymns: "Crown Him with Many Crowns," Bridges
"He Lives," Ackley
"We Have Heard the Joyful Sound," Owens
Offertory Prayer: Our Father and our God, you have given to us and for us your very best in Jesus Christ, your Son. You have given us your Holy Spirit and the fellowship of the church. You have given us the assurance of heaven at the end of our earthly life. Today we give ourselves to you as we come bringing tithes and offerings. Use these gifts to help others come to know your love. We pray in Jesus' name. Amen.

Introduction

There is much drama in the Gospels among various groups of people. The legalistic Pharisees opposed the liberal Sadducees. The intensely nationalistic Zealots despised the politically accommodating Jewish tax collectors. Yet sometimes these diverse groups worked jointly on a project—usually to attack Jesus.

Beyond the conflicts of people groups was the conflict of ideas. Judaism was established. It was the old and traditional way with hundreds of detailed laws. For example, Scripture informed the Jewish religious person to observe the Sabbath and to keep it holy, but that was not good enough for the zealous legalists. In the codified scribal law, the *Mishnah,* rules regarding the Sabbath extended for twenty-four chapters. The argument was about what constituted work. For instance, to tie a knot was work—but what was a knot? Certain knots were illegal, such as a knot on a rope to hold the bucket used to draw water; but some knots were legal, such as on a woman's girdle. So, on the Sabbath, the enterprising Jew would draw his or her water with a bucket attached to a girdle! Jesus came along and thought all of that was silly. He said that if one's ox falls in a ditch on the Sabbath, then he should get it out—after all, the day was designed for humankind's welfare. Jesus was practicing new religion, and the old religious structures couldn't hold it in. If the masses began to follow this young religious fanatic, Judaism would crumble from within.

I. Nicodemus came to Jesus seeking truth.

The Jewish leaders sent one of their best to visit with Jesus. Their envoy was Nicodemus, a man with impeccable credentials. He was a Pharisee, a member of the most select brotherhood in their religion. Upon entry Pharisees vowed to scrupulously keep the entire law. The Pharisees had become the dominant religious body of Judaism during and after the exile because they had preserved the faith in strict adherence to the law. Nicodemus was also a member of the Jewish ruling council, the Sanhedrin. This group was comprised of only seventy members and was the supreme court of their religion. Although their powers were limited somewhat by Roman occupation, they still held extensive powers and were responsible for the religious and moral well-being of the land. Nicodemus was also a teacher of Israel, which meant that he was a trained theologian. Nicodemus came to Jesus by night representing the religious establishment, which was concerned about Jesus' rise in popularity among the populace. It was their privilege and duty to check him out.

The night questioner spoke in the plural—"we." He spoke not only for himself but also for the distinguished religious bodies he represented. His faith, or his diplomatic gesture, was not precise: he referred to Jesus as "a teacher who has come from God" (v. 2 NIV). He saw Jesus only as a teacher, one among many, with no real specialness.

The conversation developed around questions and misunderstandings. Jesus did not always answer the actual question Nicodemus asked but moved the conversation on to a deeper level. This learned teacher of Israel misunderstood at every point, and this prompted Jesus to go into a longer, more detailed explanation.

Jesus clearly told him, "I tell you the truth, no one can see the kingdom of God unless he is born again" (v. 3 NIV). Nicodemus misunderstood the figure, as have we. The same word can mean "again" or "from above." Jesus was talking about supernatural birth, birth that comes from the heavenly Father. Nicodemus was stuck, for he comprehended only one kind of birth. He understood only the earthly, the possible, the temporal, while Jesus was speaking of the heavenly, the actual, the eternal.

Jesus' statement was clear and simple. To enter into the kingdom of God necessitates a radical reorientation of life in which we are born from above. But this shattered Nicodemus's feeling of sufficiency. He thought that he was able on his own to make it to God. If anybody could make it on his own, it would be Nicodemus. Remember, he was a Pharisee. He had endeavored with his entire being to be righteous. He had kept the sacred law with every ounce of energy he possessed. But according to Jesus, that path would lead toward beating one's head against the wall. Nicodemus was a very religious man, but his religion was insufficient.

Not being able to earn his way into God's kingdom by keeping the law, doing good works, practicing religion, and being moral; not being able to think his way in through learning, theology, and philosophy; and not being able to gain entrance because of his own impeccable credentials, Nicodemus then attempted to reduce Jesus' teaching to absurdity: "How can a man be born when he is old? . . . Surely he cannot enter a second time into his mother's womb to be born!" (v. 4 NIV). He misunderstood both who Jesus was and what Jesus had said. He was stuck on the idea of being born physically a second time. But what Jesus really wanted him to do was bow before the heavenly Father's throne. But how?

To answer this question Jesus moved from the analogy of birth to the analogy of breath. The most basic test of whether or not life is present in a human being is whether or not that person is breathing. In both the Hebrew and Greek languages, the same word means breath, wind, and spirit. Jesus was making the point that as a human is born into this world as a mortal, so also a human is born immortal into the heavenly kingdom as a son of God. God, because he wanted to, breathed into man the gift of natural life; and now, again because he wanted to, God breathed into man the gift of eternal life. God does it because it pleases him.

Nicodemus still wanted to know how. His question implied disbelief, and with this question he left the scene. His failure to understand prompted Jesus to continue, but the dialogue became a monologue. Now Jesus occupied center stage—alone.

II. Nicodemus received truth from Jesus.

Jesus began by declaring that he spoke of what he knew. He could speak of birth from above because he had been there; he was the only one who could speak of such things. He is unique. He is supreme. He is preexistent. He is unbegotten. He is one of a kind. And he has come. That little, helpless infant in the cradle in Bethlehem is the preexistent, eternal Word whose hands cradle the whole world. And that is the key! Here is the Good News! No one can be born from above unless the Unbegotten One comes down. He descends so that we can ascend.

Jesus descended, but he also ascended. He began his return to the Father as he was lifted up on a Roman cross. In John's gospel the cross is not Jesus' agony but his glory: "When I am lifted up from the earth, [I] will draw all men to myself" (12:32 NIV). He continued his marvelous ascent when he was raised up from the grave. The final stage of this fantastic story of descent and ascent was when he was lifted up to heaven. And there it is. No one can go up unless Jesus comes down; but because he goes up, he takes us up, and that is what it means to be "born from above." It has happened to me, and it can happen to you. Can you believe it?

Conclusion

Nicodemus left the scene, causing us to wonder, *What did he decide?* Did he decide to quit trying to make it to heaven on his own? Did he decide to allow God to give birth from above?

The question today is not, "What did Nicodemus decide?" but rather, "What are *you* going to decide?" Some of you are hoping good works will cause you to make it. You are a good person. You try to help other people. You're better than most. *You* must be born from above. Some of you are trying religion. You are here every time the door is open, or maybe you're just here on Sunday morning—either way you say, "I've got religion and I've got it made." *You* must be born from above. Some of you figure one way is as good as another and your philosophy keeps you from total surrender to any way. *You* must be born from above.

Indications are that Nicodemus finally understood and accepted the *gift* of eternal life from Jesus. And if Nicodemus had to do it, with all of his impeccable credentials, you can bet that you have to do it too. "Unless a man is born from above he cannot see the kingdom of God" (MLB).

SUNDAY EVENING, FEBRUARY 23

Title: I Challenge You!

Text: "Dear friends, this is now my second letter to you. I have written both of them as reminders to stimulate you to wholesome thinking. I want you to recall the words spoken in the past by the holy prophets and the command given by our Lord and Savior through your apostles" **(2 Peter 3:1–2 NIV)**.

Scripture Reading: 2 Peter 3:1–4

Introduction

The church was being attacked on every front—both without and within. Without was the persecutor of the Roman Empire as Christians were being put to death daily. Within was the false teaching of immoral men who used God's grace as an excuse for sinning.

In his first letter, Peter countered the attack from without. In his second letter, he counters the attack from within. Rather than offering comfort, Peter offers a challenge to the Christians who are threatened by the efforts of those who would sabotage their faith from within.

In our time, when there are still those who would destroy the church from without or sabotage it from within, we hear the words of Peter, "I challenge you!"

I challenge you:

I. To spiritual productivity (2 Peter 1:5–10).

"The more you go on in this way, the more you will grow strong spiritually and become fruitful and useful to our Lord Jesus Christ" (v. 8 TLB). False teachings and immoral lifestyles were threatening to destroy the church. Peter saw in spiritual productivity an effective force in countering the efforts of the enemies of the church.

Edmund Burke said, "All that is essential for the triumph of evil is that good men do nothing." Notice that spiritual productivity begins with the people we are and then moves on to the good we *do*. Peter challenges us to take eight steps to spiritual productivity (vv. 5–7).

A. *"Faith" (v. 5).* Spiritual productivity begins with faith; everything goes back to that.
B. *"Virtue" (v. 5).* Faith must express itself, not in a retreat to a monastery, but in a life that moves forward courageously.
C. *"Knowledge" (v. 5).* This is the knowledge of what to do and when to do it, practical knowledge.
D. *"Temperance" (v. 6).* This means, literally, the ability to take a grip on oneself, to practice self-control.
E. *"Patience" (v. 6).* Cicero defines patience as "the voluntary and daily suffering of hard and difficult things, for the sake of honour and usefulness." It also represents steadfastness.
F. *"Godliness" (v. 6).* This implies real trust in God.
G. *"Brotherly kindness" (v. 7).* To be spiritually productive, we must care enough about others to become involved in meeting their needs.
H. *"Charity" (v. 7).* The first seven steps to spiritual productivity must culminate in charity, or Christian love.

In light of Peter's challenge to spiritual productivity, we must ask ourselves, "What on earth am I doing for heaven's sake?"

Peter says, "Not only do I challenge you to spiritual productivity, but also to doctrinal integrity—for what you believe determines how you live!"

II. To doctrinal integrity (2:1, 18–19).

Peter's stated purpose of this letter is to warn Christians of the destructive effects of certain false teachers who have infiltrated the church.

A. *William Barclay points out four characteristics of a false prophet:*
   1. He is more interested in gaining popularity than in telling the truth.
   2. He is interested in personal gain.
   3. He is undisciplined in his own personal life.
   4. He leads men further away from God rather than closer to him.
B. *Like so many "false prophets" today, they did not try to start their own religious movements but rather infiltrated the local church.* America alone has more than 350 sects and cults, and most of them claim to base their doctrines on the Word of God. The only sure way to maintain doctrinal integrity is by staying true to the Bible.

III. To joyous expectancy (3:1–18).

At the ascension of Christ, the angel said to the disciples, "This same Jesus, which is taken up from you into heaven, shall so come in like manner as ye have seen him go into heaven" (Acts 1:11). From that day until this, the literal, physical return of Christ has been our joyous expectancy.

In the 216 chapters of the New Testament, there are 318 references to the Second Coming, or one out of thirty verses. Twenty-three of the twenty-seven New Testament books refer to this great event. For every prophecy on the first coming of Christ, there are eight on Christ's second coming.

A. *Which some do not share (2 Peter 3:3–4).* The thing about the heretics that most concerned Peter was their denial of the second coming of Jesus.

B. *The delay of its fulfillment is an expression of God's grace (vv. 8–9).* We must view time as God does. With God one day is as a thousand years, and a thousand years are as one day.

C. *Which will be fulfilled (v. 10)!*
   1. Unexpectedly—as a "thief in the night."
   2. Dramatically—"the heavens shall pass away with a great noise . . ."

D. *Which requires preparation (v. 14).* The thing in which Peter is supremely interested is the moral implication of the Second Coming. If these things come, then we must be prepared.

But how can we be found to be "without spot, and blameless"? Only by the cleansing power of Christ's shed blood for our sins.

Conclusion

Would you be found "without spot and blameless" should Christ return today? You can be so through faith in Jesus Christ as God's Son, who died in your place on the cross.

I challenge you to make the most noble, the most courageous, and the wisest decision you will ever make. Make it today.

WEDNESDAY EVENING, FEBRUARY 26

Title: A Psalm of Repentance
Text: Psalm 51

Introduction

An eternal pattern for sinning saints of God who come back into full communion with their Lord is contained in this poignant psalm. Historically, it is the account of David's pathway to restored fellowship with God after his sin with Bathsheba. Many of the constituent elements included in the doctrine of repentance and restoration are found in the text of this haunting psalm.

It can be divided into seven steps that one can take to regain the fellowship with God that was lost because of sin.

I. Sin judged by God (vv. 1–6).

A. *The first petition in the repentant prayer is for pity (vv. 1–2).* David calls for this mercy on the basis of God's lovingkindness, which is his nature of goodness toward all. David knows that he cannot appeal to God's justice. The second petition is a plea to "blot out" his transgressions—expunge them completely from the divine record. "Wash me thoroughly from mine iniquity" is the third petition. "Wash" is a strong word describing the action one would take in scrubbing an exceedingly soiled garment.

B. *Verses 3–4 constitute David's confession: "I acknowledge my transgressions: and my sin is ever before me."* He does not blame anyone or anything else for his sin. He takes full responsibility for what he has done. David's contrition has resolved into confession.

C. *The doctrine of original sin, or the total depravity of man, is revealed in verse 5.* David understood the essential sin nature of man. Therefore, there must be an "inner change," or "truth in the inward parts" (v. 6). The "turning over of a new leaf" would not do.

II. Forgiveness and cleansing through the blood (v. 7).

A. *"Hyssop" (v. 7) was used in the cleansing ritual performed when a person was cured of leprosy.* It made him "ritually clean," and thus he became qualified to worship in the temple. Leprosy was a picture of sin; and as leprosy had to be cleansed before one could participate in corporate worship, so must sin in the individual's life be cleansed by the blood of Christ before that individual can stand in God's presence.

B. *"Wash me"—this cleansing was for the continual state of fellowship between the believer and God (1 John 1:7).*

III. Cleansing (vv. 8–10).

A. *David desires a sense of forgiveness.* Forgiveness is accepted by faith; the "feeling" follows in due time (v. 8).

B. *"Create in me a clean heart" (v. 10).* This is indicative of the new birth. David insists upon a "creative" act of God. Paul reminds us that the individual who is "in Christ" is a "new creature," or creation (2 Cor. 5:17).

C. *"Renew a right spirit within me."* A new and regenerated attitude and personality must be followed in the life of the believer.

IV. Spirit-filled for joy and power (vv. 11–12).

A. *"Cast me not away . . . take not thy holy spirit from me" (v. 11).* The New Testament sheds comforting light on this verse. We know that even though it is possible for us to "grieve" or "quench" the Holy Spirit in our lives, it is impossible for us to eject him. For, upon conversion, we are no longer our own, but we are bought with a price.

B. *"Restore . . . the joy of thy salvation" (v.12).* David had not lost his essential relationship with God as child when he sinned. But he had severed the line of communication and had jeopardized his fellowship with God. Now that he has repented and his sin has been forgiven, he prays that God will give him back that which had been so precious to him—the overflowing joy he had had with God because of his unique relationship with the Lord.

C. *"Uphold me with thy free spirit" (v. 12).* "Free" is best translated "gracious" or "willing." Our God is not reluctant when it comes to dispensing blessings to his people. Once we meet the requirements, we can expect the floodgates of heaven to open.

V. Service (v. 13).

Only when sin is confessed and forgiven in a believer's life is that person able to share his or her faith effectively with unbelievers. Results, in the winning of the lost, are assured.

VI. Worship (vv. 14–17).

David's concern now is that his sin not be the cause of others' sin. This forgiveness and restoration will cause rejoicing. He has come to the realization also that God does not require sacrificing, except that of a broken heart and a contrite spirit.

VII. The restored believer (vv. 18–19).

Only the believer in fellowship with God can experience true concern for others. In short, the forgiven, restored believer is in a position to be an even greater blessing to God, because his or her testimony comes out of the furnace experience.

Suggested Preaching Program for the Month of

March

■ Sunday Mornings

For the first two Sundays of the month, continue the series "God's Provisions for Our Salvation." The weeks preceding Easter provide an appropriate time to preach about the great salvation God has provided for us through the death of Jesus Christ on the cross. Transition into a series of messages with the theme "The Death of Christ and His Victorious Resurrection from the Dead."

■ Sunday Evenings

"Messages from the Book of Ruth" is the suggested theme for a series of topical sermons based on the experiences of Ruth, Naomi, and Boaz.

■ Wednesday Evenings

Continue and complete the series "Let God Bless You through the Psalms."

Sunday Morning, March 2

Title: For God So Loved

Text: "For God so loved the world, that he gave his only begotten Son, that whosoever believeth in him should not perish, but have everlasting life" (**John 3:16**).

Scripture Reading: Romans 5:8

Hymns: "Love Divine, All Loves Excelling," Wesley
"Love Is a Name I Love to Hear," Whitfield
"Love Is the Theme," Fisher

Offertory Prayer: Holy and loving Father, thank you for the supreme expression of your love in the person of Jesus Christ. Thank you for his willingness not only to give his time and energy, but also his blood on a cross that we might experience forgiveness and receive the gift of eternal life. Today we give our tithes and offerings and ourselves into your service that others might come to know your love through him. Amen.

Introduction

The gospel according to John could be called a "Re-Genesis" or "Genesis Revisited." You recall those immortal words that begin the Old Testament: "In the beginning, God . . ." Even casual readers notice the obvious influence when they read John's first phrase: "In the beginning, the Word . . ." Genesis is about creation and the beginning of life, while John focuses on re-creation and the beginning of eternal life.

In the beginning the earth was dark, void, and formless. And the Spirit of God moved. The Lord God said, "Let there be light" and, because God spoke, it was. After six days, after the creation of light, water, land, sky, vegetation, the sun, moon, stars, birds, sea creatures, land creatures, and ultimately humans, God saw all that he had made and declared that it was good—indeed, in delight he said that it was very, very good. Creation, all that is, arose from God's love, enjoyment, and creative energy.

But the lights went out. Again it was dark—this time spiritually and theologically. A catastrophe had happened. The created had willingly rebelled. Free people had preferred darkness. Apparently irreparable damage had been done, and they were without light from on high.

But again God, who is love, moved. Again he said, "Let there be light," and there was light from the *Son* and re-creation (redemption) was made possible.

Now, after recalling humankind's creation and rebellion, hear the text, which Martin Luther fondly referred to as "the gospel in miniature": "For God so loved the world that he gave his one and only Son, that whoever believes in him shall not perish but have everlasting life" (NIV). Any adequate "theology" can be summed up in John 3:16: God loves you; Jesus came to save you; believe and you will be saved.

I. God's motive: "For God so loved the world."

"For God so loved the world" reminds us to get our picture of God back in focus. The world-renowned Scottish New Testament interpreter William Barclay commented:

> Sometimes Christianity is presented in such a way that it sounds as if God had to be pacified, as if He had to be persuaded to forgive. Sometimes men speak as if they would draw a picture of a stern, angry, unforgiving God and a gentle, loving, forgiving Jesus. Sometimes men present the Christian message in such a way that it sounds as if Jesus did something which changed the attitude of God to men from condemnation to forgiveness. But this text tells us that it was with God that it all started. It was God who sent His son, and He sent Him because He loved men. At the back of everything is the love of God. (Clarence E. Macartney, *The Greatest Questions of the Bible and of Life* [Nashville: Abingdon-Cokesbury, 1948], 213)

Jesus did not die to change God. Before the crucifixion was reality in the life of the Son, it was actuality in the mind of the Father.

God is not trying to keep us out; he's trying to get us in. He is not the closed door; he is the open door. He is out to get us—but he is out to get us in the sense of a lover wooing his beloved; he is not out to get us in the sense of annihilating us. That is exactly what God, because he so loved the world, hopes to stop. This leads to our second word.

II. God's method: "He gave his one and only Son."

John's point is that God loved the world so much that he *gave*. God's love had a result: the sending of his Son. Here is a real miracle: that God would send his only Son. Thus this verse points us back to a manger in Bethlehem and forward to a cross in Jerusalem.

Jesus' coming declares and acts out the message of divine love. Love always leads to action. The great American preacher Henry Ward Beecher said it well: "We never know how much one loves till we know how much he is willing to endure and to suffer for us; and it is the suffering element that measures love." By this test God gets an A+. He was willing to endure and suffer mockery, insults, injury, pain, threats, thorns, thirst, nails, spears, betrayal, denial, desertion, rejection, death, and more—all because he loved and acted out his love.

God's sending his Son means everything. We know the way to God because he sent Jesus. Jesus—who is the Way, the Truth, and the Life—can lead us to God and his gift of eternal life. We can go to him because he came to us.

Would you believe that a person wanted you to go over to his or her house to eat and visit if he or she never invited you? Of course not. But we know that we are invited to God's house because Jesus is God's personal invitation: "Here I am! I stand at the door and knock. If anyone hears my voice and opens the door, I will come in and eat with him, and he with me" (Rev. 3:20 NIV). He would not have come nor would he have gone through what he did if he did not want to have an intimate relationship with us.

Another word from our text needs to be heard, namely:

III. God's message: "Whoever believes in him shall not perish but have everlasting life."

The primary purpose of the life and death of Jesus, God's one and only Son, is humankind's salvation. God's desire is to save all persons, as Jesus himself said: "[I] came to seek and to save what was lost" (Luke 19:10 NIV); and again: "I have come that they may have life, and have it to the full" (John 10:10 NIV). God's last and ultimate word to humankind is a word of salvation.

Since Christ confronts humankind with the ultimate expression of God's love, salvation or condemnation is determined by whether one does or does not believe. God loves all persons and desires to save them all, but salvation only becomes effective among those who believe in Christ. For the rest, love turns to judgment. It is only those who believe in Jesus who do not perish but have everlasting life.

Jesus was sent to save, but there is a negative aspect to justification by faith. That some should reject him was not part of God's plan, but their rejection brings judgment on themselves. Hear this: God does not condemn us; rather, we condemn ourselves in our refusal to accept God's offer of love. The very fact of salvation for all who believe implies judgment on all who do not. It is the person's reaction to this revelation of God in the personal presence of Jesus the Christ that determines his or her end. The coming of Jesus divides humankind into the redeemed and the condemned. Jesus' coming gives people the opportunity of salvation and challenges them to a decision. To accept God's gift is to be saved; to refuse his good gift is to be judged. The choice is yours.

Conclusion

What will you do with the gospel proclamation: Believe and have eternal life or not believe and perish?

Sunday Evening, March 2

Title: Ruth and Naomi

Text: "But Ruth said, 'Entreat me not to leave you or to return from following you; for where you go I will go, and where you lodge I will lodge; your people shall be my people, and your God my God'" **(Ruth 1:16 RSV)**.

Scripture Reading: Ruth 1:1–18

Introduction

Once upon a time, long ago and far away, in the small village of Bethlehem (which means "house of bread"), there lived a man named Elimelech, his wife, Naomi, and their two sons, Mahlon and Chilion. Elimelech owned a small plot of ground. He grew seasonal grains, and around the border of his plot olive and almond trees grew.

Then one winter the life-sustaining rains failed to fall. Without them crops failed and springs and even the deepest wells dried up. Panic struck the area. A man could not feed four hungry adults, so Elimelech and his family gathered up their meager belongings and, like a hundred million refugees before and since, made their way to another land. The family traveled east, down the steep hills of Judea, across the Jordan River to Moab.

Imagine that family making their sad trek into a foreign land. They were Judeans living among the ancient enemies of their own people.

Not long after settling in Edom, Elimelech became ill and died. But Naomi still had her sons, her source of pride and security. Shortly after the death of their father, the boys married Moabite girls, Gentile pagans. With the passage of two years, both sons died, leaving three widows in one household in a day when one's financial security was tied up in one's extended family. Naomi and her daughters-in-law were bereft indeed. In fact, Naomi changed her name to Mara, which means "bitterness." She felt that she had been dealt a bitter blow by God.

Finally, Naomi got word that there was rain and fertility again in Judah.

So she decided to return to the only place in the world where her husband had owned a piece of ground. She would make her way back to Bethlehem. It must have been a tearful scene when those three women reached the border between Moab and Judah. They lifted up their voices and cried. Naomi said, "Go back to your homes. There's no hope that I can have other sons whom you can marry, and even if I could, who'd want to wait so long?"

They said, "No, we won't go!" But the mother-in-law insisted. Orpah saw some good sense in it and returned. But Ruth refused to go back. She returned instead to Bethlehem with her mother-in-law, Naomi.

I. Making the best of a bad situation.

When Naomi and Ruth reached Bethlehem, the neighbors said, "Is this Naomi come home again?" She said, "No, call me Mara, for my name is now bitterness."

Even though they were home, there was no work and no security. Ruth was young, vigorous, and healthy and decided she would do what she could to meet their needs. She went into the barley fields during the harvest and gleaned behind the harvesters. It was there that Ruth gained the attention of the workers and then the owner of the field, Boaz. He passed the word to the harvesters: "Leave a little extra for her." When she went home that night, in her apron she carried a half bushel of barley. How excited the two women must have been! But that was nothing compared to Naomi's excitement when she learned the name of the man who owned the field and who had been generous to her daughter-in-law. Boaz was a kinsman of Elimelech, and that had great implications. But that's another part of the story.

II. Ruth's conversion to faith in Naomi's God.

Ruth was a gentle woman and a woman of faith. She gave up her family, her nationality, and her gods in order that she might give her allegiance to Naomi and to Yahweh, the Lord God of Israel.

I wonder why Ruth gave up her home to go with Naomi. The text doesn't really tell us, and so we are left to our imaginations. I wonder if it was the quality of life she had seen in the family of Elimelech and Naomi that attracted her. Or it could be what she had observed in Naomi when she lost her husband and sons. Maybe it was the way in which Naomi handled grief that caused Ruth to feel such an admiration for her mother-in-law that she wanted to know her God and embrace her faith. Is your faith attractive?

III. They lived happily ever after.

The lovely story was played out. The young woman gleaning in the barley field caught the eye of the owner. She went home to tell her mother-in-law that his name was Boaz and discovered that he was a kinsman. This meant that he could claim Elimelech's property, including his daughter-in-law. Naomi and Ruth would have security and know love again.

But there was a complication. Boaz was not the next of kin; he was not first in line.

A drama was played out at the city gate. Boaz and his relative bargained back and forth. Boaz said to the next of kin, "Would you like to redeem Elimelech's property?"

"Oh, yes, surely," he said.

"Along with the property you must marry Ruth, his daughter-in-law."

"Not so fast," said the next of kin.

You see, if he married Ruth, the law of levirate marriage would mean that their children, not his other children, would inherit Elimelech's property. It would complicate his inheritance. So he backed down. Boaz acted promptly and claimed the property and Ruth's hand in marriage. Like all good love stories, it came to a happy ending.

But the rest of the story is this. In the course of time, Boaz and Ruth's son Obed would have a son named Jesse, and Jesse would have a son named David, the great king of Judah from Bethlehem. With the passing of centuries, one of the descendants of Ruth, also born in the village of Bethlehem, was Jesus, who was none other than the Messiah.

Conclusion

The story of Ruth teaches us the providence of God in the lives of ordinary people. The next time you read Romans 8:28, remember the story of Ruth. And the next time you read the story of Ruth, remember Romans 8:28: "In all things God works for the good of those who love him, who have been called according to his purpose" (NIV).

God can bring good out of suffering, grief, disappointment, and loss. If you don't believe that, just look at the cross!

Wednesday Evening, March 5

Title: When the Wicked Prosper
Text: Psalm 73

Introduction

The problem presented in this psalm is similar to that presented in the book of Job: man finds himself plagued with problems for which he has no solutions. This particular problem has to do with the apparent inequity that exists when the wicked prosper and the righteous suffer.

The author of this psalm was a prominent music leader in the temple. He was a man who doubtlessly gave his life, his talents, and his time to the ministry of music among God's people. He came to a point in his life when Satan succeeded in causing him to succumb to self-pity. This psalm can be divided into four parts.

I. An introductory summary (vv. 1–2).

A. *These opening words (v. 1) were written after the problem was solved and the difficulty overcome.* However, the psalmist had been uncertain at one time about the basic truth of God's goodness. Because of circumstances, he had begun to doubt. When a person doubts solid truth, he or she has nothing but slippery ground under his or her feet.

B. *These first two verses portray a steadfast, unmovable God who is unwavering in his goodness to his people over against a poor man who is struggling for footing and is on the verge of a severe fall.*

II. The prosperity of the wicked (vv. 3–14).

A. *At this point the psalmist presents that which caused his dilemma and almost brought him to spiritual ruin.* It was the fact that persons who made no attempt to honor and serve God were, as far as he could tell, "getting ahead" in the world!

B. *It is a fallacy of man's interpretation of God's nature that he always rewards the good with tokens of his favor and punishes the evil by withholding good or sending trouble into their lives.*

C. *Asaph's feelings were more than mere indignation (as Luther suggests in his commentary); they were actually the result of envy that had begun to rankle in his heart.*

D. *Next, the psalmist begins to list several things that prove the wicked are prospering.* He notes that they do not seem to have to endure the troubles that are the lot of so many good people (v. 5). And when it comes time for them to die, they die easily, without the suffering and agony that so often accompanies the death of the righteous.

E. *He caricatures them by saying that their "eyes stand out" in fatness.* They are overweight from their surfeiting and drunkenness, so much so that their eyes actually protrude in their puffy faces! They are vicious and overbearing; they are sarcastic toward God (v. 8).

F. *Again, in verse 13, Asaph contrasts his life, in which he has attempted to honor and serve God, with theirs.*

III. The solution of the difficulty (vv. 15–26).

A. *Even though Asaph had poured out the bitterness of his soul to God, he had not spoken openly (v. 15).* In other words, in spite of his spiritual depression and lack of understanding, he held his tongue and did not risk weakening the faith of others by sharing openly his doubts and misgivings.

B. *In fact, Asaph continued to fret and fume until he went into the sanctuary of God (v. 17).* Asaph's withdrawal into the presence of God enabled him to gain a perspective he could not have attained while he was outside grappling with doubts. Also, he hushed for a while and let God speak, heeding God's admonition, "Be still, and know that I am God" (Ps. 46:10).

C. *God revealed to him plainly "the end" of those who refuse to honor him.* Even though they may appear to be prospering in this life, they live always on the precipice of eternal disaster. They are "in slippery places" (v. 18). In the dark watches of the night, their hearts experience the terror of uncertainty and fear.

Conclusion

Verse 28 records a masterful discovery Asaph made: "But it is good for me to draw near to God: I have put my trust in the Lord God, that I may declare all thy works." He would never be the same again.

SUNDAY MORNING, MARCH 9

Title: Reaffirming Our Relationship
Text: "So Jacob called the name of the place where God had spoken with him, Bethel" **(Gen. 35:15 RSV)**.
Scripture Reading: Genesis 35:1–15
Hymns: "We Gather Together," Baker
"Count Your Blessings," Oatman
"Make Me a Channel of Blessing," Smyth
Offertory Prayer: Father God, we thank you for your leading us throughout the journey of life. We thank you for your protection over us. We are grateful for your provisions for us. We thank you especially for the gift of faith in Jesus Christ that has opened the door for us to receive the bounty of your many blessings. In response to your goodness, we come bringing tithes and offerings as symbols of our desire to be dedicated to your work in the world. Bless these gifts to that end we pray. In Christ's name. Amen.

Introduction

Homecoming is always one of the highlights of the high school or college year. It is a time when school spirit and support are worked up. Alumni return to renew their acquaintance with friends, to revisit their old haunts, and to relive their experiences. It is a happy occasion, a time to reaffirm relationships.

Jacob had a different sort of homecoming when he returned to Bethel. Bethel was the place where he had met God when he fled from his home and from the wrath of his brother, Esau. There he had seen a ladder stretching from earth to heaven and had seen the messengers of God ascending and descending between earth and heaven. There he had received a promise from God and had made a vow to God. It had been a place of meaningful spiritual experience. Twenty to thirty years had passed, and life had brought a variety of experiences to Jacob. He had married, had a large family, and become wealthy. And he had fled again—this time from Laban, who was both his uncle and his father-in-law. He had reconciled with Esau and was back home in Canaan.

So Jacob went back to Bethel. He renewed the vow he had made with God so many years before, which had included a vow to tithe. He reaffirmed his relationship with God.

A time of stewardship emphasis, particularly a pledge day or commitment day, gives us the opportunity to reaffirm our relationship with God.

I. In reaffirming our relationship we remember the beginning.

A. *What had happened at Bethel?*

1. Jacob had met God personally. This was the beginning of Jacob's personal experience with God. It was only after these times that God could be identified as the God of Abraham, Isaac, and Jacob (Gen. 28:16–19).
2. God had given a promise to Jacob. It was the reaffirmation of the promise God had made to Abraham, Jacob's grandfather, and to Isaac, Jacob's father. God would work through Jacob (Gen. 28:13–15).
3. Jacob made a vow to God. In response to the promise made by God to Jacob, Jacob made a vow to God. He vowed to serve God and worship him. With this he included a vow of stewardship, to tithe (Gen. 28:20–22).

B. *What had happened since Bethel?*

1. Jacob had become rich and self-sufficient. Jacob was no longer the wanderer fleeing from his family, looking for a place of refuge. He had become a success.
2. Jacob had disappointment in his family. His daughter Dinah had been raped by Shechem. It was terrible disappointment and a tough personal blow.
3. Jacob had trouble with his neighbors. Following Dinah's personal tragedy, Jacob's sons had acted deceitfully and had massacred the Shechemites in revenge.
4. Jacob and his family had apparently drifted from the vow.

C. *Why do we need a Bethel?* In a time of personal need, Jacob went back to the place of beginning. He went back to the place where he had first affirmed a relationship with God to reaffirm that relationship.

Often we need to make that journey emotionally and spiritually, if not physically. Our needs may be the same as Jacob's needs. When we look at what had happened to Jacob since Bethel, we realize that there is hardly a contemporary family that has not faced those same problems in some measure—more affluent than ever before, with the accompanying self-sufficiency, disappointments, problems with interpersonal relations either at home, at work, or with the neighbors; and drifting away from the commitment made to the Christ. To Bethel, to God, we go to reaffirm our relationship.

II. In reaffirming our relationship we return to the basics.

As well as "back to Bethel," we could also say "back to the basics"! Athletic teams continually go back to the basics in order to compete well. As Christians we too need to go back to the basics. What are those basics?

A. *Cleansing (35:2–3).* Jacob had his family cleanse themselves from idolatry. One cannot go into the presence of God with the vestiges of idolatry clinging to him or her. We need to cleanse ourselves from the idolatry of self-sufficiency, self-righteousness, and self-interest.

B. *Conversion.* Christ must be personally accepted. It was at Bethel that Jacob first met God personally and made a commitment to God. It was at Bethel that Jacob followed God.

C. *Commitment.* In his vow to God, Jacob made a commitment. At Bethel, for the first time, Jacob pledged to tithe. If one is hesitant about pledging to give, perhaps he or she ought to look to this scriptural precedent for pledging.

D. *Continuation (35:14–15).* Jacob made an altar at Bethel, and there he worshiped God. We continue the commitments we make to God through regular worship. Our commitments take on meaning as they are reinforced through the regular worship of God.

III. In reaffirming our relationship we receive the blessings.

A. *The blessing of an enlarged promise from God.* In looking at the blessings Jacob received from God, we are aware that we can receive the same blessings. Blessings are not always defined materially. In fact, the greatest blessings are spiritual.

B. *The blessing of renewed fellowship with God.* In this account we are told again of Jacob's name change to Israel. *Jacob* means "the supplanter," and his whole previous history had been an attempt to supplant someone, to get the upper hand, whether with Esau or Laban. *Israel* means "he who strives with God." A whole nation now carries that name.

How long the silence between Jacob and God had lasted we do not know. But we do know that fellowship between Jacob and God was renewed. The renewing of fellowship with God is always a great blessing.

Conclusion

This is a day for reaffirming your relationship with God. It begins with an act of faith. Take that step of faith for the Savior now.

Bethel means "house of God." Here in the house of God you can reaffirm your relationship to him.

Sunday Evening, March 9

Title: Three Widows in One Home
Text: "Now Elimelech, Naomi's husband, died, and she was left with her two sons. . . . Both Mahlon and Kilion also died, and Naomi was left without her two sons and her husband" **(Ruth 1:3, 5 NIV)**.
Scripture Reading: Ruth 1:1–22

Introduction

Benjamin Franklin used to refer to the book of Ruth as the most beautiful story ever written, a story all the more appealing because it is true.

One must become acquainted with the times of the book of Ruth to understand some of the great truths God has for us there. The events of the book took place during "the days when the judges ruled" (1:1 NIV). The days of the judges were rough and bloody days, days of arms and treachery, days of violence and murder.

The characters in the book are God, Elimelech, Naomi (or Mara), Mahlon, Ruth, Chilion, Orpah, Boaz, and Obed.

The story of the book of Ruth takes place in Moab and in Bethlehem. Bethlehem is in the hill country of Judea, on the main highway to Hebron and Egypt.

The book of Ruth has a threefold purpose: (1) to give a picture of domestic life during the period of the judges, (2) to show how faith and piety are rewarded in this life, and (3) to trace the lineage of the Messiah (through the Gentile women Rahab and Ruth).

Our text and the Scripture reading tell us of three widows in one home—Naomi, Ruth, and Orpah. Chapter 1 has valuable lessons for us all.

I. Three widows in a home teach us there is light in the midst of darkness.

Even in stormy times we can find green pastures. Sometimes the blackest times are not as dismal in reality as they look in history. Men and women loved and worked, wept and laughed; and the gossips of Bethlehem talked over Naomi's return. We need to learn to look for the silver linings in the dark clouds of life. There are blessings for us even though the wolf of hunger comes to prowl.

II. Three widows in a home teach us that some who turn back are not far from the kingdom.

Orpah left Naomi and went back home to her gods. She is the first in the series of those who were not far from the kingdom of God. She needed a little more resolution at this critical moment in life; and, for want of it, she shut herself out of the covenant and sank back into a world she had earlier renounced.

Many turn back. How tragic! How sad!

III. Three widows in a home teach us of the godly influence of a loved one.

In spite of Naomi's great losses, in spite of her sharp afflictions, she should be cheered for her spiritual gain. She lost her home in Moab, but she gained the conversion of her daughter-in-law Ruth.

We can influence our loved ones by spending time with them, helping them, loving them, valuing them, and instructing them. When Christians become consistent, their loved ones will be converted.

IV. Three widows in a home teach us that God is working out his will.

What is the theme of the book of Ruth? Dr. Eric W. Hayden says it is "rest in weariness." I believe it centers around Boaz, the kinsman-redeemer and type of Christ. God was working out his will through Ruth and Boaz.

Conclusion

Our hearts are ever pulled on by new hopes. Naomi went back to Bethlehem for bread, but she found more than bread. Ruth went to Bethlehem to help Naomi, and because God was at work in her life, her hope for life would be far more than she realized.

WEDNESDAY EVENING, MARCH 12

Title: The Lord, My Refuge
Text: Psalm 91

Introduction

Few psalms paint such a delightful picture of trust and confidence in God as Psalm 91. It has been used in times of trouble and distress throughout the generations. It is a cheerful song of faith in God and is appropriate whatever the circumstances.

Though the psalm carries no title or mention of its author, Hebrew tradition ascribes it to Moses, based principally on the many close resemblances between it and Deuteronomy 32 and 33.

The theme of Psalm 91 is the security of the person who thoroughly trusts in God. The psalm has an antiphonal arrangement, in which the first speaker delivers verses 1–2; the second, verses 3–4; the first again responds with verses 5–8; and the second with verses 9–13. A third speaker, making himself the mouthpiece of Jehovah, brings the psalm to a conclusion by stating the blessings that God himself will bestow on his faithful ones (vv. 14–16). We might imagine three great choirs in the temple singing this psalm antiphonally.

I. Summary of the theme (vv. 1–2).

A. *To "dwell in the secret place of the most High" (v. 1) is to have the Almighty for one's constant companion.* "The shadow of the Almighty" to the Jew meant the presence of God in the Holy of Holies, and the Jew entered there vicariously in the person of the high priest on the Day of Atonement. Today, because of the work of Christ on the cross, all believers can "come boldly" to the throne of grace and thus rest beneath the shadow of the Almighty.

B. *The psalmist rejoices in God as his "refuge" (v. 2), the place of security and protection from whence we successfully fight spiritual warfare.* The result of this awareness is an open confession, "I will say of the LORD," in which the psalmist delights.

II. Deliverance from evils (vv. 3–8).

A. *The second speaker addresses the first and says, in effect, "Yes, certainly God will deliver you from whatever dangers beset you.* Let me name a few of them for you!" And then he proceeds to do so.

1. "The snare of the fowler." Like a bird, the soul of man is exposed to many dangers, including those that are hidden, such as the snare of the bird-hunter (the "fowler"). It is a hidden peril from which only God can deliver us.
2. "The noisome pestilence." Leprosy was no doubt the most feared pestilence among the Hebrews, for it suggested to them the curse attached to some sin that had greatly displeased God.
3. "The terror by night." Robbers constituted the chief nighttime menace.
4. "The arrow that flieth by day" probably referred to open warfare.
5. "The destruction that wasteth at noonday" may have referred to sunstroke (see Ps. 121:6).

B. *Verse 8 declares that without suffering himself the believer will look on and see the punishment of the ungodly.* This was true of many of the plagues of Egypt, during which time the Hebrews witnessed the calamities befalling the Egyptians (cf. Ps. 23:5).

III. Security for those who trust in the Lord (vv. 9–13).

A. *In verses 9–10 the second speaker addresses the first with a reaffirmation of the first speaker's words.* He adds that the faithful are under the constant care of angels (v. 11; see Heb. 1:14), who guide and direct them.

B. *There is much mystery concerning angels, and perhaps their visibility is limited because we would tend to worship them, as John did on the island of Patmos.* The suggestion is strong, however, that God assigns them to protect his children.

IV. God's promise to those who trust him (vv. 14–16).

A. *In these last three verses, Jehovah himself becomes the speaker.* It is not enough that the faithful should encourage one another by their anticipations of God's blessings and mercies, but God himself now speaks by the mouth of his prophet and makes promises directly.

B. *Verse 14 is a ratification of verses, 3, 7, and 10–15.* Verse 15 is a marvelous prayer promise, like many in the New Testament.

Conclusion

All in all, Psalm 91 is a source of continuing comfort for God's people, especially when they are called on to suffer or to wage warfare for that which is right.

SUNDAY MORNING, MARCH 16

Title: When Love Makes a Choice
Scripture Reading: John 10:10–18
Text: "'The reason my Father loves me is that I lay down my life—only to take it up again. No one takes it from me, but I lay it down of my own accord. I have authority to lay it down and authority to take it up again. This command I received from my Father'" **(John 10:17–18 NIV)**.
Hymns: "Love Lifted Me," Rowe
"In the Cross of Christ I Glory," Bowring
"Christ Receiveth Sinful Men," Neumeister
Offertory Prayer: Our heavenly Father, we thank you for the blessings of life. We thank you for the gift of this day and this time of worship. We thank you for strength to work, the opportunity to work, and the money that we receive from the labor of our hands and our heads.

We give to you freely of our money, for we know that you have freely given to us the gift of life and the greater gift of eternal life through faith in Jesus Christ. Receive our gifts as we give them in Jesus' name and for his sake. Amen.

Introduction

In 1949 when it became apparent that the Chinese Communists were going to take all of mainland China, Baker James Cauthen, who later became executive secretary of the Foreign Mission Board of the Southern Baptist Convention, was then area secretary for the Orient. Dr. Cauthen told the missionaries with the South China Mission that each would have to make his own decision whether to stay in China, to transfer to another field, or to return home.

In the mission station at Wuchow, where the Stout Memorial Baptist Hospital was located and where the now-famed Dr. Bill Wallace, a modern missionary martyr, was the chief surgeon and administrator, five missionaries chose to go and three chose to stay. In explaining his decision to stay to one of the other missionaries, Wallace said, "I'm just one piece of man without other responsibilities."

"One piece of man" was an old Chinese saying used courteously to depreciate one's value. As Jesse Fletcher pointed out in *Bill Wallace of China*, it indicated a single, unencumbered, expendable person. By it, Wallace meant that his life was the one so seated by circumstances that it was prepared by God for that moment. He did what he felt was right in his own heart. He was later martyred by the Chinese Communists. He made love's choice.

Jesus made love's choice in the garden of Gethsemane. His choice was a cross, and John 10:17–18 makes it clear that the cross was indeed his own choice. His struggle in the garden was not in knowing the will of God but in accepting it.

I. Since the cross was love's choice, it was an act of obedience.

A. *There is a task to do.* God had given Jesus a task to do. That task was the redemption of persons from their sin. It could be accomplished only by the death of Christ. When Christ gave himself as a sacrifice for our sin, it was in obedience to God and to his will for him.

God has given each one of us a task to do. For us, it is not the redemption of humankind; it is the carrying of the message of God's love and the truth of God's redemption to hurting humanity in many personal and practical ways.

B. *The task can be accomplished only through obedience.* Sonship for Jesus, and childhood for us, can never be based on anything except obedience. For Jesus to have been disobedient to God's will would have short-circuited God's plan for the redemption of humankind.

When Paul was giving his testimony before King Agrippa, he said, "So then, King Agrippa, I was not disobedient to the vision from heaven" (Acts 26:19 NIV). Jesus could have said the same thing. He was not disobedient to God's will.

But what of us? God has given us many visions—to witness, tithe, and pray, and to express compassion, love, and mercy. Have we been obedient?

C. *The reason for obedience.* We are obedient to God because God can have no rivals in our hearts. God must claim first place. Obedience to him and to his will must come first.

II. Since the cross was love's choice, it was an act of glory.

A. *The cross was the means of Christ's glory.* From this passage it can be seen that Jesus expected to die. He never doubted that he would die. And he equally never doubted that he would rise again.

Jesus could have this confidence that the cross was the way to glory and that he would rise from the dead because he had confidence in God. He knew that God would never abandon him.

B. *The suffering was for a moment; the glory is eternal.* Jesus believed that the suffering was but for a moment. The glory that would come through the cross was for all eternity. It has been stated before: "No cross, no crown." Without the cross there would be no coronation of Jesus as King of Kings and Lord of Lords.

In general anything worth getting is hard to get. This is true in academics, sports, and other learned skills, crafts, and techniques. The world is filled with people who have missed their destiny because they would not pay the price. The price may be sacrifice, even self-sacrifice. But the suffering that lasts for a moment gives rise to eternal glory. It was true for Christ, and it is true for us.

III. Since the cross was love's choice, it was an act of voluntariness.

A. *Jesus repeatedly stressed that his death was voluntary.* Throughout his ministry Jesus pointed to the cross. When the woman in Bethany anointed the feet of Jesus with precious ointment, some saw it as a waste, but Jesus saw it as an anointing for his burial (Matt. 26:12). Following Peter's great confession at Caesarea Philippi, Jesus repeatedly told the disciples of his death and resurrection even though they did not catch the references until after the resurrection.

Jesus knew what the cross was—it was an instrument of death. He was not unacquainted with the agony of the cross when he made love's choice.

B. *The death of Christ on the cross was for us.* Jesus gave himself for us. It was not for himself that he died. He died for us. He gave himself for our sins. In the First World War a magnificent young French soldier was seriously wounded. His arm was so badly injured that it had to be amputated. The surgeon was grieved that the soldier would have to go through life maimed. When the boy regained consciousness, the surgeon told him that he was sorry he had lost his arm. The young man replied that he did not lose his arm; he gave it—for France. Jesus gave his life—for us.

Conclusion

The work of Christ on the cross was for us. It is effective in dealing with our sin. It enables us to triumph in the situation that sin created inside us, between us and others, and between us and God.

In *World Aflame* Billy Graham tells of a hill overlooking the harbor of Macao on the south coast of China. Portuguese settlers once built a massive cathedral on a hill, but a typhoon proved stronger than the work of human hands, and the building fell some centuries ago. The building fell in ruins except for the front wall. High on the top of that jutting wall, challenging the elements down through the years, is a great bronze cross. In 1825 Sir John Bowring was shipwrecked near there. Clinging to the wreckage of his ship, at long last he caught sight of that great cross, which showed him where he could find safety. This dramatic rescue moved him to write the words familiar to millions:

In the cross of Christ I glory,
Towering o'er the wrecks of time;
All the light of sacred story.
Gathers round its head sublime.

When love made a choice, it chose a cross. By that cross we can know and experience the love of God, and we can have life. What is your choice based on love's choice?

SUNDAY EVENING, MARCH 16

Title: Romance in a Field

Text: "She bowed down with her face to the ground. She exclaimed, 'Why have I found such favor in your eyes that you notice me—a foreigner?'" **(Ruth 2:10 NIV).**

Scripture Reading: Ruth 2:1–23

Introduction

The book of Ruth is a small book consisting of four chapter divisions and eighty-five verses. This little book is one of the rarest and most beautiful stories in all literature. We need to remember that the author had three major thrusts in mind as he wrote it: (1) to portray domestic life during the period of the judges, (2) to show how faith is rewarded, and (3) to trace the lineage of the coming Messiah.

In chapter 1 the scene takes place in the land of Moab, where we see three widows in one home. When we come to chapter 2, the scene shifts to a harvest field. Naomi and Ruth have arrived in Bethlehem, and because they are poor, Ruth goes to glean grain in the field of a rich kinsman of Elimelech by the name of Boaz. Boaz comes into the field and inquires of his reapers, "Whose young woman is that?" (v. 5 NIV). The answer is given: "She is the Moabitess who came back from Moab with Naomi" (v. 6 NIV). Boaz is immediately attracted to Ruth, admonishes her to glean in his field, and assures her of safety. So the beautiful romance in the field begins.

Some wonderful truths come out of chapter 2 in the presentation of the beginning of the romance between Boaz and Ruth.

I. One great truth is that all honest work is honorable.

Naomi and Ruth came to Bethlehem with sadness in their hearts over the loss of their husbands. They also came destitute and in need of food. Ruth was young enough to work, so she went out into the harvest field to glean. All honest work is honorable. Ruth was not lazy. She was willing to work and do what was necessary for survival.

II. Another great truth is that we should be kind and inspire others.

When Boaz came into the field, he said to his employees, "The LORD be with you!" And they answered him, "The LORD bless you!" (v. 4 NIV). Not only was Boaz kind to his reapers, he inquired about Ruth and was kind to her. "Why have I found such favor in your eyes that you notice me—a foreigner?" (v. 10 NIV). Ruth had been kind and courteous to her mother-in-law, and in turn Boaz was kind and gracious to her.

Two graces that all of us need to develop are gratitude and respect. They will do wonders for us. The world needs kindness and inspiration.

III. Another truth for us is to learn to trust in God.

Ruth had turned from the gods of the Moabites and had turned to trust in the Lord God of Israel (2:12).

It is a great day when we learn to trust the Lord. Evidently there was something in Naomi's life and in her words to Ruth that caused Ruth to trust the Lord. The same ought to be true in our lives. Our lives and our words should lead others to receive Jesus Christ as Savior. Let us be in the business of leading others to trust our Lord.

IV. Still another truth for us is to be generous toward others.

Boaz commanded his young men, "Even if she gathers among the sheaves, don't embarrass her. Rather, pull out some stalks for her from the bundles and leave them for her to pick up, and don't rebuke her" (vv. 15–16 NIV).

Ruth was able to take home an ephah (about three-fifths of a bushel) of barley.

Conclusion

When Ruth went home and told Naomi of the events of the day and of the kindness of Boaz, it was shouting time for Naomi, for Boaz was a near kinsman.

Isn't it wonderful how God works out his plan even in a field of romance?

WEDNESDAY EVENING, MARCH 19

Title: The Mercies of the Lord
Text: Psalm 103

Introduction

This psalm may well be called "a pure note of praise." It has a rather sober undercurrent at one point, yet it ascribes well to the description given to it by Alexander Maclaren: "There are no clouds on the horizon, nor notes of sadness in the music of this psalm. No purer outburst of thankfulness enriches the church."

As the psalm progresses, it swells into grander and grander chords of praise to the Almighty. It can be divided into four sections for study.

I. Self-exhortation to bless the Lord (vv. 1–5).

A. *We must remind ourselves to praise the Lord for all his benefits to us.* David, for some reason, was overcome with the multitude of God's blessings. He calls on his "soul" (his personality) and his entire inner being ("all that is within me") to address this outflow of praise to God.

B. *He begins by enumerating some of these blessings.* Forgiveness of sin properly heads the list. The healing of diseases points out the truth that God's concern for us includes the physical as well as the spiritual.

II. Exhortation to Israel to bless the Lord (vv. 6–13).

A. *In this section of the psalm, David transfers the blessings he has received in his personal life to the way in which God has dealt with his people, Israel.* Yet in these words there are excellent applications for God's dealings with us today.

B. *Verse 8 is a case in point.* How often have we benefited from these gracious virtues of our Lord! Verse 9 provides a good comparative statement about God and his relationship with his people. He will not chasten us interminably; yet he will not withhold his chastening forever when we persist in our disobedience.

C. *In verse 10 David reminds us that God has not dealt with us to the degree that our sins deserve.* Verse 12 is the magnificent statement assuring us of the way in which God considers our past sins that had separated us from him. Verse 13 is a cherished portrait of God in his role as a loving and understanding heavenly Father.

III. God's consideration for human weakness (vv. 14–18).

A. *What a magnificent contrast we find in verse 14!* Humans are frail, yet the Almighty God treats these frail beings with exceedingly great compassion.

B. *Because of man's frailty (resulting from his fall in Eden), "his days are as grass" (v. 15).* Here David is underscoring the transiency of man's existence.

IV. A call to all in God's kingdom to bless him (vv. 19–22).

In this sweeping conclusion to the psalm, David calls on the angels, the hosts of heaven (possibly the cherubim and seraphim), and finally all of creation ("all his works") to praise God.

Conclusion

This psalm undoubtedly stands among the most exalted and thrilling expressions of praise to God from man's perspective in all of Holy Scripture. The psalmist exhibited not merely a "general praise" attitude, but an excitement over specifics! Too often our praise and thanksgiving sink to the level of the perfunctory and become little more than a ritual.

SUNDAY MORNING, MARCH 23

Title: When the Religious Are Wrong

Text: "Then the high priest rent his clothes, saying, He hath spoken blasphemy; what further need have we of witnesses? Behold, now ye have heard his blasphemy. What think ye? They answered and said, He is guilty of death" **(Matt. 26:65–66)**.

Scripture Reading: Matthew 26:57–68

Hymns: "Hope of the World," Harkness
"O Jesus I Have Promised," Bode
"Love Is the Theme," Fisher

Offertory Prayer: Our Father, we are grateful to you this day for your blessings to us. As we think of the blessings, we think particularly of your love, of your strength, of the ability to earn money, of the opportunity to share our substance with you. Help us never to forget the extent of your sharing Christ with us—even to death. Help us never to forget the length of our commission from you—to the ends of the earth.

So with gratitude for your grace to us and your strength in us and with acknowledgment of our debt to you, we give to you this day this offering. Bless it with your presence, we pray. Multiply it with your power, we ask. Accompany it with your presence, we plead. In Christ's name. Amen.

Introduction

People can be wrong in their judgments. Harry Emerson Fosdick, in his book *What Is Vital in Religion,* told of a newspaper editor in Harrisburg, Pennsylvania, who heard Lincoln's Gettysburg Address at the dedication of the national cemetery. But he was a hardheaded realist who would not fall for the words expressed by the president of the United States during those crucial Civil War years. He wrote in his paper: "We pass over the silly remarks of the President, for the credit of the nation, we are willing that the veil of oblivion shall be dropped over them and that they shall no more be repeated or thought of." But that newspaper editor was wrong in his judgment of Lincoln's Gettysburg Address.

The priests in Israel once made a wrong judgment too. They decided that Jesus was not the Messiah. The storm had been gathering for some time. The plot thickened as Jesus continued his ministry and the people responded to his love and his teachings. For the priests the issue was decided when Jesus raised Lazarus from the dead. They determined then that he must die.

The priesthood was well established in Israel. According to one source, there were one hundred thousand priests in Jesus' time. The only qualification for the priesthood was unbroken physical descent from Aaron. Moral qualifications and spiritual power did not enter into the matter. The only disqualifications were certain physical blemishes.

In the illegal trial of Jesus, the priests came to a definite decision: Jesus must die. They were the religious of their day. But on that day the religious were wrong.

What happens when the religious are wrong?

I. When the religious are wrong, we see the results of pride.

A. *The pervasion of pride.* It is easy to see that the priests were pervaded with pride. Since they qualified for the priesthood by their ancestry, they had an unusual pride in their paternity. They also had pride in their position and power. And they were pridefully convinced that their position was right and that Jesus' position was wrong.

B. *The place of pride.* Pride has a proper place in our lives. We should have pride in certain things. The pride in oneself that causes one to live and serve with confidence is one instance. The pride in the gospel that causes one to share it with others is another. But pride can also be harmful. As with the priests, pride can easily cause one to make wrong decisions and to follow destructive courses of action.

C. *The price of pride.* The Bible warns, "Pride goeth before destruction, and a haughty spirit before a fall" (Prov. 16:18). The price of pride can be very high; pride can indeed lead to destruction.

Our pride can keep us from reaching the things we desire most. Supposedly, the priests desired to reach God most of all. But their prideful rejection of Jesus kept them from entering into the presence of God. The priests' pride kept them from God. Our pride can keep us from attaining our goals.

II. When the religious are wrong, we see the effects of prejudice.

A. *The fact of prejudice.* Prejudice refuses to take into consideration the individual himself. The religious leaders were prejudiced against Jesus. To them he did not have the right credentials. They prejudged him, deciding that he could not properly represent God.

B. *The faults of prejudice.*

1. Prejudice blinds us to God. Those who are prejudiced cannot see what God wants them to see. God wanted the priests to see the revelation of himself through Jesus Christ, but their prejudice blinded them.
2. Prejudice limits the love of God. The priests did not like the people with whom Jesus associated, and they were willing to cut those people off from the love of God. Through their prejudice toward those individuals they in effect limited the love of God.

Jesus showed God's love to people like Zacchaeus, whom they had labeled a sinner. Jesus showed that a good Samaritan had carried out the commandment of God to love another as he loved himself, while the priests would have no dealings with the Samaritans, good or otherwise. By their prejudice, the religious leaders were asserting that God loved them but not others.

III. When the righteous are wrong, we see the completion of the plot.

A. *Causes of the plot.* The priests' plot against Jesus thickened. Several causes of the plot can be traced through the account.

1. Jesus brought people directly to God. This destroyed their pride in position. The priests were no longer necessary for persons to come into God's presence.
2. Jesus cleansed the temple and called for it to be used only for its original purpose. In doing this he put an end to some of the religious leaders' profits, for they had profited from the exchange of currency used in the temple. They had also profited from the sale of animals to be sacrificed at the temple.
3. Jesus was inclusive in his love. This undercut the religious leaders' prejudice. They were exclusive in their love. Only religious Jews of their own kind came under the umbrella of their love. But Jesus showed the true heart of God in an inclusive love that reached out to all persons.
4. Jesus raised Lazarus from the dead. This showed up the religious leaders' power. They did not have power over life and death. They did not have the power to act directly for God.

All of these things fit together to cause the priests to plot against Jesus. In the trial the plot was completed.

B. *The course of the plot.* The priests found a weak link in Jesus' organization. By the betrayal of Judas, they were able to arrest Jesus. Then they tried him.

Follow the course of the plot. First, the religious leaders brought out false witnesses. In their search for false witnesses, they could not find witnesses who would agree with their accusations against Jesus (Matt. 26:60–61). The law said that two witnesses had to agree before a person could be found guilty. Finally, they found two people who twisted and misapplied the statements of Jesus to assert that he said that he would destroy the temple and rebuild it in three days. Of course, the reference was to the temple of his body and his resurrection from the dead.

Next the religious leaders tried direct confrontation. When the false witnesses made their charges against Jesus, they directly confronted him, asking him if he was the Christ, the Son of God. Jesus refused to answer them. Then Jesus simply stated that the high priest had said it himself and that one day they would witness the Son of Man in his power and glory (vv. 62–64). This was too much for the high priest, who accused Jesus of blasphemy (v. 65). The priests found him guilty and announced the penalty of death (v. 66). In the course of the plot, they confronted Jesus directly.

In the end, each one of us must confront the Christ directly.

Conclusion

The religious can be wrong. When the priests decided against Jesus, they were wrong. But the religious can also be right. They are right when they recognize in Jesus the one who can forgive sin and bring them to God. We must decide for Jesus. Won't you decide for Jesus this day and pledge your life to follow him in faith?

Sunday Evening, March 23

Title: How to Find a Mate
Text: "So Boaz took Ruth, and she was his wife" **(Ruth 4:13)**.
Scripture Reading: Ruth 4:7–17

Introduction

Dr. Clarence E. Macartney, in his book *Great Women of the Bible*, describes Ruth as "the woman who got her man." When one reads the book of Ruth, one becomes aware of the love manifested in the story—Naomi's love for Ruth, Ruth's love for Naomi, Ruth's love for Boaz, Boaz's love for Ruth, and God's love for all. Certainly one of the great themes of the book is love—domestic love.

If you are looking for someone to marry, you would do well to read the book of Ruth until you are thoroughly acquainted with the book. What kind of person do you want to marry? The book of Ruth has suggestions to offer you.

I. Some negative things to consider when trying to find a mate.

A. *Don't chase the opposite sex (3:10).* No one likes a woman-chaser or a man-chaser.

B. *Don't go out with others for what you can get out of them (3:10).* Don't be a gold digger.

C. *Don't be too timid (3:1–5).* At Naomi's insistence Ruth took the initiative. Ruth was willing to be the aggressor, but she acted in good taste and according to the customs of that day.

D. *Don't react against those who want you to marry.* Naomi, a gracious mother-in-law, wanted her daughter-in-law to marry. Of course, no one can choose your life's companion for you, but others can encourage you when you are not willing to take the initiative.

II. Some positive qualities to consider when trying to find a mate.

A. *Look for an industrious person (2:7).* If you marry a lazy person, you will have a marriage full of trouble.

B. *Look for a considerate, loving person (v. 11).* Ruth was a loving person, and so was Boaz.

C. *Look for an expressive person (v. 13).* Many marriages are on the rocks because the partners do not talk with each other, do not compliment each other.

D. *Look for a thoughtful person (v. 18).*

E. *Look for a physically attractive person (3:3–4).* In other words, marry a person who will endeavor to make herself or himself attractive.

F. *Look for a person wise enough to listen (v. 5).*

G. *Look for a person of integrity (3:11; Prov. 31:10–31).*

H. *Look for a person who is willing to follow God's leadership (Ruth 2:1–3).* Ruth was willing to follow the person whom God had provided for her. Boaz was willing to obey the laws of God, to follow God's leadership. Two laws are involved in this love story: (1) the law regulating redemption of property (Lev. 25:25–34) and (2) the law concerning a brother's duty to raise children for the deceased (Deut. 25:5–6).

Conclusion

Ruth was the wife of Boaz, the mother of Obed (Ruth 4:13–17), the grandmother of David (vv. 18–22), and the ancestor of Christ (Matt. 1:5). She found her mate, and what a mate she found! Exercise wisdom and follow the guidance of God in choosing your mate.

WEDNESDAY EVENING, MARCH 26

Title: The House of the Lord
Text: Psalm 122

Introduction

"The house of the LORD," which is the theme of this psalm, could only have been the "tent of meeting," or the tabernacle, the prototype having been built in the wilderness by Moses. The temple on Mount Moriah was not completed until the reign of Solomon, David's son. Still, the tabernacle was repeatedly called "the house of the LORD" (see Judg. 19:18; 1 Sam. 1:7, 24; 2 Sam. 12:20) long before the temple was built.

Though Psalm 122 is a record of David's own personal feelings about Jerusalem and the house of God, he doubtlessly wrote the psalm for the people to sing as they came up to Jerusalem for the three great annual feasts of the Jews: Passover, Pentecost, and Tabernacles.

I. The joy on the way to Jerusalem (vv. 1–2).

A. *"I was glad when they said unto me, Let us go into the house of the LORD" (v. 1).* What are some truths implied here? First, it is the will of God that we should worship him corporately, in a congregation. We encourage each other; enthusiasm and joy are contagious emotions. We learn from each other; we observe the ordinances together by way of "remembrance" as God's people. Our attitude toward the church, when expressed to others, should always be positive and upbuilding, never pessimistic and derogatory.

B. *Historically, many of the Jews coming to Jerusalem for the Feast of Weeks came from long distances and often found the journey tedious and wearying.* Yet always they comforted themselves with the thought that it would be worth it all when they came to stand in the Holy City and before the tabernacle, which housed the ark representing the glory of God among his people. Satan often sees to it that we have many hindrances when we start to come to God's house.

II. The great esteem for Jerusalem (vv. 3–5).

A. *David was impressed with the natural, physical beauty of Jerusalem.* The houses were not scattered here and there, without thought in planning and building. They were built with forethought and design, and the streets were beautiful and spacious. David's description of Jerusalem could be compared to the ideal spiritual design of the church, which is formed in spiritual unity, love, and communion.

B. *There were two general reasons why the Israelites rejoiced in coming together in Jerusalem.* First, they received instruction from God; they came to hear what God had to say to them through his prophets and teachers of the Law. Second, they came to worship before the glory of the Lord and "to give thanks to the name of the LORD." Thanksgiving was always a vital part of the worship of the Hebrew people.

C. *The people had a reason to be in love with Jerusalem, because justice was administered there by a king who was concerned about the material and physical needs of his people as well as their spiritual needs.* "Thrones" (v. 5) refer to courts where civil disputes were settled. Christians ought also to be concerned about the civil needs and problems of their society.

III. The great concern for Jerusalem (vv. 6–9).

A. *"Pray for the peace of Jerusalem" (v. 6).* David calls on others to intercede for Jerusalem. This injunction is equally appropriate today, for the "peace of Jerusalem" has a definite effect on the whole world. It is often true that this tiny land bridge in the Middle East controls the international "temperature" of the world.

B. *In verse 7 David prays for peace among the people ("within thy walls") and also for the leaders who sit in the palaces, who give direction and leadership to the people.* For as the leaders prosper and are blessed by God, so will those blessings be passed on to the people. Furthermore, David was a people's king (v. 8). He loved his people and longed to see them happy and prosperous. David summarizes in verse 9 by returning to his opening theme. He loves the house of God.

Conclusion

We could easily translate "the house of the LORD" to mean "the body of Christ." We should seek the good of all our brothers and sisters in Christ. So what can we say about this delightful psalm? It is obvious that David loved the house of the Lord. He longed to see God's people strengthened through corporate worship. May God give us a commensurate love for his church and for our fellow believers.

SUNDAY MORNING, MARCH 30

Title: When the Innocent Are Guilty

Text: "'What shall I do, then, with Jesus who is called Christ?' Pilate asked.

"They all answered, 'Crucify him!'

"'Why? What crime has he committed?' asked Pilate.

"But they shouted all the louder, 'Crucify him!'" **(Matt. 27:22–23 NIV).**

Scripture Reading: Matthew 27:1–2, 11–26

Hymns: "At the Cross," Watts

"Great Redeemer, We Adore Thee," Harris

"Jesus Is All the World to Me," Thompson

Offertory Prayer: Our Father, for the beauty of this day and for the bounty of your care, we thank you. And for the love of your Son, Jesus Christ, who gave his life for our sin, we thank you.

We come to offer to you the strength of our bodies as represented by a tithe and a gift from the wages of our work. We offer to you the love of our hearts as seen in our worship to you. We offer to you the commitment of our lives as seen in our profession of faith in Christ.

Accept our gifts, we pray. Bless our lives, we ask. In the name of Jesus Christ, your Son and our Savior, we pray. Amen.

Introduction

The refrain of a popular song some years ago asserted that "the lights went out in Georgia" the night they hanged an innocent man.

There was once a day when the lights went out all over the world. In the middle of the day the earth was plunged into darkness. The reason was that people had hanged an innocent man—Jesus, the Christ. Accepting the guilt of the world's sin upon himself, he was innocent of sin.

A central figure in the crucifixion of Jesus was Pontius Pilate, the Roman governor. Pilate was never very popular among the Jews. For one thing, he had no understanding of them and their ways. Also, he had little sympathy for them. But it was to Pilate that the Jews brought Jesus to be judged guilty, for only the Roman government could pronounce the death penalty.

Pilate knew that Jesus was not guilty, and three times he affirmed it. Political pressure was exerted on him, however, and he pronounced a sentence with which he did not personally agree.

What happens when the innocent are judged guilty? Notice that in this account Pilate asked three questions. These three questions are significant in helping us see what happens when the innocent are judged guilty.

I. When the innocent are judged guilty, one must give a description.

Consider the first question that Pilate asked Jesus: "Are you the king of the Jews?" (v. 11 NIV).

A. *It could be considered a political description.* When Pilate asked Jesus if he was the king of the Jews, Jesus forced Pilate to answer the question himself. Answer it he did as he put the sign on the cross: "THIS IS JESUS, THE KING OF THE JEWS" (v. 37). The sign was erected in derision of the Jews. But it gave the answer in the only way Pilate knew to describe a kingship: a political description of a king.

   Jesus was not king as Pilate understood kingship, in a political way. Jesus was not king as the Jews understood kingship, in a messianic way, with all their presuppositions and dreams of a messiah. Jesus was King as God intended, in a spiritual way. When Jesus established the rule of God in a human heart and the kingship of God over a human life, he was expressing himself as King in a spiritual way. But it was a way that both Pilate and the Jewish leaders had trouble understanding.

B. *It could be considered a personal description.* How would you describe Jesus? In the end each one of us must make his or her own personal description of Jesus. He is the loving Son of God who wants to rule over each life. When you accept Jesus Christ as personal Savior and make him Lord over your life, you are giving the personal description of Jesus as King that accurately describes his kingship.

II. When the innocent are judged guilty, one must deal with determination.

The second question Pilate asked was, "Which one do you want me to release to you: Barabbas, or Jesus who is called Christ?" (v. 17 NIV).

A. *There is a determination to bring death.* The Jews were determined to put Jesus to death. Pilate would not consider a religious charge. So, according to Luke's account, they fabricated a threefold political charge against Jesus.

Jesus was charged with being a revolutionary. The Jewish leaders left the impression with Pilate that Jesus had gathered a revolutionary group around himself. The Romans were intolerant of revolutionary activities, while they could be extremely tolerant of religious practices.

Jesus was also charged with inciting people not to pay taxes. Rome, as most governments, was interested in its subjects paying their taxes. The Jews implied that Jesus had taught people not to pay their taxes to Rome.

Finally, Jesus was charged with claiming to be a king. The implication was that Jesus would usurp the throne of Caesar in that area. It related to the charge as a revolutionary.

The religious leaders attempted to get witnesses against Jesus. But what kind of witnesses could they get? What could anyone say against him? The apocryphal *Acts of Pilate* says that a continual stream of witnesses came demanding to be allowed to give evidence in favor of Jesus. One man said that he had been an invalid for thirty-eight years and that Jesus had healed him. Another man said that he had been blind and that Jesus had given him sight. Another person testified that he had been a leper and that Jesus had cleansed him. And there came a woman called Bernice (Veronica in Latin) who said that in the crowd she had touched the hem of Jesus' garment and that an issue of blood that had troubled her for twelve years had stopped. These were true witnesses for Jesus in the face of the religious leaders' determination to put him to death.

B. *There is a determination to shift blame.* As determined as were the Jewish leaders to bring death to Jesus, so determined was Pilate to escape the responsibility for it. What shifted his decision toward their demand for the death penalty for Jesus was their hint of blackmail. The Jewish leaders threatened to report Pilate to Rome. He could not stand another negative report from Judah to Rome, so that settled the matter for Pilate.

But still Pilate tried to shift blame, to escape responsibility. He wanted the crowd to make the decision for him. But the crowd had been instigated by the priests to call for the death of Jesus. And when Pilate put the decision before them—Who would they release as an act of mercy at the Passover time: Jesus, the innocent lover of all humankind?—they chose Barabbas.

But there are some responsibilities that we cannot escape. We must accept these responsibilities for ourselves. There is no way we can shift the blame for failing to accept the Christ as our Savior. There is no way we can avert the responsibility to recognize Jesus as the Son of God. These are our personal responsibilities. We cannot shift the blame for them to others no matter how hard we may try.

III. When the innocent are judged guilty, one must make a decision.

The third of Pilate's questions is the most significant: "What shall I do, then, with Jesus who is called Christ?" (v. 22 NIV).

A. *It is a personal decision.* Each of us must honestly and personally face this same question: What will I do with Jesus? We cannot evade the question. Although Pilate tried to evade it, washing his hands to symbolically indicate that he had washed his hands of the whole affair, his guilt remained. Each person must face Christ and bow the knee to him as Lord—either on this earth or after death.

B. *It is a pressing decision.* Just as Pilate was pressed to make a decision about Christ, so are we. Our decision cannot be put off indefinitely. Each of us has to answer.

Conclusion

The innocent one may have been judged guilty and killed, but the truly guilty ones are those for whose sins he paid. You can come to him now. He will forgive you. When the innocent are judged guilty, the guilty may become innocent.

Sunday Evening, March 30

Title: A Happy Marriage

Text: "So Boaz took Ruth, and she became his wife. Then he went to her, and the Lord enabled her to conceive, and she gave birth to a son" **(Ruth 4:13 NIV)**.

Scripture Reading: Ruth 4:1–22

Introduction

We come again to the book of Ruth. We remember that the purpose of the book is to portray domestic life during the period of the judges, to show how faith and dedication to the Lord is rewarded, and to show the line of the coming of the Messiah, the Lord Jesus Christ.

The happy marriage of Ruth and Boaz takes place in chapter 4. Let us learn some precious truths from this chapter about a happy marriage.

I. A happy marriage takes place when believers are brought together by the Lord.

When we read the book of Ruth, we become aware that the providence of God is at work. God is in the process of bringing two believers together in marriage, two believers with different backgrounds but who love the Lord very much. Likewise, a wedding of Christians should take place only if the two parties believe God is bringing them together for life, that he is leading them to link their lives together.

II. A happy marriage takes place when the couple receives the blessings of God.

It is evident that God was blessing Ruth and that God wanted Boaz to have a companion for life. Surely they were rewarded by God.

A. *Ruth was rewarded with a husband (vv. 1–12).*
B. *Boaz was rewarded with a wife (v. 13).*
C. *Ruth and Boaz were rewarded with a son (vv. 13–17).*
D. *Ruth and Boaz were rewarded with a lineage (vv. 18–22).*

We need the blessing of God if we are to have happy marriages.

III. A happy marriage takes place when children are considered a gift from God (v. 13).

Children should not be perceived as accidents. Children should be wanted and should be considered gifts from God.

IV. A happy marriage takes place when old age brings happiness.

Both Boaz and Ruth were true to God. One was of the covenant and the other was a Moabite. Boaz was loyal to God in the midst of defections. Ruth, by conviction, said, "Whither thou goest, I will go; and where thou lodgest, I will lodge"—but don't stop there—"thy people shall be my people, and thy God my God" (1:16).

Neither Boaz nor Ruth knew what the union of two righteous souls would bring. Their union would bring a child, then grandchildren, and rejoicing forever. The union of Boaz and Ruth would bring happiness to their barren lives; and from this union would come the Lord Jesus Christ, who would bless all who would come to him by repentance and faith.

Conclusion

You too can have a happy marriage when your marriage is the result of the Lord's leadership and when you love each other as did Ruth and Boaz.

SUGGESTED PREACHING PROGRAM FOR THE MONTH OF APRIL

■ Sunday Mornings

Continue and complete the series "The Death of Christ and His Victorious Resurrection from the Dead." Christ died, was raised to life, and now lives; and Christianity is a life of fellowship with the living Lord. We need to respond to this great truth every day.

■ Sunday Evenings

"The Ministry of Jesus to Individuals" is the title of the series that begins this month and continues through June. As Jesus came into contact with various individuals, he ministered to them on a one-to-one basis. He showed insight and concern for each one's situation. As we study Jesus' encounters with individuals and recognize his ability to minister to our needs today, our faith will be strengthened.

■ Wednesday Evenings

From the days of Adam, humans have been questioners. Some of our questions are directed to God, others to self, and still others to peers. "Questions Christians Ask" is the suggested theme for the next three months of Wednesday evenings.

WEDNESDAY EVENING, APRIL 2

Title: What Is the Kingdom of God Like?
Text: "And when one of them that sat at meat with him heard these things, he said unto him, Blessed is he that shall eat bread in the kingdom of God" **(Luke 14:15)**.
Scripture Reading: Luke 14:15–24

Introduction

Brian A. Nelson, in his book *Hustle Won't Bring in the Kingdom*, tells of his son Barry's involvement in a community vacation Bible school. One of the leaders, urging Barry to attend, promised a party. The last day of the school came, and each of the different age groups presented a commencement program. During the presentation the five-year-old Barry turned to the teacher who had invited him and said, "You promised me a party, but all we've had so far is church."

Often we make a distinction between something that is joyful and what takes place in church services. The Bible doesn't view things that way.

Throughout Scripture the kingdom of God is compared to a party. Festivals and celebrations are prominent in both the Old Testament and the New. And many of Jesus' parables contain the idea of a party.

Parties are happy occasions of fun, games, and interacting with other people. The kingdom of God may be compared to a great party. Let us compare the kingdom of God with a joyous celebration.

I. To have a party, preparations must be made.

The householder in the parable of the banquet made extensive preparations. In keeping with Middle-Eastern customs, a general announcement was sent to inform people of the event. Servants later went to tell the people that all the preparations had been made.

A. *God has been making general preparations for the kingdom.* From the earliest beginnings of the "holy history" recorded in the Old Testament, God has been preparing for the kingdom. The selection of Abraham, the making of a nation, the coming of the prophets, and many other matters represent general preparations for the kingdom.

B. *God sent his Son for the final preparations for the kingdom.* The life and ministry of Jesus Christ represent the completion of God's preparation. After Jesus taught, healed, died, and rose from the grave, God's servants could say, "Come; for all things are now ready" (Luke 14:17).

II. To have a party, invitations must be extended to people.

Parties are not to be enjoyed only by the host or hostess. People are a necessary part of a party.

A. *God is pictured as a great inviter.* Lloyd Ogilvie wrote a book on the parables entitled *God's Autobiography.* Ogilvie claims that the parables disclose the nature of God. In this parable about the great banquet, God is portrayed as the Great Inviter. He wants people to come to the kingdom.

B. *God grants the invited the privilege to choose.* When the servants invited people to the party, they were confronted with three different excuses. One wanted time to look at a field. Another wanted to test some oxen. Still another wanted to spend time with his wife. These excuses were not valid, but the householder allowed the people the privilege of choosing to come or not to come to the party.

III. To have a party, activities must take place.

The host had a great banquet so that his guests could eat, enjoy one another's company, and maybe participate in party games.

A. *At God's party there is a variety of guests.* The parable teaches that God first invited the Jews to the kingdom, and then he turned to the

Gentiles. Even though God invites both Jews and Gentiles, "still there is room."

B. *At God's party it is proper to conform to the Host's wishes.* Gracious guests eat the food prepared for them and take part in the planned activities. To be genuine participants in God's party, we need to submit to God's rule.

Conclusion

Although the kingdom of God is far too exhaustive a topic to cover in one message, we can gain insight by comparing the kingdom to a joyous party.

SUNDAY MORNING, APRIL 6

Title: When the Savior Is Substituted
Text: "As they came out, they found a man of Cyrene, Simon by name: him they compelled to bear his cross" **(Matt. 27:32)**.
Scripture Reading: Matthew 27:27–37
Hymns: "Must Jesus Bear the Cross Alone?" Shepherd
"Face to Face with Christ My Savior," Breck
"He Is Able to Deliver Thee," Ogden
Offertory Prayer: We come to you this day, Father, with hearts grateful for your love, which we will try to express through a life of gratitude to you; with hearts thankful for your grace, which we will try to express through a life of devotion to you; and with hearts full of joy because of your continuing presence, which we will try to express through a life of service to you. Enlighten our minds to know your will and strengthen our hands to do your will, Father. We return to you this day our offerings, our tithes, and our gifts in gratitude for all that you have done for us. Please accept our gifts and bless our lives. We pray in the name of our Savior, Jesus Christ the Lord. Amen.

Introduction

How many times have you read in the newspaper an account of an athletic event something like this: "John Jones came off the bench to lead the Wildcats to victory!" The article implies that a substitute has carried the day.

Any coach will tell you that one of the keys to victory is a strong bench—having tough players who are able to substitute for the regulars when they are injured, tired, or ineffective.

But sometimes substitution is not by choice; some are substituted for others by force. And so it was that Simon of Cyrene substituted for the Savior on the road to his crucifixion. As far as we can ascertain, Simon was an innocent bystander. From North Africa, he was a Jew of the Dispersion, that large group of Jews who lived away from Judea.

For Simon this Passover in Jerusalem may have been the culmination of a lifelong dream. He may have saved his money for years for the trip. It seems as though he had just arrived when he felt the tap of a Roman spear on his shoulder and he was forced to carry a cross too heavy for a prisoner who was exhausted by trials and beating.

That day Simon of Cyrene, without realizing it, substituted for the Savior of the world. He was at the cross when the Savior for whom he substituted died for him as well as for all of us. What happens when you substitute for the Savior?

I. When you substitute for the Savior, the plan may come quite unexpectedly.

A. *It may come with no advance warning.* The last thing Simon of Cyrene had planned to do was carry a cross. One account mentions that he came in from the country. He may have just arrived in Jerusalem and not had any idea of what was going on when he joined the crowd that lined the street as Jesus carried his cross to the place of execution.

We never do get much advance warning about how we can substitute for the Savior. During the Civil War when Clara Barton, the "Angel of the Battle Field," who founded the American Red Cross, was ministering to a wounded soldier, he said to her that she was like Christ to him. To that soldier at that time, she substituted for the Savior. And that particular act may have come with no advance warning.

B. *It may change your plans.* We have no idea what Simon's plans were. We really do not know why he had come to Jerusalem or what he had planned to accomplish during his visit there. But we can be sure that his plans were radically changed. And his life was changed also.

Quite suddenly you might be stopped in the midst of your activities and the routine of life to stand for Christ, to substitute for him. And that one act of witness could well change the whole direction of your life.

II. When you substitute for the Savior, you will need to be prepared in advance.

A. *The need for preparation.* If you do not know when or under what circumstances you will be called on to substitute for the Savior, you will need to be prepared in advance for your ministry. Opportunities come suddenly and unexpectedly, and if you are not ready to serve, you will not have time to get ready. Preparation must always be made in advance.

Jesus gave us some parables about preparation that point out this truth. For instance, the parable of the ten virgins, five of whom were prepared for the coming of the bridegroom and five of whom were not, shows the need for preparation.

B. *The method of preparation.* How does God prepare us for this service? We do not always know. He prepares us in many small ways of which we may be totally unaware. God moves in our lives in small and mysterious ways. The Holy Spirit can be working without our realizing what he is doing. Later we may see that God was using an experience to prepare us for his service in a way we were unaware of at the time.

III. When you substitute for the Savior, you become a participant and not just a spectator in the world.

A. *One can come as a spectator and leave as a participant.* That happened to Simon of Cyrene. He came to Jerusalem and the crucifixion scene as a spectator. Possibly he was just standing in the crowd trying to see what was going on. But he left as a participant in the crucifixion of the Christ.

In reality we cannot just look on the world and not become an active participant in it. One philosopher took what he called "a balcony view of life." He proposed to look on life as one would view it from a balcony, always being a spectator and never being a participant. But suddenly he was changed from spectator to participant.

B. *God calls us to be participants.* As we look at the needs of the world, we realize that we must participate in witnessing of Christ to the world and in helping to meet those needs.

Consider world hunger as just one area. We can be involved in the attempt to alleviate world hunger and to minister to those who hunger. Someone has expressed the futility of simply acting as a spectator:

> I was hungry and you circled the moon.
> I was hungry and you told me to wait.
> I was hungry and you set up a commission.
> I was hungry and you talked about bootstraps.
> I was hungry and you told me I shouldn't be.
> I was hungry and you had war bills to pay.
> I was hungry and you said, "Machines do that kind of work now."
> I was hungry and you said, "The poor are always with us."
> I was hungry and you said, "Law and order come first."
> I was hungry and you blamed it on the government.
> I was hungry and you said, "So were my ancestors."
> I was hungry and you said, "We don't hire those over age thirty-five."
> I was hungry and you said, "God helps those who help themselves."
> I was hungry and you said, "Sorry, try again tomorrow."

The same thing is true in world mission, world evangelization, and world ministry. The needs are here right now. And response to them must be here right now if anything is to be done about them.

Conclusion

We all can help the Savior by substituting for him when a need arises and our time to serve comes. The legend of Saint Christopher, whose name means "Christ-bearer," is that he was a ferryman who carried people over a bridgeless river. One day he carried a child over the river on his back, the child seeming to grow heavier at each step. When they reached the shore, he remarked that one would think he had been carrying the burden of the world. To this the Christ child replied: "Thou hast borne upon thy back the world and him who created it." According to this story of the saint who died about AD 250, he carried the Christ himself. Simon carried his cross, and we carry on his ministry.

Actually, we are all Christ-bearers. We are all called on to carry his cross. You may never know when you will be asked to substitute for the Savior. Will you be ready?

Sunday Evening, April 6

Title: Nicodemus: Hampered by Intellectualism

Text: "Jesus answered and said unto him, Verily, verily, I say unto thee, Except a man be born again, he cannot see the kingdom of God. Nicodemus saith unto him, How can a man be born when he is old? Can he enter the second time into his mother's womb, and be born?" **(John 3:3–4)**.

Scripture Reading: John 3:1–21

Introduction

One of the amazing facts about the creation of humans is that each person is unique. No two personalities are exactly the same. It is true within a family. There may be two or even a dozen children in a family, yet each one is different and has his or her own unique personality. For example, one child may be a dreamer and live with his head in the clouds. The other is practical and down-to-earth, a realist.

If this is true in the family, how much more is it a fact among people as a whole? And if it is true in physical and social relationships, it is equally true in spiritual matters. Nowhere do we see this demonstrated more vividly than in Jesus' encounters with individuals. The Gospels are filled with beautiful and poignant vignettes in which we observe Jesus dealing with persons in one-on-one relationships. Never did he handle those meetings in exactly the same way. Rather, he met people where they were. He didn't demand that they first adjust their "receiving sets" to his channel; instead, he tuned in to them.

He spoke their language; he identified with their problems. He established a genuine rapport—a climate in which he could freely transmit his truth to their minds. This became the basis for the birth of faith.

For the next several Sundays, we will be examining individuals Jesus encountered, whose stories are told in the Gospels. We begin with Nicodemus, perhaps one of the most famous personalities in the New Testament.

I. The personality of Nicodemus (vv. 1–2).

A. *This was Jesus' first trip to Jerusalem after he had begun his public ministry.* Already he had performed many miracles, and the word of what he was doing had spread far and wide. Thus, on this trip to Jerusalem, Jesus' popularity poll was soaring. The latter part of John 2 tells of the great crowds of people who were attracted to Jesus out of curiosity. Perhaps there should be no chapter division at this point, for it seems that John 3:1 draws a contrast between the people who were superficially following Jesus, and Nicodemus, who exhibited a much deeper level of sincerity. Jesus recognized this instantly.

B. *Who was Nicodemus?* He was wealthy, for when Jesus died, Nicodemus brought "a mixture of myrrh and aloes, about seventy-five pounds" (19:39 NIV). Only a wealthy man could have afforded that. He was also a Pharisee. In many ways, the Pharisees were the best people in the land. They had taken a vow that they would spend their lives observing every detail of the scribal law. To the Jew, the Law was the most sacred thing in the world. It consisted of the first five books of the Old Testament—the Pentateuch. They believed that it was the perfect Word of God. So they set about to extract from the great principles of Moses' law an infinite number of rules and regulations to govern every conceivable situation in life. Nicodemus, as "a ruler of the Jews," was a member of the Sanhedrin, the seventy-member "supreme court" of the Jews. It was the most influential governing body in Palestine.

C. *In Nicodemus, then, we have a wealthy man of the Jewish aristocracy, a fanatically devoted religious leader (a Pharisee), a man of national prominence as a member of the Sanhedrin.* And this man was coming to Jesus, a homeless prophet who had been a carpenter in the backwoods Galilean town of Nazareth! The fact that Nicodemus came at night does not necessarily indicate a fear of being seen by others. The rabbis declared that the best time to study the law of God was at night when a man was undisturbed.

D. *So, as we examine the personality of Nicodemus, we discover a cultured, refined, educated gentleman who was not experiencing the deep soul satisfaction in life for which he longed.* In a quiet, simple way, the Holy Spirit was maneuvering him into position where he could receive what he needed and what he so deeply wanted in life.

II. The approach of Jesus (3:3).

A. *Nicodemus had expressed his opinion of Jesus.* In essence, Jesus was saying to Nicodemus, "Nicodemus, your knowledge of me is quite correct. I am indeed 'a teacher come from God.' But that is not enough. You must receive a new kind of life that will give you a clear vision of what the kingdom of God truly is. You are a student; you are trained in academic matters. But the life you need now comes from above, and it will enable you to see clearly and experience genuinely that which you desire. You must be 'born again,' Nicodemus!"

B. *No doubt Nicodemus was perplexed.* Perhaps he expected Jesus to say something profound and learned to him. The problem was that Nicodemus's approach was intellectual, whereas Jesus' approach was spiritual.

III. The exciting conversation between Jesus and Nicodemus.

A. *We can sense immediately the great consternation Nicodemus was experiencing, for he asked, "How can a man be born when he is old? Can he enter the second time into his mother's womb, and be born?" (v. 4).* It is possible that Nicodemus may have been referring to the physical impossibility of what Jesus had said. It would seem, though, that Nicodemus was wiser than that. More than likely, if he had understood Jesus literally, he would have walked away from such absurdity.

B. *It is possible that Nicodemus could have been implying: "Master, how can a man whose habits and ways of thinking are already fixed be expected to change so radically?* Physical rebirth is impossible; but is spiritual change any more possible after the die has been cast, after habits and lifestyles have been formed and deeply ingrained?"

C. *Thoroughly convinced of Nicodemus's genuineness, Jesus began to teach him the truth of his gospel.* He told him that unless he was "born of water and of the Spirit, he [could] not enter into the kingdom of God" (v. 5). The "water" may have been Jesus' way of referring to John the Baptist's water baptism, which was symbolic of repentance. New birth (spiritual birth) is possible only when persons repent of their sins and confess that they are sinners before God.

D. *Verse 9 represents the climax, the turning point, in the conversation between Jesus and Nicodemus.* Nicodemus asked, "How can these things be?" (v. 9). His question may not have had a negative note of doubt at all. He may not have been implying that Jesus' words strained the intellect and reason of a man almost past the point of credibility. Rather, Nicodemus may have been appealing for some direction.

E. *Then Jesus told Nicodemus that "just as Moses lifted up the snake in the desert, so the Son of Man must be lifted up, that everyone who believes in him may have eternal life" (vv. 14–15 NIV).* This was the moment of decision for Nicodemus.

Conclusion

John does not tell us how Nicodemus responded. But based on the future appearances of Nicodemus in the gospel story, we can surmise that he became a believer in the Lord Jesus. Jesus met and dealt with Nicodemus where he was, and from that point he moved him to the threshold of the kingdom. God starts with all people where they are. From that point, he lovingly and patiently leads them to repentance and the new birth.

WEDNESDAY EVENING, APRIL 9

Title: How Can a Church Grow?
Text: "And the Lord added to the church daily such as should be saved" **(Acts 2:47)**.
Scripture Reading: Acts 2:37–47

Introduction

Once a man moved to a new neighborhood. At his previous residence he had grown vegetables. Yet in his new place he failed two consecutive years to grow tomatoes. He shared his failure with a neighbor who encouraged him to get his soil tested. The man did, and an agricultural expert told him that the soil lacked the proper chemicals to grow tomatoes. The next year he added the chemicals, and the soil produced a bountiful tomato crop. Conditions in the soil had to be right to grow tomatoes.

Christians often try to grow churches and fail. They ask, "How can a church grow?" To find the answer to such a question, we need to turn to a resource for church growth, namely, the book of Acts. The church in Jerusalem from its beginning was a growing church. It grew because the conditions were right. Let us examine those conditions.

I. A growing church is an evangelistic church.

One of the conditions that produced church growth was an evangelistic concern. The church in Jerusalem was interested in reaching others with the gospel.

A. *Evangelism grows out of basic beliefs.* "And they continued stedfastly in the apostles' doctrine" (2:42). The concept of the "apostles' doctrine" seems to be diverse. More than likely, some of these doctrines included: (1) people are lost; (2) Christ can save; (3) people can be changed by Jesus Christ; and (4) eternal destiny depends on a person's response to Jesus Christ. These kinds of beliefs motivate one for evangelism.

B. *Evangelism extends to various groups.* The church at Jerusalem made the Jews their target group. Later the Christians aimed at Samaritans (half-Jews) and pagans.

II. A growing church is a worshiping church.

From the earliest records of the New Testament church, the congregation engaged in worship. Worship of Jesus Christ made the conditions right for the church to grow.

A. *Genuine worship has praise of Jesus Christ as its object.* The Lord Jesus Christ was the object of the church's affection.

B. *Genuine worship has personal evaluation as its result.* Whenever one directs thoughts and affection toward Christ, painful realization comes of human finiteness and sin. Christians see themselves as they really are.

III. A growing church is a caring church.

Careful study of the Jerusalem church indicates another condition that is imperative for church growth. It is the care the believers had for others.

A. *The church recognized their union with each other.* A prominent word that describes the union of believers with Christ and with each other is *fellowship*. The word is descriptive of a joint partnership because of a union with Christ in faith.

B. *The church practiced fellowship.* The more one studies the New Testament churches, the more one can see their Christian relationships with one another. They respected one another, helped one another, and forgave one another. Furthermore, the church ministered to the needs of those who were not in their fellowship.

IV. A growing church is a praying church.

No church can grow without the prevalence of prayer in its life. The early church prayed constantly. "And they continued stedfastly . . . in prayers" (v. 42).

A. *Prayer represents a communion with the Lord.* The New Testament Christians prayed as an act of enjoying the presence of God. John Killinger wrote a book entitled *Prayer: The Act of Being with God.* Perhaps that title gives the best definition of prayer.

B. *Prayer represents a dependence on the Lord.* The early Christians prayed in order to seek God's will and to ask for God's power. Their prayer life represented a dependence on the Lord.

V. A growing church is a giving church.

A casual study of the New Testament will disclose that the early church had a sacrificial spirit. They were willing to give.

A. *Giving comes from the willingness to give oneself.* Many of the New Testament believers loved the Lord so much that they gave their lives.

Stephen was a prominent example of one who did not love his life more than Christ.

B. *Giving demonstrates itself in the areas of time and possessions.* The first-century believers took time to accomplish Christ's mission. They gave of their possessions so his mission could be completed.

Conclusion

If the right conditions prevail, fruit and vegetables may be grown. You cannot grow oranges in Alaska because the conditions are not right. Similarly, to grow a church, the proper conditions have to be present.

Sunday Morning, April 13

Title: When Christ Is Confessed

Text: "Now when the centurion, and they that were with him, watching Jesus, saw the earthquake, and those things that were done, they feared greatly, saying, Truly this was the Son of God" **(Matt. 27:54).**

Scripture Reading: Matthew 27:45–56

Hymns: "Beneath the Cross of Jesus," Clephane
"The Old Rugged Cross," Bennard
"Victory in Jesus," Bartlett

Offertory Prayer: Our Father, we concentrate this day on the great gift that you have given us through the death of Jesus Christ, your Son, for our sins. May we concentrate also on the gifts that we give you: the greatest gift of a humble and contrite heart and the gifts of our money earned through toil. Amen.

Introduction

Ernest Gordon, former dean of the chapel at Princeton University, wrote in his book coauthored with Peter Funk, *A Guidebook for New Christians*, that for six years he saw active service as a soldier in the Highland Regiment. That service included tragic battles, wounds, and imprisonment. He became accustomed to fear, hate, brutality, torture, and despair. He lost his fear of pain and death and of what other men could do to him. He was hardened by the laws of nations and the experience of survival. Death and hell could not scare him. What changed his life was the "love profound" he saw in the lives of converted men. They showed him the way to Jesus and to the activity of the Father.

Gordon was not the first hardened soldier affected by "love profound" as seen in the cross of Jesus Christ. Probably the first was the centurion who presided over Jesus' death. Although callused by death, he was sensitive to the difference between Jesus and other men he had seen die. This difference caused him to confess, "Truly this was the Son of God."

How much the centurion knew about Jesus previously we don't know. How much of the trial he attended and the impressions he had from the trial we don't know. What we do know is his confession of Christ.

At the cross the centurion who presided over Jesus' crucifixion confessed the Christ. Our confession of Christ is much the same. And it comes at the cross.

I. In the confession of Christ there is the observation of events.

A. *This Roman leader would be a keen observer of events.* He could not have reached such a place of leadership without the ability to observe the events taking place around him. As the centurion in charge of the crucifixion detail, he would have been aware of at least the things that happened on the way to the cross and at the cross. These events must have made a profound impression on him.

Jesus' behavior at the trial also would have impressed him. Jesus stood at the trial with regal bearing. One gets the impression that Pilate was on trial before Jesus rather than Jesus before Pilate.

The acceptance of the sentence and the cross by Jesus was impressive. Whereas many others had likely protested, cursed, and sought to escape the sentence, Jesus never said a mumbling word. Likewise, Jesus' actions on the way to Golgotha were impressive. There was no bitterness, no protestation of innocence, no shrieking or crying out. Instead, he comforted others along the way.

The words from the cross that we have collected and called the "seven last words of Christ" must have had some impact on the observers.

And one certainly cannot overlook the supernatural occurrences that took place at the time of the crucifixion.

As a keen observer of events, the Roman centurion would have been impressed at the crucifixion of Jesus.

B. *Any sensitive person becomes aware of these same events.* As we transport ourselves from the time of the crucifixion to the present, we perceive that any sensitive person becomes aware of these same events. We know something out of the ordinary was happening as Jesus was crucified. This is the application of Jesus' statement in John 12:32: "And I, if I be lifted up from the earth, will draw all men unto me." As he was lifted up from the earth in crucifixion, he drew people to himself in confession and faith. One of those drawn to him was the centurion in charge of the execution squad that killed him. Likewise, sensitive people of all time have been drawn to him by his death.

II. In the confession of Christ there is the reversal of opinion.

A. *An initial opinion.* Whatever opinion the centurion originally had of Jesus, it was not that he was the Son of God. We cannot, of course, know his initial opinion of Jesus, but we can surmise what it was. And from what we know of Roman military officers, we can imagine that he did not initially consider Jesus to be the Son of God. Nevertheless, he had a complete reversal of opinion. And it can happen to you. How do you view Jesus?

1. Some would look at Jesus only as a great teacher. A teacher he was. "No one ever taught like this man" was a current opinion of Jesus. He was called "Teacher" more than any other title in the Gospels. Jesus *was* a great Teacher. But he was more.
2. Others would look on Jesus as an inspired and inspiring religious leader. And that he was too. He inspired others to follow him and to rise above themselves. He was obviously inspired by God in his teaching and his activities. He *was* an inspired religious leader. But he was more.
3. Still others would see Jesus as a significant historical figure. When one looks at the historical figures of the ages, Jesus stands out among them. To grant his historicity and to acknowledge his place in history is one thing, but it is not to accept him as Savior. He *was* a significant historical figure. But he was more.
4. He was the Christ, the Son of God. That is what the centurion confessed when he witnessed the crucifixion of Jesus.

B. *A reversed opinion.* It is not until a person makes that reversal of opinion and begins to look on Jesus as the Son of God and his or her personal Savior that salvation occurs.

Until you are ready to confess him as the Son of God, he is not your Savior.

III. In the confession of Christ there is the realization of redemption.

A. *An objective element in the atonement: Jesus died to redeem humankind from their sins.* The atonement was real. The crucifixion really happened. When we look at all the events at the cross, we realize that they actually happened. The crucifixion was not a charade or a staged event. Objectively, Jesus died on the cross. And his death on the cross was for the redemption of humankind from sin.

B. *A subjective element in the atonement: the acceptance of Jesus Christ as one's personal Savior.* The subjective element is the confession that Jesus is the Christ, the Son of God, and the acceptance of him as one's own personal Savior. This is how redemption is realized.

There is no way that one can view the death of Christ for humankind and come away unaffected. People see this act of suffering love, and it makes them ashamed of their sins. It awakens their gratitude and releases within them new springs of love that make them new creatures reconciled to God. Jesus' words "And I, if I be lifted up from the earth, will draw all men unto me" (John 12:32) are the theological basis of many of our great hymns, for example, Isaac Watts's "When I Survey the Wondrous Cross":

> When I survey the wondrous cross,
> On which the Prince of glory died,
> My richest gain I count but loss,
> And pour contempt on all my pride.

Conclusion

No theology is big enough to contain the whole truth about the cross of Jesus Christ. The objective fact is that Jesus died on the cross and that he died for me. The subjective fact is that I must confess him as the Christ and receive him as my Savior.

When Christ is confessed, salvation is received and sin is forgiven. We must confess Christ to receive the forgiveness of our sins. This we can do. Why not make your own personal confession of Christ as Savior today?

SUNDAY EVENING, APRIL 13

Title: The Invalid at the Pool of Bethesda: Paralyzed by Hopelessness
Text: "'Sir,' the invalid replied, 'I have no one to help me into the pool when the water is stirred. While I am trying to get in, someone else goes down ahead of me.'

"Then Jesus said to him, 'Get up! Pick up your mat and walk.' At once the man was cured; he picked up his mat and walked" **(John 5:7–8 NIV).**
Scripture Reading: John 5:1–18

Introduction

It was the time for the Jews' annual Feast of Pentecost, one of the three great religious feasts celebrated during the year. Jesus was in Jerusalem to observe this feast. But on this particular day, instead of finding Jesus in the temple precincts, we find him instead in the northeastern section of Jerusalem in an area known as Bethesda. Here was a certain pool called "the Pool of Bethesda," which had attached to it an interesting tradition and superstition. It seemed to have in its floor a spring that bubbled at certain times. Superstitious Jews believed that when this happened, an angel had come down into the waters with healing power to cure the first person who entered the pool. It was a cruel and ridiculous superstition.

I. The depressing scene (John 5:1–4).

A. *There were five porches or "porticoes" around this pool.* We can imagine scores of sick people on cots and mats. In their desperation to be healed, they had been brought here by friends or relatives. This was their last hope. Many of them may have been told that medically there was nothing that could be done for them. All that was left for them was a "miracle cure," so they sought out the magical waters of this pool.

B. *Probably the mass of people around the pool swelled considerably during the feast weeks, for no doubt many of the pilgrims would bring their sick relatives or friends and place them on the porches around the pool.* Such was the depressing scene.

II. Now let's focus on one person in that mob of people around the pool—the destitute man (vv. 5–7).

A. *John tells us that this man had been an invalid for thirty-eight years.* We do not know how long he had been coming to the pool, how many long, weary days he had lain here crying, praying, hoping for someone to come and help him down to the pool's edge, then help him slip into the waters quickly when they were stirred before someone else could get in before him.

B. *So what do we have here?* We have a double paralysis. This man was paralyzed physically, and that was bad enough. But another kind of paralysis had slowly but surely crept up on this man—the paralysis of hopelessness. The fires of hope that had blazed so brightly in his heart in the beginning had begun to die down. Just a dim, vague flicker of hope was left.

C. *There is no way to overemphasize the importance of hope in a person's life.* Humans are made so that they must have hope of some kind or they cannot function for very long. Medical science has supported the fact that people have actually died because they lost hope. Hopelessness is a terrible paralysis, and it can destroy a person.

D. *One other thing added a tragic dimension to this man's condition.* We discover it because of something Jesus said to the man later, after he met him in the temple: "See, you are well again. Stop sinning or something worse may happen to you" (v. 14 NIV). The inference is that this man's condition may have been due to a moral sin. In some shameful way, he may have brought this physical condition on himself. We know that it is not true that every sickness is the outcome of personal sin, but apparently this man had brought sickness on himself.

III. Now there comes the beautiful and thrilling part of this story: we see the delivering Savior in action (vv. 8–15).

A. *Note the command Jesus gave to this man: "Get up! Pick up your mat and walk" (v. 8 NIV).* Jesus told him to do three things that were vital to his healing.

1. First, he was to "get up." Sometimes Jesus would take people whom he was helping or healing by the hand and lift them to

their feet. But in this case, Jesus insisted that this man, who had for so long lain in helpless and torturous pain, get up by himself! It was necessary for him to exercise his faith that Jesus could do this miraculous thing for him. And the instant he made the slightest effort, in the form of a response to the faith God was giving him, healing power surged through his body like electricity. His crippled and distorted limbs were straightened, and he got up.

2. The second thing Jesus told the man to do was to pick up his mat. What did he need now with that filthy mat on which he had lain for so many years? That man's mat represented his former condition of helplessness and hopelessness. As long as it remained on the ground, it beckoned him to come back, to submerge himself again in his state of helplessness. So Jesus was saying, "Pick up that thing! Roll it up! You will not be needing it anymore. Don't leave it here as a reminder of your past days. Destroy the evidence of that part of your life, the sad result of your sin!" This says to us that if God is willing to forget our past sins—to cast them as far from him as the east is from the west—he wants us to do the same. We must forgive ourselves just as God has forgiven us.
3. The third command Jesus gave this man was, "Walk!" He was not just asking him to walk around on the porch and demonstrate his newfound ability to move about. Rather, Jesus meant, "Walk away from here! Leave this place, this scene of your hopelessness."

B. *There is one other thing we see about this man that is somewhat unusual.* He was not able to take in all that was happening at once. Such a fantastic thing had happened to him that it was going to require some time for it to sink in.

John says that later Jesus found the man at the temple (v. 14). Jesus in no way intended to let this man get away. He was not finished with him. But he had a purpose in allowing him to experience his healed body first without knowing who it was who had healed him. So, at the proper moment, in Jesus' perfect timing, he found the man in the temple, revealed himself to him, and warned him about the disaster that would happen to him if he continued to sin.

Conclusion

Sin is depressing—however enjoyable it may be at the moment one is committing it. One can never sin and escape the inevitable consequences. It ultimately produces destitution, hopelessness, and despair. But the good news is that there is hope! The paralysis of sin need not be terminal. For Jesus can bring a hope that cannot be taken away. And with the hope comes the joy of salvation—truly a joy that is “unspeakable and full of glory.”

Wednesday Evening, April 16

Title: What Does Real Repentance Involve?
Text: “Create in me a clean heart, O God; and renew a right spirit within me” **(Ps. 51:10)**.
Scripture Reading: Psalm 51:1–17

Introduction

One of the more intriguing scenes of English literature comes from James Hall and Charles Nordhoff’s historical novel *Mutiny on the Bounty*. Some seamen accused of seizing a ship and casting the captain and crew adrift in a small boat were tried before a British Navy court and sentenced to die. Roger Byam, one of the sentenced, was a young man. An emotional scene in the novel depicts the friends of Roger Byam pleading for mercy.

The Bible also has a famous scene of a person making a plea for mercy—King David’s plea recorded in Psalm 51. His plea for mercy is an excellent disclosure of genuine repentance. Let us notice what happened to David in Psalm 51 when he received God’s pardon.

I. Real repentance involves an appeal to a loving God (vv. 1–2).

The prominent person to whom a believer turns in a crisis is God. David turned to the Lord to make an appeal for the consideration of his sins.

A. *The sinner needs to be aware of God’s attitude.* The psalmist used two expressions that were descriptive of God’s character—“lovingkindness” and “tender mercies.” The expression “lovingkindness” depends on God’s steadfast love. The expression “tender mercies” is derived from the Hebrew word for “womb.” The expression relates God’s love to a mother’s love for her child.
B. *The sinner must be aware of the reality of sin.* As soon as one catches a glimpse into the nature of God, one gets a view of his or her sin. David used three words to describe his condition: *transgression*, *iniquity*, and *sin*.

Being aware of sin is not enough. Drastic action by the Lord is needed. David made appeals for action: “blot out,” “wash me,” “cleanse me.” David recognized that only God could remedy his condition.

II. Real repentance involves confession to a listening God (vv. 3–6).

Confession never comes easy. It means a painful confession of wrong on our part.

A. *Confession involves an acknowledgment of guilt.* "For I acknowledge my transgressions: and my sin is ever before me" (v. 3). Genuine repentance comes when we see ourselves as God sees us.
B. *Confession involves an admission of personal responsibility.* David did not blame anyone but himself: "my transgression," "my sin."

God is willing to listen to one who admits the reality of his or her condition to him. The Lord always hears the sounds of genuine confession.

III. Real repentance involves a call for action to a powerful God (vv. 7–12).

The truly repentant person wants a radical transformation in life. David longed for the good days he experienced before Bathsheba. Only God had the power to redirect his life.

A. *The repentant person has a cleansed life.* "Purge me with hyssop, and I shall be clean: wash me, and I shall be whiter than snow" (v. 7).
B. *The repentant person has a renewed happiness.* "Make me to hear joy and gladness; that the bones which thou hast broken may rejoice" (v. 8).
C. *The repentant person can face God again.* "Hide thy face from my sins, and blot out all mine iniquities" (v. 9).
D. *The repentant person will have a new kind of life.* "Create in me a clean heart, O God; and renew a right spirit within me" (v. 10).
E. *The repentant person wants to be in continuous fellowship with the Lord.* "Cast me not away from thy presence; and take not thy holy spirit from me" (v. 11).
F. *The repentant person wants his or her joy restored.* "Restore unto me the joy of thy salvation; and uphold me with thy free spirit" (v. 12).

IV. Real repentance involves commitment to a demanding God (vv. 13–17).

Genuine repentance does not lead one back to old ways. It involves a commitment to the commands of the Lord.

A. *Commitment involves the sharing of experiences.* "Then will I teach transgressors thy ways; and sinners shall be converted unto thee" (v. 13).
B. *Commitment involves the offering of oneself.* "The sacrifices of God are a broken spirit: a broken and a contrite heart, O God, thou wilt not despise" (v. 17).

Conclusion

Repentance is no casual matter. It involves self-examination, confession, and commitment. Mere wails of sadness do not comprise repentance. True repentance comes from a broken heart that wants to be remade by God.

Sunday Morning, April 20

Title: When Defeat Is Turned into Victory
Text: "And he saith unto them, Be not affrighted: Ye seek Jesus of Nazareth, which was crucified: he is risen; he is not here: behold the place where they laid him" **(Mark 16:6)**.
Scripture Reading: Mark 16:1–8
Hymns: "Christ the Lord Is Risen Today," Wordsworth
"All Hail the Power of Jesus' Name," Perronet
"Low in the Grave He Lay," Lowry
Offertory Prayer: Our Father, our hearts overflow with joy on this day that marks the resurrection of our Lord Jesus Christ from the dead. We are thankful for the privilege of worship and for the pleasure of giving. Take our gifts, given in gratitude, expressed in praise, and offered in love, we pray. Bless these gifts and use them for your glory and honor throughout the world, as well as in our community. We ask in Jesus' name and for his sake. Amen.

Introduction

An aged custodian of Winchester Cathedral in England loved to stand on the cathedral roof and relate the story of how the news of Wellington's victory over Napoleon reached England. News of the history-making battle came by a sailing vessel to the south coast, and by semaphore it was wigwagged overland to London. Atop Winchester Cathedral the semaphore began to spell out the eagerly awaited message: "W-e-l-l-i-n-g-t-o-n d-e-f-e-a-t-e-d . . ."; and then a dense English fog settled oppressively over the land. The semaphore could no longer be seen, and thus the heartbreaking news of the incomplete message went on to London. The country was overwhelmed in gloom and despair: "Wellington defeated."

But later the fog lifted. Again the signaling semaphore atop the cathedral became visible, spelling out the complete message of the battle: "W-e-l-l-i-n-g-t-o-n d-e-f-e-a-t-e-d t-h-e e-n-e-m-y!" Now the message meant all the more because of the preceding gloom. The joyful news spread across the land and lifted the spirits of the people: "Wellington defeated the enemy." An apparent defeat was turned into a victory.

It was just such a turnabout that occurred with the resurrection of Jesus Christ from the dead. The message had gone out that Jesus was dead; the Jesus problem was solved as far as the Jewish authorities were concerned. Now that Jesus' body was safely laid in Joseph's tomb, the Passover festivities could go on; Sabbath would be observed. Jesus would bother the religious leaders no more.

That was the message the world received when the wind blew and the lightning flashed. But on the third day, the rising sun illuminated the world, and its illumination brought about a light they had not anticipated, a light that could not be put out: Jesus was raised from the dead!

We stand today before the open door of that tomb. The resurrection was an open door to life. The door to the tomb was opened, and Jesus walked from death to life. The apparent defeat of the cross was turned to victory in the resurrection. By his resurrection we have that same promise. It is life that we celebrate today. With the resurrection, defeat was turned into victory. And because of the living Lord, we have life.

I. When defeat is turned into victory, we have an assurance for life.

A. *The resurrection was an unexpected event.* We often approach the resurrection as though we think the first followers of Jesus expected it. They did not. Jesus had tried to prepare them by predicting both his death and resurrection, yet still they were surprised. Furthermore, they were frightened and confused by the unexpected turn of events. They hardly knew what to make of the empty tomb. Therefore, Jesus' first words to them were, "Do not be afraid."

B. *The resurrection is a reassuring event.* We surely need those same words of reassurance today, for much of life frightens us. Just as the resurrection reassured Jesus' first followers, so it reassures us today in the face of apparent defeat, the unknown, even death.

II. When defeat is turned into victory, we have an announcement of life.

A. *An announcement.* In the place of death came an announcement of life. The last word one expects to hear in a cemetery is the word of life. The last announcement one expects to be proclaimed from a tomb is the announcement of life. But that was the announcement Jesus' followers heard on that first Easter morning: "He is risen!"

B. *The content.* Notice the content of the announcement made from the grave itself: "He is risen!" Life is its content.

Easter is about life. All the symbols of Easter have to do with life: eggs are symbols of fertility; flowers are symbols of new life in the spring; new clothes are symbols of life in people. Yet the most significant symbol of Easter is the open tomb, for it announces that Jesus Christ is risen.

III. When defeat is turned into victory, we have an affirmation of life.

A. *There is a statement of affirmation.* To affirm his statement, the angel said, "See where they laid him." They could examine the place. It was apparent that he was not there.

B. *There is an instruction for affirmation.* The greatest affirmation of life came in the instruction the angel gave them. He quoted the risen Christ, who said to tell the disciples and Peter to meet him in Galilee.

The continuing presence of Christ is the greatest affirmation we have. The most convincing proof of the empty tomb is his continuing presence with his original followers. He was with them in their confusion and their struggle. And he is with us in all our struggles. He affirms life for us. He enters the fray with us.

IV. When defeat is turned into victory, we have an authorization for life.

A. *The authorization for life is in a command.* To the women the angel said, "Go . . . tell . . ." This command was their authorization to share the story of Christ's resurrection.

These words are also our authorization. This Easter Sunday we do not gather here just to celebrate an event of two thousand years ago. We don't gather here just because it is the thing to do on Easter. We don't gather here just to praise the resurrection of Jesus from the dead and to reassure ourselves. We have come here for authorization to "Go . . . tell . . ." We have a message to share, and Jesus has authorized each one of us to proclaim that message.

B. *The authorization for life brings a new meaning to life.* All of life is turned around because we have met Christ. Those women went to the tomb with sagging spirits and aching hearts. They had the sad task of anointing Jesus' body for burial, something that should have been done earlier but was not because of the time and day of his death. But when they heard the news that he was risen from the dead and looked into the empty tomb and saw that he was not there, their lives were turned around. And when they heard the authorization to share that story, their lives would never be the same again. Christ's resurrection gives lives new meaning.

Conclusion

It looked like certain defeat for Jesus when he was crucified. But at the resurrection three days later, defeat was turned into victory. And Jesus still turns defeats into victories. He can do it in your life if you come to him by faith this day, putting your life in his hands. That is the Easter message!

Sunday Evening, April 20

Title: The Man with Leprosy: Plagued by Loneliness

Text: "A man with leprosy came and knelt before him and said, 'Lord, if you are willing, you can make me clean.'

"Jesus reached out his hand and touched the man. 'I am willing,' he said. 'Be clean!' Immediately he was cured of his leprosy" **(Matt. 8:2–3 NIV)**.

Scripture Reading: Matthew 8:1–4

Introduction

There are times when all of us like to be alone. In fact, we need these occasional periods when we can retreat from the noise and pressures of life in order to get "reacquainted" with ourselves. It is a way of backing off from life far enough to get perspective, to get the whole picture. Sometimes we can live so close to situations that we cannot see them as they really are.

But there is a difference between "being alone" for periods of time as a constructive and recharging experience and being "lonely." Though the words are closely related, the experiences of being alone and being lonely are not necessarily related.

"Loneliness" suggests isolation, whether self-imposed or caused by others. Some people are so introverted that they withdraw from all social relationships. Others may have unpleasant personality traits; they are abrasive to people, even obnoxious. Eventually they find themselves isolated, left alone. Any way you look at it, loneliness is a suffocating experience.

In our series of studies involving persons Jesus met and ministered to—each with a unique and different problem—we discover in this encounter a man who was plagued by loneliness. His loneliness, however, was not because of an unpleasant personality, nor was he necessarily an introvert. Rather, his problem was the most serious anyone could have in ancient times—he had leprosy. To understand the deep implications of his encounter with Jesus and the miracle that occurred, we need to establish the setting.

I. The contrast (v. 1).

A. *"When he came down from the mountainside" (NIV).* Where had Jesus been, and what had he been doing? The preceding three chapters record the Sermon on the Mount. Jesus had just come down from the hillside where the people had listened as he taught his disciples the incomparable principles of his gospel. The people, as well as the disciples, doubtlessly were overwhelmed with the radically different things Jesus had taught. There was both authority and a magnetism about him.

B. *"Large crowds followed him" (NIV).* Never had they heard one speak as Jesus had! There was a piercing power in his words; he captivated them with his divine personality.

II. The confrontation (v. 2).

A. *Jesus' encounter with the man with leprosy added another dimension to his teaching.* The people had heard his words; now they were about to see a demonstration in action of what he had said. Not only did he have the power to declare, but also to perform.

B. *What do we know about leprosy?* Today it is called Hansen's disease. Because of the wisdom and skill God has granted to men and women in the medical profession, this dreaded disease has just about vanished from the earth. So horrible was the disease that in Old

Testament times it was considered a curse from God. So the person with leprosy bore a double burden: the stigma of believing that he had been cursed of God because of his sin, and the horror of watching himself die, little by little, knowing that the possibility of being cured was extremely remote.

C. *The "law of the leper" is found in Leviticus 13–14.* It demanded that if a person appeared to have the symptoms of leprosy, he was to be examined by the priests. If they determined that he had leprosy, he was isolated for eight days. In that period of time, if he did not have leprosy, the symptoms would likely go away. But if he was found to have leprosy, he was put outside the community so that he could not come in contact with any person, including members of his family. Thus the confrontation between Jesus and this leper is all the more arresting. Here is Jesus, sinlessly perfect and pure, standing before one who epitomized the horror of moral depravity and sin.

D. *But what about this particular leper?* Matthew says that he came and worshiped Jesus. He threw himself on the ground before Jesus. There are many unanswered questions about this leper. Something obviously had happened to convince this man that Jesus could do the impossible for him. Note his statement: "Lord, if you are willing, you can make me clean." There was no doubt in his mind that Jesus had the power to heal him. There was only one problem remaining in his mind: *Would Jesus be willing to heal him?* Given the fact he was considered morally as well as physically unclean, was there hope for him? One rabbi had boasted that he had thrown rocks at a leper to keep him away from him. Would this rabbi be any different?

III. The contact (v. 3).

A. *The leper had said, "You can, Lord, if you are willing!"* And Jesus had said, "I *am* willing!" We can imagine that the crowd gasped in horror as Jesus reached out his hand and touched this leper. Touching a leper rendered one unclean, and that person would not be permitted to worship in the temple until he had gone through an elaborate ritual of cleansing and purification.

B. *Did Jesus actually break the law by touching him?* It is entirely possible that this man was cleansed of his leprosy before Jesus ever touched him. The miracle likely took place instantly, as soon as the man's faith reached out and made contact with the power of God in Jesus. Therefore, in the instant before Jesus' hand came in contact with this leper, he was already clean. There are two reasons why this is probably true: First, Jesus' healing power was capable of being instantaneous. Second, Jesus was "a son of the law." He revered and observed the true law of Moses. There were times when he rejected and ignored the "traditions of men" that purportedly had been extracted from the law. But never did Jesus break the stated law of God in the Old Testament. He came to "fulfill" it, not to do away with it.

C. *Furthermore, this man's healing was visible.* We are not told to what stage his leprosy had progressed or what kind of leprosy he had. But there is no doubt that the people could see, plainly before them, that this leper's condition was healed. We know this is true, because Jesus told him to go and show himself to the priests and "offer the gift Moses commanded" (NIV).

D. *We are not told what this man did.* No doubt he could not contain his joy. Perhaps the people were not yet ready to receive him with open arms. But this did not bother him. He knew he was healed! He doubtlessly leaped for joy. Not only was this disastrous physical disease gone, but the suffocating loneliness that had surrounded him, perhaps for years, was also gone. He was about to experience "community" once more with his loved ones.

Conclusion

As we noted before, we can thank God today that we do not have to dread the horrible prospect of the disease of leprosy as humankind once did. But the "plague of loneliness" is still with us. It is caused by many things. Most often sin separates us, both from God and from our fellow humans. Misunderstanding contributes to the loneliness of many people. But the touch of God can dispel the terrible shadows of loneliness and bring into one's life an awareness of the constant presence of the Lord Jesus, who loves us, and who has promised to be "with us always, even to the end of the world."

WEDNESDAY EVENING, APRIL 23

Title: What Is a Christian?
Text: "And the disciples were called Christians first in Antioch" **(Acts 11:26)**.
Scripture Reading: Acts 11:19–30

Introduction

Perhaps the question seems elementary, but it is an important one: What is a Christian? All kinds of answers are given to this question. The label *Christian* has been abused. It has been used to describe a person born into a family of believers, one who belongs to a church, one who believes certain doctrinal propositions, and one who acts benevolently toward others.

Perhaps it would be helpful to investigate the Scriptures for the meaning of the word *Christian.* The name originated in Antioch as a means of jest. Literally it means "belonging to Christ's party." People would look at the followers of Jesus and call them contemptuously "those Christ folk." They were right, for a Christian, simply stated, is a person who is a follower of Jesus Christ. Let us examine some implications of being a Christian.

I. A Christian is one who believes.

A. *The disciples in Antioch became Christians as a result of believing in Christ.* "And the hand of the Lord was with them: and a great number believed, and turned unto the Lord" (v. 21). The beginning of their Christian life happened the moment they believed. Nothing other than belief marks the origin of becoming a Christian.

B. *People deserve the name Christian because they believe in Christ.* The term *believe* deserves consideration. In the Bible the word *believe* means more than knowledge or intellect; it means to put one's trust in the Lord. The moment one opens his or her life to the Lord is the moment that person becomes a Christian.

II. A Christian is one who belongs.

A. *The disciples in Antioch bound themselves together in an assembly.* "Then departed Barnabas to Tarsus, for to seek Saul: And when he had found him, he brought him unto Antioch. And it came to pass, that a whole year they assembled themselves with the church, and taught much people" (v. 25–26). Those persons who had united their lives to Jesus Christ joined together in a body of believers. They felt that they belonged in a life together called the church.

B. *People who join their lives to Jesus belong to each other.* Christians belong to each other because of a union with Christ. Branches have kinship because they draw life from a common vine. Sheep belong to a flock because they belong to the same shepherd. Believers belong to the family of God because, out of a new birth, they have been born into God's family.

III. A Christian is one who behaves.

A. *The disciples in Antioch were identified by their behavior.* The outsiders observed their lifestyle. These outsiders knew of Christ's teaching, so they called these disciples "Christ folk," or "Christians." Notice a few signs of their lifestyle. First, they assembled regularly for worship. Second, they wanted to know more of Jesus. Third, they expressed sympathy and concern for needy people.

B. *Believers who belong to Jesus Christ are to act like Jesus.* The Lord is our pattern for life in character, values, motives, and ideals. The believer's behavior is to resemble the lifestyle of the Master. In fact, Paul wrote to the Corinthian believers that others could actually "read" their lifestyle: "You show that you are a letter from Christ, . . . written not with ink but with the Spirit of the living God, not on tablets of stone but on tablets of human hearts" (2 Cor. 3:3 NIV). In other words, a Christian is one who exemplifies Christ.

Conclusion

One need not be confused in defining a Christian. A Christian is a person in relationship with Christ through faith. Because of this relationship with Jesus, there is a sense of belonging to other believers, and there is a behavior that results from union with Christ.

SUNDAY MORNING, APRIL 27

Title: When You Leave Too Soon
Text: "'Don't be alarmed,' he said. 'You are looking for Jesus the Nazarene, who was crucified. He has risen! He is not here. See the place where they laid him. But go, tell his disciples and Peter, 'He is going ahead of you into Galilee. There you will see him, just as he told you'" **(Mark 16:6–7 NIV)**.
Scripture Reading: Mark 16:1–8
Hymns: "God of Grace and God of Glory," Fosdick
"Majestic Sweetness Sits Enthroned," Stennett
"Dear Lord and Father of Mankind," Whittier
Offertory Prayer: Our Father, a week after Easter we thank you for the risen Christ. Help us, Father, to reflect our gratitude for your grace by practicing the grace of giving. Make us openhearted and openhanded. Use our gifts for your purpose. Bless the gifts as well as the givers this day, we pray. In Jesus' name and for his sake. Amen.

Introduction

There is a Baptist pastor in Austin, Texas, who is a graduate of Baylor University in Waco, Texas. This pastor loves football and is an ardent fan of the Baylor Bears. To his great discomfort, he serves a congregation in Austin, which is the hometown of the University of Texas and the famous Texas Longhorns. As one can imagine, he has, at times, fallen on some lean years in that situation. In fact, at one time it had been eighteen years since the Baylor Bears had beaten the Texas Longhorns. But this pastor faithfully bought season tickets each year and drove from Austin to Waco to see every home football game.

He and his wife attended the Baylor–University of Texas game on November 9, 1974, which was played in Waco that year. At halftime he decided that enough was enough. The old nightmare was recurring, with Texas leading 24 to 7. So he threw one more handful of ashes upon his sackcloth and left for home. Baylor rallied in the second half and won by a score of 34 to 27, winning the Southwestern Conference football title for the first time in fifty years!

On the next Sunday morning he told his congregation that he had waited eighteen long years to see his dream come true. He had always believed that it would happen, and it did happen the day before. But the sad news is that he did not get to see it because he gave up thirty minutes too soon.

How often have we left too soon? How often have we turned away too soon from that which we desperately hoped to see come to fruition?

Look at Simon Peter. He had hitched his wagon to Jesus' star. Jesus had crossed his path near the Sea of Galilee and said, "Come, follow me." And follow Jesus he did.

Things went well for a while; then things began to slip. Jesus' opponents closed their ranks against him. After that memorable Thursday night supper in the upper room, Peter had tried to help Jesus' cause by the swift use of his sword in the garden of Gethsemane, but all he got for his trouble was a rebuke and a demonstration of Jesus' healing mercy.

Then came in swift succession the traitor's kiss, Jesus' instant arrest, and his trial before the high priest Caiaphas. The big fisherman saw the handwriting on the wall. The record tells us that he "followed [Jesus] at a distance, as far as the courtyard of the high priest, and going inside he sat with the guards to see the end" (Matt. 26:58 RSV). While Peter was warming himself around a fire in the courtyard, a young woman questioned him about being a follower of Jesus. Peter denied Christ—three times. Then came Jesus' crucifixion. Jesus was dead. It seemed to Simon Peter that the curtain had come down with a thud.

But Peter left too soon. Had he stayed with Jesus for three more days, he would have seen the resurrection. In his despair, disappointment, and disillusionment, what he thought was the end was not.

It is significant that on the resurrection morning the message given to the disciples was not only that Jesus would meet them in Galilee, but that specifically he would meet Simon Peter with them. The only one specified by name was Simon Peter. He who had left too soon would be included with the other believers in seeing the end of the story.

On this Sunday following Easter, when we are so aware of the resurrection of Jesus Christ from the dead, we can see what happens when we do not leave too soon.

I. If we do not leave too soon, disappointments can be changed.

A. *Great expectations bring great disappointment.* This is one reason Simon Peter was so disappointed that fateful day. He had expected so much. The ideas of love, hope, and faith had crept into the burly fisherman's heart. But it seemed that they were all dashed with the death of Jesus.

B. *Disappointments bring a mood of despair.* With his great disappointment, Peter sat in the courtyard waiting for the end. It looked as though all had failed. A mood of despair, of waiting for the end, had fallen on him.

C. *But Christ can change disappointments.* Against all our disappointments is the message of Christ: disappointments can be changed into victories! In the midst of Peter's great disappointment came the message of the resurrected Christ: he would meet Peter in Galilee!

That one who was most disappointed in his own actions as well as in the turn of events saw his disappointments changed. Christ's message to us following Easter is that disappointments can be changed. If we do not leave too soon, we can have that assurance.

II. If we don't leave too soon, defeats can be overturned.

A. *Death seems to be the greatest defeat, but even it was overturned.* For Simon Peter, Jesus' death was the greatest defeat. It seemed to Peter that the end of his dreams had come. But that defeat was overturned by the resurrection.

B. *The lesser defeats can be overturned too.* If death is the greatest defeat we face and it was overturned by the resurrection of Jesus, we have the assurance that the lesser defeats in our lives can be overturned also.

We can go about the Father's business here on earth with this principle firmly entrenched in our minds. Remember what Paul told us in 2 Corinthians 4:8–9: "We are troubled on every side, yet not distressed; we are perplexed, but not in despair; persecuted, but not forsaken; cast down, but not destroyed." In spite of these things, we know that we have been given another day, another opportunity to overturn defeat and to serve the Lord Jesus Christ.

III. If we don't leave too soon, destiny can be rerouted.

A. *We wonder about our destiny.* Don't you think Peter wondered about his destiny? Sitting in the courtyard waiting for the end, he thought he saw Jesus' destiny stamped out. But what about his own destiny? He had followed Jesus, but he had also denied Jesus. What would happen to him?

Peter found out later. In three days all of his hopes were realized. In three days not only was Jesus raised from the dead, but he also was sending personal messages to Peter. Peter had a destiny after all, and it rested with Jesus.

B. *We find our destiny with Christ.* Three days later Simon Peter found out that his destiny had been rerouted. He had a destiny as a leader in the early church. He had a place within the circle of Christ's followers. He was still accepted and loved. And God had something yet greater for him to do. He had a destiny far greater than he had ever imagined. In Christ he found his destiny. And so do we.

Conclusion

Do not leave too soon. What may seem to you to be the end may be, instead, only the prologue to the beginning. You can have a new beginning in Jesus Christ. God's grace can be known and his acts seen. If you don't leave too soon, you too may see God act in your life in ways that you had never dreamed possible.

SUNDAY EVENING, APRIL 27

Title: Matthew Levi: Imprisoned by Things
Text: "And after these things he went forth, and saw a publican, named Levi, sitting at the receipt of custom: and he said unto him, Follow me. And he left all, rose up, and followed him" (**Luke 5:27–28**).
Scripture Reading: Luke 5:27–31

Introduction

Materialism, "the quest for things," has been a sin of humankind in every generation, but perhaps because of our twenty-first-century affluence, it is more common today. And the irony of this is that "things" within themselves are not bad. There is no virtue in poverty for poverty's sake. Many Christians in the world are poor by the standards of their society. They may have food enough to eat, clothes to cover their bodies, and a roof over their heads yet not have the "extras" in life that add to human happiness. But they have learned to be content with what they have, and they are joyful Christians.

On the other hand, Satan can have a field day with material possessions. He can wreak untold havoc with the love of money. He can cause a person to become so obsessed with material things that such is all that matters in life.

The encounter we will study tonight has to do with just such an individual. All three of the Synoptic Gospel writers, one of whom was this man himself, tell us his story. His name is Matthew.

I. Matthew's encounter with Jesus (vv. 27–28).

A. *The name Matthew is significant; it means "gift of God."* Jesus may have changed this man's name from Levi to Matthew, and in so doing he may have been indicating how much Matthew was going to mean to the kingdom of God in the years to come.

B. *Luke states that Jesus "saw" Matthew; and the word he used for "saw" means more than a casual glance; it means a close, penetrating look.* In the split second that Jesus' eyes rested on Matthew, he saw everything about him. Not only did he see his past, but he saw what he could become.

C. *Luke describes Matthew as a "publican," a word that carried with it a terrible stigma.* As a publican, or tax collector, he was helping to perpetrate one of the grossest injustices of the day on his own people—the collecting of exorbitant taxes for Rome. The fact that Matthew had chosen this profession tells us something significant about his priorities—about what was important to him. Money was his god! Material possessions were of extreme importance.

D. *Since Jesus had made Capernaum his Galilean headquarters, it is likely that Matthew had come in contact with Jesus many times—not personally perhaps, but he had seen him, heard him preach and teach, and witnessed the miracles he had performed.* The authority of Jesus' words and the divine magnetism of his personality had pierced through the hard, callused exterior of Matthew, as they had for so many others. Perhaps all of the excitement and thrill had gone out of his job.

E. *The wonderful thing about the omniscience of Christ is that he knew about the discontent in Matthew's heart and soul.* So on this particular day Jesus walked by Matthew's tax booth.

F. *The time was so right that Jesus may not even have stopped.* Perhaps he just looked at Matthew and uttered those two words, "Follow me." But there must have been tremendous persuasive power in those words, for Luke tells us that after Matthew heard Jesus, he "got up, left everything, and followed him" (NIV). He left his ledger books and the money he had collected that day. Most important, he closed the door; he burned the bridge on his past life.

II. The expression of gratitude (vv. 29–30).

A. *We have only two incidents in Holy Scripture where Matthew appears, as they are recorded by all three of the Synoptic Gospel writers.* Those two incidents are his calling and the feast in his house. We have on record no single word that Matthew ever spoke, even though we know that he did bear vocal witness to Christ, for he had to invite all of his friends to the banquet!

B. *Although no mention is made of any sermon Matthew ever preached, he was a writer, and he has drawn for us a magnificent portrait of our Lord as King of Kings and Lord of Lords.* The authority of divine inspiration can be detected in every word he wrote.

C. *Note that Luke tells us "a large crowd of tax collectors and others" was present at the banquet Matthew gave for Jesus.* All of the tax collectors did not live in Capernaum. We do not know how far Matthew sent his invitations or from how far these men came. But some days had to elapse for the word to get out, and we can be sure that those were glorious days for Matthew as he was telling far and wide what had happened in his life.

D. *Matthew's guest list was predictable: publicans and sinners all!* Matthew had defiled himself; he was an outcast, a sinner, in the sight of the temple crowd. He may indeed have invited his neighbors who were not engaged in the profession of tax collecting. But they obviously had refused quickly; they could not afford to be seen in his presence.

E. *While the banquet was in progress—which likely was a testimonial by Matthew to all of his friends and associates concerning what had happened to him when he decided to follow Jesus—the Pharisees and scribes were observing it all.* They could not help but be impressed by Matthew's sincerity and fervor. Yet completely ignoring the change that had taken place in Matthew's life, they came to Jesus' disciples with the bitter and insinuating question: "Why do you eat and drink with tax collectors and 'sinners'?" (NIV). In other words, "How dare you be seen with people like this, much less break bread with them?"

III. Definition of need (vv. 31–32).

Jesus overheard these hypocrites, and his magnificent answer amounts to a timeless definition of need.

A. *Jesus' words dripped with divine sarcasm.* Though these religious critics had not addressed him directly, but had addressed his disciples instead, Jesus knew they were talking primarily about him. So he turned, and no doubt with righteous anger flashing from his eyes, he said to them: "I did not come to help people like you, for you do not think you need any help. You are the 'healthy' ones. I came instead to call those who are spiritually sick and know it, who are sinners, and know it! A doctor has no business wasting his time with people who are well, for there are multitudes who are sick and need his care. This is my mission on earth."

B. *Probably as Matthew listened to Jesus answer his critics in this fashion, his heart filled with gratitude because Jesus, the Great Physician, had reached out to him and healed him of his moral illness.* The prison bars, which had been built around his life by materialism, the love of things, had been broken asunder. He was free for the very first time in his life!

Conclusion

Just as Jesus knew Matthew completely—his past, present, and future—so God knows us. He never calls people to himself on the basis of what they are and certainly not because of what they have been. Rather, in his omniscience he knows what they can become when they are changed by his saving grace.

Wednesday Evening, April 30

Title: What Is a Believer's Best Gift?

Text: "And now these three remain: faith, hope and love. But the greatest of these is love" **(1 Cor. 13:13 NIV)**.

Scripture Reading: 1 Corinthians 13:1–13

Introduction

Frequently I am asked, "What is the best gift a Christian can possess?" Some think the gift of prophecy is best. Others think teaching is superior. Still others think speaking in tongues or working of miracles is the greatest gift.

No doubt the Corinthian church was a gifted church. Paul devoted a large section of his first letter to the Corinthians to helping them with spiritual gifts (chaps. 12–14). In the midst of his discussion, he told them of the believer's best gift: "Eagerly desire the greater gifts. And now I will show you the most excellent way" (12:31 NIV). The believer's best gift is love. Let us examine the features of the gift of love.

I. Love is preeminent (vv. 1–3).

A church may possess many qualities, but if it does not have love, it is not a vital church. Other gifts are commendable, but without love they are nothing.

A. *Love is preeminent over ecstatic emotionalism.* "If I speak in the tongues of men and of angels, but have not love, I am only a resounding gong or a clanging cymbal" (v. 1 NIV).
B. *Love is preeminent over intellectual speculation.* "If I have the gift of prophecy and can fathom all mysteries and all knowledge . . ." (v. 2 NIV). Churches may be gifted with intellectual people, but the gift of intellect is not preeminent over love.
C. *Love is preeminent over religious activism.* "And if I have a faith that can move mountains, but have not love, I am nothing" (v. 2 NIV). Love cannot be absent from religious activity.
D. *Love is preeminent to asceticism.* "If I give all I possess to the poor and surrender my body to the flames, but have not love, I gain nothing" (v. 3 NIV).

II. Love is performance (vv. 4–7).

Here Paul turns from the preeminence of love to its practice. This paragraph contains fifteen verbs. This construction would indicate that love is performance-oriented.

A. *Love is introduced by two positive qualities.* "Love is patient, love is kind" (v. 4 NIV). These are the qualities of God.
B. *Love is described by what it will not do.* "It does not envy, it does not boast, it is not proud. It is not rude, it is not self-seeking, it is not easily angered, it keeps no record of wrongs. Love does not delight in evil but rejoices with the truth" (vv. 4–6 NIV).
C. *Love is involved in meaningful performances.* "It always protects, always trusts, always hope, always perseveres" (v. 7 NIV). These are four positive actions of genuine love.

III. Love is permanent (vv. 8–13).

Love will never end. It will outlast all of the other gifts.

A. *Love will outlast the gifts of time.* "Love never fails. But where there are prophecies, they will cease; where there are tongues, they will be stilled; where there is knowledge, it will pass away" (v. 8 NIV).

Prophecies will have their fulfillment. Tongues will serve their temporary purpose. Partial knowledge will vanish. Love will outlast all of the gifts of time.

Paul used two comparisons to illustrate the permanency of love. First, he talked about the growing child. Some gifts belong to the stage of spiritual infancy. Second, Paul used the illustration of a mirror. Our present experience with the Lord is somewhat dim, like looking into a mirror; but in the future we shall see clearly.

B. *Love will last throughout eternity.* "And now these three remain: faith, hope and love. But the greatest of these is love" (v. 13 NIV). Love abides and surpasses because it is God's nature and because it gives people a basis for faith and hope.

Conclusion

The best gift a person can possess is Christian love. It is the most excellent way.

SUGGESTED PREACHING PROGRAM FOR THE MONTH OF MAY

■ Sunday Mornings

With the secular calendar calling for the observance of Mother's Day, Children's Day, commencement ceremonies, and Father's Day, this is a good time for a series of sermons using the theme "Christ and Life in the Family."

On the last Sunday of the month, celebrate Memorial Day with a sermon that calls listeners to remember those who have gone before us.

■ Sunday Evenings

Continue the series "The Ministry of Jesus to Individuals."

■ Wednesday Evenings

Continue the series "Questions Christians Ask."

SUNDAY MORNING, MAY 4

Title: The Christian Family
Text: "Be subject to one another out of reverence for Christ" **(Eph. 5:21 RSV)**.
Scripture Reading: Ephesians 5:21–6:5
Hymns: "God, Give Us Christian Homes," McKinney
"Friend of the Home," Lewis
"Happy the Home When God Is There," Ware
Offertory Prayer: Lord of all gifts, including the gift of life, we bring our gifts to you as an act of worship. We rejoice in your providential care and generous provision. You have given us all our needs—and many extras as well. We rejoice in those whom we love, in friends near and far. Accept the gifts of our hand as a measure of our love. Through Jesus Christ our Lord. Amen.

Introduction

"In the name of God, I, John, take you, Mary, to be my wife, to have and to hold from this day forward, for better, for worse, for richer, for poorer, in sickness and in health, to love and to cherish, as long as we both shall live."

"In the name of God, I, Mary, take you, John, to be my husband. . . ."

"Since John and Mary have consented together in holy matrimony before God and these witnesses, and have joined hands and exchanged vows and rings, by the ordinance of God, I pronounce that they are husband and wife, in the name of God the Father, Son, and Holy Spirit. Amen."

It requires a lot of living and love to understand these sacred words. The home was divinely established and is the oldest institution on earth. Its purposes are companionship and parenthood. But the biblical view of marriage is under attack—it always has been.

I. Biblical view of the home.

A. *The Christian wife (Eph. 5:21–23).* Counselors Henlee and Helen Barnette contend that a Christian marriage is to be a "coarchy" based on Ephesians 5:21, "Be subject to one another out of reverence for Christ." The passage literally says, "Take your proper role." Each is superior in his or her proper role. This is a lofty passage in light of the woman's role in the Jewish and Greco-Roman world of the first century.

B. *The Christian husband (5:24–33).* Husbands are to love their wives sacrificially "as Christ also loved the church." Their love is to be sanctifying and holy. And men are to love their wives as they love themselves.

C. *Children in a Christian home (6:1–4).* The modern home has been called a domestic cloverleaf on which we pass each other en route to someplace else.

Parents' love is not repaid—it is passed on. The home's highest welfare is spiritual.

II. Historic view of the home.

Church historian Roland Bainton has given us helpful background material on how human sexuality has been viewed historically.

A. *The biblical view was celebrative.* Sexuality was to be received with gratitude as part of God's good creation.

The early church overreacted to the abuse of sex in the pagan world. They came to exalt celibacy as the ideal and to view marriage as an inferior state. It was considered merely a "remedy for sin."

B. *During the Middle Ages, marriage was enriched by the idea of romantic love.* That view is still very much with us. While it has made a contribution, we must remember that the essence of romance is the unattainability of the object of one's affection. A classic example of this is the romantic love between Queen Guinevere and Sir Lancelot in *Camelot.*

C. *The Puritan view of human sexuality was "hush-hush."* As that attitude carried over into the Victorian Age, there was a lot of hypocrisy about sexual matters.

D. *The modern sexual revolution has brought a healthy openness about sexuality but greater permissiveness and a preoccupation with sex.* We need to recover the biblical perspective, which views sex as God's gift to be received with gratitude and expressed within marriage.

III. Jesus and women.

Jesus was the original liberator of women, men, and children. Indeed, he did more to liberate women from an inferior status and injustice than any other person in history. He is unique among the world's religious leaders.

Jesus elevated the status of women. He treated them as persons and took their questions seriously. No act of Jesus nor parable he told was at a woman's expense. He never made fun of women or belittled them. Jesus' attitude was revolutionary in his day, even among the Jews.

Women were prominent in the New Testament. Luke is called "the women's gospel." Consider Mary, the mother of Jesus, Mary Magdalene, Mary and Martha of Bethany, Joanna, Philip's daughters who were inspired preachers, Lydia, and Phoebe. It is noteworthy that women were the first at Jesus' cradle, the last at his cross, and the first to discover his resurrection. How do we apply this truth to woman's role today?

Conclusion

Consider the importance of family faith. Deuteronomy 6:6–9—Joshua's challenge—is a useful text.

The home is the greatest academy, for faith is both caught and taught in the home. The religion we teach our children can be unhealthy and repressive. It can even cripple, as in the case of the cults. Or the faith we share can be healthy: firsthand, constructive, and life-affirming.

SUNDAY EVENING, MAY 4

Title: The Lawyer: Blinded by Legalism

Text: "On one occasion an expert in the law stood up to test Jesus. 'Teacher,' he asked, 'what must I do to inherit eternal life?'

"'What is written in the Law?' he replied. 'How do you read it?'

"He answered: '"Love the Lord your God with all your heart and with all your soul and with all your strength and with all your mind"; and, "Love your neighbor as yourself"'" **(Luke 10:25–27 NIV)**.

Scripture Reading: Luke 10:25–37

Introduction

The human mind is a strange and marvelous creation of God with fantastic potential. It can handle reason and logic; it can make judgments in accord with its own sense of values; it can store innumerable facts and experiences from the past and recall them to act on the present; it can dream and aspire to the highest acts of benevolence toward one's fellow humans; and it can, with cold calculation, devise the most diabolical acts of destruction imaginable.

At the same time, the human mind can trigger the emotions of the heart. And when linked with heaven, it can conceive enough of the glory and reality of God to surrender to him, not only as Creator, but also as Savior and Lord. Thus it is the mind that sets humans apart from all other species of God's creation. This is why, in God's first efforts to call an individual to himself, he works through the mind. "Faith comes from hearing," says the Scripture (Rom. 10:17 NIV). "'Come now, let us reason together,' says the LORD" (Isa. 1:18 NIV). Then, once a person's *mind* is captured by the Holy Spirit, God has an entrance into his or her heart and soul.

Tonight we will observe Jesus dealing with a man whose mind was highly trained, almost to the point of keeping him out of the kingdom of God. He was a lawyer; thus his very profession suggested that he was a man accustomed to ferreting out all of the details of a matter and sifting them through all of the levels of his human reason.

I. The test that this lawyer placed before Jesus (vv. 25–29).

A. *Luke calls him "an expert in the law."* This means that he was more than just one who gave opinions or pleaded cases; he most likely was a teacher of the law and was thoroughly acquainted with all of the details of Moses' law. The question he was asking Jesus had a definite relationship to the law, in which he was "an expert." Under any other circumstances, his professional pride would not have allowed him to ask Jesus, who had no formal training in the rabbinical schools of the day, such a question of interpretation. So in the presence of at least Jesus' own disciples, and possibly others, he was deferring to the wisdom of Jesus.

B. *He asked, "Teacher, what must I do to inherit eternal life?"* The fact that this lawyer asked about "eternal life" may have been proof that he was not satisfied with life as he knew it. No doubt he was well educated and exposed to the finer things in life and enjoyed a position of respect and influence as a lawyer. Still he was not satisfied!

C. *Note that, in his answer, Jesus approached this lawyer at the point of his need—at the place where he was in his progress toward understanding the truth about life.* Sometimes zealous believers assume that unbelievers to whom they witness know all of the "religious terminology" they use, and the result is that the unsaved persons are totally confused. We must not limit the Holy Spirit to one particular way of dealing with an individual. Note what Jesus did with this lawyer. He said a totally unexpected thing to him: "What is written in the Law? How do you read it?"

D. *It was as though Jesus was saying, "You have asked a question that is answered only in the law, and you are an expert in that field.* Tell me, what does it say, and how do you interpret it?" The lawyer replied with one of the most familiar passages in the Old Testament—in fact, he combined two passages, one from Deuteronomy and the other from Leviticus (v. 27). Then Jesus, as though he were about to close the conversation, said, "You have answered correctly. Do this and you will live" (v. 28 NIV).

E. *Of course, Jesus knew that the lawyer would not be satisfied with that answer.*

And that is exactly what Jesus wanted! He wanted him to understand that the law is far more than legalism or a set of rules and regulations. Indeed, it had been at this very point that the lawyer had had his problem. Although he knew these words, he could not bring himself to admit their true meaning. He revealed his real problem when he opened another door in his conversation with Jesus. Luke states, "But he wanted to justify himself, so he asked Jesus, 'And who is my neighbor?'" (v. 29 NIV).

F. *Before whom was this lawyer wanting to "justify himself"?* His peers? Jesus, this itinerant teacher from Nazareth? Most probably he was wrestling with himself. The Holy Spirit was using this very Word of God the man had studied for years to prick his conscience. So naturally, he was trying to justify himself to himself! He knew that his actions did not match what he confessed with his mouth. And strangely enough, the point in all of this which God used to show him his spiritual deficiency was the matter of his neighbor. It was at the point of his prejudice that the felling blow came to his pride and his ego.

II. The interpretation of the law of God that Jesus gave to him (vv. 30–37).

A. *Here we have one of the most beautiful and moving of all the parables Jesus told.* Only Luke records it, and we have come to know it as the parable of the good Samaritan. Having portrayed the wretched condition of the man lying beside the highway on the treacherous Jericho Road, Jesus had told the lawyer of three men who passed by and saw this injured, bleeding, possibly dying man lying there. They all looked at him, but the first two men, the Levite and the priest, were not moved to help him at all. They "passed by on the other side." However, when the third man, the Samaritan, saw this wounded man, he was filled with compassion.

B. *When Jesus asked the lawyer, upon completing the story, which of the three was "neighbor" to the wounded, bruised, half-dead man, he immediately gave another "right" answer.* This is the amazing thing about this lawyer. All of his "answers" had been correct. Jesus did not have to "straighten him out" on his understanding and interpretation of the Scriptures. So often unbelievers have terribly distorted concepts of what the Bible teaches, but this lawyer's understanding of what the law of God taught was flawless. He knew it well.

C. *Therefore, when Jesus asked him, "Which of these three do you think was a neighbor to the man who fell into the hands of robbers?"* he answered, "The one who had mercy on him" (vv. 36–37 NIV). Now the question Jesus asked the lawyer was not so much "Who *is* your neighbor? as it was, "To whom are you willing and prepared to *be* a neighbor?" This is what is going to prove to you, as well as to the world, whether or not you have any idea what eternal life really means.

D. *What had the Samaritan done for the wounded man?* First, he had been moved with compassion. His compassion moved him to stop and do all that he could for the man. He poured oil and wine into his gaping wounds, placed him on his own beast, and apparently walked alongside the animal bearing the wounded man until they came to an inn. There he put him in that place of safety where he could recuperate, paid the bill, and thus acted as a true neighbor.

E. *Jesus was saying to the lawyer, "If you truly know God, you will love him and you will love his children in whatever circumstances and under whatever conditions you come in contact with them.* That will be proof that you have eternal life in the truest sense of the word!" We do not know what happened to the lawyer after that. Jesus dismissed him with the command, "Go and do likewise." Whether it was at that moment the lawyer came to experience eternal life, or if it came later, perhaps on the way home as the words of Jesus dawned even more clearly on his conscience, we do not know. Or, in fact, if he *ever* opened his heart to receive eternal life, we cannot say. But whatever happened, we can be sure this lawyer left Jesus with a clear understanding of what it meant to have eternal life.

Conclusion

People cannot "embrace Christianity" and claim that they believe that Jesus is God's Son, that he died on the cross and rose again, and yet show no change in their lifestyle. We are not saved by "being good neighbors." But having the heart of a Christian neighbor is undeniable proof that we have received eternal life.

WEDNESDAY EVENING, MAY 7

Title: Why Do Bad Things Happen to Good People?

Text: "And as Jesus passed by, he saw a man which was blind from his birth. And his disciples asked him, saying, Master, who did sin, this man, or his parents, that he was born blind?" **(John 9:1–2)**.

Scripture Reading: John 9:1–25

Introduction

Rabbi Harold S. Kushner has written an intriguing book titled *When Bad Things Happen to Good People.* Prompted by the untimely death of Kushner's son, the author investigated that ancient question of why bad things happen to good people.

Evidently Jesus' disciples were concerned over the prevalence of evil. Once the disciples pointed to a blind man and asked Jesus, "Master, who did sin, this man, or his parents, that he was born blind?" (John 9:2). The popular

Jewish mind-set of the first century was that suffering was a direct cause of some evil in a person's life.

The question of why bad things happen to good people is not just an ancient one. It continues to be investigated. Using the case of the man born blind, let us examine some insights about suffering.

I. Suffering provokes questions.

The case of the blind man prompted queries from the apostles. Suffering often causes people to ask questions.

A. *People always ask questions about suffering.* The disciples did what was normal. They wanted to know the specific cause of the man's suffering.
B. *Questions about suffering are hard to answer.* People often bring on their own suffering because they try to live by selfish rules in a God-made universe. Sin does bring misery and suffering, but not all suffering is brought on by one's own sin.

II. Suffering provides opportunities.

Jesus offered no explanation for the blind man's problem. Instead, he used the situation as an opportunity to show what God can do.

A. *Suffering provides an opportunity for the one who is suffering to find God.* The blind man had an opportunity to encounter Jesus Christ, and his life was changed as a result of that encounter.
B. *Suffering provides an opportunity to live for God.* Being blind and then being healed gave the man the opportunity to testify to what God can do in a life.

   Henri Nouwen wrote a book entitled *The Wounded Healer.* The basic premise of the book is that one who has been wounded can be a skilled healer.

III. Suffering produces benefits.

Sufferings, or "bad things," are not always negative. At times "bad things" happen and positive benefits result.

A. *Suffering gives a perspective on what is really important.* Have you ever considered what was important to the blind man? Was it clothes or cash? No, it was his sight. More than anything the man wanted to see.
B. *Suffering builds character.* The blind man's character resulted from the stress. The trials of life have a capacity for building and strengthening character.
C. *Suffering lengthens compassion.* The blind man would have compassion on those who could not see. Those who suffer tend to have greater compassion on others.

Conclusion

Bad things do happen to good people. We cannot always understand why they happen, but we do know what good things can come from experiences when one's faith is in the Lord Jesus Christ.

SUNDAY MORNING, MAY 11

Title: The Times of Your Life

Text: "For everything there is a season, and a time for every matter under heaven: . . . He has made everything beautiful in its time; also he has put eternity into man's mind" **(Eccl. 3:1, 11 RSV)**.

Scripture Reading: Ecclesiastes 3:1–8, 11

Hymns: "How Great Thou Art," Boberg
"Lead On, O King Eternal," Shurtleff
"To God Be the Glory," Crosby

Offertory Prayer: "The heavens declare the glory of God and the firmament showeth his handiwork." Father, we rejoice in the beauty and bounty of the good earth. You have not been tightfisted in your gifts to us. Teach us that same open generosity in our stewardship. You have entrusted us with resources, opportunities, and love. Make us faithful stewards of all. Through Jesus Christ our Lord. Amen.

Introduction

What time is it in your life? The wise man said, "There is a time for everything." Sophocles wrote the Greek classic *Oedipus Rex,* wherein the queen of Thebes asked a riddle: "What walks on four legs at sunrise, on two legs at noon, and on three legs at sunset?" The answer was man. He crawls on all four as an infant, walks on two legs as an adult, and he moves with the help of a cane when he is old.

Interestingly, the church is the one institution that speaks to those of all ages and in all stages of life. It is there with a word from God when we are born, when we are converted, when we marry, during our working years, and at the time of death. Only the church and its message touch us at so many routine and crisis times of life.

I. Childhood, the stage of dependence.

Childhood is the period of our greatest growth, and yet it is usually the most carefree time of life. Jesus blessed children. He had real affection for them, and they must have been comfortable with him.

Surely God intends for us to delight in our children, to enjoy them. Human sexuality and parenthood are part of God's "very good" creation.

Recall the "encouragers" of your childhood. Who was your "encourager"? It may have been one of your parents, a grandparent, an aunt, or a teacher.

Recall that person with gratitude. If you can, express your appreciation to that person for the contribution he or she made to your life.

II. Adolescence, the stage of transition.

Adolescence can be a time of the most intense and painful change. It is an in-between time. Adolescents are no longer children but are not yet fully adults. They are moving from dependence toward independence and self-support. It can be a scary stage of life.

The adolescence of their children can be a tough time for parents too. Some parents contend that the only thing harder than being a teenager is having one.

III. Adulthood, the longest stage.

Adulthood can be life's most demanding period. There is no official rite of passage into adulthood, no ceremony in which some authority figure says to us, "I hereby declare you to be an adult, with all the rights, privileges, and responsibilities apertaining thereto." Thus we each must make our transition from youth into adulthood.

Adulthood can be both joyous and stressful. Remember that the phrase "and they lived happily ever after" occurs only in fairy tales. As long as we are alive, we will experience struggle and stress, growth and change. We will go both up the mountain and down again. There are both peaks and valleys. Life is not an "up" escalator.

Adulthood can be a time of fulfillment but also one of disillusion. Be careful not to neglect family relationships and personal growth during your adult years.

IV. Senior adulthood, continued usefulness.

In senior adulthood our emphasis shifts from "doing" and "having" to "being." The important thing becomes not what you have acquired so much as what you are as a person.

Senior adulthood can be a time of greater usefulness and freedom. Retirement should be viewed as a new chapter in our lives. We can be liberated to do what we enjoy most without the burdens of a job.

Senior adulthood can be a time for strengthened faith and a surer trust in the future. Death itself need not be a dark prospect for those who are in Christ. Every exit is also an entrance. Death is like blowing out a candle because the sunrise has come. With growing assurance we can sing, "I only know I cannot drift beyond his love and care."

Conclusion

What time is it in your life? It is important to live your life in chapters—to know what stage of life you are in. Live life to the fullest where you are. The past has already been and cannot be recalled. Nostalgia is a sad game.

Someone has said, "Nostalgia is not what it used to be!" The future is not yet. Live where you are to the glory of God.

May the Father enable us to be our best selves at every stage of life, with a continually growing faith. Every age has its special compensations and rewards. Be thankful. Drink deeply. William Blake suggested that we "kiss the joy as it flies."

SUNDAY EVENING, MAY 11

Title: A Father and His Son: From Tragedy to Victory

Text: "Jesus asked the boy's father, 'How long has he been like this?'

"'From childhood,' he answered. 'It has often thrown him into fire or water to kill him. But if you can do anything, take pity on us and help us.'

"'"If you can"?' said Jesus. 'Everything is possible for him who believes.'

"Immediately the boy's father exclaimed, 'I do believe; help me overcome my unbelief!'" **(Mark 9:21–24 NIV)**.

Scripture Reading: Mark 9:14–29

Introduction

Under normal circumstances, few human relationships are more admirable than that which exists when there is a strong bond between a father and his son. Yet, when the son is the helpless victim of an incurable disease and his parents must watch him suffer without being able to do anything to relieve his suffering—that is a scene that will melt the hardest heart!

Such is the case in this poignant story, which all three of the Synoptic Gospel writers have recorded.

I. A scene of extremes (vv. 14–19).

A. *Imagine for a moment that we have been waiting with the other nine disciples down in the valley, somewhere at the base of Mount Hermon, for Jesus and the other three disciples to return.* A serious problem has developed while Jesus has been gone. When Jesus and the three disciples finally descend, they discover a group of people engaged in a heated debate. A group of scribes is challenging Jesus' disciples. The disciples are certainly a frustrated minority, for a father has just brought his demon-possessed son to them after hearing that Jesus can cast out demons. Instead of detaining the man and his son until Jesus returned to deal with the problem, the disciples proceeded, with a tragic kind of presumption, to handle the matter themselves.

B. *Here is evidence of a common human fallacy within these disciples.* During the preceding months, they had observed Jesus performing many miracles, including the exorcising of demons. They had heard the words he had spoken. They thought they had the "formula," the magic words, all down pat! They may even have thought within themselves, "Aha! Here's our chance! When Jesus is here, we are always in the background. But after all, we have given up much to follow him. We are always promoting him and giving him first place. Well, he isn't here right now, and we know the words he uses when he performs these miracles. Why don't we just take care of this one ourselves? Why don't *we* cash in on a little of this glory?"

C. *So what do we have thus far?* Utter, total, shameful defeat! The scribes certainly couldn't help the demon-possessed boy; and Jesus' disciples, whose Master had cast out demons in their presence, had *tried* to do it, but they could not. So when Jesus arrived, the disciples were silent, for they were embarrassed and humiliated. The scribes were strangely quiet, perhaps because of the striking brilliance of Jesus' appearance (this may be the implication of the statement in v. 15).

D. *One did speak, however.* A man, grief-stricken, walked dejectedly up to Jesus. Agony, frustration, and deep grief contorted the features of his face. He shared with Jesus the torture suffered by his son and the failure of Jesus' disciples to help him (vv. 17–18). Jesus' response was one of the saddest statements he ever made. "O faithless generation, how long am I to be with you? How long am I to bear with you?" (v. 19 RSV). Jesus was saying that he lived in the midst of a generation without faith. His cry was a soliloquy coming from his heart. It revealed his awareness of the overwhelming difficulties in which he must carry out his ministry in the world.

II. A scene of tragedy (vv. 20–24).

A. *When some of the friends of this distraught father led the boy to where he and Jesus were talking, the demon in the boy seized him, and he lapsed into what may have been the worse convulsion he ever had had.* The demon in the boy knew full well whom he was facing, as well as the power Jesus had over demons.

B. *The father said to Jesus, "If you can do anything, take pity on us and help us" (v. 22 NIV).* In that little phrase "If you can," there is a trembling, pitifully small residue of faith, of hope. It was just about gone, yet a shadow remained. Quickly Jesus seized on that bit of hope left in the man's heart. "'If you can'?" said Jesus. "Everything is possible for him who believes" (v. 23 NIV).

C. *"I do believe; help me overcome my unbelief!" was the father's reply (v. 24 NIV).* This man had reached the end of his rope and could go no further. It was all or nothing—Jesus or the end for him and his boy. In times like that God moves in and takes over. We have to get all of self out of the way first. We must stop all of our interfering. We must "let go and let God."

III. A scene of victory (vv. 25–29).

A. *Perhaps Jesus took the father and son aside for this conversation.* Jesus addressed the evil spirit and demanded not only that it come out of the boy but also that it never again enter into him. Realizing the torture that awaited a disembodied demon, the evil spirit made one last, violent attempt to hurt the boy. Mark tells us that the evil spirit cried in the agony of its leaving the body of this young man.

B. *"Jesus took him by the hand and lifted him to his feet, and he stood up" (v. 27 NIV).* Luke adds a beautiful statement to this part of the story: "Jesus . . . gave him back to his father" (9:42 RSV). Why had the disciples failed so utterly and made such fools of themselves before the enemies of Christ—giving them such fuel to feed the flames of hatred and contempt they had for Christ?

C. *When Jesus and the disciples had left the scene, they asked him, "Why couldn't we drive it out?" (v. 28 NIV).* Jesus answered plainly, "This kind can come out only by prayer" (v. 29 NIV). In effect, he was saying to them, "You don't live close enough to God!" God's power was available for their use, but that which activates that power is prayer. God would say the same thing to you and me when we fail miserably in our Christian witness and testimony.

Conclusion

Does your "performance" match your "profession"? Paul said, "I can do everything . . ." If he had stopped there, we would be justified in calling him an egotist of the highest order. But that is not all of his statement. He said, "I can do everything through [Christ] who gives me strength" (Phil 4:13 NIV). That's the secret.

Like the boy's father in this story, "we believe"—but our belief is often weak, unsupported by prayer and obedience toward God. Do we try to use the gifts and talents God has given us in our strength—and then wonder why we fail, why we are so often ineffective?

The disciples became overconfident, and they failed miserably. May God help us to be certain that our confidence is always in him and not in ourselves.

Wednesday Evening, May 14

Title: What Will Worship Do for Me?

Text: "Until I went into the sanctuary of God; then understood I their end" **(Ps. 73:17)**.

Scripture Reading: Psalm 73:1–28

Introduction

Once when I was doing some pastoral visitation, I visited a family who had not attended worship services for some time. After a time of interpersonal exchange, I invited the people to become active in our worship services. The man of the house asked me quite candidly, "Why should I attend the services?" I spent some time telling the man some of the benefits of worshiping the Lord each week.

The writer of Psalm 73 had also discovered the benefits of worship. The psalmist was caught in the circumstances of life. Doubt filled his mind. He was concerned about the prosperity of the unrighteous and the suffering of the righteous. He wondered how a good God could allow evil to go unchecked and good unrewarded.

The only help the psalmist received was to go to the sanctuary of God. "Until I went into the sanctuary of God; then understood I their end" (v. 17). Let us notice the benefits of worship.

I. Worship will help us with our perspective.

A. *While observing life about him, the psalmist's vision of life became quite distorted.* He was particularly troubled over the prosperity of the wicked. He shared his perspective in Psalm 73:3–14:

1. He thought that the wicked were exempt from physical maladies (vv. 4–5).
2. He took special notice of the pride of the wicked (vv. 6–9).
3. He was distressed because of the popularity of the wicked (v. 10).
4. He became dismayed over the wicked person's contempt for God (v. 11).
5. He was puzzled over the material prosperity of the wicked (v. 12).
6. He was disturbed about the seeming inequities of life (vv. 13–14).

Today, becoming absorbed in the media's accounts of world events can lead to a distorted perspective.

B. *When the psalmist went to the sanctuary of God, he gained a new perspective.* His visit to the sanctuary made the difference. Look at the psalmist's new perspective.

1. He saw that the rich were not in impregnable positions (v. 18).
2. He saw that the destruction of material things was inevitable (vv. 18–19).
3. He compared the wicked to a fantasy (v. 20).

Worship will help us with our perspective.

II. Worship will help us strengthen the inner person.

The psalmist was a troubled man. Invariably, he was turbulent and possessed great fears. He doubted the goodness and justice of God. Furthermore, the first part of Psalm 73 gives the picture of a person in a severe case of depression. Many people are troubled inside. They search for rest and tranquillity.

Worship will help strengthen the inner person. Until this psalmist went to the sanctuary of God, he was a troubled man. But when he went to the sanctuary of God, he was strengthened within.

III. Worship will lead to a task.

The psalmist was not content to gain a new perspective and to be strengthened in the inner person. He wanted to serve the Lord. He said, "That I may declare all thy works" (v. 28).

Worship leads us to service. Once a person came to a church service just as the congregation was about to be dismissed. The person asked the usher, "Is the service over?" Wisely, the usher replied, "The worship is over, but the service is about to begin."

Conclusion

Worship has immeasurable benefits. Listen to the psalmist and learn of his benefits. Ask others who worship weekly how worthwhile it is. Best of all, come to the sanctuary of God and encounter God's presence.

SUNDAY MORNING, MAY 18

Title: He Took a Child

Text: "Train a child in the way he should go, and when he is old he will not turn from it" **(Prov. 22:6 NIV)**.

Scripture Reading: Mark 9:33–37

Hymns: "O Teacher, Master of Skill," Reid
"O Master, Let Me Walk with Thee," Everest
"God, Give Us Christian Homes," McKinney

Offertory Prayer: Lord Jesus Christ, you chose to enter your world as a baby, and we give you thanks for the gift of childhood with its openness and trust. By our faithful stewardship of life, make us worthy children of the King. In the strong name of Jesus we pray. Amen.

Introduction

One of our earliest memories from Sunday school is the picture of Jesus blessing the little children. He had one on his lap and other boys and girls standing or seated all around him. Looking at that picture, before we could read or write, we learned that Jesus is a child's friend. We learned the most wonderful lesson of all: God loves us and cares about us, and we have worth even as children.

Another memory from long before we were old enough to go to school is singing, "Jesus loves me, this I know; for the Bible tells me so." And again we learned about God's love and care for us.

I. The importance of children.

Children are tremendously important. Look at the prominence of children in Jesus' ministry. Not only did he take them in his arms and bless them, but on one occasion he placed a child in the midst of the disciples and used the youngster to teach that we must become as little children if we are to enter the kingdom of God.

When God came to earth, he came as a child. He grew up in the person of his Son, Jesus, a child in a working-class home in Nazareth in Galilee. As a child, Jesus grew physically, mentally, spiritually, and socially just as our children grow today.

We have recognized the importance of children throughout the years. President Abraham Lincoln wrote these words: "A child is a person who is going to carry on what you have started. He is going to sit where you are sitting when you are gone. He will attend to those things which you think are important. You may adopt all the policies you please, but how they are carried out depends on him. He will assume control of your cities, states, and nations. The fate of humanity is in his hands—in the hands of a child."

II. The rights of children.

Every child has a right to be loved and cared for. Not every child receives affection, but every child deserves it. Every child has a right to nourishment and health care. Every child has a right to education and training that will equip him or her to live as a useful citizen. Society has the responsibility to provide these things.

A. *The rights of children often come into conflict with the concerns and rights of adults.* In recent years we have been hearing a great deal about overpopulation. There has been a call for responsible family planning so that children may have an opportunity for a quality of life that provides human dignity. One negative effect of the problem of overpopulation is that children may very well come off feeling as though, just by their existence, they have caused the problem.

B. *Abortion is another violation of the rights of children.* Many see abortion as a casual method of birth control, and this leads to a cheapening of the value of life. Children in the womb have rights as well as adults. We have to keep those rights in balance.

C. *Still another matter that needs to be addressed is child abuse.* Millions of children in America are abused by their parents or guardians each year, and thousands of them die as a result. Moreover, adults who have been abused as children in turn are likely to abuse their own children.

III. The discipline of children.

To say that we are to communicate love and worth doesn't mean that we are to be permissive with our children. Many people in America grew up deprived of a lot of material things, many of which they really needed. People of that generation say, "My child will not have to do without the things I did." Therefore, some of those parents have been overly permissive, overly generous, and lacking in discipline in the home. It's an understandable reaction, but it is not the healthiest response.

We need to let our children know our expectations of them. Discipline is a sign of our love for them. We desperately need the wisdom to strike a balance between disciplining our children in anger and being too permissive with them. Children are not human pin cushions whom we can jab at will because we happen to be their parents. But neither do children need their parents to be their pals. They need for us to be their parents, emphasizing love and worth and caring discipline.

IV. Children and priorities.

We don't own our children. They are given to us as a trust from God. We need to communicate our love for them and our expectations of them. The most important thing we can do is to set the right example before our children—an example of integrity and faith.

Our children know what our priorities are. They know when we are more concerned about golf than God. They know when we are more concerned about sleeping in on Sunday than being in worship. By ordering our priorities right, we set the best example for them. Children need the affirmation of our love. They need to know the expectations of our discipline. They need our example. And they need our time and interest.

Conclusion

Wayne Oates said, "We need to give our children two things. The first is roots, and the second is wings. We need to give them a sense of belonging. We need to give them freedom to prepare to be on their own."

Our greatest dream for our children is that one day we will be instrumental in placing their hands in the hand of God. This is not automatic, nor is it something we can force. There is no guarantee that our children will grow up to be Christians. The church must join parents in helping them place their children's hands in the hand of God. Training children in the way they should go calls for dedication of parents, extended families, and the church. God, give us Christian homes!

Sunday Evening, May 18

Title: Zacchaeus: Isolated by Wrong Choices

Text: "A man was there by the name of Zacchaeus; he was a chief tax collector and was wealthy. . . . When Jesus reached the spot, he looked up and said to him, 'Zacchaeus, come down immediately. I must stay at your house today'" **(Luke 19:2, 5 NIV)**.

Scripture Reading: Luke 19:1–10

Introduction

Ironically, the name Zacchaeus means "pure," yet the man who bore this name symbolized the littleness in character with which he was physically identified. He was a cheat, a traitor, a turncoat to his own people. He was selfish, greedy, and uncaring in his attitude toward others. His wrong choices in regard to betraying his own people had isolated him. Yet Jesus saw something in Zacchaeus. Through all of those outer layers of ugliness and sin, Jesus saw *potential.* He saw what this man could become.

I. The condition of Zacchaeus.

A. *Luke's description of Zacchaeus is contained in one statement: "A man was there by the name of Zacchaeus; he was a chief tax collector and was wealthy" (v. 2 NIV).* That sounds like a note one would put on a man's application for the loan of a large sum of money! It tells us about his occupation—it was a lucrative one—and about his financial condition—he was "rich."

B. *Luke further states that Zacchaeus was a "chief tax collector."* There were many tax collectors in the land, and they in turn were under the direction of "chief" tax collectors. This means that Zacchaeus, a Jew, had "sold out" his people by agreeing to represent the pagan Roman Empire in this position. A whole district was under his supervision. The rate of taxation was fixed, and the chief tax collector was required to remit to Rome the amount of money assessed his district. Then the chief tax collector was free to add to the taxes as much as he dared, no questions asked. Thus he extorted money from the Jews, making himself rich.

C. *Tax collectors were held in contempt for two reasons: they had chosen to represent a pagan power, and they bled the people mercilessly in high taxes.* Because of this, they were banned from social life and excommunicated from the temple and synagogue.

II. The curiosity of Zacchaeus.

A. *If all we knew about Zacchaeus was that he was a chief tax collector and that he was rich, it would be a depressing picture.* We could almost write him off as a hopeless case. But then we discover, like a breath of fresh air, that he was curious. A healthy curiosity is always a hopeful sign about a person. "He wanted to see who Jesus was, but being a short man he could not, because of the crowd" (v. 3 NIV).

B. *Not only was Zacchaeus curious, but he also was determined to satisfy his curiosity.* He did not let his shortness of stature deter him. Not being able to see over the heads of the people, he positioned himself on the low-hanging limb of a sycamore tree, right over the roadway where Jesus was to pass.

C. *The Holy Spirit often takes advantage of a person's natural, inherent curiosity to bring them to an awareness of their lostness and of their need for the Savior.* Unbelievers who observe a dedicated Christian respond to pressure, crises, or sorrow may become curious as to how he or she could bear those blows with such calmness and serenity. Thus they are drawn to Christ.

III. The encounter with Jesus.

A. "When Jesus reached the spot, he looked up and said to him, 'Zacchaeus, come down immediately. I must stay at your house today.' So he came down at once and welcomed him gladly" (v. 5–6 NIV). Jesus "looked up." Why? Why just at this place, just at this time? Because Jesus knew there was someone "lost" in that tree, and he "came to seek and to save what was lost" (v. 10 NIV). Always, the compassionate, loving eyes of Jesus were searching the crowds for those who were responding, even if ever so slightly, to the convicting ministry of the Holy Spirit.

B. *Jesus called out to Zacchaeus by name.* He knew all about Zacchaeus. An eminent Methodist preacher of long ago, George Stuart, gave this interesting legend about Zacchaeus: "Zacchaeus was a publican, and so was Matthew. When Matthew began to follow the Lord, one of the first things he did was to gather together those of his own class. I often think that probably he said to his Lord, 'Master, if one day you should happen to be passing through Jericho, I wish you would find a man named Zacchaeus.'"

C. *Jesus asked Zacchaeus to extend hospitality.* Only one other time did Jesus ask for some gesture of hospitality—from the Samaritan woman at Jacob's well, when he said to her, "Give me something to drink." Isn't it interesting that both of these persons were outcasts? Jesus wanted to finish in their lives what the Holy Spirit had started.

IV. The response of Zacchaeus.

A. *The events that transpired following this initial encounter between Jesus and Zacchaeus are glorious and beautiful indeed.* Luke tells us that when Zacchaeus came down from the tree, he welcomed Jesus "gladly" (v. 6 NIV). Can you imagine what a delightful stroll Jesus and Zacchaeus had en route to Zacchaeus's home? No one would dare be seen in Zacchaeus's presence. He always walked alone. It was almost as if he were a leper. Indeed, more compassion would have been shown him if he had been a leper!

B. *Of course, Jesus' critics quickly and soundly condemned him for going home with Zacchaeus.* They murmured and criticized, pulled their sanctimonious robes about them, and acted proud of themselves because they were "spiritual." But note verse 8: "Zacchaeus stood up." How long the interval was between verses 7 and 8 we have no way of knowing. But it was long enough! A radical change had taken place in the heart and life of Zacchaeus during that time.

C. *He walked out into the courtyard where all the people had gathered, and turned and addressed Jesus, who apparently had followed him: "If I have cheated anybody out of anything, I will pay back four times the amount" (v. 8 NIV).* What had been the habit of Zacchaeus's life? It could have been expressed in the words "I get." Now he is saying, "I give." This is the way of Christianity. Before Zacchaeus met Jesus, he was mastered by greed. Now he was mastered by grace.

Conclusion

What, then, was the glorious ending to this story? "Jesus said to him, 'Today salvation has come to this house" (v. 9 NIV). This was Jesus' mission. "For the Son of Man came to seek and to save what was lost" (v. 10 NIV). The man who had made "wrong choices" had now made the right choice! The songwriter has said:

> Down in the human heart, crushed by the tempter,
> Feelings lie buried that grace can restore;
> Touched by a loving hand, wakened by kindness,
> Chords that were broken will vibrate once more.
>
> —*Fanny Crosby*

Wednesday Evening, May 21

Title: How Can the Drudgery Be Taken Out of Giving?

Text: "Each man should give what he has decided in his heart to give, not reluctantly or under compulsion, for God loves a cheerful giver" **(2 Cor. 9:7 NIV).**

Scripture Reading: Acts 20:35; 1 Corinthians 16:1–2; 2 Corinthians 9:6–8

Introduction

Scientists have worked over the past decades to take the drudgery out of many of life's activities. Travel has been made easier with automobiles and airplanes. Housework has been lightened with the invention of washing machines, clothes dryers, dishwashers, microwave ovens, and other household appliances. Life has been made easier, and we hope for greater ease of living in future years.

Some believers conceive of many religious activities as drudgery. This is especially true in the area of Christian giving. Many believers do not give regularly to their local churches; and when they do give, they do it with complaining or a lack of joy. Paul said that God loves cheerful givers. So that is what we need—people giving out of a sense of joy, not drudgery. How can we put happiness into our giving?

I. Happiness in giving comes by loving that to which you give.

A. *People love to give money to something they consider important.* According to Scripture, nothing is more important to society than the church.

B. *People love to give money to something that pays great dividends.* Search the Scriptures, and you will see the results of the church's work. People find a right relationship with God. The hungry are fed, the sick are ministered to, and the homeless are given refuge by the church. There can be no greater investment than to put your money into that which promotes the kingdom of God.

II. Happiness in giving comes by acknowledging that God owns everything.

A. *A human-ownership attitude toward possessions makes giving a drudgery.* Basically speaking, the human-ownership attitude is the failure to acknowledge that God is the owner of everything. A prominent case study of one's thinking that he owned everything is Jesus' parable of the rich fool. The productive farmer in the story refers to "my barns," "my crops," and "my soul." The human idea of ownership makes one dread to give from "his" or "her" possessions to God.

B. *A divine-ownership attitude toward possessions takes the drudgery out of giving.* To give with the realization that God has given us what we have is to give with joy and appreciation. We do not own anything—talents, time, life, or possessions. These have been loaned to us by the Lord, and we express our genuine gratitude to him by giving.

III. Happiness in giving comes by dedicating self to the Lord.

A. *The gift God really wants is you.* Christianity is predicated on self-giving. "God so loved the world that he gave" (John 3:16). The Lord is interested in people giving themselves to him. "They did not do as we expected, but they gave themselves first to the Lord and then to us in keeping with God's will" (2 Cor. 8:5 NIV). The apostle Paul expressed the fact that the gift he really wanted from the Corinthians was not their money but themselves. "Now I am ready to visit you for the third time, and I will not be a burden to you, because what I want is not your possessions but you" (12:14 NIV).

B. *When we give God our best self, giving our other gifts will be no problem.* When we are willing to deny ourselves, take up the cross, and follow Jesus, the drudgery of giving the Lord his tithe and our other offerings will hold no dread.

Conclusion

Do you experience a feeling of dread when confronted with the offering plate? The drudgery can be taken away from the giving experience. Simply put, you need to open your life to the leadership of Jesus Christ. Living under the lordship of Jesus Christ will help you to learn to become a cheerful giver.

Sunday Morning, May 25

Title: Lest We Forget

Text: "Therefore, since we are surrounded by so great a cloud of witnesses, let us lay aside every weight, every sin to which we cling, and let us run with perseverance the race for which we are entered, our eyes fixed on Jesus, the pioneer and perfecter of our faith, who for the joy that was set before him endured the cross . . . and is seated at the right hand of God's throne" **(Heb. 12:1–2, author's translation)**.

Scripture Reading: Hebrews 12:1–2

Hymns: "O God of Our Fathers," Pruden
"Mine Eyes Have Seen the Glory," Howe
"My Country, 'Tis of Thee," Smith

Offertory Prayer: "Greater love has no man than this: that he lay down his life for his friends." Father, our giving is a reflection of our love. We cannot give without vividly recalling the greatest gift of all—your Son. He is your gift to humankind. He came to show us the Father and to bring us into right relationship with you. As we give, let us always do so in honor of your gift to us—Jesus Christ our Lord. Amen.

Introduction

Hebrews 11 is the Bible's hall of fame. It presents an impressive list of the heroes of the faith, noting their accomplishments. Each entry begins with the phrase "By faith . . .": "By faith Abel . . . By faith Abraham . . . By faith Moses . . . By faith the people crossed the Red Sea. . . ." They were persons who lived by unseen realities—triumphantly.

In God's grandstand sit a "cloud of witnesses." They surround us, tier upon tier, watching how we run. In faith's relay race, they have passed the baton on to us. Our faith is built on the foundation they have laid. This is what is meant by "the communion of the saints."

I. The race.

A. *In the race "for which we are entered," sin and temptation constitute our handicap.* They need to be put aside like so much excess baggage.

B. *Our assets are the worthy example of those who have gone before and our own dogged endurance.* Therefore, we can run with patience and perseverance.

C. *Our goal is Christ—"our eyes fixed on Jesus."* He is the pioneer of our faith. As our example he went before us, blazing the trail.

Years ago Jack Robinson, U.S. Olympic basketball star, described the opening of the summer games in London in 1948.

The participants circled the track before a crowd of ninety thousand spectators, which included King George VI. There were athletes from almost every nation.

Framed in the entrance to the stadium stood the runner with his torch. It had been lighted at Mount Olympia and run by relays across Europe. He circled the track to the cheers of the crowd. Then, with an emphatic stroke, he put the torch into the oil, and the flames flared up against the English sky.

Simultaneously, the sky was darkened as hundreds of pigeons were released to fly to capitals of the world, proclaiming that peace would reign during the fourteenth modern Olympic games.

Representatives of many nations were there, and God was the Creator of them all. The imagery of Hebrews 12 is a great stadium filled with believers of earlier times, watching our race of faith.

II. Gratitude.

In a memorial service we recall with gratitude those who have gone before us. This is an appropriate practice. However, we also want to remember to appreciate persons prior to their death, because gratitude is an emotion for all seasons. It is an attitude we should cultivate and practice frequently. Recall persons who have contributed to your life: parents, grandparents, an uncle or aunt, teachers, stalwart Christians. Look for an opportunity to affirm them, to express sincere appreciation for what they have meant to you. Don't wait too long to do so. Value your friends now while you may.

Rudyard Kipling's poem "Recessional" sounds a useful note for Memorial Day. Written in celebration of Queen Victoria's Jubilee, its message is amazingly modern and applies to our country as well as it did to Great Britain:

God of our fathers, known of old,
    Lord of our far-flung battle-line,
Beneath whose awful Hand we hold
    Dominion over palm and pine—
Lord God of Hosts, be with us yet,
Lest we forget—lest we forget!

The tumult and the shouting dies;
    The captains and the kings depart:
Still stands Thine ancient sacrifice,
    An humble and a contrite heart.

Lord God of Hosts, be with us yet,
Lest we forget—lest we forget!

Far-called, our navies melt away;
    On dune and headland sinks the fire:
Lo, all our pomp of yesterday
    Is one with Nineveh and Tyre!
Judge of the Nations, spare us yet,
Lest we forget—lest we forget.

Memorial Day reminds us of the reality of life and death. All life is a gift, undeserved grace from the Father. We are to receive it with gratitude and live for his glory, whether for a long time or a short while.

Recall the heroes of the faith and what they endured that we might have an English Bible, that they might bring the gospel to our shores, that we might have religious liberty in this land. List the heroes of the faith to whom you feel indebted.

Conclusion

While we are grateful for our roots and spiritual heritage, we want to be faithful in handing on that legacy to those who come after us. We have often been reminded that we are only one generation away from paganism.

Sunday Evening, May 25

Title: Martha: Troubled about Many Things

Text: "'Martha, Martha,' the Lord answered, 'you are worried and upset about many things, but only one thing is needed. Mary has chosen what is better, and it will not be taken away from her'" **(Luke 10:41–42 NIV).**

Scripture Reading: Luke 10:38–42

Introduction

Martha of Bethany, the sister of Mary and Lazarus, had the rare and cherished privilege of preparing a meal for Jesus. She was a woman who loved her Lord deeply but who at times had difficulty sorting out her priorities.

It is difficult to consider Martha's story without bringing her sister, Mary, into the picture. In fact, on all three occasions in the Scriptures where these women appear, they are seen together. It is the contrast between the two that tells us so much about each one of them.

These three word pictures of Martha and Mary present three days out of their lives. There is great contrast among these three days and the events that transpired within them, yet there is a strange continuity among them as well.

I. Luke describes the first day as a day of joy.

A. *It is somewhat unusual that Luke does not mention Lazarus here, for as the brother, he must have been the breadwinner in the home.* Nonetheless, the inference is that Martha ran the household in Bethany. As we view this first scriptural portrait of Martha (vv. 38–42), we see her as a loving hostess determined to do everything she could to make Jesus' visit to her home a perfect one.

B. *Something else unusual about Martha, Mary, and Lazarus is that there is no mention in the Scriptures as to how they came to be followers of Jesus.* Rather, when they enter the story, they are already believers. There is something special about the relationship between Jesus and these three. It is obvious that their home became more than just a place to stop for a visit when he was passing through Bethany. It was a refuge. It was the one place where Jesus could be "at home."

C. *On this first day, which we have described as a day of joy, we find Martha busily occupied in a loving attempt to give Jesus a worthy welcome.* This was a "day of days" for Martha; it was very special, and she wanted it to be perfect. Yet into this day of sunshine and joy there crept a shadow. In Martha's loving attempt to make Jesus welcome and comfortable, she was almost overcome by her "busyness."

D. *Perhaps there was a bit of an edge in her voice when she spoke to her sister, Mary.* Maybe something happened during the course of that day that was the proverbial straw that broke the camel's back for Martha. Obviously, she was at her breaking point when she came to Jesus with her complaint: "Lord, don't you care that my sister has left me to do the work by myself? Tell her to help me!" (v. 40 NIV). Martha may have called Mary several times, but Mary was so preoccupied with Jesus that she probably didn't hear her sister.

E. *Jesus had no rebuke for Martha, although he did have a word of reproof.* He was not angry with her; he merely wanted her to see her misplaced priorities. She had become so occupied with many things that she had forgotten the one thing that was by far the most important in her life.

II. John describes the second day as a day of calamity (John 11:1–44).

A. *Again we find Martha's temperament surfacing.* The ideal for new Christians would be to surrender so completely to the Lord that all unpleasant personality traits would be removed, but that is rarely what happens. Instead, most of us Christians wrestle throughout our lives with some quirk in our personalities. We must be on guard at all times. Perhaps it is an ungovernable temper; or maybe we tend to gossip or to talk too much when we should be listening; or perhaps we are too sensitive to what others think or say about us.

B. *In John 11:21 we read Martha's first words to Jesus when he and his disciples arrived in Bethany, four days after Lazarus had died.* She said, "Lord, if you had been here, my brother would not have died" (NIV). Then in verse 32, Mary, who had remained in the house and had not rushed out to meet Jesus as had Martha, said exactly the same thing that Martha had said. Yet there was a difference in attitude. Martha was perfectly honest, but she was perturbed. She blamed Jesus. Mary's statement was made with an attitude of acceptance.

C. *But note again that Jesus did not rebuke Martha.* He looked with compassion and tenderness on her hot, troubled, tempest-tossed soul, and said, "Your brother will rise again" (v. 23 NIV). But before Jesus could finish (and we know, from what he said later, that he was not through speaking), Martha impatiently answered, "I know he will rise again in the resurrection at the last day" (v. 24 NIV). Again, Jesus did not rebuke Martha. He simply continued with one of the greatest and most majestic statements he ever made about himself: "I am the resurrection and the life. He who believes in me will live, even though he dies; and whoever lives and believes in me will never die. Do you believe this?" (vv. 25–26 NIV).

III. Finally, in the third picture of Martha in the New Testament—this time in John 12—we have a day of mystery.

A. *The cross was now only days away.* Jesus had tried to prepare his followers for his approaching crucifixion. Scripture says, "Six days before the Passover, Jesus arrived at Bethany, where Lazarus lived, whom Jesus had raised from the dead. Here a dinner was given in Jesus' honor. Martha served, while Lazarus was among those reclining at the table with him" (vv. 1–2 NIV).

B. *Perhaps it is significant that, even though Martha is found here doing the same thing she had always done, she is not speaking.* She is not protesting or arguing with Jesus about his determination to go to the cross. Under any other circumstances, that is likely what Martha would have been doing. In all probability, by this time Martha had found her Lord in a new way. She was still doing many things, but she was doing them in the power of the "one thing" she had placed at the center of her life.

C. *We do not read that Jesus said anything at all directly to Martha that day.* But he was receiving her hospitality; he was eating the delicious food she had placed on the table for him. Could Jesus' silence toward Martha indicate that he had accomplished his purpose in her life?

Conclusion

Here is the lesson from Martha's story: she was honest with Jesus. She expressed her frustrations, her protests, even her anger. God wants his children to be honest and open with him. Jesus never rebuked a single soul for honest doubts and questions. The one thing that angered him was hypocrisy. He knows, and we know, that when one is honest with another, the grounds are established for understanding and reconciliation. So it is with God.

Wednesday Evening, May 28

Title: Why Are There So Many Spiritual Dropouts?
Text: "From that time many of his disciples went back, and walked no more with him" **(John 6:66)**.
Scripture Reading: John 6:53–71

Introduction

The number of high school dropouts is alarming. Equally or maybe more alarming is the evidence of many dropouts from the church. Even a casual observer will detect that over one-half of the people who join a church will become relatively inactive in its life.

During the life and ministry of Jesus, he too experienced dropouts. "From that time many of his disciples went back, and walked no more with him" (John 6:66). The word *disciple* can mean a true follower of Jesus, or it can mean a person who has an interest in Jesus' ministry. The latter usage is the meaning in John 6:66. The writer is referring to persons interested in Jesus who never became committed to him. Let us examine closely why people choose to investigate the way of Christ then choose to drop out.

I. Those who act on mere impulse become numbered with the dropouts.

A. *People often act on impulse.* During Jesus' lifetime, many people were attracted to the power of Jesus reflected in his miracles and the depth of knowledge disclosed in his teaching. Yet they were not attracted to Jesus' conditions for following him.

B. *Impulsive followers give a semblance of a decision, but as time passes, their impulsive manner becomes known.* On the surface many people seem to have decided for Christ, but time and adverse circumstances will disclose the nature of their profession. Impulsive followers become dropouts.

II. Those who seek to follow Christ amid other pursuits become numbered with the dropouts.

A. *People often want to follow Christ amid many other pursuits.* The text of John 6:66 helps us to see that people sought Christ, but they did not want to give up other matters for the cause of Jesus Christ.

B. *Following Jesus Christ means an exclusive commitment to him.* Jesus will tolerate no rivalries. No one can serve two masters, and to try to serve two masters is to exclude Jesus Christ. He wants a disciple to love him, follow him, and serve him with no other master claiming an equal loyalty or devotion. Many people drop out of the church because they are not willing to give exclusive allegiance to Jesus Christ. When Jesus talked about sacrifice, many walked away.

III. Those who cannot have life their way become dropouts.

A. *People come to Jesus and want Jesus to fit into their scheme of things.* The potential followers who are disclosed in John 6:66 wanted to change Jesus. They soon discovered that they could not manipulate the Master into their cultural religion, so they dropped him. Many people drop Jesus when they cannot have him on their terms.

B. *Jesus wants to change his followers.* When a person decides to open his or her life to Jesus Christ, the Holy Spirit begins a miraculous process of change in that person. The more one opens life to Christ, the more one is changed. It is possible to open life to Jesus Christ in an initial relationship, but it is also possible for that relationship to remain undeveloped. Though these people are immature disciples, they appear as dropouts.

Conclusion

Jesus wants committed followers. Are you a follower who has continued in your commitment? Examine your decision. Check to see if you are a genuine follower of the Lord.

SUGGESTED PREACHING PROGRAM FOR THE MONTH OF
JUNE

■ Sunday Mornings

The messages for this month continue to focus on life in the family. The suggested theme is "Facing the Crises of Family Life with Christ's Help." On the last Sunday of the month, the Sunday before Independence Day, celebrate with a sermon titled "Finding Freedom in Christ."

■ Sunday Evenings

Continue and complete the series "The Ministry of Jesus to Individuals."

■ Wednesday Evenings

Continue and conclude the series "Questions Christians Ask."

SUNDAY MORNING, JUNE 1

Title: The Master and Youth
Text: "Let no one despise your youth, but set the believers an example in speech and conduct, in love, in faith, in purity" **(1 Tim. 4:12 RSV)**.
Scripture Reading: Mark 10:17–22
Hymns: "Footsteps of Jesus," Slade
"I Have Decided to Follow Jesus," Clark
"Now I Belong to Jesus," Ellsworth
Offertory Prayer: Father, we offer our best to you, including our youth. They bring you their enthusiasm and energy, their dedication and potential. As you accept the gifts of our hands, accept as well the gift of ourselves—our total selves in your service.

Father, show us your will and give us the courage to walk in it. We give our all to you. In Jesus' name. Amen.

Introduction

The story of Jesus' encounter with the rich young ruler shows us how the Master looks at youth. Jesus himself was a young man, barely thirty. Neither were the apostles very old. Many of them were quite young, some perhaps in their late teens. Jesus led a youth movement full of excitement, enthusiasm, and the idealism of the kingdom of God.

I. The Master understands your problems.

Jesus identifies with youth's impatience. He knows the competitive pressures you feel. He understands your need to discover who you are, to be accepted, and to belong.

Modern youth are assaulted by the media, brainwashed by hidden persuaders that appeal to base and selfish motives. Youth often feel depersonalized, exploited, and threatened. The Master understands and is there to help you. Call on him.

II. The Master sees your potential.

A. *He knows your possibilities and wants the best for you.* Some youth are rebellious, but most are decent and fun-loving. Most have lofty ideals and high ambition to make the world better. They are hard workers. Many dream of a career and marriage. Jesus "looks intently" at youth, seeing them as they are and what they can become.

B. *The Master cares for you.* "Jesus looked at him and loved him" (Mark 10:21 NIV). Parents may not care, teachers may be impersonal, friends may take advantage of you, but Jesus loves you and cares for you.

III. The will of God for your life.

One of the serious concerns of Christian youth is how to discover God's will for their lives. While this is a worthy goal, attaining it is not automatic nor easy. In fact, it will take a lifetime to discover God's will for your entire life.

J. Winston Pearce gives some helpful suggestions for discovering the Father's will:

A. *"Follow the gleam."* What is your sense of intuitive leading? God will reveal his purpose for us in time. He does not play "I've Got a Secret."

B. *"Favor your bent."* What are your gifts, talents, and strengths? What do you enjoy most? Ask how these could be used in serving the Lord and your fellow humans.

C. *"Watch for the open door."* What needs could you help meet? They may well constitute your call to service. Look for opportunities for service.

Conclusion

We are taught by Jesus to pray, "Thy kingdom come, thy will be done on earth. . . ." He intends that we pray like that and also work to answer the prayer. Let Jesus be Lord of your life.

SUNDAY EVENING, JUNE 1

Title: A Man Born Blind: Suffering for God's Glory

Text: "His disciples asked him, 'Rabbi, who sinned, this man or his parents, that he was born blind?'

"'Neither this man nor his parents sinned,' said Jesus, 'but this happened so that the work of God might be displayed in his life'" **(John 9:2–3 NIV).**

Scripture Reading: John 9:1–7, 35–41

Introduction

Can you imagine what it would be like to be born blind? Can you conceive of never having seen, even for a fleeting moment, a flaming sunset, a bed of roses, a flock of sheep, or a graceful swan gliding across a lake? Such was the condition of a man Jesus met in Jerusalem one day.

When the apostle John sought to describe the works of Jesus, he did not merely chronicle miracles and healings at random. Rather, he chose, carefully and deliberately, eight "signs," as he called them. Each sign was outstanding in its revelation of the power of God operating through his Son. There was a definite design and meaning in the choice of each miracle. This incident revolves around one of these eight signs.

I. The setting in which the healing of this man born blind took place.

A. *Just before this encounter with the man born blind, Jesus had been attending the Feast of Tabernacles in the temple at Jerusalem.* It was during this third of the three major feasts during the Jewish year that the magnificent and impressive ritual of the lighting of the giant candelabra on the porch of the temple took place. Four great candelabra, each containing four golden bowls of oil, would cause such a brilliant, blazing light reflecting off the white marble walls of the temple that the whole city of Jerusalem would be illuminated.

B. *As Jesus observed this impressive and symbolic ritual, he thought of the spiritual and moral darkness that still enveloped the souls of these people.* He could hold back no longer. He shouted for all to hear, "I am the light of the world: he that followeth me shall not walk in darkness, but shall have the light of life" (John 8:12). Then, as he left the temple, after encountering the hostility of the Jews who took up stones to stone him, he passed by this man born blind. What a perfect demonstration this would be to illustrate what he meant when he said to them that day, "I am the light of the world"!

C. *This, then, was the setting in which this meeting took place.* For here, in this man born blind, was one who had experienced the most complete *physical* darkness humans could experience. Now he was about to know not only what *physical* light can do but *spiritual* light as well.

II. The situation itself.

A. *"As he went along, he saw a man blind from birth"* (v. 1 NIV). To see blind people in Palestine was not uncommon. Particularly would this be true around the temple area and during feast days and holy days, when many more Jews than usual would be in the vicinity. The beggars—the blind and handicapped—were wise. They had learned that people coming to and leaving the temple were generally a bit more compassionate and benevolent than they were at other times.

B. *Thus, for Jesus and his disciples to see a blind man on the temple porch was a common sight.* But this blind man was different from the others. In fact, this is the only incident recorded in the Gospels where Jesus healed a person blind from birth. No disease had attacked and destroyed the eyesight of this man, nor had an unfortunate injury blinded him. He simply was born blind.

C. *Jesus must have stopped and looked at the man, for the disciples seemed constrained to "make conversation," for they obviously thought it was a bit unusual for Jesus to do this.* One of them asked Jesus what was responsible for this blindness—the man's own sin or that of his parents. The Jews, like many Christians today, had a tidy little belief concerning things they couldn't explain any other way. For, reflected in the statement the disciples made to Jesus was, "It's obvious, Master, what has happened here. Somebody 'had it coming' to him. He got what he deserved. Was it this man himself or his parents?"

D. *Let's analyze the disciples' question.* First, they were sure that there was some connection between human disability and sin. And they were right. When God created man, he intended for him to have the gift of sight. Well, something had happened in the creative process as far as this man was concerned. Somewhere one of God's laws had been broken. But it is not necessarily true that every tragedy like this is the result of some personal sin. From ancient times, this had been man's belief. It is reflected in the Old Testament story of Job. Certainly we do often suffer when we sin, but not every tragedy that comes into our lives is the result of our personal sin.

E. *Another ridiculous fallacy in the disciples' question is reflected in their suggestion that this man had sinned.* If that were the case, he would had to have sinned before he was born! Some of the Jewish teachers believed in the preexistence of human personality, and even a few accepted the idea of the transmigration of souls. This, obviously, was so far afield from the truth that Jesus did not even bother to reply. But about this blind man's handicap—what is the answer? Is there an answer?

III. The statement Jesus made.

A. *Jesus stated plainly that the man's congenital blindness was not because of personal sin, neither his nor his parents'.* But at the same time, Jesus did not give a solution to the problem. He removed its cause, in the healing of the man's blindness, but he did not explain its reason. He did take the opportunity, however, to show what God can do.

B. *So the question still remains: Why didn't Jesus give a solution to this age-old problem of suffering?* Why do the righteous suffer? There are some mysteries within the sovereign will and wisdom of God that are beyond human understanding. It is the height of presumption for humans to think that they must know and understand everything that happens to them. Here is where the miracle and mystery of faith come in. How wonderful indeed when we learn to rest our soul—our yesterdays, our today, and all of the tomorrows God may grant us—in the hands of God.

IV. The solution Jesus provided for this man's dilemma.

A. *Why did Jesus use clay in the healing of this man's blindness (vv. 6–7)?* Surely there was no healing virtue in the clay. Many other times Jesus had healed—even blind eyes—without the use of any means. But obviously there was a lack in the ability of this man to believe.

B. *After Jesus anointed the man's eyes with the clay, he bade him go wash in the Pool of Siloam.* The man obeyed, and he was healed. There are few details as to exactly what happened when he received his sight. There is a sequel, however. Because of his testimony, he was cast out of the synagogue. Jesus found him and revealed himself fully to him, and the man acknowledged him as Messiah.

Conclusion

This blind man learned about Jesus slowly, progressively; but each step was more and more glorious. He had suffered—why, we do not know. But for whatever reason, his suffering was compensated when he was able to appreciate the glory of God in the receiving of his sight.

WEDNESDAY EVENING, JUNE 4

Title: Can Human Nature Be Changed?

Text: "And I will give them one heart, and I will put a new spirit within you; and I will take the stony heart out of their flesh, and will give them an heart of flesh" **(Ezek. 11:19)**.

Scripture Reading: Ezekiel 11:17–25

Introduction

On December 2, 1982, Dr. Barney Clark experienced a first in medical history. His diseased heart was replaced with a mechanical heart. He suffered from cardiomyopathy, an extreme weakening of the heart. The surgeon, Dr. William DeVries, replaced Barney Clark's diseased heart with a new one, which gave him 112 more days of life.

The prophet Ezekiel realized that Israel needed a new heart. The nation suffered from rebellion, which led to captivity. The only thing that could change Israel was a new heart, or spirit.

Human nature needs to be changed. The question has been asked, "Can human nature really be changed?" The answer is yes. But human nature can be changed only by the miraculous working of God.

I. Everybody needs a new heart.

A. *Human beings have ruined their nature by willful rebellion against God.* Jeremiah, recognizing the ruin that rebellion had caused human nature, said, "The heart is deceitful above all things, and desperately wicked: who can know it?" (Jer. 17:9).

B. *A ruined nature is a universal problem.* The sinful condition of human nature is not something restricted to a few; it is the condition of all. "For all have sinned, and come short of the glory of God" (Rom. 3:23).

C. *The condition of the human heart is a hopeless condition.* People cannot change themselves. Neither can rituals or religious works change the human heart. The human heart needs the changing power of God.

II. Everybody can get a new heart from God.

A. *The first step in getting a new heart is to admit your condition.* Recently I spoke with a woman who had experienced some heart problems. She told me, "I don't know why, but I refused to admit that I had a problem." Later she acknowledged that she had a problem; and after having a medical examination, she found she needed heart surgery. No one can be helped without the admission of a need.

B. *The second step in getting a new heart is to believe in Jesus Christ.* To receive a new heart, one must submit to the Great Physician, Jesus Christ. Whenever one puts himself or herself in God's hands, it is the beginning of a new kind of life. Only Jesus is capable of changing the human heart.

C. *The third step in getting a new heart is to experience a new creation.* God makes people different when they open their lives to him (see 2 Cor. 5:17).

III. Everyone who receives a new heart has a new life.

A. *A new heart means a new relationship with God.* Human rebellion has created a gap between God and a human being. The fault is not with God but with the person. When Jesus Christ is allowed into a life, the relationship with God is restored (see 2 Cor. 5:18–19).

B. *A new heart means glorious fellowship with other changed human beings.* Two men came to visit a patient before he was to have open-heart surgery. They were members of Mended Hearts, a fellowship of people who had experienced heart surgery. These men gave the patient encouragement and hope. Similarly, the church is a group of people who have had their nature changed by the power of Jesus Christ.

C. *A new heart leads to a new quality of life.* When Jesus changes a person, he gives a new life. Dr. Barney Clark died on March 23, 1983, 112 days after he received his new heart. Before he died, Clark told reporters that the new heart had given him life. Jesus gives a quality of existence that will never end.

Conclusion

Human nature can be changed by the marvelous power of Jesus Christ. Everyone can receive a new heart.

SUNDAY MORNING, JUNE 8

Title: Is That All There Is?
Text: ". . . the destruction that wastes at noonday" **(Ps. 91:6 RSV)**.
Scripture Reading: Psalm 91:1–6
Hymns: "Make Me a Channel of Blessing," Euclid
"Teach Me, O Lord, I Pray," Keegan
"When We Walk with the Lord," Sammis
Offertory Prayer: Father, we have come into this place of worship with our gifts. We offer our tribute of praise for your grace and love. We offer our silent adoration. We bring our gifts of money, representing the investment of our lives returned in part to you. We come to hear a clear word from above to apply in our daily living. Accept our gifts in the Master's name. Amen.

Introduction

A popular song tells about a young woman who tried everything in life and concluded each experience with a haunting refrain: "Is that all there is?" She failed to find significance in anything. She would probably ask the same question of St. Peter on Judgment Day.

"Is that all there is?" That can become the theme song of the middle years. We are witnessing the "graying" of America. Mickey Mouse is now more than three-quarters of a century old. And even Charlie Brown is more than a half-century old. We're not as young as we used to be either.

I. Middle age defined.

Middle age is an interesting time of life, the longest part of life. It is the "continental divide"—when we reach the top and can look in both directions.

Some have called it "middlescence" to correspond with adolescence. But the middle years are aptly described as "that time in life when paunch and wrinkles appear and hair disappears." At least those are some of the indications. It can be a traumatic period.

The middle years are a time when we are assaulted by the media and brainwashed by youth-oriented culture. You know you are middle-aged when you have lived through the widening of neckties at least three times. Middle age is a time when we are depersonalized by technology. It's a time when we are exploited by inflation and staggering interest rates. Who's getting ahead? Worse than that, our annuities are threatened.

II. The taffy years.

I came across an apt description of the middle years. Someone called them the "taffy years"—when we are pulled in several directions. We are pulled by our children, pulled by our aging parents, pulled by our business or profession, pulled by civic needs, pulled by the church. These are demanding years in which we bear the heat and burden of the day. The psalmist spoke about "the destruction that wastes at noonday."

A. *Think for a moment about how middle-agers relate to their children.* First, these are staggeringly high-cost years. I have read so many things about the cost of rearing a child or putting a child through college that I have just about given up reading! Then, suddenly, after we've spent all that money, we experience the empty nest. This is especially tough on the mother, who has been so needed. All at once those piles of laundry disappear and she has to adjust to cooking for two again. But children leaving can be a positive thing as well. Expenses are cut, more room is available in the house, and the family car will be at hand when you need it.

B. *Consider the taffy years with reference to our aging parents.* Earlier generations lived in a simpler, agrarian society. They married earlier but could afford to because a couple's father would give them forty acres of the family farm and a mule and build a house for them to start housekeeping. They had an extended family of grandparents, aunts, uncles, and cousins with all kinds of support systems built into it. With our nuclear family, we don't have that. Then with the aging of our parents, we develop all kinds of complications. Primarily, there is the problem of distance. Few children live and work near their parents today. There may also be great expense involved in their illness and care. This may be complicated by longer life expectancy. When the time of death comes, all of a sudden a part of our past is gone, and we are the older generation. That is a sobering experience.

C. *Our workload and professional life put pressures on us, some wonderful and some difficult, but pressures nonetheless.* In a survey of nearly three thousand people, 56 percent of them said they were dissatisfied with their work, unhappy in their jobs. That's not true with everybody. For some people, middle age is a time of great achievement, when their professional life really comes together. They taste the sweetness of success, only to discover that it's rather hollow. What happens once we achieve our goal and find no other worlds to conquer and no other achievements for which to strive? Others in middle age discover they are not going to achieve. Their life's work is a dead end.

III. Problems of middle age.

A. *Middle age can be a time of job security, but it can also be a time of job insecurity.* We used to think that if a person landed a job, stayed there, and did it well that he or she had it made. But that's not true any longer. Many men and women at mid-career get laid off when their companies downsize or relocate.

B. *Middle age can also be a threatening period for marriage.* When you study the statistics, it's rather alarming to find people who have been married twenty to twenty-five years suddenly divorcing. Many marriages by that time have gone stale; boredom has set in. That can mean the death of any relationship. Many couples at middle age begin to experience what lawyers call "incompatibility." I've read that there is no such thing as incompatibility—that's just an argument dreamed up by an attorney who doesn't have a strong case!

Middle age is a time of high risk. You've heard of mental fatigue—middle age can be a time of *moral* fatigue. When a marriage goes stale, one partner may have an affair, and the couple may suddenly wake up to the fact that they don't have a marriage any longer. It has disintegrated.

C. *Middle age can be a time when one's health is threatened.* Health problems may occur at any age, but they seem to increase in the middle years.

D. *The middle years can be a traumatic period as we go through physical changes.* Our appearance begins to change, and we suddenly get interested in that historical character who discovered Florida. Ponce de Leon was fifty-two years of age when he heard from the Native Americans about a fountain from which a person could drink to halt the aging process. He went looking for the fountain of youth and found it at St. Augustine. If you've taken a drink out of it, you know it's sulfur water! The fear of losing one's youth, physical strength, and potency can be devastating, causing a person to feel trapped with no way out.

E. *Middle age can be a time when pride works havoc in our lives.* We have achieved something, have enjoyed some success, so we begin to rest. Spiritual dry rot sets in. We may stop reading, stop growing, stop studying.

IV. Potential of the middle years.

Middle age does hold some marvelous advantages and possibilities. And we can apply some techniques for making the middle years even more productive. One is the simplification of life, something our Quaker friends call "centering down." We can learn to simplify our schedules, making life less demanding. We can learn to say no to some requests in order to say yes to more important ones. The middle years can also be a time when we simplify our wants. We don't have to keep on acquiring things in order to have a sense of worth. It is possible in the middle years to discover how much is enough. It may also be possible in the middle years, as our incomes grow, to have a part in some extras, to give to some causes more generously than we ever could before.

Middle age can be a time of great contentment and thanksgiving. Let us thank God for our children and parents and spouses, for work, for friends, for challenge, and for the family of God.

Conclusion

Middle age can be the time for self-examination and mid-course correction. We are no longer thinking the far-reaching thoughts of youth. This is time for taking stock and getting our bearings. The great Methodist missionary E. Stanley Jones said, "Everybody ought to be reconverted at age forty." Everyone at the entrance of the middle years should make an opportunity for spiritual self-examination. It can be a time of spiritual renewal in which we discover new purpose in life and exercise a new dedication to the will of God as we enter the period of our greatest usefulness. What about it? Is this a time for your reconversion?

SUNDAY EVENING, JUNE 8

Title: The Condemned Woman: Destroyed by Sin's Stigma

Text: "[The teachers of the law and the Pharisees] said to Jesus, 'Teacher, this woman was caught in the act of adultery. In the Law Moses commanded us to stone such women. Now what do you say?' . . .

"When they kept on questioning him, he straightened up and said to them, 'If any one of you is without sin, let him be the first to throw a stone at her'" **(John 8:4, 7 NIV)**.

Scripture Reading: John 8:2–11

Introduction

There is no greater tragedy in the world than that of persons who persist in traveling a particular path of sin until the stigma of that sin has destroyed both their own sense of pride and self-worth, as well as the confidence and respect of others. There is a time in such persons' lives when they pass a "point of no return" in regard to their acceptance by society.

Yet there are times when a miracle transpires and the seemingly impossible takes place. God takes persons who have destroyed themselves, and perhaps those around them, and not only forgives their sin but also reverses their lifestyle so that the stigma of sin is gone. Such is the background of the story we are considering tonight.

I. Reviewing the problem (vv. 2–6)

A. *The scribes and Pharisees were always looking for some charge by which they could discredit Jesus.* This time they were certain they had cornered him. There was no way, in their estimation, that he could get out of this one.

B. *The law was clear on this matter.* Leviticus 20:10 states that both an adulterer and an adulteress must be put to death. Whereas the method of death is not designated in that passage, Deuteronomy 22:13–21 suggests that should a girl already betrothed to be married commit adultery, she should be stoned to death outside the city gates. Therefore, from a purely legal point of view, the scribes and Pharisees were correct. This woman, caught in adultery, was liable to the death penalty.

C. *So what was the problem?* It concerned the dilemma in which the religious leaders sought to trap Jesus. If he gave the decision that the woman ought to be stoned to death, two things would happen. First, he would jeopardize his reputation with the people that he was a friend of sinners, a man of mercy and compassion. Second, he would be suggesting a violation of the Roman law, which decreed that the Jews no longer had the power to pass the death penalty. But what if Jesus had openly declared that this woman should not be stoned for her sin, that she should be pardoned, forgiven? They would say quickly that Jesus was teaching people to break the law of Moses and that he was condoning the sin of adultery. There we have the problem.

II. The confrontation (John 8:6–8).

A. *John says that Jesus did not answer the woman's accusers.* He simply stooped down and began to write in the sand with his finger. Some say Jesus may have been writing down some of the sins of which these accusers were guilty. We cannot know for certain.

B. *Whatever the case, these men were so far into this by now that they had to carry through.* Though they may well have been quite uncomfortable at this point, they continued to press Jesus for an answer. Jesus "straightened up and said to them, 'If any one of you is without sin, let him be the first to throw a stone at her'" (v. 7 NIV).

C. *In no way was this what these self-righteous scribes expected Jesus to say.* He was throwing the issue back in their faces! Jesus had reversed the scene, putting the scribes on trial both before God and their own consciences. Jesus stooped down and wrote again in the sand. He did not look at them again. He didn't have to; his words were like burning firebrands that had slammed against their hearts.

III. The reactions of the accusers, the woman, and Jesus (vv. 9–11).

A. *The reaction of the accusers.* All of a sudden, this legal and moral issue had become a spiritual one. Jesus had focused not on the sin or the legal penalty for that sin, but on the person involved. That was always Jesus' way of doing things. This did not mean that he was "soft" on sin or that he condoned so scarlet a sin as adultery. Rather, his first concern was with the victims of sin.

B. *Jesus had clearly made his point with the religious leaders.* They may have hated him for it, for not only had he caused their own consciences to hurt, but he also had embarrassed them before the crowd. Slowly they began to slip away.

C. *What about the woman?* I think she was perhaps one of the most confused individuals who had ever stood before Jesus. No doubt she knew the law on this matter of adultery and what lay in store for her. Also, the exposure of her sin had destroyed her sense of self-worth. She was at the lowest possible point in her life.

D. *What did Jesus say to her?* "Woman, where are they? Has no one condemned you?" (v. 10 NIV). Perhaps it was at that moment that she recognized who Jesus was and received him as her Savior. Her soul, which had been so soiled by sin, was now as pure and clean as the new-fallen snow.

E. *What about Jesus' reaction?* We must not misunderstand Jesus here. He was not considering the sin of adultery lightly. Whatever else may have been involved in Jesus' reply to her, we do see here the truth that Jesus was giving her another chance. She had made a mess of her life, but he was handing her the marvelous privilege of starting over again!

Conclusion

Louise Fletcher Tarkington wrote this delightful little poem:

> How I wish that there was some wonderful place
> Called the Land of Beginning Again,
> Where all our mistakes and all our heartaches
> And all of our poor selfish grief
> Could be dropped like a shabby old coat at the door
> And never put on again.

In Jesus Christ, this is gloriously possible.

WEDNESDAY EVENING, JUNE 11

Title: What Does It Mean to Be Lost?
Text: "For the Son of Man came to seek and to save what was lost" **(Luke 19:10 NIV)**.
Scripture Reading: Luke 15:1–7

Introduction

There are words we commonly hear, but when it comes to explaining these words, the task is difficult. For example, we often hear the word *lost,* but do we understand what it means to be lost?

Jesus used the word *lost.* Our text declares that "the Son of Man came to seek and to save what was lost" (Luke 19:10 NIV). The Lord also spoke of a lost sheep, a lost coin, and a lost son (cf. Luke 15). The word used for *lost* in 19:10 means "to be wasted." For a life to be apart from God means that one's life is being wasted. Let us examine what it means to be lost.

I. Being lost means not to be where you belong.

A. *Jesus illustrated the concept of lostness with three unique stories (Luke 15).* These stories have many facets, but the primary thrust is that lostness means to be out of place. The sheep belonged with the shepherd and the other sheep. The coin belonged in the possession of the woman. The son belonged at home with his father. None of these was in the proper place.

B. *Being out of place with God has many implications.*
   1. To be out of place means not to be in the right place. Someone has said, "Birds belong in the air, fish belong in the sea, and humans belong with God."
   2. To be out of place implies a uselessness. For example, if I lose a dollar bill in a field, the bill cannot be used.
   3. To be lost does not imply meanness or corruption, though that will sometimes be the case. Lostness means not going in God's direction where one belongs.

II. Being lost means to have lost a sense of direction.

A. *Jesus' story of the lost sheep illustrates that lostness means a lost sense of direction.* The shepherd had to go and search for the straying sheep. Many other animals have a sense of direction, but a sheep does not. The shepherd had to come and rescue the lost sheep.

B. *Losing a sense of direction has serious implications.*
   1. To lose your sense of direction could lead to panic.
   2. To lose your sense of direction could lead to useless activity of trying to find your way. Often people lost in the woods will walk in circles. Likewise, many people seek to be right with God, but their human attempts are futile.
   3. To lose your sense of direction could cause you to go to the wrong destination. This is exactly what happens spiritually. A person who is lost without Christ is heading toward hell, a destiny of life apart from God.

III. Being lost means to have a spirit of rebellion.

A. *The stories of Jesus recorded in Luke 15 illustrate that lostness means an obstinate attitude.* This truth is noticed in the sheep and especially in the rebellious son. The son's attitude may be noticed in his words "Give me my share of the estate" (v. 12 NIV). The meaning of lostness is graphically illustrated by the Master's story. Lostness means to live life by your own wishes.

B. *Living life in defiance of God has some serious implications.*
   1. To rebel against God is to go against the one who loves and cares for you.
   2. To rebel against God leads to an excessive selfishness. It means to be preoccupied with oneself.
   3. To be defiant of God means to live a lonely life. It is a life of alienation, or separation, from God both now and forever.

Conclusion

One of the worst words in the human language is *lost.* To be lost means not to be where you belong, to be going in the wrong direction, and to be defiant of God himself. The opposite of *lost* is *found.* To be found means to be where you belong, to be going in the right direction, and to be submissive to God. Being found is better. What is your condition?

SUNDAY MORNING, JUNE 15

Title: A Father's Faith

Text: "Honor your father and your mother, that your days may be long in the land which the LORD your God gives you" **(Exod. 20:12 RSV)**.

Scripture Reading: Luke 15:11–32

Hymns: "God of Our Fathers," Faber
"Faith of Our Fathers," Roberts
"Christian Men, Arise and Give," Young

Offertory Prayer: Father, we are here to worship in glad expectation of your presence and your blessing. Our gifts are a token of our gratitude for your gifts to us. They represent a portion of our time, energy, and talent returned to you in worship. We pray that you would accept them—and us. Through Jesus Christ, our Lord. Amen.

Introduction

Father's Day is not a conspiracy of the shirt and tie manufacturers of America, though one could suspect as much. Nor is Father's Day the invention of men jealous of the attention given to women on Mother's Day.

Fathers have a bad press image, as do all authoritative figures, such as teachers, police, and military officers. Fathers have been caricatured in comic strips and sitcoms. Frankly, I wouldn't choose any of these for my ideal!

I do not mean to sound defensive, but being a good father is one of the toughest jobs around. The typical father is forty-two inches around the chest, thirty-six around the waist, ninety-eight around the golf course, and a nuisance around the house! The family complains that Dad is never home.

Then when he is, he is underfoot and in their way. He fouls up the family's schedule like a French chef making McDonald's burgers.

Charles Duningston has given us a profile of a father: he is one who endures childbirth without benefit of anesthetic; he is angry at his son's poor grades though he knows it is really the teacher's fault; and he gives his daughter away (at the cost of several thousand dollars) to a man who is not good enough for her so that he can have grandchildren smarter than anybody else's.

His kids have the youth revolution movement; his wife has the woman's liberation movement; his employees have the labor union movement; and his government has the tax-reform movement. The only movement poor Dad has is the receding of his hairline and the expanding of his waistline and the cost-of-living spiral, which may land him on the bread line.

I. Luke 15 is a story about a father and his two sons.

A. *The first son strayed from home.* He was selfish. He said to his father, "Give me my share of the inheritance now." The boy was rude; he was not willing to wait until his father died to receive his legacy. He sounds much like today's generation.

The boy took a journey into a foreign country where he "spent all." He soon discovered that credit does have limits. Only then did the boy come to himself and return to his father and home.

B. *The elder brother stayed at home.* However, he too was self-centered. His every thought was only of himself. He was offended at the father's generosity to his younger brother. This son was lost too, even though he never left home.

C. *The father is the hero in this story.* What a great dad he was! The father let the boy go. He was willing to let him learn for himself even though it had to be the hard way. At the close of the story, when the boy returned, the father didn't say, "I told you so." He didn't make the boy crawl on his hands and knees and beg to be restored as a servant. The father welcomed him home, forgave him, and lavished affection on the returning son.

Between the beginning and the end of the story he was "the waiting father." How hard this must have been! When a son is away in a strange city making his start in life or away in military service, how hard it is for the father to wait for him to come home. Those are days of quiet agony. The point of Jesus' story is that the father loved *both* boys.

II. The father in the story represents God.

God is the true hero, and his fatherhood is the pattern for our fatherhood. God is not a father as we are fathers, but we are to be fathers as God is. This means that as a father you are to be a priest in your home. You are to be the religious educator of your children. You are to give them a sound moral footing, both by what you say and what you do.

Once a man told Samuel Taylor Coleridge that he had decided not to teach his children religion. He was going to let them grow up and make religious choices for themselves. That sounded enlightened and benevolent, but the truth is, it is a demonic attitude. Coleridge did not comment on his friend's statement. He waited until the visit was concluded and then said, "May I show you my flower garden?"

As the two men walked to the back of the house. Coleridge took his friend to a weed patch. The friend exclaimed, "This is not a flower garden!"

"Oh, yes, it is," said Coleridge. "I decided not to inhibit my garden. I have just left it at liberty to grow as it chooses." How foolish it is for parents to shirk their responsibility to educate their children in religion.

A father teaches his children kindness by being thoughtful at home. He teaches patience by being understanding at home. He teaches honesty by keeping his promises to the family (ouch!). A father teaches justice by being fair with everyone. No less a theologian than Dr. Seuss has said, "A person is a person no matter how small."

A father is to share affection with his children. That affection is to be a two-way street. Dr. Kenneth Chafin was professor of evangelism at Southwestern Seminary in Fort Worth, Texas. One night after dinner, his five-year-old daughter, Nancy, asked the inevitable question, "Daddy, are you going to be home tonight?"

Dr. Chafin said, "No, I'm going to the PTA to speak on 'An Ideal Father.'" Then he got an idea. He asked, "Nancy, what makes a good daddy?"

Little Nancy began to list the qualities she thought would make a good father. She said, "A good daddy knows how to fly a kite." Chafin recalled a day they had flown a kite together earlier that week. She said, "A good daddy knows how to build a fire." They had done that the night before. "A good daddy knows how to catch a fish," she said. They had gone fishing and caught a small fish; Nancy had been duly impressed. On she went until she listed ten things. Chafin stuck the list in his pocket and left for the PTA meeting.

During the preliminaries that night, he took the list out and glanced over it. Suddenly it dawned on him: The qualities Nancy had said make a good father did not require him to buy anything for Nancy; but every one of them required that he give himself to Nancy. That is what God has done for us. He has given us himself in the person of his Son (John 3:16). He is our heavenly Father, and we are his children.

Conclusion

O God, our Father, we give you thanks for your provision of our every need. We are grateful for your protective power in our lives day by day. Most of all we are grateful that you love us.

We pray for fathers. Make us worthy. Help us to be strong but not possessive. Help us to be liberating but never careless.

Grant that we may remember that we are also your children, willful and foolish and always in need of your patient grace. This we pray through our Lord Jesus Christ. Amen.

Sunday Evening, June 15

Title: The Samaritan Woman: Cursed by Guilt
Text: "Jesus answered, 'Everyone who drinks this water will be thirsty again, but whoever drinks the water I give him will never thirst. Indeed, the water I give him will become in him a spring of water welling up to eternal life.'

"The woman said to him, 'Sir, give me this water so that I won't get thirsty and have to keep coming here to draw water'" **(John 4:13–15 NIV).**
Scripture Reading: John 4:1–42

Introduction

One of the most awesome and chilling statements in the English language is that which comes from the foreman of a jury when he or she stands to say, "We find the defendant guilty!"

What is "guilt"? It is both a fact and a feeling. The dictionary says that guilt is "the fact or state of having done wrong." It is also "a feeling of being to blame." When the fact of guilt is proved in a court of law, and the guilty person pays his or her debt to society for the wrong done, then in the sight of the law that person is no longer guilty. Payment or restitution has been made, and for all practical purposes the "fact of guilt" is gone.

But the feeling of guilt isn't always so easily resolved. Sometimes it attaches itself to us like a malignancy. It distorts our emotions; it affects our attitudes; it sours our relationships with others. Sometimes it can drive a person to self-destruction. Then there are some who compensate for these feelings of guilt in other ways. They withdraw; they build fences around themselves, barriers that they allow no one to penetrate. And they live out their lives in loneliness and rejection.

As we continue our study of the way in which Jesus dealt with individuals, adapting his approach to meet them at the points of their unique and particular needs, we find a woman who was cursed by guilt. We shall attempt to discover how Jesus dealt with her overwhelming guilt.

I. The caring Savior (vv. 1–6).

A. *It was never as easy for Jesus to minister in the southern part of Palestine—in Judea, in Jerusalem—as it was in Galilee in the north.* Politics and prejudice found their focus in the city of Jerusalem and in the temple precincts where the Pharisees had their headquarters. The Sanhedrin held court there. Naturally, in that concentration of scribes and Pharisees, there were always those watching Jesus for the express purpose of discrediting him before the people who were eager to hear him preach and teach.

B. *This brings us to a cryptic but significant statement in verse 4: "Now he had to go through Samaria" (NIV).* This did not mean that, geographically, that was the only route available to Galilee. Rather, it was God's will for him to travel this road. This was not the regular route the Jews traveled from Judea to Galilee. Because of their hatred of the Samaritans, they would cross the Jordan River and travel through Transjordan and then cross back over the Jordan River into Galilee in the north.

C. *Presently Jesus and his disciples reached a famous and beloved landmark for every Israelite—Jacob's well—about a half-mile from the town of Sychar, most likely the modern Israeli town of Shechem.* It was high noon and doubtlessly a hot day. Jesus chose to sit on the well curbing while the disciples went to Sychar to purchase food. So the stage was set. In God's sovereign planning, an appointment had been made. Jesus was right on time.

II. The hardened woman (vv. 7–9).

A. *Who were the Samaritans?* They were descendants of two groups, one being the remnant of the Israelites who were members of the tribes that formed the northern kingdom of Israel. In 722 BC the northern kingdom fell to the Assyrians, and all but a remnant of Israelites were carried away captive. Then the Assyrians brought in foreign colonists from Babylonia and Media. Eventually and inevitably, these Israelites who remained in northern Palestine intermarried with the foreigners, thus losing the purity of their Israelite nationality. The Jews considered them unclean, and any association with them would render a Jew "unclean" and thus unfit to worship in the temple. Understandably, the Samaritans hated the Jews because of this bigotry and prejudice expressed toward them.

B. *Not only did this woman's nationality pose a problem, but her gender did as well.* The Jewish custom forbade a rabbi to greet a woman in public. Yet Jesus spoke to her. Because he knew what was in the hearts of people, he was fully aware of her moral character. Thus we have an amazing picture: the Son of God in conversation with an immoral woman! Jesus was breaking through the barriers of nationality and orthodox Jewish custom. Here is the beginning of the gospel for the whole world, not just for the Jews. Here is God "so loving the world," not just in theory, but in action.

III. The cultivating conversation (vv. 10–15).

A. *Can you see the subtle way Jesus approached this woman?* Here was a woman who had long since lost all self-respect; she was a "nobody." Her immoral life had isolated her even from her own Samaritan people. That is the reason she came to draw water in the heat of the noonday sun. The women of the village came in the cool of the early morning to draw their water.

B. *Jesus began his approach by asking the woman for something.* Nobody ever asked her for anything! There is nothing more devastating to the human personality than to feel unneeded. So, in spite of her initial reply to Jesus, we can't imagine what it meant to this woman for someone, even this Jew whose motives she did not yet understand, to ask her for some legitimate favor.

C. *After the woman had brought up the obvious problem that existed between Jews and Samaritans, Jesus dropped his bombshell.* Already she was confused about this whole incident. And Jesus countered with the offer to give her a drink. Of course, she thought that he referred to the water in Jacob's well, and she saw that he had nothing to draw with. Jesus had her attention.

IV. The condemning guilt of this woman (vv. 16–27).

A. *Jesus' reference to her husbands was the last thing she expected to hear.* This was the "sore spot" in her life. Night and day she lived with this burning guilt. Jesus had brought her sin out into the open. Her natural response was to change the subject.

B. *She brought up an entirely unrelated subject—she asked about the proper place to worship.* Jesus took care of that question in quick order. Then he revealed himself to her. In response to her remark about the coming Messiah, Jesus said, "I who speak to you am he"" (v. 26 NIV).

V. The cleansing experience (vv. 28–29).

A. *How much was said after Jesus revealed himself to the woman we do not know.* Somewhere after this point the miracle of salvation took place. The woman proved her newfound faith by her compelling desire to go and tell someone.

B. *She, like every other person, had to discover the reality of the Lord Jesus for herself; thus the people of Sychar came to see and hear.*

Conclusion

Perhaps the Samaritan woman became the "resident missionary" of Sychar. God took an individual who was cursed by guilt and led her through the dark tunnel of her guilt into the light of eternal life. He is still doing that today.

Wednesday Evening, June 18

Title: How Much Does It Cost to Be a Christian?

Text: "When he had called the people unto him with his disciples also, he said unto them, Whosoever will come after me, let him deny himself, and take up his cross, and follow me" **(Mark 8:34)**.

Scripture Reading: Mark 8:27–38

Introduction

A common question in today's world is "How much does it cost?" More than ever before there is a price consciousness, for it is the day of discount stores, bargain sections, and factory outlets. Smart shoppers search for the best food prices.

Everything of value has its price. It costs to become a physician, a musician, an athlete, or numerous other things. Generally speaking, one can get anything and become almost anything if one is willing to pay the price.

Jesus never deceived anyone about becoming a Christian. He described the cost involved.

I. To be a Christian involves renunciation.

A. *There are erroneous interpretations of Jesus' statement "Let him deny himself."* Second-century followers of Jesus began to disdain all forms of materialism. Some professing Christians began to have gnostic tendencies of viewing material things as evil. Jesus did not mean that one had to withdraw from the world to be properly related to it.

Some professing Christians in the twentieth century have unusual interpretations of Jesus' statement "Let him deny himself." Some think that denying self involves denying some kind of food, some pleasure, or some comfort.

B. *There are some implicit instructions about Jesus' words "Let him deny himself."* To deny oneself means nothing less than the complete renunciation of one's own life. It means to say no to every situation that is selfish. Paul amplified the meaning of renunciation in Galatians 2:26.

II. To be a Christian involves dedication.

A. *There are erroneous interpretations of Jesus' statement "take up his cross."* Some people have taken the idea of a cross as a burden to be endured, a suffering to be experienced, or an annoyance to be tolerated. According to Jesus, taking up one's cross means to follow the will of the Father; the suffering that results constitutes the cross.

B. *There are some strong implications of taking up one's cross.*

1. To take up the cross is to dedicate oneself to God's will. Jesus yielded to the Father's wishes and desires.
2. To take up the cross is to expect results. Jesus obeyed the Father's will, and it meant the world's opposition. When a Christian decides to do God's will, he or she needs to expect the world's opposition. Some Christians have had to give up their lives. To be a Christian means to be dedicated to the Master.

III. To be a Christian involves imitation.

A. *There are erroneous interpretations of Jesus' statement "Follow me."* Some have tried to imitate Christ by imagining what Jesus would do in many circumstances of life. To follow Jesus means to adopt his manner of living in words and actions.

B. *There is a manner of life reflected in imitating Jesus.* The pattern for life may be seen in the way he lived. Let us mention some of Jesus' practices.
   1. He attended worship regularly in the synagogue and in the temple.
   2. He practiced the habit of systematic prayer.
   3. He accepted people for who they were, and he sought the highest good for people.
   4. He disdained rebellion against God, whether in the form of sensuality or attitude.
   5. He obeyed the Father in every possible way. Of course, as one studies the life of Jesus, many other manifestations may be seen. The Lord gave his followers a pattern for living. As Christians look at Christ's pattern, they can rely on Christ's power to help them imitate the Master.

Conclusion

Consider the cost of becoming and being a Christian. It involves renunciation of self, dedication to the Lord's way, and imitation of Christ's life. The Lord never marks down his demands. There are no sales in discipleship. I urge you to follow the Lord, and you will have the most thrilling adventure life brings.

SUNDAY MORNING, JUNE 22

Title: Come, Grow Old Along with Me

Text: "I have been young, and now am old; yet I have not seen the righteous forsaken or his children begging bread" **(Ps. 37:25 RSV)**.

Scripture Reading: Psalm 37:25

Hymns: "Onward, Christian Soldiers," Baring-Gould
"We Are Climbing Jacob's Ladder," Traditional Negro Spiritual
"Sweet, Sweet Spirit," Akers

Offertory Prayer: Father, forgive us when we become overly familiar with holy things, including worship. May we hold you in awe, and respect one another as your children. Hide great hopes within us and give us a vision of yourself. Show us your will and make it the desire of our hearts. In Christ's strong name we pray. Amen.

Introduction

The stage of life we know as old age has been called "the sunset years." To call these our "sunset years" is to give them a touch of class—they can be very special. This time period can be a significant chapter in our human pilgrimage—a time for growth, learning, and greater maturity. Sometimes we get the idea that our later years must be that time when we are put on a shelf, but that should not be.

I. Defining the sunset years.

The sunset years are not isolated from the rest of life. We are becoming now what we will be in old age. If you pollute a stream at its source, then you pollute the whole stream. But if you make it pure and sparkling at its source, then you have the potential of keeping it useful throughout its flow.

Age is not just a matter of the calendar. Age is more than just chronology. A cardiovascular surgeon said, "Some of the patients I see are forty, but their vascular system is seventy. Other men who are seventy have a vascular system with the elasticity of a man who is thirty-five or forty." Some have concluded that we are as old as our arteries. While this may be true medically, it is not the whole truth. We are also as old as our attitudes. In old age we can still be hopeful as we face the future.

General Douglas MacArthur wrote: "People grow old by deserting their ideas. Years may wrinkle the skin, but to give up interest wrinkles the soul. You are as young as your faith, as old as your doubts; as young as your self-confidence, as old as your fears; as young as your hope, as old as your despair."

Age is a process from which none of us is exempt. It is one for which all of us might as well learn to be grateful. Some cultures honor age. They have a tradition of honoring those who have gray hair, those who have wisdom that comes from experience. But in our youth-oriented culture, it's the opposite. We glorify and turn the spotlight on youth while we despise age. Denial of the aging process keeps plastic surgeons in business.

II. A growing group.

There are more elderly among us than ever, and there are going to be more still. There are good reasons for this, and we can rejoice in them. In 1900 there were some 5 million Americans 60 years of age and above. They made up 6 percent of the population of our country. Life expectancy at that time was 47 years. A woman could expect to live only two years after her oldest child left home. Today the case is much different, with life expectancy being 76.9 years.

III. Aging problems.

A. *The coming of age brings with it crises, as does every stage of life.* One of these is economic. Many men and women have worked toward retirement as a special chapter in life. They have made financial preparation for it, only to discover that as they retire on a fixed income, the cost of living doesn't remain anywhere near "fixed." They're finding themselves in an economic pinch, greater than those still in the workforce.

B. *Aging may also bring health problems.* However, we are seeing a great deal of improvement in this area.

C. *Old age can also be a time of loneliness.* One lady said jokingly to her pastor, "I think I'll go ahead and have my funeral now while I still have some friends around who can attend."

IV. Myths about aging.

Age, like every other stage of our human pilgrimage, has its problems. But it also has great potential. There are some myths about age that need to be exploded. One is that senility is inevitable. Senility may occur due to brain disease, but it is not automatic. If we keep a good diet, exercise moderately, and keep mentally alert, there is no reason why senility need be expected.

Another myth that needs to be exploded is that as soon as change occurs in one's life-status or family situation, he or she ought to move to Florida. A person ought to make that kind of change carefully and deliberately.

V. Benefits of age.

A. *Age has its special resources—economic resources, long-term relationships, family ties, and spiritual growth.* One of the joys of aging is to discover that your children are your friends. One of your richest resources is a deep and growing faith. The faith you had when you were twelve years old has grown through a variety of experiences across the years.

B. *Age can be a time of great usefulness.* The elderly have accomplished some phenomenal things. We tend to forget this. In the area of politics, did you know that Winston Churchill was sixty-five when he was elected prime minister of Great Britain? Conrad Adenauer was elected to head the government of West Germany and served for fourteen years, retiring at the age of eighty-seven. Golda Meir was seventy-one when she became the prime minister of Israel. We see this sort of thing in the business world as well. At the age of sixty-five, living on social security, an eastern Kentucky restaurateur named Colonel Harland Sanders began a new career. He made a tremendous fortune after he was retired.

These may be delightful exceptions. They are certainly examples of enormous accomplishment during advanced years. But these can be years of great productivity. They may be the time for a second career, for learning a new language, for going back to school. These years may afford the opportunity to do some things we wanted to do all along but for which we lacked the time or finances.

C. *These can be years of great ministry.* Some of the most caring, supportive people in the church are those who are in this age category. Many carry on a pastoral-type ministry to others. Let these be years of great usefulness. The difference is not in our arteries. The difference is in our attitude. Old age can be a time for self-giving, not selfishness.

Conclusion

"Come, grow old along with me. The best is yet to be. The last of life, for which the first was made." Old age offers opportunity for an exciting life and adventure. It can be a most useful chapter. It need not be a treadmill or a saga. It can be a pilgrimage, open-ended, with purpose, direction, and significance.

Like the wine at Cana—who knows but that the Master has saved the best till the last? Even the sunset and the darkness to follow need hold no ultimate dread for those who are in Christ. Remember that every exit is also an entrance. The best, by far the best, is yet to be!

SUNDAY EVENING, JUNE 22

Title: The Nobleman: Driven by Desperation

Text: "The royal official said, 'Sir, come down before my child dies'" **(John 4:49 NIV).**

Scripture Reading: John 4:46–54

Introduction

This royal official is nameless on the pages of Holy Scripture. He was a man of high station and political authority but was akin to every man, because, at this point in his life, he was a father with a desperately ill child at home.

Note the two principal characters in this encounter. First, there was the nobleman, a Gentile, accustomed to all of the pomp and pageantry of a king's court. No doubt his sympathy with the Jewish people, over whom he helped rule, was limited if it existed at all. He was stationed at Capernaum, that bustling, strategic city on the northern coast of the Sea of Galilee. He was an important man. Second, there was Jesus, the carpenter from Nazareth. A product of Jewish peasantry, Jesus had no social position. He held no rabbinical credentials, and he taught a revolutionary new gospel in the land.

At the beginning we have an unlikely setting. Here is a nobleman coming twenty miles to ask help from a carpenter! But more important than his social and political standing was the fact he was a father with a critically ill child at home. Any parent who has had a desperately ill child can identify with him. Let's try to draw into focus the unique way in which Jesus related to this man at the point of his need.

I. The man and his motive.

A. *Why did he come to Jesus in the first place?* The man was desperate; he came to Jesus not as a nobleman but as a father. No doubt he loved his little son dearly. He may have consulted all of the physicians available. Apparently they had all told him there was no hope for his child, that his illness was terminal. Thus his motive in coming to Jesus was his willingness to do anything he could to save his child.

B. *How this nobleman was encouraged to go to Jesus with his problem, we do not know.* The only thing about Jesus that attracted him was the possibility that he might save the life of his son. He did not care who Jesus was, nor did he care what method Jesus might use to heal his child. "Save my son!" That was his one compelling motive.

II. Jesus and his method of dealing with this man.

A. *We are not told what the nobleman's first words were to Jesus.* But we do have the first words of Jesus to him. In fact, they seem rather cold and abrupt—right to the point. Jesus said (and he was speaking to all of the people gathered around him, for the "you" is plural): "Unless you see signs and wonders, you will not believe!" (see John 4:48). More than harshness, there were doubtlessly sadness and frustration of spirit in our Lord's words. Anybody could get a crowd if he promised to perform something sensational. Signs and wonders were what the people wanted. Jesus knew the hearts of the people, and he knows what is in our hearts today.

B. *But Jesus also knew the desperation and agony in the nobleman's heart.* And though Jesus had compassion on him, he had a way of making sure that such an individual was in earnest. Jesus knew what was in the man's heart from the beginning, but he always desires that we express our faith.

C. *The nobleman brushed aside the apparent rebuke of Jesus and said, "Sir, come down before my child dies"* (v. 49 NIV). He did not argue with Jesus or try to defend himself. He simply refused to leave Jesus until he had done everything he could to get help for his dying child. Yet somewhere between this plea of the nobleman and the next word from Jesus, conviction and faith did their miracle work in the man's heart. This was the greatest miracle performed that day—not the healing of the child, as marvelous as that was. What happened to the boy's father was for eternity! The healing of his sin-sick soul would never be reversed.

D. *Jesus said to him, "You may go. Your son will live"* (v. 50 NIV). The nobleman had said, "Come!" but Jesus said, "Go!" Had faith not been born in the man's heart, he never would have left Cana without Jesus. For, not only was faith in Jesus as the Son of God born in this man's heart, but also hope and assurance were there. For John tells us, "The man took Jesus at his word and departed" (v. 50 NIV).

III. The servants with their message.

A. *Apparently the nobleman had come to Cana alone.* In his deep, heartbroken state, he may have wanted to be alone. His grief was so overwhelming that he did not want the bother of protocol and royal servants bustling about him. He was a solitary man, broken and desperate as he came to Jesus.

B. *Now he began the long journey back to Capernaum alone but no longer depressed and filled with sorrow.* He was not on the way very long until he discovered some of his servants approaching. Did he panic with the normal human anticipation of bad news? No! When they announced to him that his child was alive and well, the father simply asked them to tell him exactly when his son's crisis passed.

C. *For the second time we are told that this nobleman "believed."* This was like firing the "booster rocket" to this man's faith. Already it was soaring; but this confirmation from his servants caused his faith to soar higher than ever. And an interesting postscript states, "So he and all his household believed" (v. 53 NIV). There is no doubt that he told his family about this wonderful man he had met, this Jesus of Nazareth. Simply, beautifully, gently, he introduced his family to Jesus.

Conclusion

What was the progression in this meeting between Jesus and the nobleman? He had come to see Jesus with a sense of desperate need. Jesus had met the need, and the official's desperation had been replaced with hope and faith. This is always the result of a person's response to the invitation of God's love.

WEDNESDAY EVENING, JUNE 25

Title: Who Am I?
Text: "So God created man in his own image, in the image of God he created him; male and female he created them" **(Gen. 1:27 RSV)**.
Scripture Reading: Genesis 1:26–28; Psalm 8

Introduction

All age groups—not just adolescents—are concerned with self-identity. Life must have significance and value for us all. The one thing we cannot live with is meaninglessness.

Youths do experience identity crises. They have to work out their own individuality apart from their parents. They also have to develop their body images, their qualities and limitations. And youths must decide what they are going to do in life.

Adults also have varying identity crises. These may come with major changes in their work or in their health. They may occur at the loss of a parent, child, or mate.

Much is written about the middle-age crisis. During middle age we have to deal with our aging process. We may suddenly be forced to come to grips with our own mortality. Or we may feel the weight of crushing responsibilities, which makes it hard to cope.

"Who am I?" is a valid question at many stages of life. Elton Trueblood calls this "living your life in chapters."

I. A life-affirming view of creation.

This is not characteristic of Eastern religions, nor of Greek philosophy, which has infiltrated much Christian theology. Greek philosophy considered matter to be evil and only the spirit good. Eastern religions teach that it is good to eliminate all desire and achieve nirvana or nothingness. The objective is to be reabsorbed into deity and escape further reincarnations.

II. We are made in God's image.

To say we are made in the divine likeness means we bear God's stamp. We bear the mark of our Maker: "Made in the image of God." To say this means we have been created with the freedom of moral choice. That is a high compliment. God trusts us. He will not force us to do what is right. We are free to make the wrong choices as well as the correct ones.

The fact that we are made in God's image means that humankind is responsible. We cannot blame our meanness on the stars or our ancestors, on the Devil or the world system.

This doctrine also means we are capable of creative work. Work is not a curse. In fact, to be without meaningful work would be a curse.

To be made in the image of God also speaks to our stewardship of life and creation. We must answer to God. We are accountable.

III. The dignity of humans.

Humans are the crown of creation. To say so is not an ego trip; it is the truth. Both science and the Bible agree that humankind represents the highest form of life.

In *Hamlet* Shakespeare may have been a bit carried away. He spoke of the dignity of man in glowing terms:

> What a piece of work is a man!
> How noble in reason!
> How infinite in faculties!
> In form, in moving, how express and admirable!
> In action how like an angel!
> In apprehension how like a god!
>
> —*Hamlet, II, ii*

The Bible teaches that we should not think too highly of ourselves. But it makes it equally clear that we should not demean ourselves either.

IV. Humans are social beings.

Man was made for relationship. God does not intend that we be Robinson Crusoes, living in isolation from one another. Neither should nations try to exist that way. God is not a loner, nor should we be. Augustine was on target when he said, "Thou hast made us for Thyself, and our souls are restless till they rest in Thee."

Conclusion

Don't forget who you are—and whose you are. You belong to God. You are made in his image. He has a prior claim on you even if you have not yet acknowledged his lordship.

Can you say that from your heart?

SUNDAY MORNING, JUNE 29

Title: Finding Freedom in Christ

Text: "If we say that we have no sin, we deceive ourselves, and the truth is not in us" **(1 John 1:8)**.

Scripture Reading: Romans 1:18–25

Hymns: "Christ Receiveth Sinful Men," Neumeister
"Amazing Grace," Newton
"Love Lifted Me," Rowe

Offertory Prayer: Dear Father, in our unworthiness you redeemed us. In our disobedience and faithlessness you have forgiven. Now, dear Lord, take the fruit of our labor and bless it to higher use. Cleanse the stain of sin that so often mars our gifts and grant your Spirit to reign in us, through Jesus Christ our Lord. Amen.

Introduction

The age-old problem so often wrestled with in people's minds and reflected on at length in the Scriptures is the raising of lowly humans into fellowship with the divine. How are the "sons of men" to become the "sons of God"? This is a greater problem than the divine relationship to "lower" life, because the matter of human will is involved. The higher the ambition God held for humans, the greater became the problem introduced by free will. In order to form character in people, God had to take terrible risks. He had to leave people the choice of good or evil. That was both humanity's great opportunity and humanity's occasion for falling.

The Bible attributes people's sins to their willful abuse of their God-given freedom of choosing the basic course and character of their lives. Paul, in writing to the Roman Christians, outlined the truth concerning humanity's plight as sinners (Rom. 1:18–25).

I. The seriousness of sin.

A. *Sin involves the total being of people.*
   1. Sin involves not just the physical side of people's lives.
   2. Sin is more than a mental condition.

3. Sin is in the heart of people, at the very center of selfhood.

B. *The New Testament's appraisal of sin in people.*
   1. Sin in the "flesh" describes living apart from God (2 Cor. 1:17; 10:2; Rom. 8:4–5, 13).
   2. Sin in "your bodies" means sin in your personal being (Rom. 6:12–13; 12:1).
   3. Sin in the "soul" is also referring to oneself, or person. That the soul, or person, sinning "shall die" is a warning to the total person. (Use Acts 2:41 or 3:23.)

      Sin is serious, for it involves the total person. People do not have in themselves the strength to solve their problems. Their whole beings are adversely affected. Sin invades their thinking, their will, their sense of values, their natural responses, and their relationships.

II. Slavery to sin.

A. *In people's expressions of self-will, they lose their freedom.*
   1. From trusting God to self-trust.
   2. From obeying God to self-assertion.
   3. From serving God to slavery to sin.

B. *In sinning people bring community under the dominion of sin (Rom. 6:6; 7:24).*

C. *Sin snatches and exercises lordship over people (Rom. 6:14; 7:17; Gal. 3:22).* Living is described as serving either "good" or "evil." People's acts have repercussions beyond the sensations they momentarily feel. Their acts are testimonies for God or for Satan. The constant plea of the New Testament is for people to "serve God" and thus find the liberation for which people were created. When sin is served, humankind's true destiny is denied, their created role is forfeited, and they fall under the bondage of sin and death.

III. The surrender to sin.

Humanity's surrender of "sonship" to God brings into light their personal responsibility for guilt.

A. *The Bible holds people guilty for their own sin.*
   1. Sin is not the responsibility of past generations (Deut. 24:16; Ezek. 18:2–4).
   2. People are responsible for the actions of the group of which they are a part.

B. *People are guilty for the environment they help create.*
   1. We speak of *my* country, *my* city, *my* home.
   2. No person lives to self; living is influencing.
   3. People face their sin alone.

Conclusion

Humanity's problem is sin. People may have many problems in life, such as problems in finiteness, fate, and function. They are plagued with involvement in the material aspect of their lives and by their ignorance. When all is said, humanity's plight, however, is one of sin. The Bible holds people guilty for their sin. People and people alone stand responsible and in total solitude to face their sin. To meet this condition, there came the "Good News." When people are willing to admit that sin is their own and theirs alone, the Savior will bear it. "Christ Jesus came into the world to save sinners. . . ." (1 Tim. 1:15).

SUNDAY EVENING, JUNE 29

Title: Bartimaeus: The Man with One Last Chance
Text: "Jesus, thou son of David, have mercy on me" **(Mark 10:47)**.
Scripture Reading: Mark 10:46–52

Introduction

It is sad to be a beggar, whether in ancient Palestine or modern America. There is something about a person's being driven to beg for his daily bread that is tragic. Begging, day after day, will ultimately destroy the last trace of pride and human dignity a person has. But with Bartimaeus there was compounded tragedy—not only was he a victim of abject poverty, he was also blind.

What if Jesus and his disciples had bypassed Jericho on this particular day? Jesus' heart was heavy; he was on his way to Jerusalem for the last time. He knew what awaited him there. Thus preoccupied with his approaching crucifixion, it would have been a simple thing for Jesus and his disciples either to have hurried through Jericho incognito or to have bypassed the city altogether. But Jesus was never so preoccupied with things concerning himself that he was not keenly aware of and sensitive to the needs of those around him.

There were three stages to this meeting between Jesus and Bartimaeus.

I. The encounter between Jesus and this blind beggar by the Jericho roadside.

A. *When persons lose the use of one of their senses, their remaining senses become more acute.* Thus Bartimaeus's hearing was excellent, and he must have had an uncanny ability to remember, to store up for future recall, everything he heard as the crowds passed by. On this particular day the crowds passing through Jericho were larger than usual. It was the Passover season, and every day contingents of pilgrims were passing through.

B. *On this day there was a different atmosphere, a "high tension" in the air.* Immediately, the sensitive Bartimaeus knew this. Undoubtedly, he asked the meaning of this larger crowd and received an answer. Someone told him that "Jesus of Nazareth" was passing by.

C. *So with his refined sense of hearing, Bartimaeus carefully studied the sound of the crowd until he could tell that Jesus was adjacent to where he was sitting by the roadside.* Then it was that Bartimaeus cried out, "Jesus, thou son of David, have mercy on me!"

D. *Even though the people tried to discourage him, Bartimaeus cried all the louder.* Perhaps something deep within Bartimaeus told him that this was his last chance. Jesus would not pass this way again. The timing had to be perfect. He had to get Jesus' attention right then—for in just a few seconds, he would be passing beyond earshot, forever gone from Jericho.

II. The conversation between this blind beggar and Jesus.

A. *It is significant that we read, "And Jesus stood still"* (v. 49). Jesus knew all about Bartimaeus.

B. *Therefore, Mark says that Jesus "commanded him to be called."* His command was spoken with such authority that those who, a moment before, had tried to hush Bartimaeus, did an about-face! "Be of good comfort," they said. "Rise; he calleth thee!"

C. *It is doubtful that Bartimaeus waited for anyone to take his arm and lead him to Jesus.* For Mark says that "he . . . rose, and came to Jesus" (v. 50). Bartimaeus, in the joy and ecstasy of that moment, must have coursed the sound of Jesus' incomparable voice and, in his blindness, came directly to Jesus!

III. The accommodation Jesus made for Bartimaeus.

A. *As he stood before Jesus, the Lord asked him, "What wilt thou that I should do unto thee?"* (v. 51). Certainly, Jesus knew that the man wanted to see! But the man needed to state his need before the Lord. Likewise, God knows that we are sinners; we don't have to give him that information. But still he wants us to state that fact with our own mouths.

The literal translation of what Bartimaeus said to Jesus was, "Master, that I may look up." He wanted the blessing of being able to lift his eyes, and lifting them, to see! And all the while, the deeper, subconscious yearning of his soul was to lift his spiritual eyes to see and to understand the mission of the Son of David, the Savior, who was to redeem sinful humankind.

B. *Jesus' answer was thrilling: "Go thy way; thy faith hath made thee whole" (v. 52).* Jesus did not heal people indiscriminately. It was not his purpose to heal all of the sick people and to open the eyes of all the blind people. But when the healing of a sick body or the opening of blind eyes would pave the way for a spiritual victory, for the salvation of a soul, he did it gladly and enthusiastically.

Conclusion

Jesus accommodated the physical need of Bartimaeus; that is, he healed his blindness. But far more important is the fact that Jesus added another member to his spiritual family. For we read, "And immediately he received his sight, and followed Jesus in the way" (v. 52). This means that Bartimaeus became a traveling companion with Jesus and the disciples as they left Jericho and went to Jerusalem.

The story of Bartimaeus is another in a long succession of miracles in the Bible—a succession that continues to this day. For whenever a person, recognizing his or her spiritual blindness, calls out, "God, have mercy on me!" Jesus "stands still," bids that person come, and changes his or her darkness into light.

SUGGESTED PREACHING PROGRAM FOR THE MONTH OF

JULY

■ Sunday Mornings

The sermons for July and August give us the opportunity to recommit ourselves to the basic disciplines of discipleship that can help us wear the title "Christian" more worthily. The suggested theme is "The Disciplines of Discipleship."

■ Sunday Evenings

"Wise Men of the Past Speak to the Present" is the theme for a series of messages based on texts from the Psalms and wisdom literature of the Old Testament. This series will continue through September.

■ Wednesday Evenings

Genesis 1–11 provides the biblical base for a series of studies dealing with who God is and our relationship and responsibility to him.

WEDNESDAY EVENING, JULY 2

Title: God Started It All
Text: "In the beginning God created the heaven and the earth" **(Gen. 1:1)**.
Scripture Reading: Genesis 1:1–31

Introduction

Whatever method he used, God did it—he *created* the heaven and the earth! Only the fool says, "There is no God"; and he says it in his heart because his head knows better. In fact, those who deny a personal Creator, or even refuse to consider the subject, usually have moral problems rather than intellectual ones. The book of Genesis comes straight to the point and wastes no time identifying the agent of creation.

I. The creation story introduces God.

The Genesis writer says, "Let me introduce my God." One God! Not the god of mythology but the God of history! Not one of the capricious Semitic or Egyptian deities, who socialized, quarreled, and even fornicated with other gods. Not a conqueror who slew a sea dragon. Not an agricultural deity who could be bribed with offerings to a temple prostitute. Rather, a free, personal, and ethical Spirit, who combines power, wisdom, holiness, and mercy within one moral character.

God believes in orderly arrangements. In the beginning he worked logically as he brought into being the various components of the world. At the end of each division, he stopped to survey his work and make a judgment on it. Progressively pleased, he then took the next step. The recurring phrase "saw that it was good" testifies to the infinite resources of the Divine.

Placing a high value on what he created, everything God did was in order that humans might occupy, enjoy, use, and even improve the earth. The cosmos was not an end in itself but the means by which God's highest creation—humankind—could attain their best in fellowship with their Maker.

Aren't you glad you have met God? The writer of Genesis could have told you much more about him. Subsequent passages in Genesis and other books of the Bible reveal further and even more wonderful truths!

II. The creation story explains the earth.

Many people live in a limited world and therefore have limited lives. One is not required to scan the galaxies in order to see the greatness of our Creator. This planet on which we live provides enough startling facts to make us realize it came into being as a result of divine intelligence at work. To be an atheist requires far more "faith" than to be a Christian. Furthermore, the skeptic's "faith" is not only naive, it is intellectually indefensible. To accept the fact of God is simpler, easier, and smarter.

III. The creation story interprets man.

A. *God's autographs greet us everywhere.* Each lightning strike, every fresh dawn, the universe's order and unity—all of these say, "The hand that made us is divine." Most of all, however, we see the divine penmanship in man. William Stidger puts it beautifully:

> Then to complete creation's plan
> In his own image, God made man;
> And signed his name with stroke most sure—
> Man is God's greatest signature.

B. *What is man?* One "moral maverick" called the world a "gigantic flywheel making ten thousand revolutions per minute" and man a "sick fly taking a dizzy ride on it." But God sees man as made in the divine image for fellowship with his Creator.

C. *If you wish to see man's greatness, consider the star Betelgeuse that shines so brightly in the Orion constellation.* It alone is larger than an entire solar system! Yet one human being is infinitely more important than that gigantic star. Why? In spite of Betelgeuse's huge size and the incalculable energy generated by it, that piece of matter does not even know that it exists. A person, however, if properly trained, can line up his instruments toward that ball speeding through the sky and weigh, measure, and analyze the chemical elements comprising it. As he computes the physical laws that control it, God's highest creation dwarfs that distant star so completely that comparison is out of the question.

Conclusion

Many years ago a Bible professor gave his college students six facts about man. Most of these are found in the creation accounts.

1. Man is uniquely related to God, being created in his image.
2. Man is under obligation to love and obey God, who has thus loved him.
3. Man is a social being with social privileges and obligations.
4. Man is a religious being and must worship if he is to be happy.
5. Man is free to act but is responsible to God for his actions.
6. Man may be redeemed through God's mercy by believing in Christ.

If that scholar was correct who said, "Man has always been his own chief problem," the other was equally on target who said, "Thou hast made us for Thyself, O God, and we are restless until we rest in Thee."

SUNDAY MORNING, JULY 6

Title: O Come Let Us Worship
Text: "O come, let us worship and bow down, let us kneel before the LORD, our Maker!" **(Ps. 95:6 RSV)**.
Scripture Reading: Psalm 95:1–7
Hymns: "All Hail the Power of Jesus' Name," Holden
"Love Divine, All Loves Excelling," Zundel
"I Love Thee," Anonymous
Offertory Prayer: Father in heaven, we thank you for the breath of life, for the gift of continuing life, and for the gift of eternal life. Today we come bringing a portion of our lives in the form of tithes and offerings to be dedicated on your altar for the advancement of your kingdom. Bless these tithes and offerings to that end, we pray. In Jesus' name. Amen.

Introduction

A good football coach puts his players through certain physical exercises and disciplines necessary for developing the skills and physical stamina that will make it possible for them to be a winning team.

In the spiritual realm, there are certain indispensable disciplines that we must subject ourselves to if we would truly be all that God intends. Our text details one discipline necessary for experiencing the abundant life that Jesus came into the world to give (see John 10:10).

The invitation to worship that the psalmist extends is both present and perpetual in its application. To worship is to ascribe praise and honor and glory to God. It is to revere and honor him with the heart and soul. Genuine worship is a dynamic, transforming experience both for the individual worshiper and for the congregation as they worship together in spirit and in truth. Worship is a personal encounter with God as he reveals himself to us through Scripture, song, sermon, and the praises of God's people. We need to recognize and respond to the psalmist's gracious invitation.

I. The call to worship is a call to recognize and respond to the very presence of God.

A. *This is a call to conscious awareness of the presence of God.*
B. *This is a call to awe, admiration, and adoration of the living God.*
C. *This is a call to truly become acquainted with the living God.*

II. The call to worship is a call to recognize and respond to the person of God.

The God and Father of our Lord Jesus Christ is personal, and we are to respond to him personally. This living God is described in the first six verses of Psalm 95.

A. *The Lord is the rock of our salvation (v. 1).*
B. *The Lord is a great God (v. 3).*
C. *This great God is a "great King above all gods" (v. 3 RSV).*
D. *This God is in control of the heights and also of the depths of the earth (v. 4).*
E. *This God owns both the sea and the dry land because he is the creator of both (v. 5).*
F. *This great God is also our maker (v. 6).*

This great and good God is personal, and he is worthy of our awe, reverence, respect, and adoration.

III. The call to worship is a call to recognize and receive the presents of this personal God.

When God comes to meet with us, he comes to reveal himself to us and to give himself to us.

A. *God reveals himself in ways that meet the deepest needs of the genuine worshiper.*
B. *Worshipers learn something about themselves when they truly worship.* They discover that they are more than lost orphans in an empty world. They discover that God loves them and that God is for them.
C. *Worshipers also learn something about others when they worship.* Worship is not just an experience in which a person spends some time in meditation. Genuine worship gives a vision of God, a vision of self, and a vision of others.

D. *True worshipers also learn something about the resources of God that are available for life.* God does not come to oppress us or to defeat us. He comes to impart his gifts to us.

Conclusion

In the English language the word *worship* means "worthship." It means the recognition of the one who is of supreme worth. God has revealed himself and his purposes for us in Jesus Christ. We can trust the God who loves us so much. He was willing to give up his Son for us (Rom. 8:32).

SUNDAY EVENING, JULY 6

Title: The Wisdom Books of the Old Testament
Text: "Where then does wisdom come from? Where does understanding dwell?" **(Job 28:20 NIV).**
Scripture Reading: Job 28:20–28

Introduction

The books of Job, Proverbs, Ecclesiastes, and certain Psalms primarily contain the wisdom literature of the Old Testament. These writings present a viewpoint about the way to discover the meaning of life that is often neglected in Old Testament study and preaching. Wisdom is a way of looking at life, a way based on observation. The genius of wisdom is that it announces conclusions reached not arbitrarily or by special revelation but at the end experience.

For the next twelve Sunday evenings we will consider texts chosen from these books of Scripture. But first let us consider texts chosen from these wisdom writings in general terms. There are four things we should note about them.

I. The meaning of wisdom in the Old Testament.

Dr. L. D. Johnson, in his book *Israel's Wisdom: Learn and Live* ([Nashville: Broadman, 1975], 8–10), points out six different uses of the words *wise* or *wisdom.*

A. *These words are used to signify technical skill or dexterity.* Examples are found in Exodus 28:3; 35:25, 31, 35; 36:4; 2 Chronicles 2:7; and Psalm 107:43.
B. *The same word is often used to mean craftiness rather than craftsmanship, shrewdness rather than skill.* For examples, see 2 Samuel 13:3; 14:2; and 1 Kings 2:6.
C. Wisdom *is also used in the sense of intellectual acumen, as of Solomon's wisdom (1 Kings 4:29–34).*
D. *A frequent meaning of the word is "moral discernment," as in Solomon's prayer in Gibeon (1 Kings 3:9–12).*

E. *When this moral quality of wisdom is combined with the concept of reverence for the Lord, wisdom has fully flowered.* Such uses are numerous. For examples, see Job 28:28; Psalm 11:10; Proverbs 1:7; 2:6; 15:33.

F. *The writers use the concept of wisdom known as personification (Prov. 9:1–6).* It is interesting to note the progression in the meaning of *wisdom* from "skill and dexterity" through "cleverness" to "intellectual acumen" and on to "moral discernment," then finally to "reverence of the Lord and obedience to his commandments."

II. The literary characteristics of wisdom.

A. *In his book* The Way of Wisdom in the Old Testament *([New York: Macmillan, 1971], 72–74), Dr. R. B. Y. Scott points out four remarkable literary characteristics of Hebrew origin.*

1. First, we see the unstudied directness and simplicity of the Hebrew sentence structure, with nouns and verbs predominating.
2. A second feature is poetic, the parallelism of the Semitic verse form producing an echo in the mind. The poet's thought is repeated in different words but with the same or similar structure, so that the second line balances the first.
3. There is also the luxuriant use of concrete imagery in both poetry and rhetorical prose.
4. Finally, there is the supreme Hebrew gift of storytelling.

B. *Dr. Scott further says, "The word pictures are painted with remarkable economy of line and color.* What the participants say is told, but what they are thinking and feeling is left to the imagination. The effectiveness of the writing is all the greater because of such restraint and dignity" (ibid., 74).

III. Prophets and wisdom writers.

A. *In a word, it may be said that the prophet calls on men to hear, decide, and obey, expressed by his "Thus saith the Lord."* The wise man's summons to others is to understand and to learn. He does not demand, as does the prophet, but seeks to persuade and instruct.

B. *The theology of the prophet and the wisdom writer differ accordingly.* The prophet's God was the living, active, personal Deity who had confronted him in the moment of his call.

C. *The prophets preached a salvation theology to Israel as people of the covenant.* They bore testimony to the word and will of Yahweh, calling on people to believe and respond. When the religious school of wisdom undertook the intellectual exploration of theological issues, they did not preach. They did not remind Israel of her covenant relationship with God.

IV. Divergent doctrines of wisdom.

A. *The wisdom teachers did not all agree among themselves.* The book of Job represents a debate within a circle of wisdom teachers. While no doubt originally holding to the theology of an exact retributive justice, Job's personal agony proved the inadequacy of this theory and drove him in search of deeper understanding.

This conviction of God's moral judgments appears in Proverbs (see 10:3; 15:25). This is the stubbornly held conviction of Job's three counselors who insist on it with a rigidity that almost drives the sufferer to distraction.

B. *The writer of Ecclesiastes was a wisdom teacher also in revolt against the traditional doctrine of exact retribution and reward.* His revolt was different from Job's, however, in that it did not stem from his own personal experience of suffering.

Conclusion

Christians do not believe that they live in a one-story universe. With the wisdom writers, they believe that there are eternal consequences to their commitments and behavior. Christians look to another for their way of life, to him who said, "I came that they may have life, and have it abundantly" (John 10:10 RSV).

Wednesday Evening, July 9

Title: Man and Woman Need Each Other

Text: "The Lord God said, 'It is not good for the man to be alone. I will make a helper suitable for him'" **(Gen. 2:18 NIV).**

Scripture Reading: Genesis 2:18–25

Introduction

God turned in his work of creating to enhance the life of mankind. The classical words from *God's Trombones,* "I'm lonesome. I'll make me a man," reflect the desire for relationships inherent in personhood. "The Lord God said, 'It is not good for the man to be alone. I will make a helper suitable for him'" (Gen. 2:18 NIV). No part of the Genesis record shows more clearly the mark of divine inspiration than the verses that reveal God's wisdom in placing at man's disposal a counterpart who was destined to become his equal in all things. From this primitive account comes eventually the noblest concept of all—Paul's urgent command, "Husbands, love your wives, even as Christ also loved the church, and gave himself for it" (Eph. 5:25).

I. Divine surgery.

The omnipotent God is more than an architect. He is a skilled physician as well as a certified anesthetist! The beautiful story tells us that God took woman from within man, as someone has said, "Not from his head that he might rule over her, nor from his foot that he might trample upon her, but from his side that she might be equal with him and from near his heart that he might love her forever."

The home, which predates even the church, is built on a rock, and the gates of hell will never successfully prevail against it!

II. This is it!

The Hebrew text reads literally, "This the time, bone from bone, flesh from my flesh, this!" One rabbi translates, "At last, this is it!" Man had finally found that for which he had been reaching and had sought in vain! Of all the creatures brought to him by God, not one could meet his need or take over the duty and privilege of sharing his work. What a commentary for today's world! Sophisticated approaches have tried many substitutes for the simple, uncomplicated plan God presented in the Garden of Eden. Not one of them has worked. Man and woman are harmoniously suited to each other, physically, emotionally, and most of all, spiritually. One man said, "Sometimes my wife is hard to live with, but she's a lot harder to live without." God made us for each other; and we need to remember that, like all holy alliances, we separate things God has joined together only at the peril of both sides.

III. Who leaves whom?

The marriage counselor said piously, "In marriage, the two become one." The frustrated woman said, "Yes, but which one?" The truth is that the couple become neither. One minister includes a beautiful phrase in his marriage ceremony: "Marriage is a sacred calling that takes two members of different families and unites them to form a new and unique family."

Conclusion

What a marvelous creation! The Genesis account pictures man as leaving his father and mother, emphasizing the fact that he must now provide for his new companion with a separate home, assuming all the responsibilities that accompany such a decision.

SUNDAY MORNING, JULY 13

Title: The Road Map That Leads to Success

Text: "This book of the law shall not depart out of your mouth, but you shall meditate on it day and night, that you may be careful to do according to all that is written in it; for then you shall make your way prosperous, and then you shall have good success" **(Josh. 1:8 RSV)**.

Scripture Reading: Joshua 1:1–9

Hymns: "All Creatures of Our God and King," St. Francis of Assisi
"Holy Bible, Book Divine," Burton
"Break Thou the Bread of Life," Lathbury

Offertory Prayer: Father in heaven, we thank you for this day. We thank you for the gift of an inward disposition that causes us to hunger after you and to want to please you. We bow down before you in gratitude and with joy in our hearts because of your generosity to us. Help us to be generous in the support of your work through tithes and offerings. In Jesus' name we pray. Amen.

Introduction

Many young people seek the autographs of celebrities. Some Christian young people ask those who have spiritual significance to them to autograph their Bibles. One pastor always writes the Scripture passage Joshua 1:8 underneath his signature with the comment, "This verse of Scripture provides the key to success for your life." In the journey of life, everyone would like to arrive at the destination called "success." The words of our text provide us with the road map that leads us there.

If we either reject or neglect to follow God's road map, the Word of God, there is no way we can arrive at the desired spiritual destination that God has planned for us. One of the disciplines of discipleship that each believer must choose to impose on himself or herself in order to be a winner in the game of life is not only to *read* the Word of God but also to *heed* the Word of God.

The Bible is a God-breathed, authoritative book that contains the truth about God and man, as well as a disclosure of God's will for humankind. Many people believe in the inspiration and the authority of the Bible yet have not developed the habit of studying the Bible as they should because they find it difficult to understand. Some practical suggestions for productive Bible study are in order.

I. Read the Bible regularly.

Every day let God speak to you through the pages of his Holy Book. Provide time in your schedule for regular daily Bible study.

II. Read the Bible subjectively.

Attempt to identify with the characters of the Bible. Put yourself in the middle of the verses and paragraphs and stories. Find your twin brother or sister in the Bible. Let God speak to you personally.

III. Read the Bible intelligently.

Beware of the hop, skip, and jump method of dipping into the Bible and expecting some passage to speak to you in isolation from its context. To interpret the Bible accurately, you should consider four factors when studying it.

A. *Consider the historical situation.* To really understand the Bible, we need to study the historical situation of the biblical world and the people of whom the Bible speaks.

B. *Consider the genre.* We need to know the meanings of words, and we need to recognize that the Bible contains many different kinds of literature. We must not interpret legal language in the same manner in which we interpret poetic language. The Bible is a library that contains a variety of writing genres. We must be aware of this if we are to interpret it accurately.

C. *Think logically.* We need to try to find out what the inspired human author was trying to communicate. We must try to find out what the Bible meant when it was written if we want to accurately interpret it and apply it to life as we experience it today.

D. *Determine the spiritual meaning.* The Bible was inspired by the Holy Spirit, and only the Holy Spirit can cause the teachings of the Bible to grip our hearts and lives and transform us. While this may be the most important factor to remember as we study the Bible, we must not forget the historical, grammatical, and theological factors.

IV. Read the Bible systematically.

The Old Testament contains a message quite different from that of the New Testament. Many people have staggered back in helplessness as they have sought too early to understand some of the difficult sections of the Bible. Thus one should not begin reading the Old Testament, for instance, in the book of Leviticus or Ecclesiastes.

A good Bible dictionary is helpful, as is a one-volume Bible commentary that contains introductory information concerning each of the books of the Bible.

V. Read the Bible prayerfully.

We should not only expect to learn something about the ancient past when we read the Bible, but also something helpful for the present.

We should expect to find out something about God when we read the Bible.

We should expect to find nourishment for our souls and correction for our lives when we read the Bible.

VI. Read the Bible with a desire to be obedient.

Our Lord wants to help us, and he will do it through the pages of the Bible if we will let him.

A. *Look for promises from God to claim as you read.*

B. *Look for commands to obey.*

C. *Look for examples to follow.*

D. *Look for the failures of others that can serve as warnings to you.*

Conclusion

The Bible tells us about our Savior. It invites us to trust him and receive him. Furthermore, the Bible shows us God's will for us.

If you want to find success in your personal life, your marriage, and your home life, then make much of the Word of God on a day-to-day basis, and you will find in your own experience that you are not only arriving at the destination of success, but that you are living in the city of success.

SUNDAY EVENING, JULY 13

Title: A Man of Uz

Text: "There was a man in the land of Uz, whose name was Job; and that man was perfect and upright, and one that feared God, and turned away from evil" **(Job 1:1 ASV)**.

Scripture Reading: Job 1:1–5

Introduction

As the drama began, Job appeared to have much the same theology as his three friends who came to console him. The four of them held to the doctrine of exact moral retribution in which God meted out punishment or rewards according to whether a person was wicked or righteous. As they saw it, the universe was constructed along the lines of an automatic machine that distributed rewards and punishment. God, however, is the sole cause behind the workings of his universe; and he makes no mistakes.

Hence Job had a problem. He knew that his great suffering was not due to great sinning, though the problem of suffering was primarily a religious problem. So he asked, as people have asked throughout the ages, "Why?" As Job sought an answer, he passed through three encounters.

I. Job's encounter with Satan (1:1–2:10).

A. *The character of Job is described (1:1–5).*

1. Job himself is located. He lived in "the land of Uz," a place unknown to us. His religious character was impeccable. He was "blameless," one who feared God and turned away from evil.
2. The man's blessings are listed. He had great wealth, including seven sons and three daughters. He had sheep for food and clothing, and camels for transportation, which are a symbol of wealth in the Near East even today.
3. The man's religious influence is emphasized (vv. 4–5). This patriarch, Job, served in the capacity of priest for his own family just as Abraham did for his family.

B. *The scenes of Job's first encounter are given (1:6–2:10).*

1. Scene one takes place in the heavens (1:6–12). The words "came to present themselves before Jehovah" (ASV) are literally "proceeded to come for the purpose of presenting (setting themselves) against Yahweh." Satan, the adversary, would naturally be

among those present for such a purpose. After having Job called to his attention, Satan raised a question: "Does Job fear God for nothing?" (v. 9 NIV). Then he threw down the challenge, "But stretch out your hand and strike everything he has, and he will surely curse you to your face" (v. 11 NIV). God accepted Satan's challenge and gave Satan permission to touch all Job had but not Job himself.

2. Scene two is set in Job's home territory (1:13–22). When given free rein, Satan works fast. Four catastrophes hit Job in quick succession. What was Job's reaction? Read verses 20–21. The benediction is: "In all this, Job did not sin by charging God with wrongdoing" (v. 22 NIV). The adversary's first attack on Job failed completely.
3. Scene three is again in the heavens (2:1–6). Again Satan was among those who presented themselves "against Jehovah." When God reminded Satan that Job still held fast his integrity, Satan made a second challenge that would make the assault even more personal by attacking Job's body (vv. 4–5). God again accepted the challenge, permitting Satan to attack Job's body but not to take his life (v. 6).
4. Scene four is again in Job's home territory (2:7–10). The adversary attacked Job with "painful sores" (v. 7 NIV). Now bereft of everything, Job sat among the ashes and scraped himself with a piece of broken pottery. His wife counseled him to "renounce God, and die" (v. 9 ASV). Yet "in all this did not Job sin with his lips" (v. 10). So intense and prolonged was Job's suffering that his three friends came from afar to comfort him. After giving vent to the emotion of grief, they sat with him on the ground in silence for seven days.

II. Job's encounter with men (3:1–39:24).

Character descriptions of the three friends are not given; but from their speeches, we may discern broad distinctions that separate any one of the three from the other two. Eliphaz was the mystic of the group. He felt his past experiences put him in direct contact with God. Bildad was neither a mystic nor an original thinker. Rather, he was a traditionalist, a scholar, wise in the wisdom of the ancients. Zophar was a hard, orthodox dogmatist, untroubled by any doubts about the finality of his theology. In the thinking of these three men, God rules the affairs of people with a justice so rigid and so exact that it is always well with the righteous and ill with the wicked. Now note:

A. *Job's soliloquy (3:1–26).* Job broke the silence, vividly expressing his longing for death in a poignant soliloquy. He cursed the day he was born (vv. 1–10).

B. *The first cycle of speeches (4:1–14:22).* The theme is "the character of God." Job's friends had no room in their thinking for secondary causes. God is the sole cause of all that happens, both evil and good. Therefore, every happening in the lives of humans is either a reward for good or a punishment for evil. So, they argued, if Job would only accept his suffering as God's just punishment and throw himself on God's mercy, God would come to his aid and deliver him. Job must see himself as a sinner.

But it didn't work. Job knew and believed in the character of God as well as they. Although he too believed in God as the sole cause, he stoutly maintained his innocence; and he could not see why God treated him thus.

C. *The second cycle of speeches (15:1–21:34).* The theme is "the fate of the wicked." Job's friends concluded that they were dealing with one on whom pure and lofty thoughts of God made little impression.

Job dismissed his friends with their arguments as "miserable comforters." Job thought of God as his real antagonist, one with whom he could not hope to contend. His innocence would not be forever concealed. His innocent blood would cry unceasingly to heaven until he received a response (16:19).

In his reply to Bildad's second speech, Job moved by a leap of faith from the depths of despair to the summit of hope. This was the high-water mark of Job's faith (19:25–26).

D. *The third cycle of speeches (22:1–27:23).* The theme is "the sinfulness of Job." Having failed in their first two efforts, Job's friends now expressed openly and pointedly what they had previously hinted at. They charged Job with every possible sin of the Eastern rich man. Job again protested that he was innocent (27:1–23).

III. Job's encounter with God (38:1–42:6).

The purpose of God's words to Job from the whirlwind was to rebuke Job for his presumption and to heal him by lifting him out of his perplexities into perfect peace.

A. *God's first speech and Job's reply (38:1–40:5).* God asked Job ironic questions, each of which allowed for but one humbling answer, "I don't know." Job was so overwhelmed and aware of his own smallness before God that he said, "I lay my hand upon my mouth" (40:4 ASV).

B. *God's second speech and Job's response (40:6–42:6).* Ironically, God invited Job to assume the attributes of Deity and rule the world himself. He must have thought himself capable of doing so, since he questioned the way God was ruling it. Job realized that his knowledge of God was limited, academic, and speculative. Then he made a complete confession and repented "in dust and ashes."

Conclusion

Some have charged that the epilogue spoils the piece, confirming what is rebuked in the poetry section. Viewed superficially, it seems so; but this epilogue does two things: It shows that the three friends were rebuked for their rigid adherence to an inflexible orthodoxy and did not speak right concerning God. The epilogue also establishes that Job's integrity was not mere innocence but a vital relationship with God.

For the Christian the solution of suffering is religious rather than speculative. It is a heart solution rather than a head solution.

WEDNESDAY EVENING, JULY 16

Title: Sin Makes Things Different—Always Worse!

Text: "The man and his wife heard the sound of the LORD God as he was walking in the garden in the cool of the day, and they hid from the LORD God among the trees of the garden" **(Gen. 3:8 NIV)**.

Scripture Reading: Genesis 3:1–15

Introduction

By whatever name we call sin, one fierce and forceful fact remains concerning it. Departure from God—whether missing the mark, rebellion against authority, or moral crookedness—severs the relationship between humans and their Maker. Whatever other truths we glean from the story of Eve and the serpent, one surpasses all the rest: wickedness destroys all the beautiful things we enjoy, including the peace and serenity of comfortable surroundings and a well-ordered life. When we compare the origin stories of other cultures with the Hebrew account in Genesis, a startling phenomenon confronts us. Only the latter presents the moral and ethical dilemma of sin entering the human race at the inception and poisoning the whole system. Why? Because God inspired the Genesis record, and his holiness pervades every chapter and verse of Holy Scripture. Polytheism presents no moral absolute. Only monotheism has a God who says, "Be holy, because I am holy" (1 Peter 1:16).

I. A sinister suggestion.

Whether we view the serpent as Satan, the adversary, the Devil, or the deceiver, his character speaks so loudly we cannot fail to hear. The evil one knew exactly how to approach the woman, exciting her curiosity. He led Eve by three well-known steps. First, he distorted God's prohibition. Second, he weakened the divine restrictions, causing her to doubt. Third, he followed the distortion and doubt with a flat denial. Satan led the woman away by causing her to believe that serving God was a prison and that obedience was the world's master kill-joy.

II. A weakened woman.

Why did Satan tempt Eve first? Was it because she was the weaker vessel? An outstanding Old Testament professor said, "No, it was because she was the stronger. Satan knew that if he 'got her,' he could take the man into his camp easily." Whatever validity this argument contains, Satan did choose the woman as the initial target and succeeded superlatively. Eve may have realized already that she was slipping when she overstated God's command. The record does not tell us that God warned her not to touch the tree. Perhaps Eve added that part to strengthen her own crumbling resistance.

III. Gruesome guilt.

How terrible the day when sin erases the glow of innocence from one's face! Something even more tragic then takes place! Where one previously walked in intimate fellowship with God, confident and even childlike, without shame or fear, an immense spiritual distance arose between Creator and creature. One redeeming fact that promised hope remained: Adam and Eve were not beyond the sound of the divine call.

Conclusion

Today, if you hear God's voice, harden not your heart!

SUNDAY MORNING, JULY 20

Title: Take Time to Listen When You Pray

Text: "But when you pray, go into your room and shut the door and pray to your Father who is in secret; and your Father who sees in secret will reward you" **(Matt. 6:6 RSV)**.

Scripture Reading: Matthew 6:5–13

Hymns: "Praise Him! Praise Him!" Allen
"Joyful, Joyful, We Adore Thee," Beethoven
"In the Garden," Miles

Offertory Prayer: Father God, for the privilege of coming into your house to worship with your people, we thank you. We come now as individual worshipers bringing our tithes and offerings and praying your blessings on all of the offerings to the end that they be used in ministries of mercy and in the proclamation of the good news of your love for people in this community and to the ends of the earth. In Jesus' name we pray. Amen.

Introduction

To excel in the sport of his or her choice, an athlete must voluntarily submit to the physical disciplines that will equip him or her for excellence of performance. Likewise, to truly be followers of Jesus Christ, we must choose to follow certain spiritual exercises and disciplines.

Jesus' prayer life was not a mere routine or habit that he followed. His prayer life was a dynamic experience with the Father God that so enriched him that one of our Lord's disciples said to him, "Lord, teach us to pray" (Luke 11:1 RSV). The art of effective praying needs to be learned, and Jesus is the authoritative Teacher to whom we should listen and whom we should imitate.

We need to recognize that prayer was meant to be a dialogue in which communication takes place in both directions rather than being a monologue. Following several sermons that emphasized this concept of prayer, a creative young person composed a song that he entitled "Listen When You Pray." The chorus goes like this:

> Listen, O listen when you pray
> to hear what God might have to say.
> Listen, O listen when you pray
> to hear what God might have to say.
>
> —*Raymond Glover*

It is interesting to note how many times in the Old Testament the people of God are indicted for the sin of refusing to listen to God's voice. It is also interesting to note how many times in the New Testament our Lord says, "He who has ears to hear, let him hear" (e.g., Matt. 13:9). This phrase is repeated seven times in Revelation 2 and 3.

I. Jesus assumed that his disciples would pray (Matt. 6:6).

Humans pray because they must. The Greek word for man—*anthropos*—means "an upward-looking creature." Humans were made with a hunger for God.

A. *Jesus assumed that we would hunger for fellowship with our heavenly Father.* This hunger leads us to engage in both private and public prayer.

B. *Jesus assumed that we would hunger for fellowship with the family of God in dialogue with the Father God.*

C. *Probably Jesus assumed that we would pray because of an overwhelming sense of helplessness and need.*

D. *The great need of humans in their struggle with evil causes us to want to pray.*

1. There is evil within us.
2. There is evil about us.
3. The evil one walks about seeking whom he may devour. It has been said that Satan trembles when he sees the weakest saint upon his or her knees.

James said, "Draw near to God and he will draw near to you" (4:8 RSV). When we pray we need to remember: "Listen, O listen when you pray to hear what God might have to say."

II. Some misconceptions regarding prayer may lead to disappointment and skepticism.

We should not think of prayer as some kind of supernatural "grab bag" into which one reaches at "God's State Fair" in order to obtain some prize.

Prayer is not a substitute for hard thinking and hard work by which we solve many of our problems.

Prayer was never meant to be a magic shortcut to success.

Prayer is not an arrangement of beautiful religious words used to gain God's attention.

Prayer is a personal experience of dialogue with God.

It is God who invites us and moves us to come into his presence. We come into his presence with mingled emotions of fear and joy and expectancy.

As communication takes place in prayer through words and acts, we experience new clarity of vision, new understanding of reality, new strength for action, and new courage for living.

III. Prayer is communication between the Father God and his children.

We are to enter the closet, the private place, and shut the door. It is significant that we are instructed to shut the door.

A. *We are to shut the door so that God can get our attention.* We have a problem with being distracted and preoccupied and not listening when we pray. The psalmist says, "Be still, and know that I am God" (Ps. 46:10). Habakkuk declares, "The Lord is in his holy temple: let all the earth keep silence before him" (2:20).

B. *We are to shut the door so that we can hear God's voice.*
   1. The heavenly Father does not shout or scream when he speaks to us.
   2. The writer of Hebrews encourages us to listen: "Therefore, as the Holy Spirit says, 'Today, when you hear his voice, do not harden your hearts as in the rebellion'" (3:7–8 RSV).

C. *We are to shut the door so that we can speak freely to the Father God.*
   1. We need to take time to adore him, to praise him, and to thank him when we pray.
   2. With the door closed we can take time to confess our sin and to promise God that we will forgive those who have sinned against us (Matt. 6:14–15).
   3. With the door closed we can voice our petitions for others in prayer. All of the pronouns in the Lord's Prayer are plural. The God to whom we pray is "*our* Father." When we pray for bread, we are to pray that the Father will "give *us our* daily bread."

Conclusion

Take time to listen when you pray. Especially listen to the Scriptures, for reading them can be the listening side of prayer. Listen to the prayers of others when they pray in public. Listen to the needs of those around you when you pray. Listen to the voice of God's indwelling Spirit within you when you pray.

> Speak to my heart, Lord Jesus,
> Speak that my soul may hear;
> Speak to my heart, Lord Jesus,
> Calm every doubt and fear.
> Speak to my heart, Lord Jesus.
> Purge me from every sin;
> Speak to my heart, Lord Jesus,
> Help me, the lost to win.
>
> —*B. B. McKinney*

Sunday Evening, July 20

Title: God's Hedge

Text: "'Does Job fear God for nothing?' Satan replied. 'Have you not put a hedge around him and his household and everything he has?'" **(Job 1:9–10 NIV)**.

Scripture Reading: Job 1:6–12

Introduction

Of Satan Jesus said, "When he lies, he speaks his native language, for he is a liar and the father of lies" (John 8:44 NIV). Yet a pearl may sometimes be found in the mouth of a swine and truth in the mouth of the Devil.

Our text is one of God's precious pearls in the mouth of a swine, truth in the mouth of the Devil. God did not dispute Satan's statement that he had set a hedge about Job and all he owned. Moreover, God proceeded to show that his hedge around Job was higher and stronger than even Satan had imagined. This is one of the overlooked lessons of Job.

God has placed a hedge about his own. What significance does this fact have for us? Consider this from two points of view: God's and that of the Christian.

I. What suggestions does God's hedge about us make?

A. *Proprietorship.* God's hedge around us suggests that he owns us. No honest man would put a fence around another's property. God created us and redeemed us. When, in response to God's word, "I have redeemed you" (Isa. 43:1 NIV), we reply, "You have redeemed me," the pact is sealed. He owns us, and we have recognized his right to ownership.

B. *Preciousness.* There are millions of unfenced acres in the United States, wastelands not worth a fence. But fertile fields are. We sing, "So precious is Jesus, my Savior, my King." The other side of that coin is that we are precious to him.

C. *Protection.* A good fence protects a crop against its enemies. Satan walked around Job and found that hedge impregnable until God conditionally opened the gate and let him in. No anxious mother watches over her baby more carefully than Jesus over his own (see Ps. 34:7).

D. *Purpose.* God's hedge is not merely for the sake of protection. He also wants to plant and cultivate his field (1 Cor. 3:9).

II. What ought to characterize those around whom God has placed his hedge?

A. *Separation.* Jesus told his disciples, "You do not belong to the world.... That is why the world hates you" (John 15:19 NIV). He also said, "My prayer is not that you take them out of the world but that you protect them from the evil one" (17:15 NIV).

B. *Usefulness.* Jesus shows how we are to do this by two striking figures of speech.

   1. "You are the salt of the earth" (Matt. 5:13 NIV). The function of salt is to flavor, to preserve, to create thirst.
   2. "You are the light of the world" (Matt. 5:14 NIV). The function of light is to illumine, to give life and health and direction.

C. *Fruitfulness.* One should expect more from a fenced field. Abandon an orchard. Take down the fence. It will soon cease to bear fruit; and what it does bear thieves will steal.

D. *Endurance.* James writes, "You have heard of Job's perseverance" (5:11 NIV). The word here does not mean patience in the sense of waiting for something to happen. It means patience in the sense of being able to endure, to keep on going in the face of disappointment, frustration, suffering, and defeat.

Conclusion

May God help us who are God's precious and protected possession to carry out his purpose for us! God help us to keep ourselves separate from the world, useful, and fruitful! God help us to endure, to keep on.

Wednesday Evening, July 23

Title: The Gospel before the Gospel

Text: "I will put enmity between you and the woman, and between your seed and her seed; he shall bruise your head, and you shall bruise his heel" **(Gen. 3:15 RSV).**

Scripture Reading: Genesis 3:14–19

Introduction

Nowhere do we find demonstrated more profoundly, yet with greater simplicity, that "the New is in the Old concealed and the Old is in the New revealed" than in the Lord's words to the serpent following Eve's defense as to why she yielded to the tempter's charms. Cautious scholars today warn that we can read too much into a passage as we look back across the Old Testament through the eyes of clearer revelation; but few students are willing to give up the messianic thrust of the pronouncement, even though they admit Eve and her husband probably fathomed little of what the veiled reference to Christ actually contained.

I. Sin, though attractive, is deadly.

No one has ever denied that Satan's way of life offers a certain fascination that, on the surface, seems to be delightful. Eve saw immediately that three things—appetite, avarice, and ambition—could be fulfilled to some extent through indulging in the forbidden fruit. A New Testament writer picked up on this trilogy, "For all that is in the world, the lust of the flesh and the lust of the eyes and the pride of life, is not of the Father but is of the world" (1 John 2:16 RSV). Jesus faced the same categories: "Turn stones to bread and satisfy your appetite . . . fall down in homage to Satan and satisfy your desire for possessions . . . jump off the cliff, receive divine protection and satisfy your need for recognition." Basic principles never die! These sinful desires still demand satisfaction in our everyday lives.

II. A "gospel of hate."

What a strange expression of seemingly contradictory terms! Nevertheless, this ancient oracle contains a "religion of enmity," which possesses a godly sanction in order to fulfill a divine purpose. Not a vicious conflict between humans, but a feud between two opposing philosophies of life! Why? Because God still claims a foothold in his own territory and will not surrender his sovereignty to Satan nor leave the earth he created at the mercy of a beastly usurper! Humanity must be taught at the beginning the need for a "noble hatred." Ruskin was right when he said that nothing is essential for the spread of evil except that good men do nothing. God was acting with moral responsibility when he said to the serpent, "I will put enmity between you and the woman, and between your seed and her seed" (Gen. 3:15 RSV).

III. Good tidings in embryonic symbolism.

How was this ancient prophecy fulfilled in history? Satan put Jesus on the cross! Though a part of the divine plan, evil men did it. Clovis is said to have remarked, "If I and my Frankish army had been there, they wouldn't have done it"; but the deed still would have been committed, for it was a "preplanned making explicit in history of the Lamb slain from the foundation of the world." Satan bruised Christ's heal. Another fact stands out, however, and the Hebrew text places it first. The seed of the woman crushed Satan's head. All of Satan's dastardly schemes fell when Jesus made atonement on Calvary and God validated all that Jesus did by the resurrection. Don't say, "Satan will be defeated!" He has already been trampled! Christ reigns now in the hearts of those who will receive him. Satan doesn't own this world. He never did! The earth is the Lord's and the fullness thereof!

Conclusion

How much Eve understood or how she responded is not the question. We leave her salvation and that of her husband to God's infinite wisdom and mercy. We live in the full stream of divine revelation. Every one of us stands without excuse. The Savior has come and is waiting for us to repent of sin and receive the atonement. Have you done it? If not, will you? Now is the time!

SUNDAY MORNING, JULY 27

Title: The Command to Love
Text: "This I command you, to love one another" **(John 15:17 RSV)**.
Scripture Reading: John 15:12–17
Hymns: "I Will Sing the Wondrous Story," Bilhorn
"Love Is the Theme," Fisher
"Lead Me to Calvary," Kirkpatrick
Offertory Prayer: Thank you, Father God, for loving us when we were very unlovable. Thank you for giving your Son to die for our sins. Thank you for giving us the privilege of becoming members of your family. Thank you for giving us your Holy Spirit as an indwelling presence. Thank you for giving us the privilege of worship and the privilege of serving you. Accept these tithes and offerings as indications of our desire to serve you, not only in this community, but beyond as well. Through Jesus Christ we pray. Amen.

Introduction

Among the great disciplines that characterized the life of Jesus was his perpetual determination to practice genuine love toward those who crossed his pathway. If we would be true followers of Jesus Christ, we must see life as an opportunity to love, and we must see people as those to whom we have the opportunity of demonstrating genuine Christian love.

I. We are commanded to love.

John the beloved apostle declared, "God is love. In this the love of God was made manifest among us, that God sent his only Son into the world, so that we might live through him. In this is love, not that we loved God but that he loved us and sent his Son to be the expiation for our sins. Beloved, if God so loved us, we also ought to love one another" (1 John 4:8–11 RSV).

A. *We are commanded to love God supremely (Matt. 22:37).* We are to put God first at all times.
B. *We are commanded to love our neighbors as ourselves (22:39).* Most of us have a problem at this point because we do not love ourselves appropriately. Therefore, we do not have a proper measure by which to know how to truly love our neighbor.
C. *We are commanded to love our enemies (5:43–45).* Most of us have difficulty at this point because we think of love as an emotion, a sentimental attachment, or a romantic attraction.
D. *We are commanded to love one another (John 15:17).*
E. *Paul issued a command that husbands are to love their wives as Christ loved the church (Eph. 5:25, 33).* This presents problems, because the only kind of love that some people know anything about is romantic love.

II. The Greeks used different words to describe different kinds of love.

We overuse and misuse the word *love.* The Greek language was much clearer at helping people to understand the different forms and expressions of love.

A. *Storge refers to natural family love, the love of parents for children and children for parents, and the love of grandparents for grandchildren.* It is even used for the love of an animal for her young.
B. *Eros is sensual love, "need" love, or "me" love.* Love on this level is often self-seeking rather than self-giving. Love on this level seeks gratification and pleasure.
C. *Philia is "friendship" love or "respect" love.* It expresses itself in philanthropy and friendship. It is love without a romantic content. Often it is love based on the worth of the one who is loved.
D. *Agape is self-giving, Christlike love.* This is the kind of love that God demonstrated in the gift of his Son for our sins. Agape love is "help" or "gift" love. It is unmerited goodwill. Agape love finds its source in the heart of the giver rather than in the loveliness of the recipient.

   In a good marriage one can observe all four types of love as signified by these four Greek words. Not to make these distinctions can lead to confusion about the type of love that is commanded in the Scriptures.

III. "Love one another, even as I have loved you."

A. *Christian love is not instinctive.* It is not emotional. It is not a mere feeling. Nor is Christian love automatic. Christian love is an activity in which we are called to participate.
   1. Christian love is a lesson to be learned, and Jesus is the teacher.
   2. Christian love is a habit to be practiced.
   3. Christian love is a commandment to be obeyed.

4. Christian love is a principle to be followed.

B. *Jesus loved his disciples, and he wants us to love in the same manner.*

1. Jesus loved his disciples and accepted them as they were.
2. Jesus loved his disciples and affirmed them.
3. Jesus loved his disciples helpfully.
4. Jesus loved his disciples and forgave them fully.
5. Jesus loved his disciples tenderly and kindly yet firmly.
6. Jesus loved his disciples sacrificially.

Conclusion

Christian love is more than an emotion or a feeling. Christian love is an activity that follows a decision of commitment. Let us look into the face of every person and see him or her as one for whom Jesus Christ died. Let us look into the face of everyone and see one who needs the love that we can give because of the indwelling Christ. Let us look into the mirror and see for ourselves one for whom Jesus Christ died on the cross.

As we seek to love God supremely, let us decide to love ourselves appropriately, and perhaps we will find it easier to be obedient to our Lord's command, "Love one another, even as I have loved you." By doing so, we will find ourselves continually wearing the badge that indicates that we are true disciples of Jesus Christ (John 13:34–35 RSV).

SUNDAY EVENING, JULY 27

Title: Is It Possible to Know God?

Text: "Can you fathom the mysteries of God? Can you probe the limits of the Almighty?" **(Job 11:7 NIV)**.

Scripture Reading: Job 11:1–12

Introduction

The pages of history record the struggles and agony of soul of many great saints before God became real to them. Martin Luther was a brilliant and conscientious monk of the Roman Catholic Church, a model in his behavior and devotion to duty; but he was not satisfied until God used Romans 1:17, "The just shall live by faith," to speak to his heart. His experience sparked the Protestant Reformation.

John Wesley was a strict, methodical priest of the Church of England, but he never knew peace in his heart until one night in a meeting at Aldersgate Street when he felt his heart "strangely warmed." He knew that God had made him free from the law of sin and death. That date was May 24, 1738—an important date in Christian history.

Zophar the Naamathite, one of Job's "comforters," questioned Job about whether he could truly know God. He asked, "Can you fathom the mysteries of God?" (Job 11:7 NIV). He was asking, "Is it possible to know God?" Four answers may be suggested to this question.

I. The answer of the so-called atheist.

The atheist's answer is, "No! You can't know God, for he does not exist except in one's imagination."

There is no point in arguing with the atheist. That is not the way to reach him. He has troubles enough trying to explain a universe without God. Why add to his burdens?

II. The answer of the agnostic.

The agnostic believes that nothing is known or can be known about God. Is there a God? "Well, maybe yes, maybe no," she says; "we just cannot tell." She doesn't deny that there is a God. Nor does she affirm it. She just says, "We don't know."

III. The answer of the "Paul man."

A man like the apostle Paul would say, "I know him whom I have believed" (2 Tim. 1:12 ASV). This man is scorned by the atheist. When the agnostic hears him, he is puzzled. The idea of being so sure of God is beyond him. But there is something magnificent about these prophet-dreamers who are so sure of God, of his will for their lives, and of his program for his kingdom. When the people of this world are like a pack of wild beasts ready to spring at one another's throats, we need such believers.

The conductor Reichel was taking his great choir through the last rehearsal of Handel's *Messiah.* He had come to the point where a soprano soloist takes up the refrain, "I know that my Redeemer liveth." The soloist's technique was perfect. She had faultless breath control, accurate note placement, flawless enunciation. When she finished, Reichel stopped the orchestra. All of the choir expected his commendation of the soloist, for her work was mechanically perfect. But he did not commend her. Instead, he stood before her and asked soberly, "Oh my daughter, do you know him? Do you really know him as your Redeemer?"

Cut to the quick, the soloist, a sincere Christian, stammered, "Yes, Mr. Reichel, I *do* know him. He *is* my Redeemer."

Almost in a shout, the great conductor said, "Then *sing* it! Sing it so I will know!" He signaled to the orchestra.

This time, forgetting all about mechanics, and hurt for fear she had not witnessed as best she could for her Lord, the young woman poured all the power of her magnificently trained voice, undergirded by the emotion of the moment, into singing, "I *know* that my Redeemer liveth."

The choir burst into spontaneous applause, and Reichel again stood before her, tears streaming down his face, to say, "Oh, my dear, you *do* know him, for you have told me."

IV. The answer of the "Job man."

This person says, "If only I knew where to find him!" (Job 23:3 NIV). While he is not to be compared with the "Paul man," he is on the way. He is not an atheist who says, "No, you can't find God. There is no God." He is not an agnostic who says, "You can't know one way or the other." He says, "I believe there is a God. 'If only I knew where to find him!'" And one day he will!

Conclusion

After all is said and done, finding God is really letting God find us. Our search for God is simply our surrender to his seeking us. We find him as runaway children, who, weary of their escapade, find their father. They consent to be found by him.

Friend, have you let your heavenly Father find you?

WEDNESDAY EVENING, JULY 30

Title: Does God Expect Us to Care?
Text: "Then the LORD said to Cain, 'Where is Abel your brother?' He said, 'I do not know; am I my brother's keeper?'" **(Gen. 4:9 RSV)**.
Scripture Reading: Genesis 4:1–15

Introduction

Every time we hear the expression "Am I my brother's keeper?" we should remember that it was initially asked by a man with blood on his hands, a coldhearted murderer. Whether or not the question was rhetorical, Cain certainly, if he expected any answer, did not anticipate that the one to whom he addressed his interrogation would accuse him directly. He meant for his words to be a defense. Guilt was not in his vocabulary, and he refused to let anyone, especially God, place any blame on him. This is always the approach of those who wish to avoid responsibility.

I. The command.

Although we have no record of it in the Bible, some instruction must have been given regarding worship. Since Cain and Abel were grown men, their parents had, no doubt, given birth to other children by this time (Gen. 5:4); and we find it incredible to think for a moment that the race was void of any religious ritual or stewardship requirements.

Oliver Wendell Holmes once said that there was in the corner of his heart a plant called reverence that needed watering once a week. Some of us need it more often!

II. But what kind of worship?

We blush with shame concerning that "converted" sea captain who could enjoy his devotions twice a day but never have any conscience for the slaves in the pit below suffering the rigors of almost unbearable filth and toil. He had a long way to go in Christian maturity! Worship should make us more sensitive to the needs of others and cultivate within our soul a tolerance for the fact that others may do things a bit differently. Above all, we should not make a fetish of trying to outdo our friends in piling up virtue with God. Cain had some real "blinders" on when he went to the altar. Far too many times we do also!

III. When love is gone.

Cain did not lose his love; rather, he never had it. If one ounce of affection resided in his heart, he would not have, could not have killed his brother. Cain cared only for himself and ended up with no one caring about him. This is the way it happens every time. Do you know why Jesus is still the greatest person and the most worshiped in the world? It is because he cared more than anyone else about people.

Conclusion

God expects us, in principle, to do the same thing. We are to care for others regardless of how they feel about us!

SUGGESTED PREACHING PROGRAM FOR THE MONTH OF AUGUST

■ Sunday Mornings

Continue and complete the series "The Disciplines of Discipleship."

■ Sunday Evenings

Continue the series "Wise Men of the Past Speak to the Present."

■ Wednesday Evenings

Continue the studies from Genesis 1–11 that reveal that the God of antiquity is the same God today and that human nature and human needs do not change.

SUNDAY MORNING, AUGUST 3

Title: Responding with Forgiveness

Text: "Then Peter came up and said to him, 'Lord, how often shall my brother sin against me, and I forgive him? As many as seven times?'" **(Matt. 18:21 RSV)**.

Scripture Reading: Matthew 18:21–35

Hymns: "Christ Receiveth Sinful Men," Neumeister
"He Included Me," Oatman
"Though Your Sins Be as Scarlet," Crosby

Offertory Prayer: Heavenly Father, we bring our gifts of love and praise as well as our tithes and offerings to you today. Accept and bless the tithes and offerings in the proclamation of the gospel to the ends of the earth and in meeting the needs of your kingdom's work. Help us to give as you have given. Help us to be merciful and kind toward others as you have been merciful and kind to us. Amen.

Introduction

How do you respond to mistreatment and injury? All of us have to admit that when we are mistreated, we find it difficult to have the mind of Christ and to demonstrate the Spirit of Christ toward those who mistreat us. But responding with anger, hostility, bitterness, and retaliation is the Devil's way of destroying your home, your family, and your fellowship with others.

I. Dealing with the pain of being mistreated.

Every human being experiences mistreatment from others. How we deal with this will to a large degree determine our total well-being in life.

A. *Some have suffered abuse and mistreatment by their parents or by others in positions of authority over them while they were young and helpless.*
B. *Many people experience repeated mistreatment in marriage.* Dr. David Mace has affirmed that marriage provides the occasion for the experience of anger more than any other relationship in life because of its length and the close relationship it represents between two human beings, who at times may threaten one another.
C. *Parents often experience painful injury through the immature and selfish conduct of their children.*
D. *Many experience pain and agony because of the stupidity and selfishness of a brother or sister.*
E. *Many people experience pain in their vocations or on the job where they earn their living.*

Peter must have experienced discomfort and injury within family relationships, because he came to our Lord with the question, "Lord, how often shall my brother sin against me, and I forgive him? As many as seven times?"

II. The teachings of our Lord regarding forgiveness.

Our Lord comes through crisp and clear on how we are to deal with injury and mistreatment.

A. *Our Lord specifically forbids retaliation.* We are to avoid being vindictive and revengeful. We are to avoid striking out and returning evil for evil, curse for curse, blow for blow, injury for injury.
B. *Our Lord does not suggest that we suppress hostile feelings and ignore the injuries and mistreatment that we experience at the hands of others.* To do this would create a poison within our minds that would eventually produce an eruption.
C. *Our Lord does not suggest that we retreat into self-pity, which can lead to discouragement, despair, and depression.*
D. *Our Lord specifically places on us the obligation to give the gift of forgiveness to those who mistreat us.*

We often find it difficult to be forgiving, because we have a natural impulse to retaliate. We may find it difficult to be forgiving because we labor under the impression that to be forgiving may encourage continued mistreatment. Or we may find it difficult to be forgiving because we want the one who injured us to be worthy and to deserve the gift of forgiveness. Forgiveness is always an undeserved gift. God gives us the gift of forgiveness. If we wait until someone deserves forgiveness, we will harbor feelings of anger and hostility toward that person always.

Our Lord not only taught but practiced the habit of forgiving. While on the cross suffering for the sins of a guilty people, he prayed, "Father, forgive them; for they know not what they do" (Luke 23:34 RSV).

III. The rationale for being a forgiver.

When Jesus suggested that his disciples give the gift of forgiveness "seventy times seven," he was thinking of the terrible consequences that would take place in the hearts of the injured if they refused to forgive. Jesus, with perfect insight into human nature, knew that hate in the heart would be like a cancer in the soul.

A. *We are to give the gift of forgiveness because we have received the gift of forgiveness (Matt. 18:23–27).* Paul wrote to the Ephesians, "Let all bitterness and wrath and anger and clamor and slander be put away from you, with all malice, and be kind to one another, tenderhearted, forgiving one another, as God in Christ forgave you" (4:31–32 RSV).

B. *We need to consider the terrible cost of an unforgiving spirit if we have difficulty giving the gift of forgiveness (Matt. 6:14–15).* Giving the gift of forgiveness is not a price we pay to receive forgiveness. Those who harbor hate and wrath in their hearts have closed the door through which God's forgiveness would come to them.

C. *We must give the gift of forgiveness in order to prevent Satan from establishing a beachhead in our thoughts (cf. 2 Cor. 2:10–11).*

D. *A forgiving spirit will bring healing to the injured spirit.* Many people quiver with pain because they have been mistreated and sinned against. Jesus speaks to these and says we are to forgive "seventy times seven." This is a strong statement that we need to take literally. Every time we hurt, we need to give the gift of forgiveness again. Some misunderstand at this point. They think that if you do not forget, that you have not forgiven. In reality, it is impossible to totally forget. On the other hand, if we forgive and do it repeatedly, for all practical purposes we will forget to the point of no longer harboring hate or striking out in retaliation.

Conclusion

God's forgiveness to each of us is free, complete, and forever. He doesn't hold our sins against us; he offers forgiveness to each of us personally. On the basis of his forgiveness, we can be forgiving toward others. If you have been holding a grudge against someone, you can give yourself a clean heart and a clear conscience if you will ask the forgiving God to help you to give to that one who injured you the gift of forgiveness.

Sunday Evening, August 3

Title: If a Man Die
Text: "If a man dies, will he live again?" **(Job 14:14 NIV).**
Scripture Reading: Job 14:1–22

Introduction

Sooner or later Job's ancient question wells up in each heart: "If a man die, shall he live again?" There is no doubt about the answer to the first part of the question, for "it is appointed unto men once to die" (Heb. 9:27 ASV). So the real problem is "Shall he live again?" No question is more earnest or more universal than this.

What is the answer to this haunting question, with which every individual must come to terms? Many things might be said in reply, but all the answers may be summed up under three headings.

I. Some say the answer is no.

A. *This is the answer of the materialist.* This person says that all there is to humans is flesh, bone, blood, and nerve tissue. What happens after death? The materialist answers, "Nothing." Where does one go? "Nowhere."

B. *This is also the answer of the atheist.* The atheist says, "We live; we strive; we sorrow and rejoice; we reproduce ourselves; we die. And that is the end of us. Oh, we have a little more ability to think than the lower animals, but that is about the sum and substance of the difference."

C. *This is also the answer of the epicurean.* The epicurean's view is, "Let us eat, drink, and be merry, for tomorrow we die; and that's all there is."

II. Some say, "We do not know the answer."

These people say, "We cannot answer for certain. The answer may be no, or it may be yes. We just do not know." This is the answer of the agnostic, a term invented by Thomas Huxley. It is a transliteration of a Greek word that means "unknown." The agnostic does not say outright that there is no future life, rather that we cannot know one way or the other.

Without Christ the greatest minds of history have not been able to be sure of life after death. Even the great Greek philosopher Socrates, as he faced death, could do no better than to say, "The time of my departure has arrived, for me to die and you to live. Which is better only God knows."

The agnostic doesn't help us. There is no strength in a doubt, no matter how beautifully phrased; nor is there salvation in a question mark: "If a man die, shall he live again?" The agnostic says, "Maybe yes, maybe no. We cannot know for sure." There is no help in that.

III. Some say the answer is yes.

Job's question, "If a man die, shall he live again?" is answered by Christ's declaration, "Because I live, you also will live" (John 14:19 NIV). Job's question is as old as the human race. Job stated dramatically the finality of death: "So man lies down and does not rise; till the heavens are no more, men will not awake or be roused from their sleep" (Job 14:12 NIV). But Job wished that it were not so. If there is no hope, one must still hope. Job's heart literally leaped with longing as he voiced his question with bated breath, "If a man dies, will he live again?" But he never quite answered his own question. The New Testament does, however.

A. *Where are we to live?* We are to live in a city. The theme "the city of God" runs throughout the Bible. We dream of it here; our dream will be realized there. Speaking of Abraham, the writer of the epistle to the Hebrews says, "By faith he became a sojourner in the land of promise, as in a land not his own, dwelling in tents, with Isaac and Jacob, the heirs with him of the same promise: for he looked for the city which hath the foundations, whose builder and maker is God" (11:9–10 ASV).
B. *In what are we to live?* Paul tells the Corinthians, "For we know that if the earthly house of our tabernacle be dissolved, we have a building from God, a house not made with hands, eternal, in the heavens" (2 Cor. 5:1 ASV). His meaning is that we will have an eternal dwelling place with Jesus and all of his saints of all the ages (see John 14:2).
C. *How are we to live?* Again Paul tells the Corinthians, "For verily in this we groan, longing to be clothed upon with our habitation which is from heaven: if so be that being clothed we shall not be found naked" (2 Cor. 5:2–3 ASV). Each of us is going to live in a resurrection body, a body as perfectly suited for heaven's realm as our mortal bodies are for life in this realm.

Conclusion

"If a man dies, will he live again?" The answer is "Yes, if he is in Christ." Because he lives, we too will live. We will live in a city. We will live in a permanent dwelling place. We will live in a resurrection body like that of our Lord's. Christ is God's answer to Job's question.

WEDNESDAY EVENING, AUGUST 6

Title: God Never Leaves His World
Text: "To Seth also a son was born, and he called his name Enosh. At that time men began to call upon the name of the LORD" **(Gen. 4:26 RSV)**.
Scripture Reading: Genesis 4:16–26

Introduction

Because records are unavailable, we do not know what happened to Adam and Eve in the years that followed their expulsion from the garden of Eden. One thing is certain, however; life went on as it always does, and the first people on earth began to build a civilization. God told Adam and Eve, "Be fruitful . . . multiply . . . replenish the earth, and subdue it" (Gen. 1:28); and they took him seriously.

I. The bad continued.

Unfortunately, wickedness seems to spread faster than righteousness. The first record is about the "bad guys" and how they multiplied. With complete intellectual honesty, the Genesis writer made no attempt to disguise the fact that we owe much to Cain's descendants for developing the external civilization of the world. Cain built a city!

Sin intensifies and multiplies far more in urban culture than in rural. The God-defying energy of Cain's descendants, with their secular activism, produced tools and weapons of war, as well as portable tents of skin. Crafts, art, and music joined the gradual growth of culture; and soon polygamy came upon the scene. Clever, though godless, Cain's descendants, in each succeeding generation, relied more implicitly on their own skill and less on the help of God.

Our own generation needs to learn a lesson taught us by this ancient civilization. Wealth, ability, culture, and worldly success, when divorced from God, blight rather than bless.

II. The good remain.

Whatever else the book of Revelation teaches, it stands side by side with the first book of the Bible to proclaim the eternal truth that the forces of evil can never defeat God's plan nor eliminate his people from the earth. Like a breath of fresh air come the words concerning the birth of Seth's son Enosh: "At that time men began to call upon the name of the Lord" (Gen. 4:26 RSV).

III. The Lord waits.

Have patience with your God. The poet was right—God gives the key to his own when he feels the time is right. Vengeance belongs to God. He will repay. Let the Lord be God. The flood of judgment will come but not yet. The iniquity of the Amorites must always be full before the Lord acts. Why does God let the two contrasting ideologies compete when one is diametrically opposed to his will?

Conclusion

Our constant prayer should be, "Oh, God, breathe through the heat of our desire your coolness and your balm. Help us to choose and remain loyal to your precepts, making them our priorities whatever the Cains, Lamechs, and their contemporary counterparts may do." Without God, life crumbles; with him, things not only stand secure, but also everything fits together and makes sense.

Sunday Morning, August 10

Title: You Must Learn to Be a Giver

Text: "Forgive, and you will be forgiven; give, and it will be given to you; good measure, pressed down, shaken together, running over, will be put into your lap. For the measure you give will be the measure you get back" **(Luke 6:37–38 RSV).**

Scripture Reading: 2 Corinthians 9:6–8

Hymns: "Joyful, Joyful, We Adore Thee," Van Dyke
"Give of Your Best to the Master," Grose
"Since Jesus Came into My Heart," McDaniel

Offertory Prayer: Father God, we come to you today, recognizing you as the giver of every good and perfect gift. We come thanking you for your generosity and kindness to us. We come eager to respond with generosity to you and toward others. Accept our tithes and offerings, and bless them in ministries of mercy to others. Help us to learn and to believe that it is more blessed to give than to receive. In Jesus' name. Amen.

Introduction

One of the greatest gifts you can give is the gift of forgiveness to someone who has mistreated you. At the same time that you give the gift of forgiveness to others, you give yourself the gift of a heart free of hate, anger, and hostility.

It is no accident that Jesus spoke about giving and forgiving in the same breath. Dr. Charles Williams, a noted Greek scholar, translates our text into the following words: "Practice forgiving others, and you will be forgiven. Practice giving to others, and they will give to you, good measure, pressed down, shaken together and running over, people will pour into your lap. For the measure you use with others they in turn will use with you."

If we would search for the disciplines of discipleship that make it possible for us to discover the abundant life, we must focus on the privilege of being a giver.

I. There is much disbelief regarding the beatitude about giving.

The teachings of Jesus contradict the popular concept of what it takes to experience happiness. Humans in their fallen state believe that it is far more blessed to receive than it is to give. Jesus taught the opposite. We need to recognize that we have a built-in handicap at the point of believing this great teaching of Jesus Christ.

Whenever someone says something about giving, our "pocketbook-protection instinct" takes over, and we begin to put up defenses and reasons we should not participate in giving.

A. *We are fearful creatures.* We fear poverty and want.
B. *We find it difficult to trust in the goodness of God and in the provisions he will make available to us.*
C. *We find inside ourselves an acquisitive instinct that expresses itself in grasping the things that promise happiness.*

D. *We are natural lovers of comfort and luxury, and it is easy for us to be deceived into believing that happiness comes through getting and having and keeping.*
E. *We live in a world that judges success in materialistic terms.*
F. *We are spiritually short-sighted in that we act as if we were earthlings alone and not citizens of the kingdom of heaven, which has an eternal dimension.*
G. *We overly invest in the present and forget about eternity.*
H. *We experience the joy of receiving, and it is so nice that we do not even investigate the possibility of experiencing the joy of giving.*

II. We concentrate on what we cannot give.

When we come across the teachings of Jesus about giving, we offer excuses. One of our favorite verses seems to be the comment of Peter in which he said to the beggar, "Silver and gold have I none." We should move on and say, "Such as I have give I thee" (Acts 3:6). We concentrate on our comparative poverty in contrast to the riches of others.

Jesus was not talking about the giving of a specific gift or even the receiving of an offering. He was talking about a life philosophy or reason for being. That is, he was suggesting that we should commit ourselves to giving as a way of life.

III. We need to recognize the results of a giving way of life.

We often say, "Preparation pays off," or "Education pays off." The banker will say, "Saving pays off." The stockbroker will say, "Investing pays off." Jesus says, "Giving really pays off, both with people and with God."

In marriage, partners learn that being stingy with each other produces stinginess in the other. In marriage, if a husband and wife will try to outgive each other, both of them will experience an abundance of joy and happiness.

Followers of Christ discover that the more they follow this discipline of Jesus—giving—the more they find the life abundant. If you want to live a full life, become a giver. If you want God to fill your heart and your pocket, you must decide to become a giver of yourself to God and to others. Stinginess, selfishness, and a greedy grasping after things are restrictions that keep God from being able to fill our hearts and lives with abundance. The joy and profitability that come as a result of giving must be experienced. It is like swimming: you'll never learn to swim until you get into the water.

Conclusion

You would be wise today to give your mind to the God who created you. Give your body to the service of God and others that you might glorify God, making him known through your life (Rom. 12:1; 1 Cor. 6:20). Give your treasure to God, and you will discover that you can't outgive God. Give God your past and your present, then trust him for the future. Set some giving goals for yourself, and you will begin to live the abundant life. But first of all, and of primary importance, you need to give yourself to Jesus Christ and trust him as your personal Lord and Savior.

Sunday Evening, August 10

Title: The Voice of Youth
Text: "It is not the old that are wise, nor the aged that understand what is right. Therefore I say, 'Listen to me; let me also declare my opinion'" **(Job 32:9–10 RSV).**
Scripture Reading: Job 32:1–10

Introduction

Here speaks the voice of youth, the perennial sophomore whose mission in life is to set his elders straight. Having listened to Job and his three friends throughout their dialogue, Elihu is fed up. So he breaks in with, "It is not the old that are wise. . . . Therefore I say, 'Listen to me.'" Here also is exhibited the abiding clash between youth and the aged, two groups who often do not see eye to eye.

Read all of Elihu's speeches and you will see that he did say some wise things and also some stupid things. He illustrates the "voice of youth." He did get a hearing; his elders heard him through.

I. Youth has some things that those of us who are mature could use.

A. *We could use some of the enthusiasm of youth.* Speaking to youth, a French writer once said, "Lay up for yourselves a good many enthusiasms in your youth, for you will lose many of them along the way."

B. *We could use some of the impressionableness of youth.* We could profit by being more flexible. It takes one-seventh of a second to send an electrical impulse around the world, but often it takes five years to get a good idea through one-fourth of an inch of human skull. Some people have concrete minds, "all mixed up and permanently set."

C. *We could use some of the idealism of youth.* The younger generation with its sharp insights and its idealism is often an embarrassment to its elders.

II. Those who are mature have some things that youth could use.

A. *Youth could use a little of the hard-earned knowledge that comes from study, time, and experience.* It may be said of many young people, as Paul said of Israel, "For I bear them witness that they have a zeal for God, but not according to knowledge" (Rom. 10:2 ASV). Zeal is a wonderful thing, but apart from knowledge it can get off the track. This was true of Elihu. The Bible seems to believe in the superior wisdom of those who have been taught by the years. That fact that children are urged to obey their parents (Eph. 6:1) is based on the assumption that, having lived longer, parents know more than their children.

B. *Youth could use a little of the humility that comes from a few setbacks and defeats.* Humility is a costly commodity. The tuition is high, but the lesson is priceless.

C. *Youth could use a little of the tolerance we learn along the way through our follies and failures.* This young man, Elihu, was also sharply critical. At times those of us who are older strike sharp blows with our tongues. But for criticism at its sharpest, youth can sometimes outdo their elders. Generally speaking, if we live with any purpose at all, we learn through our own failures and follies, if not by the grace of God, to be a little more tolerant. An unknown writer has said:

> There is so much good in the worst of us,
> And so much bad in the best of us,
> That it ill behooves any of us
> To talk about the rest of us.

Now, having looked at this matter from both points of view, to what conclusion are we to come?

III. Youth and maturity need one another.

A. *We must see that we are a team and that the team is not complete without both young and old.* In a college town a few faculty members and some workers in a nearby children's home conceived the idea of a church to serve, primarily, these two institutions. They met in the chapel of the children's home on Sunday afternoon to discuss the matter. It was thrilling when 100 college students and 122 children from the home, fourth grade through high school, sang a hymn; but the discussion didn't get anywhere. After a few minutes a college boy saved the day. "We need a church in this part of the city," he said, "but this won't work. We have 200 young people and children here but only a handful of adults, and all but one of them is under forty years of age. We need more older people, fifty to sixty years old." A church was later successfully organized there but on an all-age basis.

B. *We must see that life is for everybody.* The cynic's view is that life is for nobody. In the days of the Roman Empire, when there were no eyeglasses, no dentures, no surgery to correct the ills of the aging, no vitamins, and no treatment for hypertension, life was only for youth. Old age was unrelieved tragedy. In later times there was the attitude, "Youth are to be seen and not heard." But now the pendulum has swung back the other way. Youth are on the stage, front and center. Life, however, is for everybody: the young with their strength and enthusiasm, the old with their knowledge and wisdom, and the middle-aged with their know-how and drive.

C. *We must have a common faith that results in the sharing of a common spiritual life.* We are told that after Pentecost "the multitude of them that believed were of one heart and soul" (Acts 4:32 ASV). In the power of the Spirit every kind of chasm was bridged.

Conclusion

This is good news for everybody. To continue in God's fellowship is to be one of God's evergreens. Life is not a matter of the calendar but of the Spirit.

Wednesday Evening, August 13

Title: Let's Go to God's House Today
Text: "Enoch walked with God: and he was not; for God took him" **(Gen. 5:24)**.
Scripture Reading: Genesis 5:21–24

Introduction

Someone has called the fifth chapter of Genesis a "monotonous chronicle of nobodies." The writer brings before us, one by one, the descendants of Seth and tells us that they were born, produced children, and died.

In the midst of the long and dreary list is a delightful variant. Enoch came on the scene and received special treatment. He did more than follow the dull routine of his predecessors. In the midst of what must have been a stale and slowly deteriorating society, gradually moving toward the philosophy of Cain's descendants, Enoch "bucked the trend" and walked with God. What is involved in "walking with God"?

I. You must begin.

"The first step of a thousand-mile journey," say the Chinese, "begins at home," and the first step in the Christian life is to become a Christian. One dedicated missionary of another generation said, "Becoming a Christian is surrendering as much of myself as I understand today to as much of Jesus as I understand today."

The classic statement of Amos that two cannot walk together unless they are in agreement implies that they have made an agreement to meet for the trip. Back then people did not accidentally stumble on one another in the wilderness. Conditions were dangerous, and people did not walk alone. They planned in advance for fellowship. Likewise, people must decide they want to walk with God before they do it.

II. God in the same direction.

In a hard-fought Rose Bowl game many years ago, a player became confused and, with only a few yards to go for a touchdown, ran more than ninety yards in the wrong direction. His mistake cost his team the triumph they might have gained. He later testified that he thought the yelling crowd was cheering him on, so he ran that much harder. The problem was that he was headed in the wrong direction. To have the same goals as God means we must have an insight that is uncluttered by side aims. Enoch not only had the faith that enabled him to see things in proper perspective, he also had the faith that kept him moving in the same path as his heavenly Father.

Enoch was called upon to walk with God during days that were becoming progressively more evil. Scorn, ridicule, and even violence must have thrown opposition across his path, but he persevered. Enoch walked forward against difficulties, but what made it all worthwhile was his intimate companionship with the God he knew and loved.

III. Climax of the journey.

Fanny Crosby wrote, "Someday the silver chord will break." Every life must end; and those who, like the blind hymn writer, know Jesus will stand "within the palace of the King." Someone has said that death and God are the two greatest ideas of which the human mind is capable. What the former means to us is determined by what the latter means during our days on earth.

Conclusion

Recounting the story of Enoch for her parents, a small child said, "God and Enoch used to take long walks together, but they would always return to Enoch's home. One day they walked farther than usual. God said, 'Enoch, it's closer to my house than yours. Let's go there!' They did, and Enoch liked it so much he never wanted to return to his own."

SUNDAY MORNING, AUGUST 17

Title: Locating and Serving on Your Mission Field

Text: "Return to your home, and declare how much God has done for you" **(Luke 8:39 RSV)**.

Scripture Reading: Luke 8:38–39

Hymns: "We Have Heard the Joyful Sound," Kirkpatrick
"I Know Whom I Have Believed," Whittle
"Tell Me the Story of Jesus," Crosby

Offertory Prayer: Father God, thank you for your generosity and every expression of your kindness toward us. Help us to respond to your goodness by being gracious and merciful and helpful to others. Accept our tithes and offerings and bless them to the end that others shall come to know of your love and of the great redemption that is available through Jesus Christ our Lord. In his name we pray. Amen.

Introduction

The biblical account of the deliverance of the man from the legion of demons is one of the most dramatic accounts to be found in all of the New Testament. In this miraculous event Christ took the initiative to deliver this man from the destructive powers of the demonic. As a divine and benevolent mediator, he confronted the evil forces in this man and persisted until the man was set free, and we see him "sitting at the feet of Jesus, clothed, and in his right mind" (Luke 8:35).

This dramatic and inspiring account portrays the fact that Jesus Christ came into this world to do more than just deliver people from the power of the demonic in an initial experience of conversion. Jesus needed the potential of this man for the good of others. He had a chosen place of service where this man could be God's messenger and helper and man's minister and servant. We can deduce from this that God has a mission field for each of us, and we must locate that mission field and begin to serve him there.

Dr. Russell Conwell, founder and president of Temple University, had a famous lecture entitled "Acres of Diamonds," which he delivered more than five thousand times. The point of this exciting lecture calls our attention to the fact that we will find our diamonds at home rather than in some distant and exotic place. Jesus was affirming this same great truth when he spoke to the man and said, "Return to your home, and declare how much God has done for you" (v. 39 RSV).

I. The proper response of a saved man.

This man who was delivered from the power of the demonic provides us with an interesting study in motivation. Verse 38 declares, "The man from whom the demons had gone begged that he might be with him; but he sent him away" (RSV).

A. *Gratitude could have caused the man to want to be with Jesus always.*
B. *A new affection and love for Jesus could have caused this man to want to be as close to him as possible for the rest of his days.*
C. *It is possible that the fear of a reoccurrence of demonic possession could have caused the man to want to stay close to the one who could deliver him.* The closer we stay to Christ, the less opportunity Satan has to take charge of our lives.

The man's motive for wanting to be with Jesus was a worthy and commendable motive. We should imitate him at this point.

II. A prayer request that was not granted.

The Scripture tells us that even though the man wanted to be with Jesus and his apostles, Jesus "sent him away, saying, 'Return to your home, and declare how much God has done for you'" (vv. 38–39 RSV).

There are a number of recorded prayers that were offered to Jesus that he did not grant.

A. *A greedy brother prayed that Jesus would insist that his covetous brother divide the inheritance properly (Luke 12:13).* Jesus declined to grant this request.
B. *A mother requested preferential treatment for her two sons (Matt. 20:20–28).* Jesus declined to grant this request as well.
C. *Jesus' enemies taunted him and prayed, "Come down from the cross" (27:40).* We can rejoice that he did not grant their request.
D. *The man in this morning's passage offered a very proper prayer:* "The man from whom the demons had gone begged that he might be with him." And Jesus had chosen the apostles "that they might be with him."

   Jesus declined to grant this request because he had a greater need for the man and a greater purpose for him. We can conclude that Jesus did not come into this world merely to make us feel good or to give us a feeling of inward security.

   Later Jesus was to go to the area where this man's home was located, the Decapolis (Mark 7:31–8:10). This was an area made up of ten gentile cities located east and south of the Sea of Galilee. This man went back to the area and gave his testimony. When Jesus arrived, thousands of people were waiting to see and hear him. No doubt they had heard the man's report concerning the miraculous and merciful power of Jesus Christ. It was here that great crowds gathered and followed him to the extent that they became weary and in need of food. With seven loaves of bread, our Lord miraculously fed a crowd of four thousand people.

   These mighty events took place because of the man's personal response to the wishes of the Lord who had set him free from the dominion of evil.

III. Our Lord's personal request and our continuing commission.

"Return to your home, and declare how much God has done for you." When many people think of the mission field, they think of some far-off, exotic place where they might experience adventure and excitement. It is true that our Lord commissioned his church to carry the gospel to the ends of the earth and to all peoples of the earth. Perhaps individual believers and the church as a body have missed the point by failing to recognize that the mission field begins at home.

A. *Christianity begins at your home.* It is in our homes that we are to believe and behave as followers of Jesus Christ. The faith that does not ring true at home will not be effective in some faraway place.
B. *Service to our Lord begins at home.*

1. By a changed lifestyle in the home we can demonstrate the reality of the presence of God in our hearts and lives. It is at home in the most important of human relationships that we are to demonstrate the *agape* love that the Holy Spirit of God pours out into our hearts through faith in Jesus Christ.
2. By word of mouth we are to relate to others the good things that God has done in our lives. Our Lord desires each of us to serve him in our homes, and this refers not just to our families but to the network of our family relationships. Recent studies in personal relationships have indicated that the average person today has regular contact with about eighty different persons. In a sense that means that our world, though we live in the midst of billions, is really quite small. It is in this smaller world where we are to verbalize the good news of what God has done for us in and through Jesus Christ.

IV. Christians are in the communication business.

"Return to your home, and declare how much God has done for you."

Jesus was specifically requesting that this man get into the communication business. He wanted this communication to take place where the man was known. He wanted him to communicate about the goodness of God in the area where people had known what he was before he became a believer.

A. *The silent witness of a transformed life is incomplete.* It is tremendously important that we be different.

B. *If Christ has made a difference, then we must verbally give testimony to his goodness and kindness to us.*

Conclusion

When we give expression to the joy and gratitude of our hearts and when we give voice to praises for God, if these are genuine, they will create hunger and thirst in the hearts of our "home folk" to come to know Jesus Christ also.

The man who had been demon possessed did what Jesus asked. He went home and shared the good news of what God had done for him. Let each of us follow his example.

Sunday Evening, August 17

Title: The Proof of the Pudding
Text: "O taste and see that the Lord is good!" **(Ps. 34:8 RSV)**.
Scripture Reading: Psalm 34:1–22

Introduction

Our text reminds us of an ancient proverb: "The proof of the pudding is in the eating." The psalmist's challenge is to make the pragmatic test—"Taste and see."

But to many this does not dispose of the questions, "If God is good, how could he have made a world where suffering, tyranny, crime, injustice, poverty, and disease exist? If God is good, then having made a world like this, must he not be lacking in power?" How can God be good? As we deal with this question that arises involuntarily in our hearts, we want to approach the matter from two points of view—the negative and the positive.

I. Consider the involuntary question that arises in every heart: "How can God be good?"

To be specific and yet not get bogged down in fine-spun theories, let us consider three affirmations, each of which may be illustrated by a typical situation in which one would likely raise this question.

A. *The fact that God doesn't make life easy is no sign that he is not good.* Perhaps something happens to you in the prime of life. You are overtaken by a disease that cripples you or you lose your position, which means the end of a promising career. In such a situation you are apt to ask yourself, "If God is good, how could he let this happen to me? Why did he not protect me from this tragic thing?" Is that your most mature understanding of the goodness of God—that if he were truly good, he would spare you from everything that makes life difficult?

   Do good parents who love their children always make life easy for them? Would Beethoven's music have been more beautiful if he had never known deafness? Would Milton's poetry have been more moving if he had not been stricken by blindness?

B. *The fact that God does not overrule our freedom to destroy ourselves is no proof that he is not good.* Suppose you drink too much, drive too fast, and then kill somebody and seriously injure yourself. Then you say, "If God is good, why didn't he stop me? Why didn't he prevent this?" If we choose to use our freedom to destroy ourselves, it is not God's goodness we need to question but our own.

C. *The fact that God does not always act in a way we can understand is no indication that he is not good.* Suppose you are young and terribly disappointed in love. The girl of your dreams deserts you for another. This seems to be the end of everything. A year later you meet the woman who is to become your wife. She is God's chosen one for you; and you begin a life that is full not only of romance but of happiness and joy and solid achievement. One day you realize that you are now thanking God for the very thing you blamed him for a year earlier. Because God's ways are higher than our ways and his thoughts than our thoughts (Isa. 55:9), things that seem at the time to be bad usually turn out for our good.

Now we turn from the negative to the positive viewpoint.

II. Consider the way to an answer, the Bible's way.

The psalmist's imperative is, "O taste and see that the LORD is good!" Three thoughts stem out of these words.

A. *This is a challenge to the unbeliever, the doubter.* The psalmist rejoices in this: "The angel of the LORD encamps around those who fear him, and he delivers them" (Ps. 34:7 NIV). By reason of this protection over his saints arises the summons to test the graciousness of God. Tasting stands before seeing, for spiritual experience leads to spiritual perception. We cannot see the beauty of a stained-glass window if we remain outside the building. A sinner cannot know the grace, mercy, and peace of God if he or she stays outside of Christ in unbelief.

B. *This is the testimony of the believer.* This is not only the saint's challenge to the unbeliever, it is his or her testimony as well. The only true knowledge comes through experience. "Taste and see!" Jesus invited the two disciples who inquired where he was staying, "Come, and you will see" (John 1:39 NIV). When Nathanael would have raised questions about Philip's testimony, Philip didn't argue. He challenged him to make the pragmatic test, "Come and see" (v. 46). Come and see Christ for yourself. Come and see what he has done for others. Come and see what Christianity has done. Inquire, analyze, and look at what has been accomplished. It is no sin to inquire. It is the only way to know.

C. *This is the ultimate ground of assurance.* To "taste and see" is the only way we may know for ourselves. Try it. Experience the grace of God for yourself. Some would say, "First I must know, then I will do." Actually, the reverse is true. First you must do, then you will know. Christianity begins as an experiment; it ends as an experience.

Conclusion

Horatius Bonar gave his testimony of his experience with Christ in a beautiful hymn, "I Heard the Voice of Jesus Say." The second stanza and chorus go like this:

I heard the voice of Jesus say,
"Behold, I freely give
The living water; thirsty one,
Stoop down and drink, and live."

I came to Jesus and I drank
Of that life-giving stream;

My thirst was quenched, my soul revived,
And now I live in him.

Wednesday Evening, August 20

Title: What Is Life All About Anyway?
Text: "Thus all the days of Methuselah were nine hundred and sixty-nine years; and he died" **(Gen. 5:27 RSV)**.
Scripture Reading: Genesis 5:25–27

Introduction

Scholars have come up with many fanciful ideas about the two genealogies of Adam's descendants. One thing, however, seems evident as we study them: The world was quickly divided into two groups—those who viewed life only in terms of the material and those who saw spiritual meaning in it.

Slightly past the middle of Seth's genealogy a man comes on the scene about whom we wish we knew more. He lived so long that a longer earthly existence is attributed to him than to any other person. Methuselah remains a mystery. What did he do for such an extended period of time? Was he good or bad? Aggressive or passive? Intelligent or stupid? A builder or a wrecker? A part of the problem or a part of the solution? His life serves as a basis for us to inquire as to the meaning of our own lives. What are we here for and how can we best use the days God has given us?

I. This was a real world.

Although the first eleven chapters of Genesis are clouded in mystery and subject to various interpretations, the people did live in a time of historical factuality. We have no reason to discount the integrity of these biblical accounts. Someone had to be first; and to call these stories parables, myths, or allegories does not solve any problems but rather raises greater ones.

What about the ages? Thoughtful, mature students are giving careful consideration to the early chapters of Genesis. No good reason can be found for refusing to allow the people life spans of several hundred years. The world was new. Iniquity had not contaminated the land. Environments had not become polluted. Common sense says, "Take these years literally. There may be some minor problems if you do, but there are major, almost insuperable, problems if you do otherwise."

II. Length does not necessarily mean depth.

Methuselah lived a long time, but what did he do? Did he talk with God? Did he help his neighbors? Did he invent anything worthwhile to assist humanity? Did he write any good books? Did he alleviate anyone's suffering? Did he champion the cause of anyone who was mistreated? If so, would not the writer have told us about it?

III. The final and universal truth.

The last words recorded about Methuselah are the same as those concerning everyone in Seth's genealogy except Enoch. The "and he died" reminds us sharply that we too will someday "go the way of all flesh." In one country in a generation gone by, the craftsmen began working on the king's coffin the day he was installed as monarch of the land. Why? To remind him that he was only mortal and would someday be called on to surrender the reins of leadership to another person. If we are tempted to be cruel and overbearing, we need to remember that death is the "great leveler" that equalizes us. Dr. Elisabeth Kübler-Ross reflects on a vital lesson that death teaches. She says it is "the denial of death that is partially responsible for people living empty, purposeless lives; for when you live as if you'll live forever, it becomes too easy to postpone the things you know you must do."

Conclusion

On the tombstone of a famous entertainer is written, "He could make the whole world laugh"; but nearby on Fanny Crosby's marker we read, "For to me to live is Christ." That's what life is all about!

SUNDAY MORNING, AUGUST 24

Title: Your Role in Proclamation
Text: "Pray ye therefore the Lord of the harvest, that he will send forth labourers into his harvest" **(Matt. 9:38)**.
Scripture Reading: Matthew 9:36–10:1
Hymns: "Throw Out the Lifeline," Ufford
"Let the Lower Lights Be Burning," Bliss
"Seal Us, O Holy Spirit," Meredith
Offertory Prayer: Heavenly Father, we pray that you will send forth laborers into the harvest. As you send us, we shall gladly go. As you call our children, we dedicate them to your service. As you use a portion of the material goods committed to us, we give it freely. In loving response for every good and perfect gift that you have sent our way, we offer our prayers, our gifts, and ourselves today. In our Lord's name we pray. Amen.

Introduction

The gospel message may be indelibly inscribed on your mind. You may have a keen awareness of the needs that surround you and know well the New

Testament plan for proclamation. But until you become involved in personal proclamation, all of your knowledge is of no avail. You stand beneath the stern judgment of God—knowing the truth but not sharing it.

Eight out of ten experiences of our Lord as recorded by John are experiences with individuals. One by one he witnessed, made plain the way of salvation, and urged people to follow him.

The modern church has tended to emphasize mass evangelism to the neglect of this simple and personal New Testament approach. Time has now forced the church either to return to the dominant New Testament method of proclamation or to abandon any serious hopes of winning numbers of people to Christ.

I. Your role in proclamation calls for compassion.

"But when he saw the multitudes, he was moved with compassion on them, because they fainted, and were scattered abroad, as sheep having no shepherd" (Matt. 9:36).

A. *Because of distress, your role calls for compassion.* Those whom Jesus saw were distressed, harassed, and worried. The normal reaction when one sees a multitude is wonder and awe, but not so with Christ. His was one of pity and compassion. He saw the wolf as well as the sheep, Satan as well as humans.
   1. Sin gives birth to distress. Cain was distressed because of sin. The rich young ruler went away "sorrowfully" because of sin.
   2. Distress develops mental agony. "And the king was much moved, and went up to the chamber over the gate, and wept: and as he went, thus he said, O my son Absalom, my son, my son Absalom! would God I had died for thee, O Absalom, my son, my son!" (2 Sam. 18:33).
   3. Distress, if unchecked by the grace and power of Christ, ends in frustration. Many who have not known the healing power of the Lord have succumbed to the cynical philosophy of life expressed in Ecclesiastes 12:8: "Vanity of vanities, . . . all is vanity."

B. *Because of instability, your role calls for compassion.* The multitudes today are as "scattered" as they were when Christ looked upon them. This word means "thrown or tossed about."
   1. False teachings encourage much of the instability that plagues people (Eph. 4:14). The Jews heard every kind of doctrine. They did not know which way to turn, and this brought compassion to the heart of Christ, and so it should to us.
   2. Spiritual and emotional instability expresses itself in endless pursuits. Sometimes it is the pursuit of physical pleasure. "Wherefore do ye spend money for that which is not bread? and your labour for that which satisfieth not?" (Isa. 55:2). Others pursue

intellectual satisfaction, "ever learning, and never able to come to the knowledge of the truth" (2 Tim. 3:7).

A statesman told of his youthful ambition to become a U.S. senator. After years of hard work and waiting, his state sent him to Congress. He entered with fear and trembling, so awesome was his responsibility. He soon began to wonder how many of the others had been elected. They seemed to care so little for their people and even less for their place of service. He had attained his goal, but now it seemed dull and commonplace.

II. Your role in proclamation urges immediate action.

"Then saith he unto his disciples, The harvest truly is plenteous, but the labourers are few" (Matt. 9:37). Christ is saying, "There is much to be done but few to do it. Whatever we are to do, we must do it now!"

A. *Your role in proclamation urges immediate action because of the scarcity of laborers—"the labourers are few."*
   1. The scarcity of laborers is accentuated by the multitudes to be won. A pastor asked twenty-nine adults on the street in a town in Missouri how a person is saved, and only seven could answer!
   2. The scarcity of laborers can be solved by prayer. "Pray ye therefore the Lord of the harvest, that he will send forth labourers into his harvest" (Matt. 9:38). Such prayer will not only call others forth, but it will thrust you forth into the fields as well.

B. *Your role in proclamation urges immediate action because of the urgency of the hour.* In John's account Christ says, "Lift up your eyes, and look on the fields; for they are white *already* to harvest" (John 4:35b, emphasis mine). In four months (April) the fields would be ripe for harvest. To wait beyond then to harvest would be to lose most of the crop. The harvest of souls cannot wait either.
   1. The urgency of the hour is emphasized by the numbers already dying without Christ. Many are characterized by Jeremiah 8:20: "The harvest is past, the summer is ended, and we are not saved." How many who died in your town last year, died without Christ? And how many of these did you even try to tell about Christ?
   2. The urgency of the hour is seen in the brevity of our lives. "For what is your life? It is even a vapour, that appeareth for a little time, and then vanisheth away" (James 4:14b).
   3. The urgency of the hour is heightened by the imminence of Christ's return (Matt. 24:42).

C. *Your role in proclamation urges immediate action because of the tragedy of a lost soul.* "The rich man also died, and was buried; And in hell he lift up his eyes, being in torments" (Luke 16:22b–23a). The tragedy of a lost soul is the hopelessness of his condition. Between the saved and the lost, between heaven and hell there is "a great gulf fixed" (Luke 16:26).

III. Your role in proclamation requires an empowering.

"And when he had called unto him his twelve disciples, he gave them *power* against unclean spirits" (Matt. 10:1a, emphasis mine).

A. *Because of the futility of human effort, your role in proclamation requires an empowering.* This truth is dramatically illustrated in the powerless disciples at the foot of the mountain on which Christ was transfigured. In the face of human need they had no power to meet that need because, as Christ pointed out, they had neglected their own spiritual lives (Mark 9:28–29).

   1. Human effort is no match for Satan's powers, "for we wrestle not against flesh and blood" (Eph. 6:12a).
   2. The futility of human effort is transformed when divinely empowered. The same men who were powerless at the Mount of Transfiguration became men of great spiritual power and healed "all manner of disease" (Matt. 10:1). Why? Because of the transforming power of God.
   3. The futility of our human effort keeps us mindful of our dependence on Christ. "But we have this treasure in earthen vessels, that the excellency of the power may be of God, and not of us" (2 Cor. 4:7).

B. *Because of the magnitude of the task, your role demands an empowering.* Matthew 9:37b reminds us that "the harvest is plenteous." Only a supernatural empowering can prepare us for such an overwhelming task.

   1. There is the magnitude of the souls to be won (Matt. 7:13b).
   2. There is the magnitude of the time to be spent. "Then said I, Lord, how long? And he answered, Until the cities be wasted without inhabitant, and the houses without man, and the land be utterly desolate" (Isa. 6:11).
   3. There is the magnitude of the effort to be expended. Christ tells us to "go out into the highways and hedges, and *compel* them to come in, that my house may be filled" (Luke 14:23b, emphasis mine).

C. *Because of the miraculousness of salvation, you need an empowering.* The disciples in Matthew 10:1 were sent out to perform miraculous deeds and thus needed a miraculous empowering.

Conclusion

Only you can fill your role in proclamation—not your pastor and not your Christian friends. You play the major role in the eternal welfare of certain souls. By the grace of God, in the power of God, and for the sake of God, play your role as a real child of God!

Sunday Evening, August 24

Title: A Plea for Patience
Text: "Wait on the Lord, and keep his way, and he shall exalt thee to inherit the land" **(Ps. 37:34)**.
Scripture Reading: Psalm 37:1–11, 25–40

Introduction

"Wait on the Lord" is the theme of this psalm. In verse 7 the psalmist says, "Rest in the Lord, and wait patiently for him."

"Wait," he says. The hardest, most tedious, most exacting, and sometimes the most exasperating work in the world is waiting. But waiting on the Lord has its rewards. The bitterest waiting in the world is that which is in vain. But waiting on the Lord is never in vain; we have his word on it (v. 34). If we need anything today, it is patience—patience to wait on God.

I. What is meant by "waiting on the Lord"?

A. *Negatively, some things are not meant.*
   1. This does not mean letting the Lord wait on us.
   2. This does not mean that we are to be idle. Millions are waiting for a better world, a warless world, a crimeless world.

B. *Positively, certain elements are involved in waiting on the Lord.*
   1. We must have the ability to endure until God's time comes. Some people do not wait on anything. Like a firecracker with a short fuse, they can't wait.
   2. We must submit to God's plan. In the prophecy of Habakkuk, we find these sublime words: "O Lord, revive thy work" (3:2). When? In the prophet's own time? No! In the next generation? No! In God's own good time.

      All Christians should pray for revival. Do we have the grace to pray Habakkuk's prayer?
   3. We must have the faith to believe that God has a plan and that he is working it out. If we have faith in God's way, his purposes, and his promises, we can wait.

II. Why should we wait on the Lord?

A. *Because, unless we do, we will find ourselves out of step with God, out of harmony with his will.* The prophet Jonah ran in three directions: he ran away from God, he ran with God, and he ran ahead of God. To his disappointment the revival in Nineveh was a success. From the highest to the lowest, everyone repented. From a safe vantage point, Jonah waited to watch Nineveh be destroyed. When it wasn't destroyed, he became angry. God rebuked him sharply. Jonah had run ahead of God.

We do that as well! We make our plans, plunge in, and then implore the Lord to bless *our* plans with success instead of first seeking his will that we might work his purposes.

B. *Because, unless we do, we will defeat ourselves by our own impatience.* If the sin of being dilatory has slain its thousands, the sin of impatience has slain its tens of thousands. Some have thought to analyze the motives of Judas Iscariot in betraying his Master by suggesting that Judas was impatient and thought Jesus' methods too slow, that he hoped by his act to precipitate a crisis that would force Jesus to use his great power.

C. *Because only he can bring it to pass.* Great purposes in this world, great programs of righteousness, great revivals of religion are not carried out ahead of God nor apart from God, but by his power. The words of the prophet Zechariah are both a warning and a prod to courage: "Not by might, nor by power, but by my spirit, saith the LORD of hosts" (4:6).

Before Pentecost the disciples had a commission to carry out, a program to carry on, and a Lord to proclaim. But they also had a command to obey: "Tarry ye in the city, until ye be clothed with power from on high" (Luke 24:49 ASV). Jesus was saying, "Wait! Wait on the Lord!" and they did. How glorious was the result!

III. What are the rewards for waiting on the Lord?

The great saints of all the ages have been those who had the grace, the faith, and the patience to wait on the Lord.

What rewards may we expect? Psalm 37 names three.

A. *Provision.* The simplest comes first. Provision is necessary. It has been promised. The psalmist says, "I have been young, and now am old; yet have I not seen the righteous forsaken, nor his seed begging bread" (v. 25). Verse 9 tells us, "Those that wait upon the LORD, they shall inherit the earth."

B. *Protection.* This is hard to believe sometimes, but the psalmist says, "Depart from evil, and do good; and dwell for evermore. For the LORD loveth judgment, and forsaketh not his saints; they are preserved for ever" (vv. 27–28).

C. *Perfection.* This may be better stated as "maturity." The psalmist begins his benediction by saying, "Mark the perfect man, and behold the upright: for the end of that man is peace" (v. 37).

Conclusion

May God give us the grace and the faith to wait on him and, until he acts, to do the best we know for him.

WEDNESDAY EVENING, AUGUST 27

Title: Even God Gets Tired!
Text: "The LORD was sorry that he had made man on the earth, and it grieved him to his heart" **(Gen. 6:6 RSV)**.
Scripture Reading: Genesis 6:5–8

Introduction

Iniquity infects faster than purity heals! Man, like an idle swimmer, drifts with the tide and carelessly floats down the stream of moral perversity far more often than he exerts himself to swim against the current and reach the safe shore. We start sinning early and never stop as long as we live. When society is thrown together closely and becomes a compact unit quickly, we find iniquity easily amplified!

I. Each "not" to his own.

A strange phenomenon developed, which grew to be a serious problem as the race multiplied. The "sons of God" and the "daughters of men" intermarried. Although several interpretations have been offered; and, with proper respect to all of them, the most likely meaning is that the wicked people of Cain's descendants became companions of the righteous (or at least not quite so wicked) descendants from Seth's genealogy. In other words, the "to each his own" did not hold up. Godly and ungodly people sought to forget religious differences in an attempt to "grow their lives together." Tragedy always comes when this happens.

II. God surveyed the situation.

Even a patient God becomes weary! How many years it took the world to get so immersed in iniquity that God decided to "take inventory," we cannot tell. Nor are we to suppose that he did not notice the increasing depravity along the way. Surely, at every stage of downward development, his heart broke, but he did not act until the situation was hopeless!

III. Why did he do it?

The gravity of the matter is made apparent by the severity with which God resolved it. Sin so predominated that only an extreme measure could cope with the situation. Corruption engulfed the world so completely that God could foresee no prospect of change in attitude on the part of humankind.

What is meant by the expression "the LORD repented"? We should realize the writer used an inadequate human term for a perfect and entirely good divine action. Does this mean God was sorry he had made the world? Of course not! This would imply a lack of foreknowledge on his part. Rather, he was grieved at the way things had turned out! The Hebrew writers were often graphic in their expressions; and even though inspired of God, they spoke with terms that they did not intend to be taken literally.

What will he do? Start over! The "land of beginning again" always holds hope for the future. The statement "My Spirit shall not always strive with man" (v. 3) was meant to impress man with how serious the issues were. The "hundred and twenty years" may have meant, as some claim, that inhabitants after the deluge would be limited to that number in their life span; but it probably refers to the total number of years he would allow his preacher, Noah, to proclaim a "gospel of grace." Even when God's patience wears thin, he stretches the limit as far as possible.

Conclusion

Not "Why did I do it?" but "What will I do about it?" is the important question concerning sin in our own lives. God always gives people time to amend their ways, but if they do not, judgment must come. As it was in the days of Noah, so today, and it always shall be!

SUNDAY MORNING, AUGUST 31

Title: Grace to Serve
Text: "I can do all things through Christ which strengtheneth me" **(Phil. 4:13)**.
Scripture Reading: Philippians 4:1–13
Hymns: "I Surrender All," Van deVenter
"I'll Go Where You Want Me to Go," Brown
"Take My Life and Let It Be," Havergal
Offertory Prayer: Almighty God, our Father, fountain of wisdom and inspirer of people, we thank you for making available to us a sufficiency of grace to save, sustain, school, and serve. We also thank you that through the presentation of our gifts and your blessing on them, we can participate in proclaiming the gospel, introducing people to Christ, and rendering ministries of mercy to those in need. Help us to know the blessedness of giving generously and cheerfully through Christ, in whose name we pray. Amen.

Introduction

God's grace is the most profound subject of divine revelation and that which is beyond the ability of the natural person to comprehend. The "God of all grace" makes full and free provision of salvation, sustenance, and schooling for those who will receive.

I. The purpose of this grace.

Grace is intended to make us disciples of and workers for Christ. We have been saved that we might serve the Lord Jesus. Are you exerting an aggressive influence toward the overthrow of Satan's kingdom, doing something to limit the reign of sin and to increase the number of Christ's followers? If so, one great purpose of this grace is being accomplished. If not, the grace of God has been bestowed on you in vain. When Paul urged his readers not to receive the grace of God in vain, he intimated that grace is intended to effect some worthy ends closely related to the Lord, ourselves, and others.

The one great purpose of this grace, which includes all others, is "that [we] may with one mind and one mouth glorify God, even the Father of our Lord Jesus Christ" (Rom. 15:6). The supreme purpose for which grace is given is that by it we may glorify God (Matt. 5:16; 2 Thess. 1:11–12). By the tone of our tempers and the tenor of our lives, we are to honor God's grace and make manifest his glory: "Whether therefore ye eat, or drink, or whatsoever ye do, do all to the glory of God" (1 Cor. 10:31). God proposes to show the world through you what his grace can do, in order that others may see the workmanship and honor the Workman.

Christians are saved so that they may work for the Lord. Never yet was a soul bought with the blood of Christ and regenerated by the Spirit of God to whom there was not given a work to do. Many church members are not disposed to do any work for the Lord. They think that there is not any work in the church in which they can use their God-given talents, time, money, or influence. Nevertheless, some spiritual work is required of every Christian. By prayer, Bible study, and watching for opportunities, we are to do more than attend worship services occasionally. We are to give time and labor for Christ and others, thereby leaving on our generation some mark for good, something that will enable Christ to say at the Judgment, "Well done, good and faithful servant."

II. The power of this grace.

The grace of God transformed Paul from a lost sinner into a child of God, from a servant of Satan into a saint of God, from a persecutor of Christians into an apostle of Christ, and from a busy person into a fruitful Christian. God's grace created within Paul the desire to serve the Lord and made his efforts fruitful.

Only the grace of God can make an effective worker out of an individual. Paul said, "I thank Jesus Christ our Lord, who hath enabled me, for that he counted me faithful, putting me into the ministry" (1 Tim. 1:12). Paul had been empowered by divine grace for a great life of Christian service. Standing at the height of his glorious career as a servant of Christ, Paul cried out, "By the grace of God I am what I am" (1 Cor. 15:10). It was the grace of God that had enabled him to do the work that he had done for the Lord.

By grace people are selected to serve God in special ways. Concerning the selection of the disciples and calling them to service, Christ said, "Ye have not chosen me, but I have chosen you, and ordained you, that ye should go and bring forth fruit" (John 15:16). Paul had this consciousness of having been selected by grace when he was called to be an apostle (1 Cor. 15:10). It was by grace that he had been saved, selected, sustained, and schooled; and it was also by grace that he had been made effectual in service. We may wonder at the abundance of his labors and their fruitfulness, but the secret of these things was the enabling grace of God.

To meet our Lord's expectation of walking habitually in good works, we need to be made "strong in the grace that is in Christ Jesus." Let us ask God to make us what we ought to be and to give us sufficient grace to do what needs to be done in Christian service.

In the sunset hour of his life, during his imprisonment in Rome, and while awaiting a violent death, Paul wrote, "I can do all things through Christ who keeps on pouring his power into me" (Phil. 4:13, my translation). He had found his way to the source of inexhaustible power. Paul had tried Christ under all conditions and circumstances of life and had found him equal to every emergency. He jubilantly testified to the measureless resources within the realm of absolute reliance on Christ. Paul did not hesitate to acknowledge that the ability to live contentedly, victoriously, and usefully came from the Lord. As long as Christ kept on pouring his power into Paul, the apostle had adequate strength for every need. Christ is the source of all power for victorious living and acceptable service. With peace in his soul and valor in his spirit, Paul was able to do all things that the Lord commanded him, because Christ continued to pour his strength into him just when and as he needed it. To us also Christ administers his undiminished strength in proportion to our needs.

Conclusion

A lesson of paramount importance for us is that we cannot do anything of ourselves but that through God's wondrous grace we can obtain sufficient strength to render the service the Lord requires of us. God's grace is sufficient to enable us to do the will of our Lord, performing to his glory the assignments with which he has entrusted us.

> Grace is flowing from Calvary,
> Grace as fathomless as the sea,
> Grace for time and eternity,
> Grace enough for me.

Sunday Evening, August 31

Title: An Ancient Saint's Experience with Doubt

Text: "But I had nearly lost confidence; my faith was almost gone because I was jealous of the proud when I saw that things go well for the wicked" **(Ps. 73:2–3 version unknown)**.

Scripture Reading: Psalm 73

Introduction

This psalm along with Psalms 37 and 49 form a trilogy, for all three deal with the problem of reconciling God's moral government with observable facts. How can an all-powerful God be good and yet allow the wicked to prosper and the righteous to go unrewarded?

Beyond doubt, Psalm 73 is autobiographical, giving evidence that faith had had a fight and won. Remarkably, this experience of doubt had come to one who appeared to stand closest to God, Asaph, a priest or teacher of the wisdom school.

Doubt plays a larger part in our lives than we would like to admit. But as Psalm 73 shows, it can have a beneficial effect if it becomes the means to a good end. Doubt can have true value in our lives if it clears away rubbish and stimulates the search for truth; but it is of no value unless it is finally swallowed up in assurance.

The psalmist here reveals four things about his experience:

I. The depth of his doubt.

A. *He had almost lost his footing in the matter of his faith.* The disparity between belief and reality led the psalmist to doubt his faith and to call into question the goodness of God (v. 2).

B. *He had almost concluded that righteousness is in vain.* It goes unrewarded, and the righteous suffer untold hardships (vv. 13–14). If this is so, how can God be good?

C. *He had reached the depths of self-pity (v. 14).* Self-pity tends to exaggerate. It feeds on itself. It weakens the fabric of faith and is the mark of spiritual immaturity. Self-pity and spiritual growth move in opposite directions.

D. *Religiously, he had sunk to the level of a beast (v. 22).* Literally he is saying, "So soured, so embittered was I and without understanding, I was as a plump colossus of flesh before thee." This surely means the hippopotamus, an emblem of colossal stupidity, says Delitzsch. When a person is nearest God, he or she is most full of self-loathing.

II. The sources of his doubt.

Doubt may be devil-born or it may be the growing pains to fuller truth. What were the sources of the psalmist's doubts?

A. *His superficial observation.* He confesses that he was envious of the wicked; and he tells us why (vv. 3–11). The wicked prosper (v. 3). They live a prosperous life and "there are no pangs in their death" (vv. 3–4 ASV). They are free of pain and trouble (v. 5). They are filled with pride, and injustice and cruelty seem to be their very clothing (v. 6). Their bodies are fat and bulge with luxurious living (v. 7). They mock at the threat of divine judgment (vv. 8–11).

But the psalmist's observations are superficial, for actual experience doesn't bear them out. The psalmist doesn't see the whole picture.

B. *His tendency to generalize from only a few examples (v. 12).* What human failing is more prevalent than this? If we try to be true to God and suffer heartbreak and misfortune, while it appears that the godless prosper and are free from suffering, we ought not to generalize.

C. *His inability, his failure, to see through to the end.* Looking back, the psalmist admitted his failure to reconcile God's ways and the seeming good fortune of the wicked "until I went into the sanctuary of God; then understood I their end" (v. 17). Might it not be that for the people of God apparent failure and suffering are God's disciplinary processes, which have for their end conformity to God's will?

III. The antidote for his doubt.

This psalmist went down into the depths. He passed through the fire. Yet he ended on a high plane of faith. What saw him through?

A. *His concern not to injure the faith of others (v. 15).* If his first reaction was to use his teaching office to tell his doubts to others, he was dissuaded from this by his concern for others.

B. *His realization that he was a man and not God (v. 16).* There are some problems the human intellect cannot solve. God's moral government of this universe is a matter too weighty for man's weak powers. The subject was above the psalmist's reach.

C. *His experience with God in the sanctuary (vv. 16–17).* The biblical way of facing problems is to take them into the presence of God. The prophet Habakkuk faced essentially the same problem, as he saw the wicked swallowing up a man more righteous than he (Hab. 1:13). How did he solve his problem? He sought God's presence (2:1). Neither Habakkuk nor the psalmist checked his brains at the door.

D. *His God-given grace to take the long look and to see the wicked as God sees them.* When he did this, he saw: (1) that the wicked are the ones in slippery places, not the saints (v. 18); (2) that the law of retribution does work for the wicked here and now (vv. 18–19); (3) that God does despise sin and all its works (v. 20); and (4) that the ultimate end of the godless is their destruction (v. 27).

IV. The joy of a mature faith.

A mature faith is one that has come out of the fire, a faith that God can give only to those who have brought their doubts and problems to him. Examples of this are the prophet Jeremiah in the Old Testament and John the Baptist in the New. As a result of his experience, this psalmist came to:

A. *The realization of God's abiding presence.* Out of the clouds of doubt his soul now came into the sunlight of glad certainty (v. 23).
B. *The assurance of God's counsel and the hope of eternal life (v. 24).*
C. *The reality of his relationship with God (v. 25).* For the psalmist, all the heaven he wanted was God. Is this not true of the New Testament saint also (John 14:3)?
D. *The security and refuge of God's unfailing strength (v. 26).* He shared this secret with another psalmist, who said, "God is our refuge and strength, a very present help in trouble" (46:1).

Conclusion

The psalmist's final benediction is this: "But it is good for me to draw near to God: I have put my trust in the Lord God, that I may declare all thy works" (73:28).

Suggested Preaching Program for the Month of
September

■ Sunday Mornings

"Standing Up to the Storms of Life," based on the Beatitudes as found in Jesus' "Sermon on the Plain" in Luke, is the theme for the September and October sermons. These messages challenge disciples of our Lord to be disciples indeed.

■ Sunday Evenings

Continue and complete the series "Wise Men of the Past Speak to the Present."

■ Wednesday Evenings

Genesis 1–11 is a profound section of the Holy Scriptures in which God was dealing with humanity prior to his choice of Abraham as the father of the faithful. God was both merciful and just at that time, and he continues to be merciful and just today. Conclude this series this month.

Wednesday Evening, September 3

Title: You Don't Have to Go with the Crowd
Text: "But Noah found favor in the eyes of the Lord" **(Gen. 6:8 RSV)**.
Scripture Reading: Genesis 6:5–9

Introduction

Whether the flood in the days of Noah covered the whole earth or was confined merely to the populated area is subordinate to the message it has for us today. The moral rather than the physical aspects of the story should excite our interest.

How quickly society degenerates when it takes the road of self-indulgence! In Noah's day wickedness engulfed the earth; and God not only became "tired of it all," he grew infuriated at the arrogant way humankind ignored his commands and flaunted his precepts. What a lesson for us today!

I. Unholy marital alliances.

Whenever ungodliness abounds in a society, the cause lies, to a large extent, in the lack of stable home life. When one is happy with his companion, he has no need to find thrills in illicit relationships. Mutual satisfaction in this area can come only when partners help each other physically, emotionally, and most of all spiritually. When the "sons of God" allowed their eyes to roam and became attracted to the "daughters of men," trouble began.

II. Sin produces strange things.

Because of sin God reacted in an unusual way. The text says, "God saw that the wickedness of man was great in the earth, and . . . it repented the LORD that he had made man on the earth, and it grieved him at his heart" (Gen. 6:5–6). Does God repent? Not in the sense that humans do!

God certainly did not admit that he had made any mistake or did anything wrong in creating man. He gave man a free will and realized this permitted the privilege of making a decision to sin. However, when it happened, God felt a deep spirit of regret, even though he, in his foreknowledge, knew from the beginning what man would do. This fact about God enhances his character. He has a free will himself and may change his mind. He acts toward people as they act toward him. This fact about God saves us from either despair or presumption. He changes his attitude as we change ours.

III. Some people stand out for God.

The words concerning Noah tower above all the descriptions of excesses that pervaded the land. The Bible says that Noah "found grace" in the Lord's eyes. We should remember that, no matter how bad things get, God always has someone "waiting in the wings" to carry on his work. When Elijah complained that everyone had forsaken the Lord, he was reminded that there were seven thousand who had not bowed their knees to Baal.

A young man attended a party, not knowing that alcoholic beverages would be served. He had been taught that total abstinence was right, but he wavered when he saw almost every person drinking. He determined he would watch one young woman, whom he respected, and do what she did. She smiled sweetly when a drink was offered to her, but without making a big scene, quietly refused. Later he married her and went on to become one of the great gospel songwriters of his day. Noah refused to take part in the sin of his day, and God used him to perpetuate the race.

Conclusion

Sometimes it costs a lot to stand unflinchingly for God; but to do so brings a rich reward, not only in the world to come, but also here on earth in personal satisfaction. We don't have to do what the crowd does! The only answer we can give to a world that despises us is a life that will not compromise. We must, however, do it in and with a spirit of love.

SUNDAY MORNING, SEPTEMBER 7

Title: Under the Rule of God

Text: "Looking at his disciples, he said: 'Blessed are you who are poor, for yours is the kingdom of God'" **(Luke 6:20 NIV)**.

Scripture Reading: Luke 6:20–26

Hymns: "Rejoice, the Lord Is King," Wesley
"I Love Thy Kingdom, Lord," Dwight
"Christ the Lord Is Risen Today," Wesley

Offertory Prayer: Holy Father, we thank you for this your church, which is also our church. We thank you for what this congregation of believers means to this community and to your work around the world. We come now, bringing tithes and offerings to express our gratitude for your goodness and our desire to see your kingdom come into the hearts and lives of people to the ends of the earth. Bless these gifts to that end, we pray. In Christ's name. Amen.

Introduction

Jesus' perspective on life is different. As the Lord of glory, he had a view of life that included both the heavenly and the earthly. As the Creator of life, he knew the essentials for life. His view of life is beautifully demonstrated in this great sermon—the Sermon on the Mount.

A clue to understanding these "beatitudes" and "woes" is found in the very first one. The "poor" are identified as the ones who have the "kingdom of God." The suggestion is that they actually possess the kingdom—the rule of God—in this present moment. While Jesus taught that there would be a future manifestation of the rule of God in a glorious fashion, he also taught that there are some who have already begun to experience the rule of God in their earthly lives.

Jesus opens his great sermon with these "beatitudes" and "woes" because they are essential in a life that will stand up to the stress of the storms of life.

The Beatitudes give us the conditions for coming under the rule of God. The "woes" give us the barriers to coming under the rule of God.

I. The conditions for coming under the rule of God.

The Beatitudes could also be called "conditions for entrance into the kingdom of God." To be in the kingdom is to be under the rule of the King of the kingdom. The things that our Lord pronounced "blessed" must have been as surprising to the first hearers as they are to us today. They go against everything the world has set up as being important.

A. *The King makes poverty a condition for coming under the rule of God.* "Blessed are you poor, for yours is the kingdom of God" (v. 20 RSV). In his account of the sermon, Matthew adds "in spirit" to "the poor." While poverty may make it easier for some individuals to realize their poverty of spirit, it does not in itself bring people under the rule of God. It is not uncommon to find rebellion and bitterness toward

God among the poor. Our Lord is speaking of an awareness of inner poverty that brings a person to God.

B. *The King makes hunger a condition for coming under the rule of God.* "Blessed are you that hunger now, for you shall be satisfied" (v. 21 RSV). Matthew's account says, "Blessed are those who hunger and thirst for righteousness" (5:6 NIV). This lets us know that our Lord meant more than physical hunger. Those who are to share in the riches of the kingdom must have an intense desire in that direction. They must desire to be right with God more than anything else in the world.

C. *The King makes weeping a condition for coming under the rule of God.* "Blessed are you who weep now, for you will laugh" (Luke 6:21 NIV). The word means to weep out loud, audibly. These are not just any tears but rather weeping that comes from sorrow over personal sin and the sin of others. Weeping is the outward expression of a "broken and contrite heart." The great joy of the kingdom comes to those who have sobbed their way into the presence of the great King of mercy.

D. *The King makes identification with himself a condition for coming under the rule of God.* "Blessed are you when men hate you, when they exclude you and insult you and reject your name as evil, because of the Son of Man. Rejoice in that day and leap for joy, because great is your reward in heaven. For that is how their fathers treated the prophets" (v. 22–23 NIV). "Because of the Son of Man" is the key phrase for understanding this beatitude. People do not come under the rule of God simply because they are cursed or mistreated by others. Rather, they come under the rule of God when they so fully identify themselves with the King of the kingdom that the world begins to treat them like they treat the King.

These four statements go together. Each is an essential condition for coming under the rule of God. As you consider them, it is not difficult to understand why so few seem to be seeking to come under God's rule. This will become even clearer as you align the conditions with the barriers to the kingdom as expressed in the "woes."

II. The barriers to coming under the rule of God.

The "woe" is not an announcement of judgment as much as an expression of sorrow and regret on the part of the King. He desires that all people come to know personally the reality of the kingdom.

A. *The King identifies riches as a barrier to the kingdom.* "But woe to you who are rich, for you have already received your comfort" (v. 24 NIV). Riches are not evil themselves, but they have the capacity to become a blockade in people's search for God. They have a way of becoming the object of their trust and the basis for their lives. They have a way of leading people to believe that they can live without God. They may begin to see God as a crutch needed only by the poor. Since almost all of us would fall into the classification of the "rich" in our world, we need to consider the word of our Lord very seriously.

B. *The King identifies worldly fullness as a barrier to the kingdom.* "Woe to you who are well fed now, for you will go hungry" (v. 25 NIV). This world does have the capacity to so fill people's lives that they begin to lose their sense of need and their hunger for God. This deadly satisfaction is a danger to you eternally!

C. *The King identifies worldly pleasure as a barrier to the kingdom.* "Woe to you who laugh now, for you will mourn and weep" (v. 25 NIV). Our Lord is referring to the laughter that grows out of the pleasure and entertainment of this world. So many who do not know God seem to spend their days having "fun." Their lives are filled with one pleasurable event after another. They ignore the fact that each individual is ultimately accountable to God. When one stands before the Judge of all the earth, he will be the only basis for joy. A life without him will not stand the storms.

D. *The King identifies the praise of men as a barrier to the kingdom.* "Woe to you when all men speak well of you, for that is how their fathers treated the false prophets" (v. 26 NIV). The approval of others is such a subtle thing. Almost unconsciously this can become the basis on which one decides his or her lifestyle.

Conclusion

Every person who has ever come under the rule of God has had to overcome these barriers and meet these conditions.

Are you ready to come under his rule?

SUNDAY EVENING, SEPTEMBER 7

Title: The Secrets and Certainties of Tomorrow

Text: "Do not boast about tomorrow, for you do not know what a day may bring forth" **(Prov. 27:1 NIV).**

Scripture Reading: Proverbs 27:1–10

Introduction

From the time King Saul went down to the cave of the witch of Endor until now, people who are desperate for certainty in the face of their fears for tomorrow have been the willing victims of soothsayers, fortune-tellers, spirit mediums, and their kind. It is a sad commentary on humankind that the elements of superstition, fear, curiosity, and insecurity are so strong within that these assorted "humbugs" are able to live by preying on others' weaknesses.

Why are people so gullible? Because they so earnestly desire to know the secrets of tomorrow. There are two things to consider.

I. The secrets of tomorrow.

The mistakes of yesterday and the confusion and tension of today are very real, but concerning tomorrow we must tread softly.

A. *What are tomorrow's secrets?*
   1. Will tomorrow bring prosperity or poverty? That secret is locked hard and fast in tomorrow's vault (James 4:13–14).
   2. Will tomorrow bring success or failure? Who can say? Sometimes we seem bound for success, and then some unconsidered factors enter in and we experience disappointment.
   3. Will tomorrow bring love, making two lives the mutual fulfillment and complement of one another? Or will tomorrow bring heartbreak, loneliness, and despair?
   4. Will tomorrow bring health with all its rosy hues of hope or sickness with its sufferings and handicaps?
   5. Will tomorrow bring joy or sorrow?
   6. Will tomorrow bring life or death?

B. *Since these unknown possibilities are real, with what attitude should we face tomorrow?*
   1. Some face an unknown tomorrow with the pagan attitude "Let us eat, drink, and be merry for tomorrow we die."
   2. Some face an unknown tomorrow with an attitude of utter futility. "What is the use?" they ask. And some even die by their own hand.
   3. Some face an unknown tomorrow with the only attitude that will see us through, that of Christian faith. Tomorrow is safe in the keeping of infinite love. Tomorrow is God's day.

II. The certainties of tomorrow.

A. *What, according to the Scriptures, are the certainties of tomorrow?*
   1. Tomorrow will bring its own light, its own revelation (Ps. 19:2; Prov. 3:6). We cannot see the end from the beginning; but when tomorrow comes, with it will come God's guidance.
   2. Tomorrow, if we have faith, will bring its material provisions. Jesus taught us this (Matt. 6:11). Do you know anyone whose experience contradicts that of the psalmist (Ps. 37:25)?
   3. Tomorrow will bring its own evil for the day (Matt. 6:34). But we can say with the psalmist, "I will fear no evil: for thou art with me" (Ps. 23:4).
   4. Tomorrow will bring its own strength for the day. "As thy days, so shall thy strength be" (Deut. 33:25).

5. Tomorrow will bring its own settlement of accounts. God may let them pass today, but he will settle with us tomorrow.
6. Tomorrow will bring Christ. Since the future is out of our control, we must trust God fully with it.

B. *As we consider these certainties of tomorrow, what ought to be the result in our lives?*

1. We ought to be receptive, responsive, and active today and every day. Jesus lived by this rule (John 9:4).
2. We ought to be warned.
3. We ought to be encouraged (1 Cor. 15:58).
4. We ought to be built up in our faith. Our God is a sovereign God. His ways are just; his laws are immutable. He will not fail.

Conclusion

God is gracious and merciful. He is a promise-keeping God. Upon those persons who today confess the error of their ways and repent, God will set his seal of pardon and will hold them secure tomorrow and on that endless tomorrow when all our tomorrows will have ceased in their cycles to reach out into endless day.

WEDNESDAY EVENING, SEPTEMBER 10

Title: When It's Too Late, It's Too Late!

Text: "They went into the ark with Noah, two and two of all flesh in which there was the breath of life. And they that entered, male and female of all flesh, went in as God had commanded him; and the LORD shut him in" **(Gen. 7:15–16 RSV)**.

Scripture Reading: Genesis 7:1–16

Introduction

The day of judgment always arrives! God is patient, for he wishes no one to perish, but he also comes to the point when he can't wait any longer for people to repent.

Beyond a doubt, Noah will remain forever as one of the greatest preachers who has ever lived. He saw the course that events were taking and, perceiving the inevitable consequences if those things continued, could not keep silent. With his heart overflowing, he became a "preacher of righteousness."

I. Sometimes we receive undeserved blessing.

We don't know if Noah's children were true believers like their father, but they did live according to his prophetic counsel. Perhaps they were just in the right place at the right time, and God, through his mercy, spared them in order to perpetuate the race.

We often receive a blessing from being in the right place at the right time. This is why we should be careful about what kind of schools we attend or to which we send our children. The friends we choose influence us for good or evil. Shem, Ham, and Japheth were in the household of Noah; and either directly or indirectly, deserved or undeserved, this allowed them to participate in the blessing of being delivered when the great day of judgment came to the earth. Thank God if you received the wise counsel of godly parents. Be sure you heed it!

II. God always provides redemption.

The one who made the world will never turn it over completely to the forces of evil! He didn't do it in Noah's day, and he is not going to do it in our generation. Those who believe in God and commit themselves to his requirements will find security when the day of judgment arrives.

III. Someday opportunity will pass.

One of the most significant verses in the entire flood story says, "And they that went in, went in male and female of all flesh, as God had commanded him: and the LORD shut him in" (Gen. 7:16). A twofold emphasis may be seen. God, of course, protected Noah; but the verse also contains a warning to every unrepentant sinner who is in the process of turning down the call of God. The "shut door" excluded those who refused Noah's message and consigned them to a watery grave. There was no further opportunity! The door of mercy had remained open for 120 years. Then it was closed!

Theologians differ as to the "unpardonable sin." Some say it is a sin of the tongue, blasphemy against the Holy Spirit, as the Pharisees were doing in the New Testament account (Matt. 12:31–32). Others say it is one's continual rejection of the Holy Spirit's wooing until he has "sinned away his day of grace." One thing is certain: continual refusing will cause one to be condemned eternally as surely as if one had committed an "unpardonable sin." Even God cannot save a person until he or she repents. We can wait too long! R. A. Torrey told a moving story about a journalist who stayed in a burning building, sending out messages to the public about the fire. He remained too long, and his way of escape was cut off. He perished in the flames! How true in our spiritual life! We can live a sinful life too long, and judgment will come upon us.

Conclusion

As the evangelist put it many years ago, "Turn or burn!" When the door is closed, it's too late!

SUNDAY MORNING, SEPTEMBER 14

Title: Love Your Enemies

Text: "I say unto you which hear, Love your enemies, do good to them which hate you, bless them that curse you, and pray for them which despitefully use you" **(Luke 6:27–28)**.

Scripture Reading: Luke 6:27–35

Hymns: "Love Divine, All Loves Excelling," Wesley
"Love Is the Theme," Fisher
"Savior, Teach Me Day by Day," Leeson

Offertory Prayer: Heavenly Father, thank you for being so generous to us. Thank you for the abundance of your gifts to us day by day. We thank you supremely for the gift of your Son and for his gift of the Holy Spirit to us. Today we come bringing financial gifts as tokens of our desire to give ourselves completely to you and to the advancement of your kingdom's work on earth. Help us to see ourselves as laying up treasures in heaven as we come bringing tithes and offerings to you. In Christ's name. Amen.

Introduction

The only life that will stand the storms of life is one that is based on love. This is an insight given to us by the Lord of life himself. In this famous sermon Jesus makes love an essential for a storm-proof life.

Twice he repeats the admonition, "Love your enemies." It must have been a shock to those who first heard it. Their best spiritual leaders had been telling them to love their neighbors but to hate their enemies. Jesus extends the admonition of neighborly love to include even the unneighborly. He used the word for "love" that was used of God's love for sinful humans.

The world has not changed. This is still the kind of world in which even the most virtuous persons have enemies. Enmity against them may grow out of political differences, competition in the marketplace, moral differences, or even differences of religion. The enemy may be in your own household or almost a stranger. You and I are to respond to each of these enemies with a Christ-like love.

I. The object of our love.

Those who first heard the admonition must have immediately thought of the Romans. These conquerors of the land of Israel were considered to be enemies, therefore Jesus' admonition must have been thought almost immoral to some who first heard it. Our Lord does not leave us in doubt about the true nature of this person we are to love.

A. *Our Lord explains the admonition with the clauses that follow.* "Do good to those who hate you" (v. 27 NIV). Hate describes the enemies' basic attitude toward you. In their hearts they have deep, malicious feelings of disrespect for you.

B. *"Bless those who curse you"* (v. 28 NIV). To curse means to call doom down on the head of a person. It is the verbal attempt to do you harm. Such are the actions of the enemies we are to love.

C. *"Pray for those who mistreat you"* (v. 28 NIV). We are to pray for those who go beyond a hateful attitude and hateful words to hateful deeds. These are people who do more than speak hurtfully; they act harmfully.

II. The actions of love.

Part of our problem with this word from Jesus is rooted in our understanding of love. Love has become sentiment and emotion in our day. We sense the impossibility of having the same feelings for an enemy that we have for a member of our family. But this word used by our Lord does not refer to emotion or sentiment. It refers to action. It is the will to do a person good and not evil.

A. *The actions are selfless.* When you realize that someone hates you, your first natural reaction is to think of yourself. Jesus describes actions in which self-interests are set aside that the interest of the enemy may be considered. He admonishes, "Do good to those who hate you." This is translating the love—the desire to be helpful to the person—into some positive action. It could involve finding some need in the life of that person and then meeting that need.

"Bless those who curse you." The natural reaction is to defend yourself from hateful words and to seek to discredit the source of such words. Love will ignore self and seek to build up the enemy. Literally, it means to invoke a blessing on that person.

"Pray for those who mistreat you." This is what Jesus did. As his enemies were spitefully nailing him to the cross, he was praying, "Father, forgive them, for they do not know what they are doing" (v. 34 NIV).

B. *The actions are generous.* Our Lord presents us with several situations we might encounter at the hand of an enemy. In each he calls for a generous response on our part (see Luke 6:29–30).

Striking someone on the cheek is more than an insult; it is an act of violence. Such an act of violence is to be responded to with kindness and generosity. The person who takes away your cloak does so violently. He robs you of your personal possession. The generous thing to do is to give him even more than he asks. The principle is that love is generous.

Many who have spoken words of admiration for the Sermon on the Mount have never listened to it carefully. The world will call you a fool if you conduct your personal life by this principle, yet this is the life that will withstand the storm.

Love will find a way to do for the enemy what you would want done for yourself. Jesus is not calling for what is naturally done in the world of sinners, but what can only be done supernaturally by those who know the Lord.

III. The reward of our love.

"Your reward will be great, and you will be sons of the Most High, because he is kind to the ungrateful and wicked" (Luke 6:35 NIV). Pragmatically, it can be demonstrated that it is better to live by the principle of love than not to do so. Those who are committed to respond to every situation in love are able to withstand the storms of life more effectively. They experience joy and peace.

There is a reward in character—this is primary! "You will be sons of the Most High" means that you will be reflecting the character of God.

There is also a reward of fellowship. Sons have access to their father. To be a son of the Most High surely carries with it the privilege of fellowship with him.

Conclusion

This word of our Lord brings a deep sense of inadequacy to each of us. While we readily admit that this is what we should do, we also know our natural tendencies toward revenge and hate. We must remember that the one who spoke these words is able to make all things new. And admission to him of our weakness and an invitation to his strength could be the beginning of a life that will withstand the storms.

SUNDAY EVENING, SEPTEMBER 14

Title: The Eyes of the Lord

Text: "The eyes of the LORD are in every place, keeping watch on the evil and the good" **(Prov. 15:3 RSV)**.

Scripture Reading: Psalm 139:1–12; Proverbs 15:1–10

Introduction

Our text is relevant to each one of us. "The eyes of the LORD" are constantly on us. Why? This is true for six reasons.

I. To rebuke us for our wrongdoing.

We are tempted to sin. We fall, and God sees us. In the book of Job we read, "For his eyes are upon the ways of man, and he seeth all his goings" (34:21).

II. To shame us for our little doing.

How little we do for God! His eyes are on us:

A. *To shame us for our little giving.* How much do we give in proportion to the whole program of the church? For how many minutes would our gift pay the electric bill?

B. *To shame us for our little praying.* How many of us threw ourselves on a prayerless bed last night? How many of us have prayed each day this past week for some lost person?

C. *To shame us for our infrequent worship.* How careless and shameless we are about this. If the average pastor could write an eleventh commandment, it would go like this: "Six days thou shalt travel and visit all thy relatives and do all thy gadding about, but the first day of the week is 'the Lord's Day,' and in it thou shalt verily go to church, thou and thy wife and thy children and thy manservant and thy maidservant, and all who live in thy house."

D. *To shame us for our little working.* In days gone by, a church in Birmingham, Alabama, used to greet prospective new members with a series of questions: "What experience have you had as a worker in the church? What kind of job would you like in our church? This is a working church. Are you willing to work?"

III. To remind us of our vows before the Lord (Ps. 116:14, 18).

There are some things we have vowed before the Lord that we would not do and some things we vowed we would do. His eyes are upon us:

A. *To keep us back from sin.* One man tells of an experience he had at a track meet many years ago when he was in high school. He gave the cashier at the concession stand $1.00 in payment for an ice cream cone, and she gave him $4.50 in change. Realizing that she had mistaken his dollar for a five-dollar bill, he was tempted for a few seconds to keep the money, but the thought captured his mind, "What would my mother think?" He returned $4.00 to a grateful salesperson. But one with higher standards and with deeper loving concern than our mothers is watching us.

B. *To bring us to repentance.* Simon Peter made a vow to his Lord, "Even if I must die with thee, yet will I not deny thee" (Matt. 26:35 ASV). After Peter did deny the Lord, however, we are told, "The Lord turned, and looked upon Peter. And Peter remembered the word of the Lord" (Luke 22:61 ASV). Jesus' look in that hour broke Peter's heart.

IV. To instruct us in the ways and things of the Lord (Ps. 32:8).

Like a father watching his small son build a toy boat and giving a word of counsel when he can, God's eyes are upon us to instruct us. Our eyes are limited in their vision. God's eyes are not.

V. To assure us in time of danger or need.

How assuring to know that someone who can and will help us is watching over us at such a time. A small child thought it was a great feat to cross the street all by herself to where her grandmother lived. But her mother was watching from her front porch until the child was safely inside with her grandmother. God is watching over us. His eyes are upon us to assure us (Pss. 33:18–19; 34:15).

VI. To encourage us, to challenge us to do our best.

In 1933 the New York Giants were helped to the National League pennant and victory in the World Series by the pitching of Carl Hubbel. In late season, but before the pennant had been won, Carl's father died on a day he pitched and won. No one expected Carl to be back three days later to take his regular turn in the pitching rotation, but an hour before game time he appeared and suited up. He pitched one of the great games of his career that day. When asked how he could do it, he said, "As you know, my father was blind. I felt somehow that he saw me pitch for the first time today. I just couldn't let him down."

Conclusion

We must not let our heavenly Father down.

Wednesday Evening, September 17

Title: The God We Serve Loves Us
Text: "I set my bow in the cloud, and it shall be a sign of the covenant between me and the earth" **(Gen. 9:13 RSV)**.
Scripture Reading: Genesis 9:1–17

Introduction

The flood was over! Noah had sent out the raven; and being a scavenger, the raven flew back and forth, feasting on what it could find until the water was gone. The dove, who had been sent out three times, returned twice. He waited patiently until the water had abated sufficiently for his normal livelihood. Finally, the day came for Noah and his family to leave the ark. He brought the animals with him and, first of all, had a worship service to praise God for deliverance. Any experience with God is meaningful; but after passing through a great crisis, a personal encounter with our Maker is essential to get us "back on the road" to balanced living. Without a continuing fellowship with the Lord, we simply cannot cope with the problems that confront us as we move from one stage of life to another.

I. Things will continue normally.

God made it abundantly clear to Noah that the earth would continue its natural functions. He said, "While the earth remaineth, seedtime and harvest, and cold and heat, and summer and winter, and day and night shall not cease" (Gen. 8:22). Great security is ours because we know that the natural laws of the universe function with regularity. Fire is hot, water is wet, the law of gravity operates—these truths enable us to move forward with definite plans in everyday living. We know that predictable patterns exist, and we can count on darkness at night and light in the daytime. Since consistency prevails in the natural realm, God has every reason to expect us to function likewise in the spiritual areas of our lives. Life will go on with regularity until God decides to end it.

II. Moral laws work also.

Although we usually think of the prophets as declaring what will happen, a seminary professor years ago thrilled his class when he said, "Isaiah does not teach so much that sin *will* be punished as he does that sin *must* be punished." Why? Because God is holy and has established the universe in such a way that right will triumph eventually because it is the expression of his character. We do not break God's laws, but we break ourselves on them. They still stand, but we fail.

If you were to jump out of a window on the tenth floor, you would not break the law of gravity. Rather, you would only demonstrate it when you hit the ground below. It is the same with God's moral principles. We do not break them. They "break us" if we violate them.

Live according to God's standards and eventually things will work out well. Ignore his precepts and you will pay a terrible price. These laws work out in this life before eternity, as we call it, begins.

III. A rainbow for the clouds.

The God we serve loves us! No greater proof can be found for this fact than the "rainbows" he sends from time to time. Many scholars believe the flood was the first time rain fell on the ground. Previously, "there went up a mist from the earth, and watered the whole face of the ground" (Gen. 2:6). If so, this "first rainbow" was adopted by God as a sign of his mercy. After every storm, a rainbow comes to remind us that, though God must send judgment, he is still a God who loves us and will continue to work with us and for us!

Conclusion

With so many things happening in this world to upset us and cause the future to seem uncertain, we need to fortify ourselves often with God's promises. He sends a rainbow of assurance for every doubt, a rainbow of forgiveness for every sin, a rainbow of faith for every fear, and a rainbow of comfort for every sorrow. God does not explain why the clouds gather and drop their gloom on us. He does, however, in his own infinite way, take all the adversities of life and make them work out for our good and his glory. When we see the rainbows of life, they tell us that God wants us to serve him in love and find joy in knowing that he will "never, no never, no never forsake us"!

SUNDAY MORNING, SEPTEMBER 21

Title: Be Merciful
Text: "Be merciful, just as your Father is merciful" **(Luke 6:36 NIV)**.
Scripture Reading: Luke 6:36–38
Hymns: "Jesus, Lover of My Soul," Wesley
"There's a Wideness in God's Mercy," Faber
"When I Survey the Wondrous Cross," Watts
Offertory Prayer: Heavenly Father, because you have been so gracious and good to us, we come today offering not only our substance but also our time and talents and energies into your service. Accept these gifts as tokens of our love and as indications of our desire that others come to know your grace and mercy. Bless them to that end we pray. In Jesus' name. Amen.

Introduction

You were created to be like God. You are to reflect the moral image of God in your character. This was basic in the teaching of Jesus our Lord. He states this plainly in our text: "Be merciful, just as your Father is merciful" (Luke 6:36 NIV).

This is another of those basic ingredients that must be in a life if it is to withstand the storms that come to test it. What did our Lord mean by this word *merciful*? The word could be translated "compassionate." It means to be sympathetic with another person, to grieve and sorrow with him or her, to be responsive to a need that is seen in his or her life.

In connection with this admonition, Jesus makes three other admonitions. Each of them brings before us situations in which we need to practice mercy.

I. We must be merciful with the faults of others.

"Do not judge, and you will not be judged. Do not condemn, and you will not be condemned" (v. 37 NIV). These two admonitions go together, comprising the one admonition to be merciful with the faults and shortcomings of others.

A. *Exegesis.* "Judge" could be translated "criticize." Our word *criticize* comes from the Greek word that is translated here "judge." It means to express a censorious spirit, to be critical of others, to judge them. "Condemn" comes after judging. It means to pass sentence, to assign a penalty. It is acting on the judgment one has formed.

Ultimately, to "judge" and "condemn" are the work of God alone. He alone has the knowledge necessary to make judgments and pass sentences.

B. *Application.* Everyone we will meet in life will have some flaw. All of us have sinned and continue to come short of God's ideal for our lives. Every one of us is in great need of the mercy of God. We need for God to be patient and sympathetic with our flaws, failures, and shortcomings.

Jesus gave a parable about the man who received God's mercy but was unwilling to extend mercy to his fellow man. In the end God withdrew his mercy and turned him over to the tormentors to collect all that he owed.

Yet how many of us are guilty of relating to other people as though we are morally superior, as though we are their judges? Parents can fall into this error in relating to their children. Marriage partners can tear a marriage apart by living this way. Many churches have been destroyed by people who did not know the meaning of "mercy."

II. We must be merciful with the offenses of others.

Sooner or later some of the flaws in others become personal. They act toward us in such a way that we are tempted to do more than judge and condemn; we are tempted to seek vengeance. It is to this situation that the Lord speaks when he says, "Forgive, and you will be forgiven" (v. 37 NIV).

A. *The meaning of forgiveness.* The word Jesus uses for "forgiveness" in our text is graphic. It is the opposite of "judge" and "condemn." It means "to pardon," "to set free." The root idea of the word is "to loose from." So, to forgive people is to release them from responsibility for whatever they have done against you.

   Can we forgive if those who sin against us don't seek our forgiveness? Technically, we cannot forgive until they seek forgiveness, but we can be forgiving. We can have forgiveness ready in our hearts and even be seeking opportunities to extend it to those who have wronged us. This is surely true of God.

B. *The reason for the forgiveness.* Forgiveness is encouraged because we will need forgiveness ourselves: "And you will be forgiven." Nothing will encourage forgiveness more than a little self-awareness. The person who refuses to be forgiving toward the offenses of others is manifesting the worst kind of pride. Such an attitude suggests that that person feels he or she will never stand in need of such forgiveness.

   Surely we must practice mercy when we are offended and extend forgiveness to the offender. When we do, we are acting like our glorious heavenly Father.

III. We must be merciful with the needs of others.

In the last statement of this paragraph, mercy is seen in yet another life situation. "Give, and it will be given to you. A good measure, pressed down, shaken together and running over, will be poured into your lap. For with the measure you use, it will be measured to you" (v. 38 NIV).

A. *We are to be a giving people.* "Give" is a present-tense imperative in the Greek text. This means that such generosity is a mandate from the Lord. It also means that this is to be a habit. Jesus is not admonishing us to be supportive of the church in this text, but rather he is urging upon us "giving" as a lifestyle. Whenever we meet a fellow human who has a need, we are to be merciful. We are to respond to that need according to our ability.

   Again God is our pattern. In the promise of wisdom that he gives, James refers to God as the one "who gives generously to all without finding fault" (1:5 NIV). Our God is a liberal giver.

B. *The promise to the giver is staggering in its implication.* You will be rewarded for your giving with the same measure that you use in giving: "Good measure, pressed down, shaken together and running over, will be poured into your lap. For with the measure you use, it will be measured to you" (Luke 6:38 NIV). If you give encouragement, it will come back to you. "Blessed are the merciful, for they will be shown mercy" (Matt. 5:7 NIV).

Conclusion

Showing mercy is a principle on which you can build your life. Spread mercy abroad in the land. Such mercy will be a welcome change in this broken, suffering world. A merciful life can be confident when the storms begin to come. If we have given mercy, we will receive the mercy of the Lord in this life and in the life to come. God help us to do it.

SUNDAY EVENING, SEPTEMBER 21

Title: Work That Lasts
Text: "I know that, whatsoever God doeth, it shall be for ever" **(Eccl. 3:14)**.
Scripture Reading: Ecclesiastes 3:1–14

Introduction

One hazard of our mechanized society is that we can become a part of the machine, endangering both mental and emotional health. A greater danger is the attitude we take toward work. We must not look on our work as a dreary monotony, a burden to be borne. We must learn to have a healthy attitude toward it.

Some people rebel at their work as an unpleasant duty. This is a problem in society, a challenge to school teachers, and an explanation for much absenteeism in industry.

Some do their work only because they must. They are immersed in a spirit of resentment and self-pity.

Some go about their work in a spirit of resignation. Theirs is the attitude,

"You can't do anything about it. You might as well take it as it comes." This is the spirit of a slave.

But some regard their work as a ministry for God. A reporter interviewed three men on the same job, asking each one, "What are you doing?" The first replied, "I am cutting stone." The second said, "I am trying to support my family." But the third answered, "I am helping build a great cathedral." He was happy because he saw his work as a ministry for God.

The work God does in this world is of eternal significance. He is to be our inspiration, our standard, our guide.

I. Work is honorable.

Work is not a part of the penalty for sin. Man had a job before the fall (Gen. 2:15). Labor is the vocation given by the Creator to every human. Labor is the dignity of man. It is the signature of each person to the image and likeness of God.

II. Work is necessary.

The psalmist wrote, "Man goes out to his work, to his labor until evening"(104:23 NIV). Work is a blessing and not a curse. It is the means by which we serve one another. Work is necessary for all humankind. The "playboy" becomes less than a man. He is little more than a parasite.

III. Work enables us to join hands with God in his work in the world.

Work is a daily blessing that makes possible our participation in a great God's creation. As Paul put it, "We are God's fellow workers" (1 Cor. 3:9 NIV; also see 2 Cor. 6:1).

IV. Work enables us to join hands with our fellow Christians.

There is a sense in which work is the real meaning of the church and the secret of its fellowship. Work holds a church together and keeps it on course.

V. Work that is of the Lord is not in vain.

So often our labor is in vain. It comes to nothing. But no labor for God is ever lost (1 Cor. 15:58). His work lasts.

VI. Work that is for God keeps on working.

Of the deceased saints, John heard a voice from heaven say, "Write: Blessed are the dead who die in the Lord from now on." "Yes," says the Spirit, "they will rest from their labor, for their deeds will follow them" (Rev. 14:13 NIV).

Conclusion

In Psalm 90, Moses prayed, "Establish the work of our hands for us—yes, establish the work of our hands" (v. 17 NIV). If the "work of our hands" is God's work, he will establish it. Whatever God does, it will be forever.

Wednesday Evening, September 24

Title: Without God We Are Confused
Text: "Therefore its name was called Babel, . . . because there the Lord scattered them abroad over the face of all the earth" **(Gen. 11:9 RSV)**.
Scripture Reading: Genesis 11:1–9

Introduction

A story has been making the rounds about a man in our nation's capital who was walking down the street with a band around his arm with the four letters B.A.I.K. Someone asked him what they meant, and he replied, "Boy, am I konfused." The questioner said, "But you don't spell *confused* with a *k*." He shouted as he walked on, "You don't know how konfused I am!" Of course, the story is fictitious, and no disrespect is intended, but in this mixed-up world today, most of us can, at times, identify with this fellow.

After the flood the world soon drifted back into the same old paths, and the people became dissatisfied with their current conditions. Perhaps they feared another cataclysmic visitation from God as they journeyed in search of a proper dwelling place (Gen. 11:2). Security is a basic need; and if people cannot find it where they are, they will often seek it elsewhere. Whatever the reason, however, the postflood people learned a tragic lesson in their search for unity and permanent closeness because they sought it through artificial means and with the wrong motive.

I. Proud people trust their own abilities.

Undeterred by the experiences of life and untaught by the lessons of history, many people refuse to admit their dependence on anything or anybody. One must have a truly humble spirit to say, "I cannot solve my problems or build my life without help from a divine source"; and many people are simply not willing to make this confession of dependence.

II. Confused people seek security in strange ways.

How do you react when you feel inadequate for the problems that confront you? Many people fight back, and the confusion grows greater. Insolent presumption and aggravated self-will cause a breakdown in communication between persons and God. Having alienated themselves from their Maker, they then seek to provide their own answers to the problems that threaten their security. Wanderlust sets in as they move from one attempted antidote to another in the vain hope that a solution will come by activity and a change of scenery. In Genesis the bewildered people "journeyed" until they found a plain.

What was wrong with the mountains? Did the peaks remind them of the flood? Or were they anxious to show their contempt for God and let him know they did not believe he had the ability to send another flood? Regardless of the cause, they decided to take matters into their own hands, feeling certain they could foil any plan of God if they "stuck together" and developed their own resources. A "building boom" began as they learned about construction materials. They envisioned a "high-rise civilization" that would honor the work of their hands. All of these things emphasized that a secular society was in the making.

III. Perplexity follows pride.

Sometimes the disenchantment comes immediately when we sin. At other times the "mill of God" grinds slowly. One thing, however, is certain. The moral law of sin and retribution, which God has established, always works! History stands witness to the stern fact that when people imagine they are independent of God and, believing man is the master of all things, seek to build for their own glory, the end is not far away.

What does the record of nations say but that God will shake and tumble down everything he has not planted? Although the "confusion of tongues" seems to be a small thing, we need only to look at the world in any time period to see that people distrust those who speak a language they do not understand. If we could talk alike, perhaps this would be the first step in reaching an agreement in other areas of life. When we rule out God and seek to take his place, the result is pandemonium, paralysis, and perversion. In God's will is our peace, but without him confusion reigns!

IV. The antidote to Babel.

Turn to the New Testament and see God's answer to humankind's confusion! Pentecost is the place. God brought unity to people who spoke differently. What a lesson for us! In the pomp of Babel, people's mouths contained alien tongues. When God's Spirit acted at Pentecost, people understood each other once more. In our perplexities today, we seem to "out-Babel" the confusion of the earlier event. In Christ, however, God's Spirit can make "one heart and one speech" among all people. An ancient prophet anticipated such an event when he said, "For then will I turn to the people a pure language, that they may all call upon the name of the Lord, to serve him with one consent" (Zeph. 3:9).

Conclusion

May our prayer be, "Lord, touch our tongues and let them proclaim praises to you." Only in this way can order come to our chaotic world!

SUNDAY MORNING, SEPTEMBER 28

Title: Watch the Planks

Text: "'Why do you look at the speck of sawdust in your brother's eye and pay no attention to the plank in your own eye? How can you say to your brother, "Brother, let me take the speck out of your eye," when you yourself fail to see the plank in your own eye? You hypocrite, first take the plank out of your eye, and then you will see clearly to remove the speck from your brother's eye'" **(Luke 6:41–42 NIV)**.

Scripture Reading: Luke 6:39–42

Hymns: "God Our Father, We Adore Thee," Frazer
"Be Thou My Vision," Byrne
"Holy Spirit, Faithful Guide," Wells

Offertory Prayer: Holy Father, help us to recognize that you are the owner of all things. Help us to know continuously that we belong to you. Help us to know that you are not impoverished and that you are not begging us to bring our gifts. Help us to know that you love the giver because you are the great Giver. Accept these gifts and bless them to your name's honor, glory, and praise. In Jesus' name. Amen.

Introduction

Jesus' words in Luke 6 are to the "spiritual." He must have turned his primary attention to the Twelve as he spoke them. In today's Scripture passage, Jesus touches on one of the primary dangers to those of us who become serious about discipleship. It is the danger of living by a double standard, or overlooking some of the planks in our own lives. We need to watch for the planks!

There must have been a smile on Jesus' face as he spoke this parable. We cannot help but see the humor in a blind man attempting to lead another blind man or in a man trying to get a small speck out of the eye of his friend while a large plank protruded from his own eye. Let us see what we can learn from this parable about living a life that will withstand the storms.

I. We have difficulty seeing the planks.

Clear perception of life is important in the Christian life. Anything that will hinder our spiritual vision is a problem. Jesus describes these impairments to vision as being "specks" or "planks." The primary difference in the two is their size. Both of them would cause a great deal of pain to the eye, and both would obviously impair vision.

A. *What is the plank?* Did our Lord have some particular sin in mind? G. Campbell Morgan thinks so. He identifies the plank as being a critical, censorious spirit. He believes that this is a greater hindrance to spiritual perception than many of the things that it would label as being sinful. This kind of spirit in people makes one want to withdraw from their presence to avoid them.
B. *Why is it difficult to see?* The difficulty is caused by human pride. While it would seem that anything so obvious would be quickly seen, human

pride blinds us to the reality about ourselves. This is especially true of spiritual pride, or pride of grace. It is the most offensive of the different forms of pride and the most common among the disciples. Such pride will blind us to the truth about ourselves. It will cause us to become so preoccupied with the specks of others that we never realize the sizable problem that has developed in our lives.

II. Removal of the planks is a painful process.

A. *The sensitivity of the spirit.* Just as a speck or plank might get into the eye, so spiritual specks or planks can get into a person's spirit. Surely Jesus uses the eye for his illustration because of its special sensitivity. Even a little speck of dust in the eye can become a painful and blinding problem. The very nature of the human spirit will make it a painful process to extract a plank from the life. You do not understand your spiritual makeup if you take this process lightly.

B. *The strength of the plank.* Jesus surely chose the plank to call attention to its size and seriousness. A plank is a much greater threat to the well-being of the eye than a small speck. Furthermore, its removal will be much more painful. While the speck would probably lie on the surface and would come away rather easily with proper care, the plank would probably be imbedded in the eye, causing great pain.

Personal holiness does not come cheap. It comes only to those who are willing to undergo the pain of removing the planks. There will be the pain of subjecting oneself to the counsel of others, the struggle of removing from one's life the offensive matter. If one expects to develop godly character in three easy steps, he or she is in for some surprises. Lives that reflect godly character have been willing to undergo the painful process of removing the planks.

III. The removal of the planks prepares us to help others.

We do have friends who have specks in their eyes, and they need our ministry. They need someone to help them extract these bothersome things from their lives. They will probably never be able to get them out without some help. Jesus says, "You hypocrite, first take the plank out of your eye, and then you will see clearly to remove the speck from your brother's eye" (Luke 6:42 NIV). The qualities needed to help others are developed as we go through the painful process of developing personal holiness in our own lives.

A. *Humility is developed.* Dealing with the plank in your life humbles you. It develops in you a proper perspective on yourself and others. Interestingly, this is the quality Paul called for when performing such a ministry (see Gal. 6:1). That "spirit of meekness" is the humility that comes as you rid your life of the planks.

B. *Understanding is developed.* If you remove planks from your life, you will know the pain a brother is feeling as you help him get the speck out of his life. Such understanding gives you the capacity to weep with those who weep.

C. *Faith is developed.* As God enables you to remove the offensive plank from your life, your confidence in his ability to help your brother with his problem will be greatly increased. You will be able to approach him with a whole new outlook. You will be able to give greater encouragement as you bear witness to God's "plank-removing" power.

God has a special school for spiritual ophthalmologists. He teaches them how to remove specks by letting them practice on themselves. They learn how to deal with the problems of others by dealing first with their own problems. You will not be qualified to minister to others until you have dealt with your own problems successfully.

Conclusion

The life that will stand the storms is marked by clear spiritual perception. The inner vision of the soul is unimpaired. Such perception or vision is gained by the careful, painful removal of planks from one's life.

Where should you begin? Why not ask God to let you see all of the planks that may be a part of your life?

SUNDAY EVENING, SEPTEMBER 28

Title: The Tragedy of Waiting for a Perfect Time

Text: "He that observeth the wind shall not sow; and he that regardeth the clouds shall not reap" **(Eccl. 11:4)**.

Scripture Reading: Ecclesiastes 11:1–10

Introduction

In our vernacular this incisive proverb says to us, "Don't just stand there; do something." The writer is saying that the Palestinian farmer who stands around wondering if the winds are going to be so high that they will blow his seed away will never sow. Summer will find his fields barren. He will have debated himself out of a crop. The same is true of the farmer who can't make up his mind to go out and harvest his crop for fear that it might rain and crush his wheat down on the ground.

This world is full of overly cautious people who are waiting for a perfect time before they do anything. This is a tragedy that may have a sixfold application to those who profess to be Christians and those who do not.

I. Many churches are waiting for a perfect time before they expand inadequate physical facilities, enlarge their work, and increase their usefulness.

They are observing the winds and regarding the clouds. Prices are too high. Materials are scarce. Some members have had financial setbacks and cannot give much. Churches have been hampered in their growth and capacity to serve for years because they waited for the perfect time to build, and it never came.

II. Many Christians are waiting for a perfect time before they accept a place of service and begin to serve God in an effective way in the church.

They observe the winds and regard the clouds; and they never quite get around to it. They will teach in the Sunday school just as soon as things are right. This means never.

III. Many Christians are waiting for a perfect time before they begin to honor God with the minimum portion of their substance that he requires, the tithe.

To tithe means to give to God's work through his church the first dollar out of ten that comes through the Christian's hands. This is the minimum, not the maximum, for Christian stewardship is not an optional matter.

An able businessman who had never tithed was made chairman of the building committee in his church. The pastor led the church to adopt an intensive campaign for new tithers as the plan for raising the funds. Seeing his pledge card, this man's daughter said, "Daddy, that is much more than a tithe for you." He answered, "Yes, I know. Maybe if the Lord will let me live long enough, I can return to him some of the tithe I owe from the years before I began to tithe." He had intended to tithe all along but had been observing the wind and regarding the clouds.

IV. Many Christians are waiting for a perfect time before they attempt to win the lost to Christ.

To find some reason, some pretext as to why it is not a good time to talk to a person about his or her soul is the easiest thing in the world to do. Many Christians do this. To wait for a perfect time is to put soul-winning off indefinitely.

Foiled twice in his efforts to win a mother of two to Christ by the untimely visits of an apparently nosey neighbor, a pastor decided that if it happened again, he would go right ahead. It did happen. He did go ahead, and he won the neighbor instead of the one he had attempted twice before to visit. "If I had only listened to him," he said. "It was the neighbor the Lord was sending me to see all the time."

V. Many Christians who are not affiliated with a church are waiting for a perfect time before they unite with a church in the community where they now live.

These dear people sign up with the utility companies, attend the public schools, frequent the local supermarkets, and participate in many things in the routine of their daily lives, but the church? Their attitude is "heaven can wait." The excuses people give for not attending to this important matter are now "old hat" to any experienced minister. For the most part, these people are observing the wind and regarding the clouds.

VI. Many unsaved are waiting for a perfect time before they accept Christ as Lord and Savior.

Like Felix of old, they say to God's Spirit, "That's enough for now! You may leave. When I find it convenient, I will send for you" (Acts 24:25 NIV). But the convenient season never comes. They observe the wind and regard the clouds. While they are musing, the fire is burning (Ps. 39:3); and one day the flame dies within them.

Conclusion

This tragedy has happened over and over again. Christian friend, don't let it happen to you anymore. Unsaved friend, while it is called today, do not harden your heart (see Heb. 3:7–8).

SUGGESTED PREACHING PROGRAM FOR THE MONTH OF

OCTOBER

■ Sunday Mornings

Continue and complete the series "Standing Up to the Storms of Life."

■ Sunday Evenings

The messages for October and November are from 1 John and make up a series called "Great Affirmations about God."

■ Wednesday Evenings

The theme for Wednesday evenings this month is "Christian Attitudes."

WEDNESDAY EVENING, OCTOBER 1

Title: Enjoying Life
Text: "These things I have spoken to you, that my joy may be in you, and that your joy may be full" **(John 15:11 RSV)**.
Scripture Reading: John 15:1–11

Introduction

An Alabama tale about the late Bear Bryant tells of his coaching his team to a one-point lead. With two minutes to play he called on his slow-but-steady fourth-string quarterback. Bryant instructed him to run the ball up the middle and then punt. The new quarterback stunned the opposition with repeated first-down runs. Deep in his opponent's territory, temptation overcame instruction. He had never had an opportunity to throw a touchdown pass. Disregarding his coach, he threw the ball. The opposing safety intercepted and broke into the clear. The sluggish quarterback struggled to his feet. He started chasing the fastest man on the field and tackled the safety before the goal line. The gun sounded. The game had ended.

Opposing coaches met at mid-field. Bryant's competition shook his head in disbelief. "How could a fourth-string quarterback catch my swiftest safety?" he quizzed. "That's easy," Bryant responded. "Your man was running for a touchdown. My man was running for his life."

What motivates you? Fear motivates some Christians. Guilt spurs on others. Yet the Bible teaches that joy should be a primary motivator. People who respond to God's joy impress us. We admire a family that faces difficulties without bitterness. The person who has suffered loss with courage will be the one we seek out in our day of loss. Joy attracts.

Negatives repel. Some people lack joy. The man who comes home to a delicious meal hurts his wife, who has worked so hard to prepare the food, when he complains about the menu. Negative personalities repel. It is always easier to criticize than affirm. Today we should rediscover a sense of joy about living. What does it mean to live in joy?

I. The source of joy is Christ.

Jesus employed a great symbol in his ministry—the vine and the branches. He pictured the branches growing out of the vine and said, "I am the vine." The concept of our abiding in him and yielding our lives to him is vital. He introduced the idea of bearing fruit, and he provides the sustenance of the Holy Spirit that flows through us. His metaphor implies constant fellowship with God.

Jesus asserted a powerful proposition. Our abiding relationship in him provides his joy in us! Joy overcomes guilt. Joy conquers fear. We are reconciled in joy!

Abraham Maslow suggested that humans seek self-actualization. We search for meaning in life. We attempt to buy and borrow joy, but true happiness comes only from the abundant life of Jesus Christ. Joy is an integral part of the Christian life. How do we get it?

II. The secret of joy is appropriation.

Paul Tillich said that where there is joy, there is fulfillment; and where there is fulfillment, there is joy. The Christian life finds fulfillment through the joy of Christ as we grow. Jesus has told us this so that our joy can be full and complete. How do we appropriate this abundant joy? Jesus suggested we obey God in a spirit of love. How may this be accomplished?

A. *First, affirm others.* Do you rejoice when someone else has success? Learn to celebrate the achievements of others so that your joy may overflow.
B. *Also, learn to give thanks.* In spite of all the troubles you may be experiencing today, take time to list the many blessings God has provided and thank him. Then joy will be yours.
C. *Finally, joy may come after a period of suffering.* Some have misinterpreted passages like John 16:22, "Your grief will turn to joy." The Bible does not suggest that we deny our sorrows. Jesus wept at the grave of Lazarus. Christ will interpret and translate the unintelligible languages of trial, tribulation, and trauma into discernible personal peace and joy. Christ counted the cross all joy, not because he cherished death, but because it would result in unveiling the joy of redemption (Heb. 12:2).

Conclusion

Jesus said, "These things I have spoken to you, that my joy may be in you, and that your joy may be full." Is your life drudgery? Abide in Christ and rediscover a sense of joy.

Sunday Morning, October 5

Title: A Good Heart

Text: "'No good tree bears bad fruit, nor does a bad tree bear good fruit. Each tree is recognized by its own fruit. People do not pick figs from thornbushes, or grapes from briers. The good man brings good things out of the good stored up in his heart, and the evil man brings evil things out of the evil stored up in his heart. For out of the overflow of his heart his mouth speaks'" **(Luke 6:43–45 NIV).**

Scripture Reading: Luke 6:43–45

Hymns: "Holy, Holy, Holy," Heber
"I Surrender All," Van DeVenter
"Take Time to Be Holy," Longstaff

Offertory Prayer: Father God, you are the giver of every good and perfect gift. You have granted to us the supremely good gift of your Son, Jesus Christ. You have bestowed within us the gift of your Holy Spirit. You have given us the privilege of being members of your family. Today we would be givers by bringing not only our money but also our very selves and offering them to you in worship and in service to our world. In Jesus' name. Amen.

Introduction

When Jesus speaks of "heart" in our Scripture passage for today, he is referring to that inner self, the core of one's being as an intelligent, volitional, and emotional self. It is that center of each of us that thinks, decides, and feels. Jesus makes it eternally important that this center be filled and overflowing with goodness.

I. The heart determines conduct.

This principle could be called the law of the heart, because Jesus states it in the absolute form—something that will always be true.

A. *The example from nature.* Our Lord, the Master of nature, viewed nature as full of spiritual lessons and turned to it for an illustration of this law of the heart. "No good tree bears bad fruit, nor does a bad tree bear good fruit" (v. 43 NIV). The law involved here is that the quality of the tree will determine the quality of the fruit it bears.

B. *The example applied to the human heart.* "The good man brings good things out of the good stored up in his heart" (v. 45 NIV). Jesus points to the parallel between man and tree. Heart determines conduct. Source provides product. This insight should help us. While the circumstances can definitely influence conduct, we do what we do because of what we are.

II. Conduct reveals one's heart.

Again Jesus resorts to the laws of nature to teach a painful and sobering truth about the laws of the spirit. Our words and deeds reveal the center of our being.

A. *The example in nature.* "Each tree is recognized by its own fruit. People do not pick figs from thornbushes, or grapes from briers" (v. 44 NIV). The fruit identifies the tree.

B. *The example in nature applied to life.* "The good man brings good things out of the good stored up in his heart, and the evil man brings evil things out of the evil stored up in his heart. For out of the overflow of his heart his mouth speaks" (v. 45 NIV).

In the context of a sermon in which Jesus was forbidding a judgmental spirit, this illustration may have been directed against a censorious spirit, which discloses a heart that is void of love and mercy.

Accepted as truth, this teaching would trace our immorality, our dishonesty, our blasphemy to the very core of the self—the heart.

III. A change of heart brings a change of conduct.

Where conduct reveals a bad heart, a change of heart is the only remedy. To change the fruit, we must change the tree.

A. *The possibility of change.* In this text Jesus' words are designed to help us acknowledge our need for change, but many other Scripture verses confirm the reality of experiencing a true change of heart (see, e.g., Ezek. 18:31). Jeremiah made such a change of heart a basic part of the new covenant. He relayed God's promise, "I will put my law in their minds and write it on their hearts" (Jer. 31:33 NIV).

B. *The plan for a change of heart.* Since the change of heart is a work of God, what can we do? The only thing we can do is admit our need for a change and ask God, in faith, for it. David prayed, "Create in me a clean heart, O God; and renew a right spirit within me" (Ps. 51:10).

Conclusion

If we are to be ready for life's storms, we must have a good heart. Our conduct is the clue to our heart's condition. Let us consider our words and our deeds. Do we need a new heart? Come today to the great heart specialist, the Lord Jesus Christ. He will give you a new heart for life everlasting.

SUNDAY EVENING, OCTOBER 5

Title: God Is Light
Text: "God is light" **(1 John 1:5)**.
Scripture Reading: 1 John 1:1–10

Introduction

There is hardly anything more beautiful than a sunrise over the Atlantic. This is true whether the sunrise is seen from a plane, a ship, or the beach. Watching the sun's triumphant conquest of the ocean is a thrilling sight. But Walter Chalmers has written in a beautiful hymn of another kind of light, the light that surrounds God, making him "hid from our eyes":

> Immortal, invisible, God only wise,
> In light inaccessible hid from our eyes,
> Most blessed, most glorious, the Ancient of Days,
> Almighty, victorious, Thy great name we praise.

The first chapter of John's gospel tells us that Jesus is the light that gives life. "The true light that gives light to every man was coming into the world," and "in him was life, and that life was the light of men" (vv. 9, 4 NIV).

I. The nature of light.

Light is the life-giving force of the universe. God's first words in the creation account are "Let there be light." This act made life possible. And light still gives life today. Light is light-making. Light does not dwell alone but shares itself, making other elements light.

II. Relationship with light.

If we can be related to light, we can be related to God, because God is light. God can be known here and now under the conditions and limitations of human life. His nature is light, which communicates itself to people made in his image until they are transformed into his likeness.

Of course we can also be related to darkness—it is our choice. Turn out the light and relate to darkness. Pull the covers over your head and relate to darkness. Close your eyes and relate to darkness. The biblical author wrote truly: "Men loved darkness rather than light, because their deeds were evil" (John 3:19).

We must be able to tell the difference between light and darkness. It is tragic when a person is blinded to both. Jesus spoke of a sin that had no forgiveness. Is self-imposed darkness a manifestation of it?

III. Psychological and practical aspects of light.

A. *A psychology of darkness involves three denials, just as a psychology of light involves three affirmations.*

1. Darkness involves the denial of the bearing of moral conduct on spiritual communion. The unbelieving individual speaks irresponsibly: "God won't mind. God loves us so much that he will overlook anything we do." But *he is light!*
2. Darkness also involves the denial of the responsibility for sinful

actions: "I won't get hooked!" Or perhaps the person will say in self-deception, "I have no sin."

3. Darkness also involves the denial of the actual fact of having sinned: "I'm not guilty!" The Scripture makes an interesting distinction. Some will say, "I have no sin." Others will say, "I have not sinned. Sin has something to do with Adam and Eve, but not with me."

All three of these are denials of the light: Turn it out, pull up the covers, close your eyes, but the light still shines!

B. *A psychology of light is more realistic, more positive, more affirming.* Three such affirmations are clear in a psychology of light.

1. Fellowship has to do with practice as well as theory. This is the meaning of "walking in the light." Those who continue to practice the works of darkness cannot be in fellowship with the light. God is light, and obedience involves walking in the light with him. The strains of "Trust and Obey" harmonize well with this concept. It is not enough to wish for such fellowship or to think about such fellowship. This fellowship is based on sound moral principles. You have to work at it!

2. God is light, and light is in the business of putting out darkness. When did darkness ever succeed in putting out light? Does not sin belong to the realm of darkness? So forgiveness accomplishes the removal of sin insofar as light is concerned. Forgiveness is like turning on the light. Sin is not concealed or denied. It is acknowledged, forgiveness is sought, and the light shines. In darkness the person says, "I have no sin." In light the person says, "I have sin—help me!"

   God is light—and it is to God that we turn when sin's responsibility finally dawns on us. Sin belongs to darkness. Forgiveness belongs to light. God is light, and light is powerful. God made it that way.

3. One quest of psychology is self-understanding. Light makes it possible. Darkness concerns deception, while light concerns honesty. Walking in the light adds the perception that reckons honestly with oneself.

Conclusion

Our universe is one of light and warmth. It is not one of cold indifference, darkness, and hostility. Even the mists of anger, prejudice, and fear are done away in the light. Light expresses not only purity and holiness, but also the concepts of God's self-revealing and his self-giving goodness. As it is the nature of light to shine, so it is the nature of God to give and to bless. He gives life and light to all who will receive them, who will walk in the light, who will accept his forgiveness, who will be honest with themselves. They will become light. You too may become light!

Wednesday Evening, October 8

Title: Humankind's Attitude toward God
Text: "But rise and stand upon your feet; for I have appeared to you for this purpose, to appoint you to serve and bear witness to the things in which you have seen me and to those in which I will appear to you" **(Acts 26:16 RSV)**.
Scripture Reading: Acts 26:11–20

Introduction

A few years ago a new pastor arrived on his church field in upstate New York. Enthusiastic and excited, he set out to minister to the needs of his people in an always-changing, pluralistic culture in America. He became concerned about the confusion caused in his congregation by an interest in the demonic. He preached a series of sermons dealing with the Devil. But to the horror of his family, he began receiving obscene telephone calls from so-called Satan worshipers. They demanded that he cease preaching against their leader, Lucifer.

The pastor continued to proclaim the truth. To the dismay of his congregation, he disappeared, presumably abducted by the Satan worshipers. What happened to the minister? No one knows for sure, but there are those who still fear he fell victim to those haters of Christ and lovers of Satan.

Throughout history there have been those who detested Christianity. Perhaps no one hated Christians more than Saul of Tarsus. He murdered them. Saul killed men and women because Christianity threatened him. Yet from a brilliant vision and voice he heard the cry of Christ, "Saul, Saul, why do you persecute me?" Upon being confronted by Christ, Saul's life was completely changed and he became the great apostle Paul. How did it happen?

I. Conversion entails an encounter with Christ.

Paul has adjusted for us the fine-tuning on the picture of humankind's attitude toward God. Salvation entails an encounter with Christ. The man of Tarsus was on his way to Damascus. He had many hours to think on his seven-day journey. As a Pharisee, he would not walk with his Sanhedrin companions. He probably spent his time alone contemplating how he would go about capturing Christians. Suddenly, a light brighter than the sun itself blinded him, and he fell to his knees as he heard the voice of the risen Lord Jesus Christ!

Just like Saul, one must meet Christ to have a change of attitude toward God. Jesus gave his word to Saul audibly. Today we have his voice in the Bible. Hear Christ again today.

II. Conversion produces a lifestyle change.

Where should one turn after an encounter with Christ?

Saul's life was altered after accepting such a dramatic invitation from Christ. Synagogues that had received notice of his coming to kill Christians found him preaching Jesus as Lord in their midst! He had directed his life against Christ. Then Christ transformed him.

True conversion should produce a converted life. Not all people are called as Saul was. God deals with persons individually. Christ meets each one where he or she is.

Equally indwelt with a new attitude toward God, Christians now have the privilege of expressing their allegiance through multiple actions called ministry. What are some ways one may serve Christ? Once again let us look at Saul.

A. *Jesus' influence transformed Saul from a teacher of chastisement to a student of charity.* Saul became Paul. Conversion produced a teachable spirit, and he became eager to follow the commands of Christ. One should always be ready to obey. When called on to minister in the church, each Christian should be prepared.
B. *God called Saul to serve.* The word employed by the writer means "helper." Christians assist the Great Physician in life's delicate operations. Believers carry the message. The church affirms the work of Christ in the world.
C. *The Lord liberated Saul to testify.* He was commissioned to witness. The word *witness* comes from the courtroom. The testimony of an eyewitness is used to prove a person's guilt or innocence. Just as witnesses testify in court to persuade a jury, a Christian's verbal witness may convince a lost person of his or her need for Christ. A true convert for Christ becomes a witness on his behalf.

Conclusion

In his second letter to the Corinthians, Paul spoke of the new person in Christ: "Therefore if any man be in Christ, he is a new creature: old things are passed away; behold, all things are become new" (5:17). Paul spoke out of his own experience of change. Christ does not produce indifference. Christ makes the difference. The person who meets him will never be the same.

SUNDAY MORNING, OCTOBER 12

Title: Jesus Is Lord
Text: "'Why do you call me, "Lord, Lord," and do not do what I say?'" **(Luke 6:46 NIV)**.
Scripture Reading: Luke 6:46–49
Hymns: "Praise to the Lord, the Almighty," Neander
"Rejoice, the Lord Is King," Wesley
"Blessed Redeemer," Christiansen

Offertory Prayer: Holy Father, thank you for your great love for a needy world. Thank you for including each of us in your personal love revealed in Jesus Christ. Help us to let your love for this world invade our hearts. Help us to give ourselves to your purposes of winning the sinful world to faith, even as you have given yourself in Jesus Christ to be our Savior. Help us to become givers rather than mere receivers and consumers. In Jesus' name we pray. Amen.

Introduction

It seems natural to address Jesus Christ as "Lord." The title belongs to him. His earliest followers felt this to be proper from the beginning, which is rather surprising since they would not have used this title to address any other. The Jews had been taught that only God is Lord. This title was their affirmation of both his deity and authority. It acknowledged his unique relationship to God and the absolute authority attending the relationship.

As we consider the nature of this life that reflects that Jesus is truly Lord, we discover that it must be a life personally related to him, fully instructed by him, and continuously obedient to him.

I. When Jesus is Lord, there is a personal relationship with him.

A. *The establishment of the relationship.* Although persons may have known about Jesus from their earliest memory, their true relationship to Jesus can begin only when they accept Jesus' invitation to come to him. This means making a faith response that admits their unique union with God and his supreme authority over humans.

B. *The continuance of the relationship.* The present participles found in the original text are more forceful than our translations of "comes," "hear," "acts." The participle form implies a continuous *coming* to Christ, *hearing* his words, and *acting* on them.

Recognizing the reality and validity of our initial response to Christ, we must continue to affirm him as the true center of our lives by our coming, hearing, and obeying. Because many mistake their relationship with the institutional church for a relationship with Christ, it is possible to be a religious leader and not know Jesus as Lord. When he is Lord, we are in a continuous personal relationship with him.

II. When Jesus is Lord, there is personal instruction from him.

A. *Through the Scriptures.* "And hears my sayings" is the second phrase Jesus used to describe life under his lordship. This grows out of a close personal relationship with him and the desire to know him better by every available means. True disciples have a hunger to know the mind of their Lord. They will approach the Holy Word regularly and faithfully so they can hear the voice of their Lord.

B. *Through the Holy Spirit.* At the Last Supper Jesus promised the coming of the Spirit, saying, "He will guide you into all truth" (John 16:13). The apostle Paul wrote, "Those who are led by the Spirit of God are sons of God" (Rom. 8:14 NIV). The Holy Spirit and the Holy Scriptures work harmoniously to provide the essential instruction for those to whom Jesus is indeed Lord.

III. When Jesus is Lord, there is personal obedience to him.

A. *Obedience is the natural result of relationship.* Just as the dancer's movements are in obedience to the music he hears, so the true disciple of the Lord hears his words "and does them."

In the upper room Jesus said, "If you love me, you will obey what I command" (John 14:15 NIV). Later that evening he added, "You are my friends if you do what I command" (15:14 NIV).

John declares, "His commands are not burdensome" (1 John 5:3 NIV).

B. *Obedience is specific.* We who would be true disciples give careful attention to the specific words of Christ and seek to implement them in our lives. We obey his words about prayer, about witnessing, about worry, about neighbors, about church and home, about love. We are concerned about the actualization of his will in every area of our lives.

C. *Obedience is continuous.* While we are yet sinners, our obedience can be substantial, though not complete or perfect. Yet as true disciples, we practice obedience as a continuing way of life.

Conclusion

This is the bottom line. The only life that will stand the storms is the one in which Jesus is truly Lord. It is a life in which his lordship is a meaningful practice rather than mere profession.

Are we living such lives?

Sunday Evening, October 12

Title: God Is Truth
Text: "The true light is already shining" **(1 John 2:8 NIV).**
Scripture Reading: 1 John 2:1–11

Introduction

A man stood on trial one morning. He spoke of truth in his plea for justice. The judge sneered: "What is truth?" The man apparently on trial (though it is difficult to say *who* was on trial) replied not at all, but previously he had said, "I am the truth." He was condemned to the scaffold, as truth frequently is.

To ask, "What is truth?" is to ask about God, for God is truth. Now truth is realism—let us not despise it. And truth is revelation—let us not isolate it. And there is my message, for to say that God is truth is to say that he is:

I. Realistic with respect to wrongdoing.

Here are three powerful words in two powerful verses: "We have an *advocate* with the Father, Jesus Christ the *righteous:* and he is the *propitiation* for our sins" (1 John 2:1–2).

A. *The first word is variously translated.* An *advocate* is one who is called alongside in a legal relationship. He or she pleads for fulfillment of that which is right according to the highest law. An advocate does not wish to set aside the law, but to fulfill it.

   As our Advocate, Jesus Christ accepts the reality of sin and of conformity to the law, but he is on the side of the person who needs him.

B. *The second word descriptive of Jesus is* righteous. In him the idea of manhood saw its absolute satisfaction. No man was ever so manly as he. In turn he asks that all who are in fellowship with him be the best that God intended. God takes sin seriously. He makes certain righteous demands on those who would follow his will. These words were written that we "might not commit a single sin." But if, as is certain, we commit sin, then we have as our advocate one who is bound to be right.

C. *The third word descriptive of Jesus is* propitiation. It could perhaps better be translated "expiation." The word is often thought of as satisfying the wrath of an angry God, but there is more to it here. Expiation describes the removal of sin, with an emphasis on forgiveness rather than satisfaction. Christ is himself the means of forgiveness. He does not simply guide, teach, and quicken: he is the way, the truth, and the life. To say that God is truth is to say that he is:

II. Rigorous with respect to righteousness.

Let us not suppose that God is some sentimental grandfather who ignores the misbehavior of children and leads them to suppose that they can get by with anything! Here, for example, in the Scripture passage is a reference to commandments. Here are rules we are expected to keep. Righteousness makes certain claims on us.

Here is a pattern of behavior: "He that saith he abideth in him ought himself also so to walk, even as he walked" (v. 6). This is the mark of truth—and it is to be lived out in the concrete, by walking on the concrete of city streets, even as he walked (though to be sure the cobblestone and dirt streets may not be an absolute parallel).

John does not say of a mere person that he is true and the truth is in him. It is rather that God is true and the truth is in him, and humans are controlled by that acknowledgment. Truth does not change. Jesus is the true revelation of God. Therefore, humans walk "even as he walked." This is the rigor of righteousness and truth.

Do you then want a sign that the remedy for your sin is really effective? Here it is! It is a twofold sign: (1) You possess a knowledge that is expressed in obedience—a knowledge of him who is truth; (2) you enjoy a union that is manifested in imitations—"the imitation of Christ." To say that God is truth is to say that he is:

III. Related to true light and true love.

Life and light and love and truth are almost interchangeable. In God they are interrelated. Jesus spoke to his disciples of a new commandment. "Again, a new commandment I write unto you" (v. 8). It is interesting to compare John's gospel with his first epistle. Jesus said in John 13:34, "A new commandment I give unto you." It sounds like the old commandment: "Thou shalt love thy neighbor as thyself." In what sense is it new? Here Paul comes to the rescue and reminds us that in Christ all things are made new (2 Cor. 5:17), for to be a Christian is to be living as a new creation.

True light means that the darkness is passing away. The light of the knowledge of God was already shining and overwhelming the darkness of lovelessness. Love sees the purpose of light and life. This is the truth about life. In the ministry of Jesus, he saw the tax collectors and aliens in a new light, and his followers in the church carried out his example by the admission of Gentiles. To be in the light, then, is to be within the newness of life that Christ has brought into the world. Love and light and life and truth are possible.

Conclusion

You have sinned. Sin will kill you unless God saves you. You must make the decision yourself, but remember that God loves you. This is the truth of the matter!

WEDNESDAY EVENING, OCTOBER 15

Title: God's Attitude toward Humankind

Text: "Restore to me the joy of thy salvation, and uphold me with a willing spirit" (**Ps. 51:12 RSV**).

Scripture Reading: Psalm 51:10–13

Introduction

John Hannah has suggested there have been six great eras of revival in America: the First Great Awakening (1720–1770), the Second Great Awakening (1785–1810), the era of Charles G. Finney (1820–1835), the Layman's Prayer Revival (1858), the era of the Great Evangelists (1875–1930), and the era of Billy Graham.

What will future historians write of our generation? Will today be known as an era of spirituality or secularism? Will we honor God or humor humanism? Will we worship our Maker or serve the god of materialism?

Revival has changed the course of history. Revival provides a time for a new beginning. God wants us to be renewed. David understood the importance of spiritual replenishment. In his great prayer of confession, David recorded for us God's plan for changing man.

I. God cleanses us and renews us in preparation for revival.

David cried, "Create in me a clean heart, O God" (Ps. 51:10). The word *create* implies God's exclusive activity. It comes from an ancient word that meant to sharpen a stick into an arrow. David knew that God must sharpen and prune us.

The Jewish king also sought a new and right spirit. The Hebrew word for "spirit" means breath. It connotes power. We need the right kind of power to flow through our lives. Wind and rain may destroy, but when tapped by a windmill or a hydroelectric turbine, nature's forces turn out vast amounts of energy.

David did not ask for just any spirit. He asked for the right spirit. The term *right* or *steadfast* comes from a term that means "to stabilize." A man was driving an automobile when the steering tie rods gave way. He grasped the steering wheel, but the car refused to respond to his guidance and went its own direction. David prayed for the stabilizing force of God's Spirit to guide him.

Arnold Bennett once said that anyone could write a good first act of a play, but it takes a good second act to develop the plot. Christians may put on a good first act, but we must not neglect the rest of life's drama. God desires that we have a proper spirit for living.

II. God reassures us of his presence.

Being alone terrifies many. King David was no exception. In David's day, long before the church came into existence, the Holy Spirit had not yet been given as a permanent gift. The Spirit of God could be poured out or withdrawn at any time. Today, when one receives Christ, the Spirit comes. One does not ever lose the Spirit's abiding presence in the church age.

When revival comes, one may be assured that God has come. Renewal does not occur without his Spirit. Encouraged by the breath of the Father, David sought restoration.

III. God sustains us by correcting us.

King David asked for restoration. He needed to celebrate God's salvation. Notice that he did not speak of this priceless commodity as "my" salvation but as "thy" salvation. Grace comes from God.

One may lose joy because of improper attitudes or actions. Yet one should learn to enjoy salvation. David asked to be sustained with a willing spirit. Today's English Version translates this verse, "Make my spirit obedient."

Conclusion

David exclaimed a great truth: "Sinners shall be converted unto thee" (v. 13). David recognized that when he got right with God, his world would be right. When we have been cleansed, renewed, reassured, and sustained, people will be saved.

SUNDAY MORNING, OCTOBER 19

Title: The Storms of Life

Text: "The one who hears my words and does not put them into practice is like a man who built a house on the ground without a foundation. The moment the torrent struck that house, it collapsed and its destruction was complete" **(Luke 6:49 NIV)**.

Scripture Reading: Luke 6:46–49

Hymns: "Rock of Ages, Cleft for Me," Toplady
"Count Your Blessings," Oatman
"Higher Ground," Oatman

Offertory Prayer: Holy Father, today we thank you for all the material, physical, and natural blessings you have so abundantly bestowed on us. Even more so, we thank you for the great spiritual realities that give strength and stability to our lives. We thank you for your presence with us always. We come today to worship you and to give ourselves to you along with our tithes and offerings. Bless our gifts, we pray. In Jesus' name. Amen.

Introduction

The conclusion is the most important part of any sermon, for it is in the conclusion that the preacher urges on the hearer the weight of the message and appeals for a response. With this in mind, we will begin our study of the greatest sermon ever preached by looking at its conclusion.

The burden of our Lord in the conclusion of his sermon is with the listeners' response to it. He uses a parable about two builders to call for a careful response to what has been heard. The conclusion warns that storms will test every life sooner or later. A proper response to the message of Christ will not enable us to avoid the storms, but it will enable us to withstand them. What are the storms that will test our lives?

I. The storms of temptation will test our lives.

Jesus gave a graphic description of a common event in the Middle East. "When a flood came, the torrent struck that house but could not shake it, because it was well built" (Luke 6:48 NIV). However, concerning the other house, "the moment the torrent struck that house, it collapsed and its destruction was complete" (v. 49 NIV). Temptation is one such storm that comes into our lives.

A. *Temptations are common in life.* The apostle Paul declared, "No temptation has seized you except what is common to man" (1 Cor. 10:13 NIV). This is one storm that will beat against every house sooner or later.

B. *Temptations come by divine permission.* While God does not tempt us, he does permit temptation. Jesus told Peter of the approaching storm of temptation. "Simon, Simon, Satan has asked to sift you as wheat. But I have prayed for you, Simon, that your faith may not fail" (Luke 22:31 NIV). The figure of sifting emphasizes the testing aspect of the temptation. Like a storm tests the foundation of a house, temptations will test the foundation of each life. Jesus wants to help us build for the storms.

II. The storms of suffering will test our lives.

What a storm is to a house, suffering is to a human life. Suffering will soon reveal the character of the life and is allowed for that very purpose. Suffering is described in Scripture under several different figures. It is often described as a "fire" into which the life is cast like metal into the fire. The fire will not change the metal, but it will surely prove it. The storms of suffering come in many different forms.

A. *Economic conditions can cause suffering.* The turbulent economic conditions of recent years have surely demonstrated this. How would you react to losing your job? This kind of storm may blow in upon us without any warning. When it does, it will test the foundations of our lives.

B. *Political conditions can cause suffering.* The early Christians often found themselves bombarded by contrary political winds and tried by political forces. It still happens in our world. Could you hold your life together if your political freedoms were suddenly taken away?

C. *Emotional stress can cause suffering.* It is impossible to live in this world without encountering stressful and depressing circumstances.

D. *Physical problems will cause suffering.* Cancer, a heart attack, a stroke, or some other dreaded disease does not fall simply on the foolish. Some who suffer the most severely are the most saintly.

Have you escaped the storms of suffering so far? This should be a cause for thanksgiving for the good providence of the Lord God. However, it should not lead you to be presumptuous. This is no sure sign that storms will not come.

III. The storm of judgment will test our lives.

The last judgment was probably primary in the mind of Jesus as he gave this sermon. He spoke against a background of the kingdom of God and the age to come. The sermon makes no sense if there is not a life beyond death and if there is no accountability to God for one's life.

A. *The storm of judgment is certain.* "It is appointed unto men once to die, but after this the judgment" (Heb. 9:27). God himself has set up this appointment for every one of us. You may be able to bribe your way out of earthly judgments, but there will be no escape from the final judgment.

B. *The storm of judgment will be revealing.* So many things will appear differently in light of the last judgment. Many lives that looked outwardly secure and prosperous will crumble into a heap before the power of this storm. Some lives that may have looked outwardly weak and vulnerable will stand strong before the wind of judgment.

Conclusion

This parable about the storms emphasizes the seriousness of life. Each of us is building for time and eternity. What we are doing with our lives will be put to the test by the great giver of life. Wise people build with an eye to the storm.

In the Sermon on the Mount, Jesus gives us the ingredients of a life that will stand storms. He says the wise person is the one who hears these sayings of our Lord and does them. He builds his life on them.

Will your life, as you are now living it, stand the storms? Storms are inevitable. Let's get ready.

SUNDAY EVENING, OCTOBER 19

Title: God Is Eternal

Text: "The world passeth away, and the lust thereof: but he that doeth the will of God abideth for ever" **(1 John 2:17)**.

Scripture Reading: 1 John 2:12–25

Introduction

"In the beginning God created the heavens and the earth" (Gen. 1:1 NIV). When the heavens and the earth pass away, God will be saying, "Behold, I make all things new" (Rev. 21:5). The psalmist declared, "Even from everlasting to everlasting, thou art God" (Ps. 90:2). To say that God is eternal is to say that he is:

I. Ageless in appeal.

It is easy to suppose that our own era or age group is the most spiritual or the least spiritual of all times, but God is ageless in appeal. It is the privilege of a pastor to minister to little children, to young people, and to adults of all ages. God's love appeals to all of them. It is not unusual to have an adult congregation break out in the pleasant strains of "Jesus Loves Me."

It is significant, then, that the writer addresses three different age groups among his readers. In reverse order he writes to the little children, the young men, and the fathers. It would be unfortunate indeed if we did not include young women with the young men, and mothers with the fathers. Little children have certain needs, and God can satisfy those needs. Young men, regardless of precise age groupings, have different needs—and so do young women. God knows that. Fathers and mothers have different needs than little children and young people. They may have depended on God's love for a long time, and he knows their needs.

For all time, from the beginning to the end, God is. The ancients worshiped and moderns worship. Communities change; churches change. God himself is the same yesterday, today, and forever. We suppose eternity to apply to beginning or end alone, but God is:

II. Contemporary in compassion.

God has compassion on us sinners. He knows us. He is not limited to our historical considerations but exists above them.

He knows our lovelessness. He knows that we are more apt to love the world and things than him or one another. The world as the object of our love is the world that exists in hostility to God. Someone has said that God's plan is for us to worship God, love persons, and use things. The tragedy of modern life is in its perverseness: we do not worship God; we love things; and we use people.

God knows and sees our temptations. They are of current design, but they are ageless in character. They are even today rooted in the desire for self-preservation and self-gratification. A person will give anything in exchange for his life. His life consists in the things he has and in the things he wants—in his pleasures both physical and mental. God knows, because he is God. Our temptations are yet based on the principles manifest on the Mount of Temptation.

A. *A man will do anything to feed himself and his family.* When challenged to make bread the easy way, Jesus replied simply, "Man shall not live by bread alone . . ." (Matt. 4:4).

B. *How much will a man give in exchange for a following?* Prestige, popularity, influence—these are things a preacher may achieve at the price of his very soul. When challenged to secure a following by performing a miracle, Jesus replied, "Thou shalt not tempt the Lord thy God" (v. 7).

In contrast with the ageless appeal of God, there is the contemporary compassion of God—he sees and knows our trials. In contrast with the ageless appeal of God, there is the temporary nature of these wants and even needs—"for all that is in the world, the lust of the flesh and the lust of the eyes and the vainglory of life, is not of the Father, but is of the world. And the world passeth away" (1 John 2:16–17 ASV). The word translated "vainglory of life" may also be translated "pride of life."

God knows our ability to love, and he would direct our love to a worthy object. His eternal nature challenges our short lives.

We may suppose that our own stage of history, with its scientific accomplishments, is the best ever. We may attempt to maintain the status quo as the best of all possible worlds, but God is:

III. Persistent in progress.

Life moves on because God moves it. Like the little girl in the cartoon who responds saucily to an adult critic, "God ain't through with me yet," so God continues to work with his creation. God is portrayed through the Old and New Testaments as leading his people onward. He appears never to be satisfied with the status quo.

It is true that there is a finality about all of life's experiences, but God expects us to make some progress too. He persists in leading his people. We suppose ourselves to be weak and our lives to be short, but God is:

IV. Generous in giving life.

God is eternal, and he shares that everlastingness with his people. He makes us everlasting too. John's object in writing this letter does not appear to have been to communicate fresh knowledge, but to activate the knowledge his people already possessed. It is activated by an anointing, or, as it is sometimes translated, an "unction." Because you have received that gift of the Holy Spirit, you have certain knowledge, and no false teaching can lead you astray if you are faithful to that knowledge.

You know the truth. You are honest in confessing your sin. You choose to remain in the Father who is eternal. You share his nature. And all of this because a man died—but not just an ordinary man. You and I might have died on a cross with no effect beyond the grief of our immediate family, but this man was God reconciling the world to himself. He came out of eternity into time, or perhaps time is a part of eternity after all.

Conclusion

Now the only "eternal" in our midst is the human soul in fellowship with God's Spirit. It is of permanent value because God has charged it with eternal value. You may experience that fellowship by faith in Christ. This too is a "last" hour. Perhaps it is a critical hour for you: "And this is the promise that he hath promised us, even eternal life" (1 John 2:25).

Wednesday Evening, October 22

Title: When God and Humankind Get Together
Text: "How lovely is thy dwelling place, O Lord . . . ; my heart and flesh sing for joy to the living God" **(Ps. 84:1–2 RSV)**.
Scripture Reading: Psalm 84:1–12

Introduction

One always appreciates home after being away. The psalmist had been away from the house of God for too long. Upon his return he celebrated the great autumn Festival of Tabernacles. The psalmist sought the Lord as a worshiper in the temple, as a pilgrim in life, and as a prodigal having been away from home. Where are you in your pilgrimage with the Lord? One may be physically close to a church but spiritually far away.

I. Do we long for God's home?

The temple provided an elaborate setting for worship. The Jews made their pilgrimages to Jerusalem. Like travelers on their first journey to Switzerland to see the Alps, the Jews were awed. God's dwelling provides a place of rest. Have you ever felt the need for rest at your home? Do we enjoy God's home with the same freedom?

David cried, "One thing have I asked of the Lord, that will I seek after; that I may dwell in the house of the Lord all the days of my life, to behold the beauty of the Lord, and to inquire in his temple" (Ps. 27:4 RSV).

A story was told of a wealthy English aristocrat who possessed fourteen houses but had not one home. Do we have the same kind of desire to be in the house of God as we do to be at home with our families? Our desire should be to worship him. Once we have learned to feel at home with God, we must depend on him.

II. Do we accept God's help?

One should not forget God's promise to Isaiah, "Fear not; I will help thee" (Isa. 41:13). Abraham traveled. Amos served God. Jesus journeyed to Jerusalem. Paul sailed the Mediterranean. God helps us get home to him. Some of you are on life's journey passing through a desert. You have crossed the barren terrain of hurts and misunderstandings. Good news awaits you. The psalmist promises that God's strength will come. In all of life's journey, God will be with us and help us.

III. Do we desire God's presence?

The psalmist has suggested that it is better to be at home with God one day than to live a thousand days without him. Mary McCullough's poem "Presence" reminds us of the nearness of God:

> God is very near to me
> In the whispering of a tree;
> And His voice I have often heard
> In the singing of a bird.
>
> I have often walked with Him
> In the twilight warm and dim;

Sure and tender, He is there
In the clover-scented air.

God is near, for He is found
In all lovely things around,
Hill, or cloud, or leaf, or star—
He is never very far.

Conclusion

David concluded with a word of commendation: "Blessed is the man who trusts in you" (Ps. 84:12 NIV). Job learned to trust God no matter what the circumstances (Job 13:15). Solomon discovered this simple truth: "Trust in the LORD with all your heart and lean not on your own understanding; in all your ways acknowledge him, and he will make your paths straight" (Prov. 3:5–6 NIV).

SUNDAY MORNING, OCTOBER 26

Title: Where Is Your Faith?

Text: "He said unto them, Where is your faith? And they being afraid wondered, saying one to another, What manner of man is this! for he commandeth even the winds and water, and they obey him" **(Luke 8:25)**.

Scripture Reading: Luke 8:22–25

Hymns: "How Firm a Foundation," George Keith
"Have Faith in God," McKinney
"My Faith Looks Up to Thee," Palmer

Offertory Prayer: Holy Father, we thank you for your blessings on us in the past. We thank you for your generosity to us today. We thank you for the promise of your providential care in the future. With faith we commit ourselves and all that we are to your work. Accept these tithes and offerings, and bless them to the end that others will come to know your love. In Jesus' name. Amen.

Introduction

Our Lord allowed his disciples to encounter a fear-provoking circumstance on the Sea of Galilee to teach them a great lesson. As they sailed over the lake, they found themselves confronted with a dangerous situation—a storm had come down the mountainside and across the lake, making sailing impossible. Because he was weary from the burdens of the day, Jesus was asleep in the front of the boat. The waves began to fill the boat with water, and it appeared that it was in danger of sinking at any moment. The fear of the disciples became such that they awakened Jesus, saying, "Master, Master, we are perishing!"

In response, Jesus rebuked the storm. He also addressed the storms in the hearts of his disciples with rebuke and encouragement. In Luke's account he simply asked, "Where is your faith?" There are two great lessons to be learned here.

I. Faith does not prevent the storms of life.

We must be clear about the purpose of Jesus' question. He was not holding his disciples responsible for the storm. He was holding them responsible for their response to the storm. They had given in to a very human fear: they were afraid they were going to die.

This brings up an interesting question. Who was responsible for the storm that beset the disciples? Scholars are not agreed about this specific incident, but there are only two possibilities.

A. *The enemy causes storms.* Some believe that Satan was actually responsible for this storm. They remind us that he is the "prince of the power of the air" and interpret this to be an open attempt on the lives of Jesus and his disciples. What I know about the Devil would incline me to believe this. I do know that he makes life as difficult as possible for those who are committed to God. Remember the experience of Job!

   The Enemy can stir up storms around your life. Your faith in God will not prevent these attacks but may actually attract them. So when the storms come, you are not to conclude that your faith has failed, but rather that it is being tried.

B. *The Lord may also stir up some storms.* No storm ever comes against us without divine permission. Even the Enemy works within limitations imposed by the loving will of God.

   But when the Lord God allows us to confront a fear-provoking circumstance, it is not a sign that our faith has failed. Jesus does not say, "Where is your faith?" because the storms come. You cannot prevent the storms by faith, but you can prevent them from destroying you. Your faith may not be able to keep you from having to face an economic storm, a vocational storm, a physical storm, a spiritual storm, or even a marital storm, but faith does make a difference in how you deal with the storm.

II. Faith does prevent fear.

The great lesson we are to learn here is that faith does prevent fear. The disciples were frightened by the threatening circumstances, but they should not have been. This prompted Jesus to ask, "Where is your faith?" If faith had filled their hearts, things would have been different.

A. *Fear is a sign of a failure of faith.* What happened to this group of disciples was a very natural thing. Any ordinary human being would have been frightened by the storm and the danger of sinking to the bottom of the Sea of Galilee. However, this little group of men was not supposed to act as just natural men. They knew Jesus Christ and, in fact, had him on board the ship. They should have been able to go through such a storm unruffled by fear.

Every one of us has known fear in some form at one time or another. It may have been the fear of failure. It may have been the fear of death. It may have been the fear of losing a job. It may have been the fear of rejection by someone important to us. But Jesus lays the blame for fear squarely on our lack of faith. The fear does not come from the circumstances but rather comes from within me.

Many of us are quite successful at hiding our fears for a while. We hide them beneath a flurry of activity. We hide them behind empty words of confidence. But sooner or later they will surface. They may surface in health problems or emotional problems, but they will surface. Fear is caused by the failure of faith.

B. *The faith that prevents fear rests in Jesus.* Jesus wanted his disciples to depend on him in this dangerous circumstance. He was calling attention to his adequacy to handle whatever situation may arise. We desperately need to learn that our faith must rest in him and not in our own abilities.

1. Faith is resting in the person of Christ. Did these disciples not know who he was? He had given them many indications of his identity. Did they really think that the Son of God would be swallowed up in a little storm on the Sea of Galilee?

   We know Jesus Christ. But do we really know who he is? Have we committed ourselves to one who cannot handle the crises of life that come to us? Indeed, he is the Lord of history, the living God. He is able to subdue all things to himself. Faith relies on who he is.

2. Faith is resting in the promise of Christ. The disciples missed it. When Jesus said, "Let us go over to the other side of the lake," his command was his promise. What he commands he enables. They should have understood that it was his responsibility to get them to the other side. Why fear? He will do what he has said he will do.

   Faith makes much of God's promises, but fear forgets them.

3. Faith is resting on the performance of Christ. Up to this point the disciples had not faced a situation in which Jesus was not the Master. Did this not encourage them to believe that all was well now? We have such an advantage over them. We have three books that remind us of his performance. We have the Bible, the complete revelation of his faithfulness and sufficiency. Oh, how the reading of the Bible encourages faith! We also have Christian history. The last two thousand years have been filled with

testimonies concerning the faithfulness and adequacy of Christ. And finally, we have the book of our own experience.

Conclusion

Are you living by your fears or by your faith? Many of you are dominated by your fears. Jesus asks you, "Where is your faith?" With that question he is offering you an invitation to cast all your cares on him for he cares for you. Won't you do that right now?

SUNDAY EVENING, OCTOBER 26

Title: God Is Faithful
Text: "Behold what manner of love the Father hath bestowed upon us, that we should be called children of God; and such we are" **(1 John 3:1 ASV)**.
Scripture Reading: 1 John 3:1–6

Introduction

You can count on God! The Bible is the story of faith and the history of God's people. God's faithfulness is the link that ties the Old and New Testaments together. The use of the word *covenant* in both the Old and New Testaments attests to God's faithfulness. His mercy in forgiveness and his continuing patience with his people also attest to his faithfulness.

God made a covenant with Abraham, the details of which are recorded in Genesis 15. Abraham took a heifer, a goat, a ram, a turtle dove, and a young pigeon and divided them into halves. He then took his position between the two halves and waited for God to meet him there. God was faithful and promised the patriarch that he would give the land to his descendants.

God also made a covenant with Israel. The nation's avowal to serve the Lord at various stages of its history appeared to be mockery, yet God was faithful to uphold his covenant. It is unfortunate that through the centuries the nation presumed on God's faithful dealings.

Later, because of Israel's faithlessness, Jeremiah introduced the "new" covenant. The adjective was necessary to distinguish it from the old covenant, which sinful rebellion had made null and void. The prophet Jeremiah was apparently at first enthusiastic about the reform movement initiated by King Josiah. However, when it became apparent that the reform movements were to have no lasting effect, the prophet introduced the "new covenant." He perceived that God's dealings with his people must be on a spiritual plane: it was here that God's faithfulness was most clearly demonstrated. So a new covenant was anticipated that would be inward and individual and eternal.

When Jesus faced his approaching death, he talked with his disciples about a new covenant. The Christian world has identified his sacrificial death as fulfilling the covenant concept of Jeremiah. "Behold what manner of love!"

In his remembrance of the Last Supper, the apostle Paul referred to the new covenant, and so does the church consistently remember God's faithfulness to his covenant at each such observance. The old was ineffective; the new is effective. The old passed away; the new continues. There are many other such points of comparison. God is faithful, and the new covenant attests to that truth.

I. The word *faithful* describes a relationship.

The new covenant is a relationship between God and man in which God bestowed grace on man. It is not reserved until death, but is characterized by liveliness. It is not a contract between equals and so transcends the legalistic. Rather, it is described in terms of our text: "Behold what manner of love the Father hath bestowed upon us!"

Although God's faithfulness was at first understood in terms of his sending rain or sunshine, in his leading the nation to victory against its foes, and in his answering of petitions for health and wealth, the new covenant has helped us to understand that the relationship is not a natural relationship, but a *supernatural* relationship. In a sense it is a creature-to-Creator relationship that includes all people. In a sense, it is a family relationship that makes room for all people to be born into the Christian family.

But it is more than that. It is a relationship between a majestic and merciful God and his people. There is no hint that any accomplishment of the most pious of persons makes this relationship possible.

II. There is a newness about it.

We are now "children" of God, by his choice, by his adoption, by his inclusion into his family.

A. *Perhaps the tradition that portrays John as an aging Christian and the writer of this letter helps to explain the frequent reference to "children."* If, indeed, the letter belongs to the last years of the first Christian century, John would have been a patriarch who considered most of his friends "children." The term describes the freshness of a new generation. God is interested not only in the patriarchs but also in the children.

B. *The term describes innocence.* Innocence is also a relative term, judged by the experience of the individual. Children are adjudged innocent, not on the basis of their sinlessness but on the basis of their lack of experience. The supposition is that experience hardens people and makes them wise in the ways of the world.

C. *But the term* children *also describes a basic trust.* Animals of most species become independent at an early age. Children depend on their parents and are nurtured during their growing years. A child trusts, and that trust is challenged by parental love. We are children of God.

D. *We are children of God by adoption.* A mother explained the meaning of adoption to her adopted son: "You see, we chose you to be our son.

We looked at you and liked you. We wanted you to come to live with us. You are our son by choice."

The relationship between parent and adopted child is much more than a legal arrangement. This is not to downplay the natural biological relationship, but something is to be said for the parent who chooses a particular child. God has chosen for Jesus' sake to claim children as his own. The future is as bright as the promises of God.

Those who are adopted are children of God with the promise of maturity. Every child enjoys his or her growth marks on the closet door, indicating an increase in height. It is not yet clear what we will be as children of God, but "we shall be like him." That's maturity for the Christian.

Our future is secure in God's faithfulness. We once sang regularly, "He has never broken a promise spoken. He will keep his promise to me." Just as children come to depend on their parents in their growing years, so we have come to depend on God in our growing years. We never grow beyond him.

Conclusion

What manner of love—how great!
What vast knowledge—of God!
What wonderful hope—in him!

And all of this is God's gift to us through Jesus Christ—"Love divine, all loves excelling." How will you respond to the God who is faithful?

WEDNESDAY EVENING, OCTOBER 29

Title: Facing Our Fears

Text: "For I have heard the slander of many: fear was on every side: while they took counsel together against me, they devised to take away my life. But I trusted in thee, O LORD: I said, Thou art my God" **(Ps. 31:13–14)**.

Scripture Reading: Psalm 31:9–15

Introduction

One of the last great sermons of the Baptist preacher George W. Truett was "The Conquest of Fear." He noted that many people are in the clutches of fear. Political instability, economic uncertainty, and the prospects of a worldwide nuclear, biological, or chemical holocaust hold the nations of this planet in constant fear. What are some of the things we fear most?

I. What do we fear?

A. *Death.* David feared death. Death represents the loss of security. In *Hamlet* Shakespeare wrote, "Death is the undiscovered country from whose bourn no traveler returns."

Death was feared in the ancient world. In Canaanite literature Baal was given an additional weapon with which to battle death. Fear was no stranger to David. But the king did not have the full revelation of victory over death that we have in Jesus Christ. Still, an individual without Christ frightfully fears life's termination. Not only did David fear death, he also suffered anxiety.

B. *Anguish.* David suggested that his strength had failed. The word comes from a term that means "to stumble."

C. *Criticism.* David feared slander. The thought of gossip terrified him. One may fear what others say, but life cannot be lived in fear. David learned this lesson. He discovered he had to overcome fear.

II. How do we overcome fear?

A. *Trust.* David said, "I trusted in thee" (v. 14). Out of his fear he cried to God. When God becomes our first priority, our fears dissipate. C. S. Lewis wrote in *Reflections on the Psalms,* "Belief in the future life is strong only when God is in the center of our thoughts." Do you want to overcome fear? Trust God!

B. *Confession.* David trusted God and confessed his commitment to God: "Thou art my God" (v. 14). First John 4:15 teaches us, "Whosoever shall confess that Jesus is the Son of God, God dwelleth in him, and he in God." Recover a sense of praise in your confession. Praise should be spontaneous and contagious. When you see something of great beauty, you tell others about it.

C. *Commitment.* David discovered a final truth about overcoming fear. He wrote, "My times are in thy hand" (Ps. 31:15). Literally, David said our future rests with God. He referred not to eternal life but to the life cycle of growing up from childhood to adulthood. He implied that we may overcome the fear of living. He suggested that we may use our fears. When you are afraid, pray, serve, and work. Put your fears to work.

Conclusion

Today parents with young children worry about the future of the world. Instead of living in fear, take time to prepare your children for living in the world. Ground them in the Word of God. Teach them. Too often our fears are only imaginary.

Some enemies are real. Others are imagined. We must face the authentic enemies of sin and secularism, but the enemies we create are ones we must learn to overcome.

SUGGESTED PREACHING PROGRAM FOR THE MONTH OF NOVEMBER

■ Sunday Mornings

The suggested theme for Sunday mornings this month is "Spotlight on Stewardship." This series of messages can be helpful to the pastor who is preaching a series of messages in connection with a stewardship campaign or budget-pledging effort.

■ Sunday Evenings

Continue and complete the series "Great Affirmations about God." On the final Sunday evening of the month, begin the series "Communicating the Message of Christmas to the World." The angels sang of Christ's birth. The shepherds shared the news of his birth. The wise men came because of his birth. It is the task of the church today to communicate to the world the meaning of his coming.

■ Wednesday Evenings

"Thanksgiving" is the theme for the meditations to be used on Wednesday evenings in November.

SUNDAY MORNING, NOVEMBER 2

Title: When It Is Good to Give

Text: "In all things I have shown you that by so toiling one must help the weak, remembering the words of the Lord Jesus, how he said, 'It is more blessed to give than to receive'" **(Acts 20:35 RSV)**.

Scripture Reading: Acts 20:31–35

Hymns: "Guide Me, O Thou Great Jehovah," Williams
"I Love Thy Kingdom, Lord," Dwight
"Take My Life, and Let It Be," Havergal

Offertory Prayer: Father God, we rejoice in this day you have made. We worship you and praise you with all of our hearts. Receive our tithes and offerings as expressions of our love and as indications of our desire that your kingdom should spread to the ends of the earth and that everyone should come to know Jesus Christ as Lord and Savior. In his name we pray. Amen.

Introduction

Shannon Randolph was fifty-three years of age. A high school dropout at the age of fourteen, he had earned his living mostly by dishwashing and odd jobs, including splitting firewood. He had first gone to the Salvation Army in Fort Worth, Texas, for lodging and food in 1969. Later he got a job at the Salvation Army as a lodge man, the man who awakened the others in the morning and got them moving downstairs for breakfast. The job paid room and board and $140 per month.

One morning in 1980 a man did not want to get up when awakened by Randolph. Jumping out of his bed, he leaped on Randolph, knocked him down, and stomped on his leg. The leg was broken in two places and the bone was shattered. After six operations and 125 days in the hospital, Randolph was released, but the leg was stiff, stuck out at an angle, and caused him to walk painfully and slowly. Upon his release from the hospital, he was awarded $7911.44 in workmen's compensation insurance. It was the most money he had ever seen. Promptly he gave $1,000 of it in cash to the Salvation Army. Shannon Randolph's comment about it was, "It just makes you feel good inside. That's all" (*The Gospel of John,* Daily Study Bible, rev. ed. [Philadelphia: Westminster, 1975], 137).

Shannon Randolph's statement that it makes a person feel good to give shadows the words of Jesus quoted by the apostle Paul in Acts 20:35: "It is more blessed to give than to receive."

Paul was on his trip back to Jerusalem following his third missionary journey. He was eager to get to Jerusalem by Passover because he wanted to deliver the gift from the Gentile Christians to relieve the suffering of the Jewish Christians.

En route the ship put in at the port of Miletus. Under the pressure of time, Paul did not visit Ephesus. Instead, he sent for the leaders of the Ephesian church to meet him at Miletus. There he delivered his farewell address to them. In this address Paul gave an account of his stewardship as an apostle. He also warned them of both their duty and their danger. William Barclay, in his volume on Acts in the Daily Study Bible, summarized Paul's address by saying that he made certain claims: he claimed that he had spoken fearlessly, lived independently, and faced the future gallantly.

In this address Paul also quoted an unrecorded saying of Jesus. We know that Jesus said a lot of things that were not recorded in the Gospels, and this is one of them. It tells us when it is good to give.

I. It is good to give when you know where the money goes.

A. *A principle.* Paul reminded his listeners that he had labored with his own hands to support himself when he ministered among them. He had set an example of giving; he had personified the principle Jesus had stated.

They knew where the money they had given to Paul went: it went to ministry.

B. *A practice.* It is important when you give money that you know where the money goes. You must know that it is used responsibly and with accountability.

That is why a church has a budget. The people in the church know where the money goes. In adopting a church budget, they agree on how the money is to be spent. In the regular reports to the church, they find out that it was spent as agreed. There is a public accounting of where the money has gone. Usually the best-accounted gift that you can give is your gift to the church. It is used responsibly and accounted for regularly and accurately.

II. It is good to give when you know what the gift shows.

A. *Involvement.* A man once wrote his pastor during a stewardship campaign complaining about the church and its ministry. He said that all he ever heard around there was giving, giving, giving. The pastor thanked him for the best definition of Christianity he had ever heard: Christianity is giving, giving, giving (*Fort Worth Star-Telegram,* September 13, 1980).

Paul indicated that these people had known of his personal involvement with them. He had not shirked his duty.

Your gift of love to the church shows your involvement in the church and its ministry. When you give, you become involved.

B. *Interest.* You give to those things in which you have an interest. Giving to the church and its ministry shows interest.

C. *Initiative.* Giving also shows the initiative to respond to God's love. God has showered his love on us. By giving we take the initiative to respond to that love. Real Christian giving should not be from compulsion, duty, threat, or guilt. It should be a person's response to God's love.

III. It is good to give when you know that the church grows.

A. *Concern.* Paul's concern was with the future of the Ephesian church. He had laid the foundation well. But he warned the leaders that problems could arise, questions could emerge, and leadership could be challenged. The very future of the gospel at Ephesus was at stake. It would depend on their faithfulness to God's principles.

Isn't it interesting and instructive that the concluding word in Paul's farewell address was the reference to Jesus' statement that it is more blessed to give than to receive? The continuation and growth of the church would depend on how they acted on that statement.

And it is still true today. Every church must give and increase its giving for the church to grow. With inflation and a need for expanded programs, a church cannot continue to give the same dollar amounts year after year and have church growth.

B. *Concept.* But how can a church grow? Paul gave some pointers for church growth to the Ephesian church leaders that will also help us to grow churches for God's glory today.

1. Be eager to work. There is no church growth without work. Growth never comes automatically. Someone has to work for it to be realized.
2. Be consistent in giving. The best way to give to the church is regularly and consistently. This is a key to strong churches and to their growth.
3. Be faithful to the gospel.

Conclusion

Jesus was right, of course. It is more blessed to give than to receive. He demonstrated that truth by giving his life for us in sacrifice for our sins. And Paul demonstrated that truth by giving his life in service to the Savior. How have you demonstrated that principle? Maybe you should begin today by giving your heart to Christ or by pledging to support his cause through the church.

Sunday Evening, November 2

Title: God Is Righteous

Text: "My little children, let no man lead you astray: he that doeth righteousness is righteous, even as he is righteous" **(1 John 3:7 ASV)**.

Scripture Reading: 1 John 3:7–12

Introduction

Righteous and *just* along with *to make righteous* and *to justify,* are often misunderstood and misused. My first consciously offensive use of the word *justification* was completely repulsive to Ed Hughes, a good friend and tough old farmer. He didn't like the word because he knew some folks who "justified" themselves, and he didn't figure the "good Lord," as he put it, "had any likin' for that." So we begin today by speaking not of man's righteousness—self-claimed or otherwise—but of God, who is consistently described as "righteous."

I. To be righteous is to be wise as to what is right.

This is the etymology of the word *righteous.* It comes from the Middle English "right-wise." To be wise about anything is to exceed mere factual knowledge and to move into the area of experience.

God was acclaimed righteous because he *did* righteousness. So he or she is righteous who does righteousness, whose life reveals its effectiveness, who realizes righteousness in conduct. Yet to be righteous is *more than* to do righteous acts, for righteousness is part of a believer's character in Christ.

Wisdom is simplicity, and to be righteous is the simplest way to live. It is simpler, for example, to tell the truth than to get involved in deceit. It is plain here, in black and white: To sin is to belong to the devil; to remain in Christ is to be righteous as he is righteous.

II. To say that God is righteous is to experience his righteousness.

No person has seen God at any time, but God's Son has revealed him. We have been exposed to the righteousness of God, and it may be seen in three different ways:

A. *Mandatory.* God gives moral laws that he prescribes for human conduct.

B. *Punitive.* God's laws are the standard of judgment. To fracture them involves fractured relationships. To fracture them exposes us to the working out of God's wrath. We must not ignore God's wrath.

C. *Redemptive.* God reveals his righteousness in his redeeming activity. God does not pass over our sins. He goes through them when he forgives us in Christ Jesus and calls us his dear children. Righteousness marks the intervention of God in human affairs, the conquest of sin down on the plains of human history. God can afford to give free, unfettered grace because his righteousness is absolute. There are no strings attached, no entangling alliances, no compromised principles. He owes no human anything!

What does all this mean to us? To say that God is righteous is to set our own course toward righteousness.

III. How shall we "be righteous"?

A. *We will not be righteous in blind acceptance of certain moral principles.* Righteousness is reasonable. It involves two positive factors: goodwill and a certain ideal of life. Righteousness is reasonable: to obey cosmic laws, moral and physical, is sensible.

B. *We will not be righteous in anguished terror.* Righteousness is submission to right in full confidence of God's love. Discipline is a part of learning and is closely related to discipleship. While the results of sin remain, the penalty becomes a discipline but blossoms into opportunity.

When a child has a genuine love relationship with his father, he does not say of sin, "I can do that. Father has forbidden it, but he is a dear father and will let me get away with it." A child who thinks like that does not really love his father. And a father who would let his child get away with sin would not be acting in the child's best interest. A few years ago, young people on a youth retreat were badgering me to let them do something I told them they could not do. In desperation they talked with our son. He complimented me before them by saying, "He won't change his mind. If he said you can't do it, he won't change." In a genuine love relationship between a father and child, the child fears doing anything the father thinks is wrong.

C. *We will not be righteous in selfish obedience.* Righteousness is involved in redemption. An illustration of this is the familiar story of Cain and Abel. Both boys sacrificed obediently, but one's sacrifice was acceptable and the other's was not. This suggests that mere agreement with the principle of sacrifice is not sufficient. Somehow the ethical element made the difference in the acceptability of that sacrifice. The violent deed of murder was only the final expression of a hostility that righteousness frequently calls out in those who reject it. To love one's brother as oneself and to acknowledge God's fatherhood to all men—this is evidence of righteousness.

Conclusion

How then does one achieve righteousness? The familiar words to the hymn ring true:

> E'er since by faith I saw the stream
> Thy flowing wounds supply,
> Redeeming love has been my theme
> And shall be till I die.

We cannot achieve righteousness, either for moral uprightness or for acceptability with God. It is God's Son whose sacrifice makes us acceptable. The Old Testament principle is clearly stated by the prophet Isaiah: My righteous servant will make many righteous (see Isa. 53:11). It is God's Spirit who assists our moral uprightness. This is the word of the apostle in Romans 10:1–3. "Christ is the end of the law so that there may be righteousness for everyone who believes" (v. 4 NIV).

It is, after all, God's righteousness, not our own, that we seek!

WEDNESDAY EVENING, NOVEMBER 5

Title: Being Thankful When the Going Gets Tough

Text: "Though the fig tree does not bud and there are no grapes on the vines, though the olive crop fails and the fields produce no food, though there are no sheep in the pen and no cattle in the stalls, yet I will rejoice in the LORD, I will be joyful in God my Savior" **(Hab. 3:17–18 NIV)**.

Scripture Reading: Habakkuk 3:17–19

Introduction

The prophet Habakkuk, born six centuries before Christ, struggled with the injustices of the Chaldean regime over the Jews. His ministerial dilemmas paralleled the perplexities of the layman Job. He lived in a day of violence and apostasy. A pandemic parade of injustice marched past Habakkuk's ministry.

Like Moses at the burning bush and Isaiah in the Jerusalem temple, God did not fail to speak to Habakkuk in a time of deep hurt. The symbolism of our text cannot be overlooked. The fig tree represented prosperity. When the fields produced no food, people starved. No sheep or cattle in the pen meant no control over the animals.

Habakkuk could have become embittered. He might have endured the injustice with a stoic passivity. Yet he discovered that some times, even the worst times, may be God's time for us to draw close to him. What did Habakkuk discover he could do in a difficult day?

I. Rejoice in the Lord.

The Hebrew word translated "rejoice" means to exalt. It does not suggest that one jump up and shout for joy when hurting. It means that when we are climbing out of the valley of despair, we must not lose sight of God. Often people start a spiritual journey but lose their joy because they have lost sight of the objective. We must keep our eyes fixed on the summit of the Christian life, Jesus Christ. Habakkuk realized he had to focus his attention on God. The battle he now faced might be difficult, but the war had been won, and that created more thanksgiving in his heart.

II. Be joyful over your Savior.

Habakkuk noted, "I will be joyful in God my Savior." When people fill a stadium and become quite excited, even ecstatic, in their enthusiasm over a sporting event, we see that as normal. Yet when someone expresses exhilaration about faith in God, we call that person a fanatic. Have we forgotten the words of Jesus, "I have told you this so that my joy may be in you and that your joy may be complete" (John 15:11 NIV)?

Habakkuk learned to be thankful for his Savior. Giving thanks to God for his salvation helped him to overcome the difficulties he faced.

III. Receive the strength of God.

Inner strength sustains us in times of trouble. Habakkuk saw God as his strength. The word used by the writer means strong, firm, and durable—the type of strength that will enable us to run like a deer or climb to new heights like wild sheep. We need to claim God's power for our lives.

Conclusion

Habakkuk learned a concept that the apostle Paul would write about many years later: "The just shall live by his faith" (Hab. 2:4; Rom. 1:17).

Five hundred years ago the profound truth of living by faith changed the heart of a priest who became a mighty man of God. Not by his own choice, Martin Luther led a reformation in rediscovering biblical faith. Perhaps you need a reformation of faith today. Begin by learning to be thankful in times of difficulty and need. Live by faith.

SUNDAY MORNING, NOVEMBER 9

Title: Giving in Jesus' Name

Text: "But Peter said, 'I have no silver and gold, but I give you what I have; in the name of Jesus Christ of Nazareth, walk'" **(Acts 3:6 RSV)**.

Scripture Reading: Acts 3:1–10

Hymns: "Glory to His Name," Hoffman
"A Child of the King," Buell
"Our Best," Kirk

Offertory Prayer: Father God, you are the giver of every good and perfect gift. We thank you for every blessing of life. We come today with joy, celebrating your goodness and contributing tithes and offerings in honor of your holy name to the end that others might come to know you as Lord and Savior. In Jesus' name we pray. Amen.

Introduction

In 1975 Daniel R. Grant, president of Ouachita Baptist University, Arkadelphia, Arkansas, wrote of an unusual check received at OBU. The Kresge Foundation had given a challenge grant to the university of fifty thousand dollars. If the university could match that amount dollar for dollar, the foundation would award OBU fifty thousand dollars to use in the renovation of their science building.

Upon meeting the challenge, Dr. Grant wrote the Kresge Foundation. In return OBU received the check for fifty thousand dollars. But it was the handwritten endorsement that accompanied the signature of Stanley S. Kresge that Dr. Grant could not forget. It read, "In the name and for the sake of Jesus Christ." Mr. Kresge wanted those who received gifts from his foundation to know that he was giving "in the name and for the sake of Jesus Christ."

When I read that, I immediately thought of the experience of Peter and John in the temple when the lame man was healed. Peter gave healing to that man in Jesus' name. His answer in response to the plea for a gift was a classic: "Silver and gold have I none; but such as I have give I thee: In the name of Jesus Christ of Nazareth rise up and walk" (Acts 3:6).

It is interesting to note that Peter did not give the man what he requested. He gave him what he needed. What he did give was of more value—and what he gave was in Jesus' name.

As you look at your church budget and your response in Christian stewardship, it is most significant that you give in Jesus' name.

I. When you give in Jesus' name, there is response.

A. *An obvious need.* The beggar's need was obvious—he was crippled. He made a request, and Peter and John made a response.

The church also has an obvious need. A building needs to be

provided and maintained. Salaries of church staff persons need to be met. Programs and ministries must be funded. The church has an obvious need for money. What will be your response to that need?

B. *Response of love and gratitude.* By giving in Jesus' name, our response is one of love and gratitude. Because they had Christ in their hearts, Peter and John had compassion on the man. Perhaps you have seen the bumper sticker that says, "Honk if you love Jesus!" But one showed up recently that expresses far better the love and gratitude one has for Jesus. This bumper sticker reads, "If you love Jesus, tithe! Anybody can honk!"

II. When you give in Jesus' name, there is a resource.

A. *The resource we have.* Peter gave to the crippled beggar from the resource he had—the power of God in Jesus Christ.

B. *Utilizing the resource we have.* Notice that Peter did not give from what he did not have. He gave from what he had. He utilized the resource he had. And that is the only way we can ever give to God.

A part of all you earn is yours to give. It should not be less than a tenth and should be given first.

III. When you give in Jesus' name, there is a reward.

A. *Something wonderful can be done in Jesus' name.* The crippled man was healed. In joy he ran and jumped as he went into the temple. Something wonderful had been done in Jesus' name.

Through Christian giving something wonderful can be done in Jesus' name. It will express itself through witness of Christ, teaching about Christ, doing ministry in the name of Christ, and engaging in mission for Christ's sake. Something wonderful that benefits and blesses many people can be done in Jesus' name.

B. *You can have the joy of being a part of it.* When something wonderful is done in Jesus' name, you can have the joy of being a part of it if you have practiced Christian stewardship. We sometimes think of the reward only in material terms. It is much more than that. There is a spiritual joy and a sense of partnership in ministry that is very rewarding.

Several years ago an unemployed electrician sued his church, claiming that he did not get his money's worth when he tithed. He wanted to recover the donations he had made to the church in response to the pastor's promise that blessings, benefits, and rewards would come to the person who gave 10 percent of his or her money to the church. The man said that after three years he had not received blessings, benefits, or rewards.

A San Antonio businessman read of the suit and sent a check to the man. The businessman said in the letter that accompanied the check that he sympathized with anyone who gives money to the church and sits back expecting God to immediately hand it back to him, with interest, by some specific act. He went on to say that he had never tried to make a deal like that with God. He and his wife had tithed for thirty-six years and had found that God honors those who honor him.

Conclusion

When you give in Jesus' name, it is a great and wonderful experience. Your life will be greatly enriched by it. Others will benefit from it. Why don't you try it?

SUNDAY EVENING, NOVEMBER 9

Title: God Is Father

Text: "And this is his commandment, that we should believe in the name of his Son Jesus Christ, and love one another, even as he gave us commandment" **(1 John 3:23 ASV).**

Scripture Reading: 1 John 3:13–24

Introduction

The simple statement "God is Father" is more an axiom than it is an affirmation. An axiom is a fundamental truth on which other truths may be based. Geometric axioms include: "A straight line is the shortest distance between two points" and "The whole is greater than any of its parts." On these axioms other truths may be developed. Let us see what some other truths are that can be based on the truth that God is Father.

I. A relationship with the world.

The example of Cain is in the immediate background of our text. Cain's resentment and hatred resulted in death—he killed his brother Abel. Love is the sign of a change from death to life.

The hatred of the world against Christ and his followers is an abiding attitude. Since God is our Father, Christians have inherited a long-term feud with the world. It stretches both backward and forward as far as the eye can see. Against the backdrop of the world's hostility, love among Christians is the sure sign of a new life.

II. A relationship with their brothers.

To speak of a common father is to acknowledge one's brothers. There may still be fussing and fuming—brothers are like that—but deep down there is loyalty and love. This brotherly love among believers must be communicated not only in word but also in deed and in truth. It is utterly ridiculous to talk of love and ignore the needs of the love object. We have a better example of love than that! A place to begin with the expression of that love is in the area of communication.

In our society it is not ordinarily a matter of dying for one another to prove our brotherhood. It is a matter of relating. Simple accessibility is a step in the right direction.

To overspiritualize religion is to weaken it ethically. It is merely sentimental slush to talk of loving God while despising one's brother.

III. A relationship with God.

Finally, of course, this is the truth of the matter: God is Father, and his children are related to him. The basic fruit of love in this relationship is confidence. Let us look at the ABCs of this confidence.

A. *Assurance.* We are "of the truth" because our love for God is true and active. Any accusations of our conscience are stilled in the presence of God's love. God is greater than we are, and we quite properly pray, "Lead us not into temptation."

   God knows all things. There is no point in our trying to hide anything from him. He already knows it. He knows us far better than we know ourselves. He knows all things and still loves us! A friend has been defined as one who knows all about us and still loves us. "What a Friend we have!" The surest ground of our confidence is that God knows all things. There is no fear of a change of status in the relationship when he finds out the truth about us; he already knows it all!

B. *Boldness.* We are bold to approach God. Think of it! And this despite the hymn writer's praise:

   > Immortal, invisible, God only wise,
   > In light inaccessible hid from our eyes,
   > Most blessed, most glorious, the Ancient of Days,
   > Almighty, victorious, thy great name we praise.
   >
   > —*Walter Chalmers*

   How dare we approach God! Why, this is the child's relationship with his father. A child can approach her father anytime. Do you remember the story of the child who found his father asleep on the sofa with the newspaper spread over his eyes? The child approached carefully, removed the newspaper, and still the father slept. Yet curious, the child looked deeply into his face and found no response. Then cautiously he lifted one of his father's eyelids and sank back in satisfaction, saying, "He's still in there!" The child could approach his father because of his relationship with him. I have always told God things that I could not tell my own father. Dad might have been ashamed of me, but not God! God already knew.

Effective prayer is possible because God's revelation brings assurance. And so we boldly pray "for Jesus' sake."

C. *Commitment.* After **A**ssurance and **B**oldness comes **C**ommitment—the commitment of faith. Faith is almost taken for granted in these verses, because we keep God's commandments. He must be followed because of who he is. Conviction then as to who he is necessarily comes before obedience to what he commands. No other peasant carpenter of Galilee had the right to command the allegiance of people. There is no union with God in Christ that is not conditioned by commitment, by loyal allegiance to the gospel, in which the clear command of love is treated as new.

Commitment is fundamental. It is his commandment. We start here. This is what "God is Father" means. Why should we refuse to enjoy a personal relationship with him?

Conclusion

Believe in God's Son. Love one another. Perhaps this is a new commandment for you—one that you have never tried. If that is the case, I urge you to try it! And in the process, enjoy the ABCs of a new relationship:

Assurance
Boldness
Commitment

John Greenleaf Whittier's hymn of commitment is a prayer. Will you make it your prayer?

Dear Lord and Father of humankind,
Forgive our foolish ways;
Reclothe us in our rightful mind;
In purer lives thy service find,
In deeper rev'rence, praise.

WEDNESDAY EVENING, NOVEMBER 12

Title: Being Thankful for God's Word
Text: "Then believed they his words; they sang his praise" **(Ps. 106:12)**.
Scripture Reading: Psalm 106:1–15

Introduction

A minister once told a joke about a local news editor who had invited his readers to send in responses under the heading "Books That Have Helped

Me." One of the responses was from an individual who stated that the most helpful books in her life had been her mother's cookbook and her father's checkbook!

Many books help us, but one book alone has life-changing power. The source of life itself may be found in the Word of God. Listen for his voice.

The writer of Psalm 106 remembered God's salvation and interpreted the Exodus experience, recounting the spiritual high of the children of Israel. They had given thanks, observed the mighty things of God, celebrated his salvation, and stepped back as he opened the sea. They were high spiritually but soon forgot to be thankful enough to apply God's words to them. What happened?

I. They believed his words.

When commenting on Psalm 106, Charles Spurgeon noted that it was not to the Israelites' credit but to their shame that they believed. Who would not have believed the facts staring them in the face! Remember the words of Jesus: "Now while he was in Jerusalem at the Passover Feast, many people saw the miraculous signs he was doing and believed in his name. But Jesus would not entrust himself to them" (John 2:23–24 NIV).

Simply to believe God's Word is not enough. A student may believe in an upcoming exam, but unless he prepares for it, what good is that belief? The problem of the children of Israel was that they believed God but were unwilling to understand him and apply his Word. They had forgotten to be thankful. How did it happen?

II. They forgot his works and did not wait for his counsel.

Note the strong Hebrew language of verse 13. They forgot God's works. How easy it is to forget your health when you have it. You may forget a good friend until you lose him or her. You may forget your family members until you need them. The children of Israel did not wait for God's counsel. These people did good things, not bad things. But they neglected to recall the things God had done. They did not wait for his counsel. The term *counsel* comes from a Chaldean word that means "the power of restraint." They had forgotten the correcting power of God's words. They wanted inspiration, not transformation.

Someone has written that the world's most critical shortage may be silence. We do not meditate on God's Word enough. The life of the Reformation came from men like Luther and Calvin who studied their Bibles. Periods of renewal in the church come when the church takes seriously the admonition to search the Scriptures.

Like the children of Israel, we believe God easily. But do we pause to listen to his counsel? When we are not thankful enough to wait, the results may be devastating.

Conclusion

What a sad commentary one finds in Psalm 106:15: "And he gave them their request; but sent leanness into their soul." Picture an emaciated, spiritually anemic person. He or she believes the Word of God but fails to respond. Belief without thankful, thoughtful practice cannot suffice.

The best book is the Bible. It will change your life. Do not simply believe it; live it. Do not simply hold it; cherish it. Do not only read it; understand it. Be thankful for God's Word.

Sunday Morning, November 16

Title: Unappreciated Values in Christian Giving

Text: You always have the poor with you, and whenever you will, you can do good to them; but you will not always have me. She has done what she could; she has anointed my body beforehand for burying" **(Mark 14:7–8 RSV).**

Scripture Reading: Mark 14:3–9

Hymns: "Love Divine, All Loves Excelling," Wesley
"Something for Thee," Phelps
"All Things Are Thine," Whittier

Offertory Prayer: Father God, today we thank you for the privilege of our being alive physically. Even more so, we thank you for our being alive spiritually. Thank you for the gift of your Spirit to us. Thank you for the gift of material substance that has come into our hands. As we bring it, take it and bless it and use it to the end that others will come to know your love and the great salvation that is available through Jesus Christ our Lord. In his name we pray. Amen.

Introduction

In 1858 a scientific expedition passed through what we now call the Grand Canyon. A young lieutenant by the name of Ives made the following entry in his report: "This region we last explored, the Grand Canyon, is, of course, altogether valueless. It can be approached only from the south, and after entering it there is nothing to do but leave. Ours has been the first and doubtless will be the last party of whites to visit this profitless locality. It seems intended that the Colorado River, along the greater portion of its lonely and majestic way, shall be forever unvisited and undisturbed."

Obviously the young man did not appreciate the values of the Grand Canyon. Rather than being the last party to visit it, his was but the first. Many people since have seen and appreciated the values of the Grand Canyon that this young officer missed. There were some unappreciated values in the Grand Canyon.

Likewise, Jesus' followers could not see the values of the unselfish and gracious act of giving when the woman anointed Jesus' head.

At this time Jesus had entered Jerusalem in the triumphal entry. The time of his death was at hand. Jesus said that by the woman's act of giving the expensive perfume so lavishly, she had anointed his body for burial before the fact. The disciples did not see the value of it. Jesus did.

From this incident we can learn about some unappreciated values in giving.

I. The extravagance of love is one of the unappreciated values in Christian giving.

A. *The fact of love.* Obviously this woman loved Jesus. And what she did was extravagant, for the value of the perfume was about equal to a year's wages for an unskilled laborer.

In Luke's gospel the woman's loving act is tied into the forgiveness of her sin. Jesus, in fact, told a parable that highlighted the love that comes from gratitude for forgiveness (Luke 7:40–43). Because we have been forgiven of our sin and have been given new life in Christ, we love him. The fact of our love for Christ grows out of our forgiveness.

B. *Love excuses extravagance.* Young lovers give gifts they can't afford, but their actions are expressive of their love. One of my favorite short stories is O. Henry's *Gift of the Magi.* Jim and Della were a young couple who were very poor but very much in love. Each of them had one unique possession. Della's hair was her glory. When she let it down, it almost served her as a robe. Jim had a gold watch, which had come to him from his father and was his pride.

It was the day before Christmas, and Della had exactly $1.87 to buy Jim a present. She did the only thing she could do. She went out and sold her hair for $20. With the proceeds she bought a platinum fob for Jim's precious watch. Jim came home that night. When he saw Della's short hair, he stopped as if stupefied. It was not that he disliked her haircut or didn't love her anymore. In fact, she was lovelier than ever. Slowly he handed her his gift. His gift was a set of expensive tortoise-shell combs with jeweled edges for her hair. He had sold his gold watch to buy them for her. Each had given the other all he or she had to give. Each had given the extravagant gift of love.

II. The worth of benevolence is one of the unappreciated values in Christian giving.

A. *The objection.* The disciples' objection to the woman's gift was its worth. They could not see past the market value. Thinking only in monetary, material terms, they were unable to see the worth of benevolence.

We must not judge church expenditures the same way we judge business expenditures. The question for church expenditures is not "What will it bring?" but "What will it do?"

B. *The question.* The profit made by selling the perfume could have been used for something else. That fact was quickly pointed out by the onlookers. The central questions is, Should it have been used for something else? True, the money could have been given directly to the poor to alleviate suffering and hunger. But would it have been used that way?

C. *The encouragement.* What encouragement this act has been to giving! By this one gracious, generous, unselfish gift poured out on Jesus that day, many more people have been encouraged to give. Three hundred poor conceivably could have been helped had that money been given to them, but many more times that number have been helped through the inspiration of that woman's unselfish act.

A pastor once told the story of a great need his church had for financial support in a crisis. One Sunday morning he told the congregation about the need and asked them to bring their gifts to the front of the church. The members loved their church and their Lord, and they soon filled the aisles as they brought their offerings.

The pastor noticed one giver above all the rest—a little girl who was using a pair of crutches. When she reached the front of the church, she removed a ring from her finger, and after great effort, she placed it with the rest of the offerings and returned to her seat.

After the service was over, the pastor looked through the gifts until he found the little girl's ring. He took it to her and said, "Honey, I saw what you did. It was beautiful, but the response of the people has been so great that we have money left over, so we do not need your ring. I have brought it back to you."

The little girl looked up at her pastor and said, "I did not give that ring to you."

III. The acceptance of opportunity is one of the unappreciated values in Christian giving.

A. *The opportunity for service.* This woman had accepted the opportunity for service to Christ. She would have plenty of opportunities to help the poor. That was what Jesus meant by his statement. It was not that he had no compassion for the poor. It was, instead, that there would always be poor people who could be helped. The opportunity to serve Christ had to be taken then or it would be lost forever.

B. *The opportunity must be taken.* Some things must be done when they can be done. How often would we like to recall times and opportunities, but we cannot.

The writer Thomas Carlyle loved his wife, Jan Welsh Carlyle. But he was a cross-grained, irritable creature, and he never made life happy for her. She died unexpectedly, and after her death Carlyle looked through her papers, her notebooks, and her journals. Old scenes came mercilessly back to him in the memory of what had happened. In his long, sleepless nights he recognized too late what she had felt and suffered under his childish irritabilities. His faults rose up in judgment against him. He had thought too little of them before, but now he began to exaggerate them to himself in his helpless repentance. Again and again he cried, "Oh, if I could see her but once more, were it but for five minutes, to let her know that I always loved her through all that. She never knew it, never."

Christian giving allows us to act while we have the opportunity.

IV. The exercise of ability is one of the unappreciated values in Christian giving.

A. *What is it we can do?* Jesus' response in verse 8 is instructive. He said, "She has done what she could." Many of us are willing to do what we can't do—preach like Billy Graham, for instance—when we won't do what we can do—tithe or teach a Sunday school class, for instance. This woman did what she could do.

B. *Giving is one thing we can do.* Norman Vincent Peale told the story of a well-dressed, affluent man who came into his office one day. He had read Peale's books and had received some help from them but still was not happy. In the conversation the man revealed that he was from a wealthy family, had no church connection, and gave no money to anything that he could keep from giving to. So Peale told him that a place he could start would be to tithe, and he explained what that meant. The man wasn't sure he wanted to do that. Peale asked him what he was doing with his money. He replied that he and his wife were about to take a trip to Europe that he estimated would cost about ten thousand dollars. Peale told him that a tithe of that would be one thousand dollars. He could start then with that amount. When the man left the office, Peale thought he would never hear from him again. However, he soon received a check for one thousand dollars mailed from London. Later the man found a church in Chicago, his hometown. He became active in the church and in the service of the Lord. What he could do was give. He did that, and it started him in Christian service.

Conclusion

There are some unappreciated values in Christian giving. Give and those values will become apparent to you.

SUNDAY EVENING, NOVEMBER 16

Title: God Is Spirit

Text: "Hereby know ye the Spirit of God: every spirit that confesseth that Jesus Christ is come in the flesh is of God" **(1 John 4:2 ASV)**.
Scripture Reading: 1 John 4:1–6

Introduction

One of the most intriguing stories in the Old Testament concerns Dagon, god of the Philistines. It was in his temple that Samson wrought havoc in a final fling of strength. Later, after the defeat of the Israelites and the tragic death of Eli, the ark of the covenant was taken by the Philistines and placed in the temple of Dagon, ostensibly to do homage to the Philistine god. After the first night of the confrontation, Dagon was down on his face before the ark. Dagon's worshipers set him back on his pedestal. After the second night, Dagon was down before the ark, but his head and his palms lay cut off upon the threshold and "only the stump of Dagon was left to him" (1 Sam. 5:4). The Philistine priests got the idea and abandoned Dagon to the ark of God.

It was not that God was confined to the ark. It was rather that God as Spirit was more powerful by far than the idol Dagon. The holiness of God was such that this holy object plagued the Philistines for a long time.

A look at the encounter between Jesus and the Samaritan woman at Jacob's well reveals the profound statement, "God is Spirit." The Samaritans sought to limit God spatially, and Jesus would not permit it. Thus his statement represents a turning point in Christian history.

I. He is not flesh.

When we were children, we imagined God to be in the flesh, a Santa Claus or grandfather figure. Then we came to identify him with Jesus Christ in the flesh. Without bogging down in problems of understanding the Trinity, let us acknowledge that God is not confined by the limitations of the flesh. He is superior, for he is Spirit.

God is superior to flesh as mind is superior to matter, as man is superior to machine. To be sure, a Frankensteinian monster is a threat to the man who is his maker. Yet the maker is superior. Even so, flesh is a threat to spirit, but hardly to God who is Spirit. He made flesh, but he is not himself flesh.

Yet God came in the flesh in the person of Jesus of Nazareth. Here is the fundamental confession of Christianity: God loved the world enough to come in the flesh. This is the central truth of the Christian faith. The fundamental doctrine of Judaism is monotheism. No prophecy, however inspired, which contradicts the principles of monotheism can be accepted as true prophecy. The fundamental doctrine of Christianity is the incarnation. No prophecy, however inspired, which denies the reality of the incarnation, can be accepted by Christians as true prophecy.

Both religious faiths recognize the freedom of the Spirit. Both owe something of their essential nature to its exercise. But both draw a line beyond which such freedom is restrained by the demands of the fundamental truth. "God was in Christ"—all Christian truth is subject to this central truth!

II. Here is the standard by which other spirits are judged.

The New Testament writers accepted the reality of other spirits without reservation. Ours is a different age, yet who can explain the demonic in Hitler, Stalin, and Amin, and in the terrorist leaders alive today apart from the reality of other spirits?

Christians are at war daily with antichristian spirits. Opposition to the gospel is everywhere, specifically in the denial of the reality of the incarnation. Here is the spirit of error. The Christian does not dare to compromise with error in any realm and certainly not in any confession so fundamental as that of the incarnation.

The spirit of evil has sent forth his messengers into the world, and their activity is known to us. They speak as of the world and act as of the world. They come under such deceptive forms as ambition, power, honor, and knowledge, and these are distinguished from mere fleshly enjoyments. The world hears them and likes what it hears. But we are of God, the Spirit of truth. We speak God's Word, and those who are of God hear us and like what they hear.

As Christians who know God's truth, we have the responsibility of sharing it with others. If we deny the need of some fleshly neighbor while presuming to worship the spiritual God, we are liars! If we satisfy our fleshly excesses while talking of our spiritual accomplishments, we deceive ourselves.

III. The God who is Spirit may be known.

A. *He made our spirits capable of knowing him.* Perhaps this is the ultimate meaning of our creation in his image. Communication is possible.

B. *He came into human experience in Jesus Christ.* Here was real man, the way God intended man to be. Here too was real God. Here was the true union between God and man just as the Creator planned. This is what God is like—the incarnate Savior is the pledge of the complete redemption and perfection of man. He is the guarantor of the restoration of the body to its proper place as the perfect organ of the Spirit.

C. *He may be depended on.* This is a part of the knowledge that is faith. It is the story of Jesus' stilling the waves and quieting the winds of Galilee—"Greater is he that is in you than he that is in the world" (1 John 4:4 ASV).

D. *He continues in our experience as the Holy Spirit.* The Holy Spirit convicts the world of sin, righteousness, and judgment. The Holy Spirit offers himself as a guide into all truth—a knowledge that is apprehended as progressive, not complete. The true disciple is one who is ever advancing in the knowledge of God, whose power of hearing and learning is given by this attitude of faith expectancy.

Conclusion

God is Spirit. He is not flesh. He is the standard by which other spirits are judged. He may be known. What does this mean to us?

1. Believe not every spiritual manifestation. Be not deceived by every spiritual mouthing.
2. God may be known, but he must be confessed. Both inner faith and outward confession are involved here. He demonstrates the Spirit's superiority over flesh. He uses the incarnation to communicate with humans. He continues to witness to truth in every form.
3. But most important of all, "God is Spirit" is the confession of Jesus Christ as having come in the flesh for our redemption because God loved us.

I urge you to confess Jesus Christ. I urge you to join his church—his body. I urge you to decide to do his will.

WEDNESDAY EVENING, NOVEMBER 19

Title: Forgetting to Return Thanks
Text: "Jesus asked, 'Were not all ten cleansed? Where are the other nine? Was no one found to return and give praise to God except this foreigner?'" **(Luke 17:17–18 NIV)**.
Scripture Reading: Luke 17:11–19

Introduction

Jesus was journeying to Jerusalem. Certain Samaritans did not allow free passage to the Jews through their territory, so Jesus had to divert his route, but this did not stop him from being available to minister.

He met ten lepers in need. We identify with these ten in that we all are spiritual lepers apart from the healing salvation of God through Christ. What happened in this exchange of conversation?

I. We may play it by the rules.

The lepers stood at a distance and cried out with loud voices. They played by the rules. According to Leviticus 13:45, lepers had to identify themselves by wearing torn clothes, covering the lower part of their faces, and crying out, "Unclean!" Apparently nine Jews and one Samaritan were brought together by the same common affliction. They obeyed the law of lepers.

How many claim to be Christians by the law but are still infected with sin? It is not enough to play by the rules.

II. We may live by faith.

The lepers cried to Jesus. They requested mercy, not healing. Jesus exhorted them in a loud voice to go to the priests. They were given an opportunity to exercise their faith. Would they take it? Will we take the opportunity to live by faith?

III. We may obey Christ's commands.

The lepers went to the priests. Their action proved their obedience. They fulfilled the law of Leviticus 14:2 by going, and Christ healed them. But they still had a problem. They forgot to return thanks. A person who comes to church and hears a word from God on prayer, tithing, or serving and then does nothing about it is unthankful.

Is there anything sadder than ingratitude? In your home, your business, and your life, have you learned to give thanks?

Conclusion

One healed leper came back and glorified Jesus. He gave thanks. What an irony! The Samaritans had closed the door to Jesus' passage. The alternate route gave Jesus an opportunity to open the door of healing for this Samaritan. The unclean had met the ultimate clean. The Samaritan rejoiced and praised God. A spirit of gratitude filled his life.

A group of students planned an evangelistic meeting under a tent on the campus of a Christian university. They heard old-fashioned preaching and gospel singing. During the week a campus cleaning woman was robbed of her cashed paycheck while walking home from the school. She returned to her cleaning job the next day brokenhearted. She had no money for food or rent. Unknown to her, some students heard of her plight and took up a special offering for her one evening at the revival.

The next day a student representative approached and asked if she had found her stolen purse. She replied that she had not and did not know what she would do. She had only prayed and asked God for his help. The young student reached into his pocket, pulled out a roll of currency, and handed her in cash as much money as had been stolen, plus more. She fell to her knees, grabbed his hand, and cried out, "Thank God! Thank God!" She had learned the lesson of thankfulness.

Jesus asked, "Were not all ten cleansed? Where are the other nine?" If God has changed your life with the power of the cross, will you demonstrate your thankfulness to him today?

SUNDAY MORNING, NOVEMBER 23

Title: Giving Thanks to God

Text: "What shall I render unto the Lord for all his benefits toward me?" **(Ps. 116:12).**

Scripture Reading: Psalm 116:12–16

Hymns: "Come, Ye Thankful People, Come," Alford

"For All the Blessings of the Year," Hutchinson

"Just As I Am, Thine Own to Be," Hearn

Offertory Prayer: O God, on this Thanksgiving Sunday, help us to be truly thankful for all your benefits to us. We wish to make our offering today a thank offering, thanking you for your many gifts to us. Most of all we thank you for the gift of your Son. In his name we give. In response to his love we express our love. Use our gifts to tell others of your great gift. In Jesus' name. Amen.

Introduction

The observance of Thanksgiving Day is a distinctively American tradition. Its practice began over four hundred years ago, in 1621, on American shores, as grateful Pilgrims gave thanks for a modest harvest on a twenty-acre plot that promised to carry them through another hard winter. For over a century our nation has observed this festive day by presidential decree.

Thanksgiving Day is a distinctively religious observance. It was set aside as a day of prayer and praise. In 1863 President Lincoln set aside the last Thursday in November "as a day of Thanksgiving and praise for our beneficent Father who dwelleth in the heavens." Reinhold Niebuhr has expressed concern that our Thanksgiving Day emphasis has departed from this religious purpose. He has said, "The Thanksgiving proclamations of the American presidents for the last two decades have increasingly departed from the original rather purely religious spirit of Thanksgiving and they have increasingly become congratulations to God for having such wonderful children in America."

Thanksgiving Day is not set aside that we might concentrate all our gratitude within the day and take God's gifts for granted the rest of the year. Someone has suggested that we change Thanksgiving Day into a day of grumbling and complaint and spend the other 364 days of the year in thanksgiving.

Benjamin Franklin recalled a childhood experience that brought a sharp rebuke from his father. An old pork barrel was situated near the table from which the father would daily draw meat for the day's need. Then his father would always pray the prayer, "We thank Thee, Father, for the meat Thou hast set before us."

One day young Ben suggested: "Father, why not say one prayer over the whole barrel and get it done with? Then we won't have to thank the Lord every meal for every piece of meat we eat." Isn't this often what we do?

Never has a generation been so blessed with material comforts and possessions as in our day. The late Dr. Gossip told of a message he brought at a meeting in a small coal-mining town in Scotland. While he was speaking, a note was handed to the chairman. He glanced at it, looked over the crowd, and passed it down the line. Dr. Gossip said he could feel the sudden, ominous, tense stillness, the unanimous agony of suspense, the holding of breath, the quickening of the heartbeats of the whole group as the terrifying note made its way nearer to the woman to whom it was directed. Her face was white as she received it. Every eye was upon her. She opened it, read it, and smiled. Instantly everyone relaxed. Dr. Gossip commented, "For always, always they live with the terror of injury and death for their loved ones brooding over them—that we might have coal."

We flip a switch on our wall and expect light. We forget the linemen who keep the electricity flowing. We are unmoved when we read of the electrocution of a worker atop a pole.

We turn the faucet in our kitchen and water flows. In the book *Wind, Sand, and Stars,* written by a pilot of the French Sahara line during World War II, we read of three Moors from the desert who had never seen a tree, a rose, or a flowing river in their native land. After the War they were guests in Europe. They were shown a waterfall in the French Alps. Now, to them, water was worth its weight in gold. This extravagance was overwhelming.

The guide was ready to move on, but they insisted on waiting. "Why?" he asked. Their amazing reply was, "We are waiting for the falls to come to an end." It was simply beyond their comprehension that God should so madly supply water. This water had been running ceaselessly for thousands of years. When they returned to their homeland they said very little about the waterfalls. No one would believe them anyway.

The psalmist, in a time when his heart sang in praise in an awareness of God's gracious gifts, asked himself, "What shall I render unto the LORD for all his benefits toward me?" (Ps. 116:12). He answered with three responses:

I. I will take the cup of salvation (Ps. 116:13).

This is the first step. The greatest gift of God to humanity is the gift of his Son. "The wages of sin is death; but the gift of God is eternal life through Jesus Christ our Lord" (Rom. 6:23). We cannot sincerely say, "God, we thank you for sending your Son to die for our sins," and not accept that Son as our own Savior. To reject God's Son and his claims on our life is to say, "So far as I am concerned, he might as well not have come to the earth." The first response of gratitude is to "take the cup of salvation, and call upon the name of the Lord." What a blessed promise is the declaration, "Whosoever shall call upon the name of the Lord shall be saved" (Rom. 10:13).

II. I will pay my vows (Ps. 116:14).

"I will pay them," the psalmist suggests, "in the presence of all [God's] people." These are public vows. They begin with a public profession of faith. We declare our allegiance to Christ and his church. Like the public vows of marriage made by two people deeply in love, the public vows of the Christian put us on record and under obligation to be consistent and faithful to our vows to Christ and his church. Think back today on all the vows you have made since that first one. Think of the high, emotional experience when that baby was born and you held in your arms a life of your own flesh. Think of that revival meeting, that camp experience, that time of great sorrow or great joy when God was so close and you vowed to love him more devotedly and to follow his will. Thanksgiving Day is a wonderful time to pay our vows to the Lord in the presence of all his people.

III. I will assume the role of the servant (Ps. 116:16).

"O Lord, truly I am thy servant," the psalmist writes. When we assume the role of the servant, we are most like our Lord. The word *minister* means "servant." The word *deacon* means "servant." The New Testament declares that all Christians are called to be "ministers," "servants," in the sense that we are to be concerned with ministering to the needs of others rather than being concerned with being served by others. Jesus said of his coming, "The Son of man came not to be ministered unto, but to minister." Let us follow his example. Let us translate our "thanksgiving" into "thanksliving."

Conclusion

When Jesus addressed Peter with the question, "Do you love me?" He followed Peter's declaration with the words, "Feed my sheep." In other words, if you love, do something about it! Thanksgiving must not be mere words. The Pharisee started his prayer with the words, "God, I thank thee," but followed those words with a bigoted, self-centered eulogy about his own self-righteousness. How does God know we love him? By our doing something about it. This begins with receiving his blessed Son as our Savior.

Sunday Evening, November 23

Title: God Is Love
Text: "He that loveth not knoweth not God; for God is love" (**1 John 4:8**).
Scripture Reading: 1 John 4:7–21

Introduction

The campus of Berry Schools is on U.S. 27 north of Rome, Georgia. Across the highway is the beautiful home of Martha Berry, founder of the schools. Years ago this cultured lady was concerned by the number of mountain boys and girls who did not get an education. She began to teach them on Sunday afternoons in the Possum Trot Church. Inside the church, the roughly hewn benches still stand. The walls are planks of wood, also somewhat roughly hewn. And on the walls there are yet the painted signs that Martha Berry used to help the boys and girls learn to read. One says, "God is love." Imagine learning to read that one!

"God is love" is one of the first memory verses I ever learned. Twice in our Scripture reading this affirmation is made (see vv. 8, 16). The word *love* neither defines nor confines God—but:

I. Without God there is no love.

God defines love. Love does not define God. As we know it in God, love is selfless, self-giving, undeserved. Regardless of what others may say about love as God defines it, it is not passive response but takes the initiative.

Without God and love, ours would be a soulless society. Women are moving to assume their rightful place in society, but without God and love, women would never have had a chance. Look at the educational institutions, the hospitals, and the children's homes. Look at the very concept of charity in our society. Without God and love, ours would be a dismal dwelling place. This is a part of Paul's meaning in his "Hymn to Love," 1 Corinthians 13.

God is the source of love, and it takes a child to know the Father's love. Jesus knew and addressed God as Father. We too are God's children and address him as Father.

II. God is always love.

Regardless of the severity of life and its continuing judgment, God is love. Paul's philosophy may be read in chapters 9–11 of his epistle to the Romans.

Sometimes that which appears to be kindness in our experience may not be love but selfishness. Here is a beneficent despot. Is this love? Here is a condescending snob. Is this love? Here is a patronizing industrialist. Is this love? Here is a doting parent or spouse. Is this love?

The continuing testimony of the Spirit is that God is love. And this is our assurance, for human love is an expression of the divine nature itself. Love's presence in a person shows an experience of new life, of new birth, of becoming acquainted with God. Where love is absent, there has not even been a beginning of the knowledge of God, for love is the nature and being of God. This is as true in the home as in the church, for God's Spirit is present in both. Where love is absent, God is absent.

The supreme sign that God is love is the incarnation. The incarnation was the only way we could learn of the true nature of the invisible God. God sent his Son as our Savior.

Love here indicates complete devotion to someone. One's whole life is built around that person. There is a sense in which creation shows God's love, but his love comes through most clearly in the new creation. When God's love possesses a person, that person is loved. When a person is loved, that love becomes love. Love is like a nuclear reactor—a tiny bit of fuel increases until all the surrounding area is illumined, warmed, or energized. It becomes a living power as a manifestation of love in a person. Like the widow's oil in the Old Testament, it never runs out. God is always love—and God defines love.

III. God's love controls us.

Paul affirmed the truth: "The love of Christ constraineth us" (2 Cor. 5:14)—that is, God's love holds us together. The stanza in the old song confesses that the old-time religion "makes us love everybody." But if the hatred and hostilities of those who sang it in my youth reveal anything, it is that they knew little of God's love and they needed a more contemporary dose of religion!

This is the perfection of God's love—obedience in confessing Christ as Savior and Lord. This too is the perfection of God's love—confidence in the day of judgment, whether at the Great White Throne or now. There is no fear in love, for perfect love casts out fear. The fearful are uncontrolled, but God's love controls us. The fearful are self-centered, but God's love is self-surrender.

Where love is absent, terrorism takes control of us. Modern mayors, for their attempts to shift responsibility for a city's crime rate, are right to focus on the home and on the church as the source of the city's healing. We ought to be ministering to and enlisting the homes of our community. We cannot maintain a heaven inside the walls of the church if we leave a hell outside. The rising crime rate reflects the love of money, the love of power, and the love of self (indulgence).

But love is kind, not cruel. Love is gentle, not violent. Love is self-giving, not selfishly demanding. Love is godly, not godless. And we learn all that about love from God, for God is love!

Not once is the emphasis of this letter about God as the object of love. The first commandment is almost ignored in the emphasis on the second. There is here no strong statement, "Thou shalt love the Lord thy God"—but over and over there is the statement, "Thou shalt love one another." This is the challenge for us. It does not exclude our love for God, but it is much easier to check on our love for one another than on our love for God. "I love God!" Do you? "I love my brother or sister." Ah, I can see that!

Conclusion

Here is the perfection of God's love—for God is love: It is the obedience of confessing Christ; it is in loving one another; it is confidence in the day of judgment. This is possible for you—for God is love. The first step is an honest confession of Christ as Savior—God's love gift. Until you do that, you cannot really know that God is love!

WEDNESDAY EVENING, NOVEMBER 26

Title: How to Stay Thankful

Text: "Giving thanks always for all things unto God and the Father in the name of our Lord Jesus Christ" (**Eph. 5:20**).
Scripture Reading: Ephesians 5:19–21

Introduction

Psychiatrists tell us that our attitudes may hurt us or help us. Anger, bitterness, and resentment actually cause us physical harm. In contraposition, feelings of love, forgiveness, and concern heal us. The attitude of revenge hurts us the most. Gratitude helps us the most.

God gives us a fundamental principle for living. He asks that we remain thankful. He understands that gratitude and continued thanksgiving produce spiritual health and mental strength. How do we keep thanksgiving going? Paul offered some practical suggestions.

I. Express your thanks by singing.

Paul emphasized the use of psalms, hymns, and spiritual songs in thanking God. He knew that music influences mood. Positive singing helps us to give thanks. He suggested three different kinds of songs.

A. *Psalms.* Here we have a representation of tradition. The Jewish influence and Hebrew tradition imply instrumental accompaniment. The earliest hymns set Scripture to music. Perhaps you could sing a favorite Scripture passage.
B. *Hymns.* These are songs of praise with festive lyrics. We have many familiar hymns in our church. Why not sing a favorite hymn?
C. *Spiritual songs.* These might be classified as new and spontaneous songs. New songs help us express our emotions with the changing times. We should be open to contemporary music to help us express our appreciation to God.

II. Make melody with the music of your heart.

Have you ever met someone walking down the street humming or whistling a tune of joy? How do you respond? When you sing in your heart, God's Spirit lifts you. Perhaps you could try praying with a hymnal close at hand, thinking about some of the great melodies in your heart as you praise God. Internalize thanksgiving.

III. Continue giving thanks to God for everything.

Verse 20 contains four phrases: (1) "always," (2) "for all things," (3) "unto God," and (4) "in the name of . . . Jesus." The Bible does not suggest that everything is good, but it does suggest that we should always give thanks for something good. Jesus never suggested we rejoice in evil. Rather, he implied that in the face of insults, hardship, and persecution we rely on God's power and find something positive.

If you are upset about your heating bill, why not thank God for the warmth that will keep you safe through the winter? Has someone been angry with you lately? Then thank God for someone who loves you. You can always find something to be thankful for if you look long enough. You could be like the man who gets up every morning, looks at the obituary column in the paper, and if his name is not in it, stops and thanks God!

IV. Submit to each other in honor of Christ.

Much misunderstanding exists in Christianity today about submission in the New Testament. T. B. Maston has suggested that we voluntarily surrender ourselves for the sake of others and the good of the Christian community for the glory of God, so that in the final analysis Christian freedom will increase rather than decrease. Submission means deference. The secret of submission comes from an attitude, not a role. The joy of thanksgiving increases as we learn to serve others.

Conclusion

A philosopher once spoke a parable from a dream. He saw a room where a number of people were sitting around a table loaded with food. The people were starving to death because they had spoons strapped to their arms, and their arms were tied so they could not bend their elbows. They had plenty of food but were starving.

He envisioned another room. The same food graced the table. These people also had spoons strapped to their arms and could not bend their elbows. They were feasting. They fed each other.

Learning to stay thankful means learning to give ourselves to others. Keep thanksgiving alive this year.

SUNDAY MORNING, NOVEMBER 30

Title: Traveling a Different Road

Text: "And being warned in a dream not to return to Herod, they departed to their own country by another way" **(Matt. 2:12 RSV)**.

Scripture Reading: Matthew 2:1–12

Hymns: "Praise to the Lord, the Almighty," Bennett
"Come, Thou Fount of Every Blessing," Wyeth
"Let All the World in Every Corner Sing," McCutchan

Offertory Prayer: Father in heaven, you have granted to us so many generous gifts that we stand in amazement before the wonder of your love. Today we would join with the wise men, and we would worship you with gifts. Help us to give ourselves into your service. Help us to give your mercy and grace to others through our tithes and offerings. In Jesus' name. Amen.

Introduction

Just as the wise men took a new direction after they met the Christ child, so our lives take a new direction after we meet the risen Christ.

The glory of God shone around the shepherds who were out in the fields guarding their flocks on the night of Jesus' birth. The shepherds actually saw a visible manifestation of the invisible God and heard an angelic choir announcing Jesus' birth. Their experience marks one of the most significant points in all of human history.

There has been much speculation concerning the mysterious wise men who came from the East. We do not know how many wise men there were, and we do not know exactly where they came from, but we can make a number of practical applications regarding their experience. Not only were they wise men by vocation, but they were exceedingly wise because they sought for and worshiped the Christ child. People today are wise when they seek Christ.

Scripture records that because of a divine communication, "they departed to their own country by another way." It is not spiritualizing too much to draw the conclusion that even today when people truly experience the presence of Christ and bow before him in worship, they travel for the rest of their lives by a different road.

I. Recognizing and responding positively to the living Christ enabled many people to travel a different road during the ministry of our Lord.

The wise men were not the only ones who traveled a different road after meeting Jesus Christ. To meet him, to believe in him, and to respond to him positively produced a revolutionary transforming effect in the lives of people during his life and ministry.

A. *Matthew the publican traveled by a different road after he responded positively to the invitation of Jesus Christ to become one of his followers (Matt. 9:9).*

B. *The woman at the well traveled a different road after meeting Jesus (John 4:39–42).*

C. *The man possessed by demons and who lived in the tombs traveled a different road after he met and was delivered by Jesus Christ (Mark 5:19–20).*

D. *Zacchaeus, the Jewish tax collector for the Roman occupational authorities, walked a different road after Jesus came into his home for dinner and remained in his heart as Lord (Luke 19:8).*

E. *The man born blind traveled a different road after Jesus came by (cf. John 1:9 with 9:25).*

F. *Saul, the proud, legalistic, religious Pharisee who persecuted the early Christians, traveled a different road after meeting Jesus on the road to Damascus (Acts 9:1–22).*

II. The followers of Christ travel by a different road in the present.

The wise men traveled by a different road as they left Bethlehem because of a divine communication that came to them. Wise men who come to Jesus

Christ today travel a different road thereafter because of the divine gift of a new nature and because of the indwelling presence of the Holy Spirit, which is the gift of God to those who receive Jesus Christ as Lord and Savior (Gal. 4:6–7).

The different road that the disciples are to follow as a result of letting Jesus Christ become Lord is demonstrated and clarified in Paul's epistle to the Ephesians. He details at least four different ways in which we are to walk.

A. *We are to "walk worthy of the vocation wherewith ye are called" (Eph. 4:1).* The apostle is affirming that belief in Jesus Christ as Lord should result in behavior that is worthy of one's new relationship to God. Believers are to respond to the highest and best that is within them because they have received through the new-birth experience the new nature that comes from God. This new nature is to be worked out in actual experience and is to result in good works that magnify and glorify God (2:10; Phil. 2:12–13).

B. *We are to "walk in love" (Eph. 5:2).* The love of which Paul speaks is *agape* love, the God-kind of love that expresses itself in a persistent, unbreakable spirit of goodwill toward others. This kind of love can demonstrate kindness and helpfulness even toward the most unattractive. This imperative does not call for an emotional attraction, but for a Christian response both to those inside the faith and to those outside the family of God.

C. *We are to "walk as children of light" (Eph. 5:8).* Verse 9 explains what this means: "(for the fruit of the light consists in all goodness, righteousness and truth)" (NIV).
   1. To walk in the light is to walk conscious of the fact that we are always in God's presence.
   2. It means to walk in complete transparency.
   3. It means to walk differently from the ungodly world.

D. *We are to walk in wisdom rather than in foolishness (v. 15).* Followers of Christ are to watch their step and not follow the ways of foolishness and stupidity that lead to self-destruction and to harmfulness to others. To accomplish this we must continually seek to know the mind of God. We can do this best by listening to the words of Jesus Christ and not only hear him, but heed him (Matt. 7:24–27).

Conclusion

To enter into a personal relationship with Jesus Christ and to worship him in spirit and in truth will make it possible for you to travel by a different road for the rest of your life. With Christ as your Savior and Friend, you can walk into the future without fear of the past, the present, or the future. If you will truly worship the Christ and let him be the loving Lord of your life, you can achieve your highest potential as you travel the road of the future. By letting him travel with you, you can avoid failure.

Furthermore, with Christ in your heart and as the Lord of your life, you can experience the joy of being one of God's helpers as you travel a different road in the future from what you have traveled in the past.

SUNDAY EVENING, NOVEMBER 30

Title: The Christmas Mission

Text: "When they were come, and had gathered the church together, they rehearsed all that God had done with them, and how he had opened the door of faith unto the Gentiles" **(Acts 14:27)**.

Scripture Reading: Acts 14:27; 16:10; 18:6; 22:21

Introduction

Evangelist Arthur Blessitt carried a large wooden cross into Beirut, Lebanon, in the midst of war. He listened to both Palestinian and Israeli troops. He prayed for both sides. Such an act of boldness might be interpreted on the part of some as too risky. For Blessitt, who has carried a ninety-pound cross more than twenty thousand miles throughout the world, his testimony represented his mission.

Remember in this season of the year the Christmas mission. Jesus came into the world that all people might come to know him. And he assigned his followers the task of taking the gospel to all nations and baptizing new believers in the name of the Father, Son, and Holy Spirit and teaching them to obey God's ways (Matt. 28:19–20). Our mission remains the same today, for millions more around the world need to hear the gospel.

What will happen to all these people if we fail? Romans 10:14–15 asks, "How, then, can they call on the one they have not believed in? And how can they believe in the one of whom they have not heard? And how can they hear without someone preaching to them? And how can they preach unless they are sent? As it is written, 'How beautiful are the feet of those who bring good news!'" (NIV). God has given us a strategy and the opportunity to take Christmas to these people.

I. What does God do?

A. *He provides opportunities (Acts 14:27).* Many opportunities for evangelism exist throughout the world. After visiting the disciples in Antioch, Paul and Barnabas went to Pamphylia and on to Attalia. They reported that an opportunity had opened to witness to the Gentiles. Luke chose the phrase, "He had opened the door of faith." Such a phrase was used for the opening of a treasure chest or the unrolling of a scroll to receive new information.

Picture the discovery of a great opportunity. God opens such doors for us today. Remember John's interpretation of Christ's mission: "With your blood you purchased men for God from every tribe and language and people and nation" (Rev. 5:9 NIV). According to Revelation 7:9, people from all nations will stand before God. God wants all kinds of people to come to him. God provides us with diverse opportunities to share Christ.

B. *He calls us to go (Acts 16:10).* We must not look at the *place* of our service as Christians more than the *call* of God to where we are. When God calls us to go, it means to begin at a point and move toward a goal. We need to know where we are spiritually and have a goal set for sharing the gospel. Do we hear his call?

II. What must we do?

A. *We must take the message to listening ears (Acts 18:6).* Paul discovered that some people resisted the gospel. Some of the Jews blasphemed Christ; they were unwilling to hear. Others responded.

Take advantage of opportunities to share with people who will listen. If people have not been hearing you, perhaps you need to take the gospel message to a group that will affirm Christ. Take the message to receptive ears.

B. *We must become missionaries (Acts 22:21).* Every Christian has the responsibility of being a local missionary. The simple concept shown by Jesus in Matthew 10:7, "As you go, preach" (NIV), established for us the precedence of witnessing as we go about our daily activities.

One church historian's analysis of the Protestant Reformation concluded that including the laity in witnessing helped to bring renewal to the church. We need to remember that a pastor is not hired to do all of the witnessing of the gospel for the church. The minister should facilitate others to exercise their ministries. The question remains: Will we share Christ?

Conclusion

When John F. Kennedy was assassinated, the entire world knew in less than an hour. Yet millions have never heard the name *Jesus.* Who will carry the message? Who will share with the world that we live on a visited planet? Through Christ, the Creator of this universe has come. He will come again. Will we be ready? We will if we have been faithful to our Christian mission.

SUGGESTED PREACHING PROGRAM FOR THE MONTH OF DECEMBER

■ Sunday Mornings

"The Good News about God for All Humankind" is the suggested theme for the series of messages provided for Sunday mornings. In Jesus Christ, God speaks of his desire to be for us, with us, over us, and in us, and to work through us.

■ Sunday Evenings

Continue and complete the series "Communicating the Message of Christmas to the World."

Close out the year with an inspirational and challenging message for the new year.

■ Wednesday Evenings

Prayer is an opportunity to communicate with God and to experience communication from God. This month's sermons are based on the Lord's Prayer.

WEDNESDAY EVENING, DECEMBER 3

Title: Established in God
Text: "Our Father which art in heaven, Hallowed be thy name" **(Matt. 6:9)**.
Scripture Reading: Matthew 6:9–13; Psalm 46:1–7

Introduction

The Lord's Prayer, or model prayer, has the potential to deliver people from their basic human fears and anxieties. It can easily be divided into four subjects: security, provision, forgiveness, and purpose. We shall divide these four themes for the focus of our next four prayer services.

Can a person in his or her frailty approach God? What is God like?

I. What is God like?

The central issue that concerned Jesus was, "What is God like?" not "Does God exist?" Many people waste time trying to prove God exists when they could be describing the revealed attributes of the God of biblical revelation whom to know is life eternal.

Is God of such nature and spirit that frail humans can approach him in their weaknesses and fears? The first-century Jews believed God's main function was to sit in judgment on the keeping of the law. Persons who came short of the expectations of the law were required to perform precise cleansing rituals and to bring sacrifices and offerings to please and appease an angry God.

The religion of the Jews had deteriorated from the teaching of the Old Testament until it was not unlike the pagan religions. Their God had become frightening and demanding. Where was mercy? Where was hope? Where was a name that could be praised? Hallowed be *whose* name?

II. God is like Jesus.

As the Son of God, Jesus embodied God's spirit and nature. It was Jesus' purpose to make plain the character of God, in whom people were to hope. Jesus said, "Believe me when I say that I am in the Father and the Father is in me; or at least believe on the evidence of the miracles themselves" (John 14:11 NIV). Jesus' miracles came from a heart of love, compassion, and power.

III. Jesus is like the gracious description of God in the Old Testament.

Jesus suggested that the Scriptures be searched, for they tell of him—that is, they tell of the nature and spirit of God, which he embodied. A search of the entire Old Testament should be made to understand the full revelation of God. It is rewarding activity to read the Old Testament with a highlighter in hand to mark the passages that describe God and his gracious promises to those who depend on him. Such a study will reveal that there are a few words that are used over and over again to characterize God. He is faithful, just, merciful, and righteous (see Psalm 103; Jer. 9:24; Hos. 2:19–20; Jonah 4:2; Mic. 7:18).

Jeremiah 9:24 gives perhaps the most concise statement, saying that God delights in lovingkindness ("steadfast love," RSV), justice, and righteousness. Each of these words has the qualities of grace and love in them. In all things God is gracious. "Our Father, who art in heaven, hallowed be thy name!"

IV. The life and death of Jesus reveal the depth of God's care.

"God, who at sundry times and in divers manners spake in time past unto the fathers by the prophets, hath in these last days spoken unto us by his Son. . . . But we see Jesus, who was made a little lower than the angels for the suffering of death, crowned with glory and honour; that he by the grace of God should taste death for every man" (Heb. 1:1–2; 2:9; see also John 1:14, 16, 18).

What is God like? He is like Jesus, who cared for every person he met, who had power over the enemies of life, who never condemned a common sinner, who opposed oppressive religion, who delivered people from the bondage of the flesh, and who gave forgiveness and new life to all who would receive him. "Our Father, who art in heaven, hallowed be thy name. Thy kingdom come. Thy will be done on earth, as it is in heaven."

Conclusion

The challenge to us from God's hallowed character is twofold. First, we must comprehend and understand the revealed, gracious nature of God. Second, we must comprehend our human weaknesses and acknowledge them to God that he might minister to our needs.

Let us acknowledge to God our inability to do all that is needed to stand for right and to care for those in need, and then ask him to help us.

Let us acknowledge the common human fear of sickness, injury, and death and ask God to increase our faith in his sovereignty, his protection, and his purpose for our lives.

Hallowed is the name of God when we know his faithfulness, mercy, justice, and righteousness and submit ourselves to him.

SUNDAY MORNING, DECEMBER 7

Title: God for Us

Text: "The Spirit of the Lord is on me, because he has anointed me to preach good news to the poor. He has sent me to proclaim freedom for the prisoners and recovery of sight for the blind, to release the oppressed, to proclaim the year of the Lord's favor" **(Luke 4:18–19 NIV)**.

Scripture Reading: Isaiah 61:1–6; Luke 4:14–19

Hymns: "O Come, All Ye Faithful," Wade
"Good Christian Men, Rejoice," Medieval Latin Carol
"Grace Greater Than All Our Sin," Johnston

Offertory Prayer: God of grace, God of glory, we look into the manger and see your gift. It is not what we expected. Sometimes it is not even what we wanted. But in our better moments the revelation comes that the Baby is you; and then we pause, bow, and say thanks. We may give our money and time, but we know that most of all you want ourselves. In the Christ child's name. Amen.

Introduction

Christmas answers the question "What is God like?" but it does so in a manner that we would not have expected—neither how we would have expected nor why. Most of us would have expected the coming of God to be like the coming of an unexpected parent when we are caught with our hand in the cookie jar. That would not be good news! We picture God as a "resident policeman" who snoops around to find illegal activities. Or we see God as a "cosmic killjoy" who is up in the sky sniffing out where anybody is doing anything fun and then snuffing it out. Or we see God as the "big boss" who controls everything and everyone as pawns. In other words, we see the coming of God as bad news.

What has happened is that we have projected on God what we saw in our parents when we were young. We felt that their love and favor were conditional. As long as we were good, we felt safe; but when we erred, punishment was sure to follow. And thus we expect the coming of God to mean judgment and punishment because we have certainly erred. We know that "we all, like sheep, have gone astray," that "each of us has turned to his own way" (Isa. 53:6 NIV). We feel guilty through and through. We feel guilty because we are. We feel estranged from God. We feel that he is against us, that all he wants to do is punish us. We expect God to come as a proud and ruling judge.

I. God became flesh.

But things are not as we would expect. When God came to earth, he did not come as a proud and arrogant ruler. He came in weakness and dependency as a tiny baby. We would not have expected the incarnation—God becoming flesh.

II. Why God became flesh.

Nor would we have expected the favor of his coming. We expect punishment. We feel that we deserve no better, and we are right. We deserve to perish in flames, but Jesus came not to condemn but to redeem, not to punish but to forgive, not to intimidate but to inspire, not to sacrifice but to be sacrificed, not to be feared but to be loved. He came not as adversary but as advocate, not as foe but as friend, not as enemy but as brother, not as condemner but as savior.

In the fourth chapter of his gospel, Luke records Jesus' inaugural sermon, Jesus' own statement of purpose. What kind of minister would he be? What kind of Savior? What is God like? Why the incarnation? Why Christmas?

A. *The Lord had anointed Jesus, first, "to preach good news to the poor."* The poor are the socially inferior. Jesus proclaimed that the poor, those persons who view themselves as inferior and are treated as such, are to hear the good news of wholeness, equality, and authenticity.

   What a relevant word to us twenty-first-century persons who feel as though God has caught us with our hand in the cookie jar. We feel of no significance, of no worth, guilty. We expect God to treat us as inferiors—as indeed we are. But no, he has come to preach Good News to us. He has come to proclaim that we can know and relate to him from the position of children. That is good news indeed!

B. *Jesus was further anointed to proclaim the "recovery of sight for the blind."* Here blindness is used in both a literal and figurative sense. People are blind to God's words and deeds, and Jesus has come to open their eyes to see what God is really like. The Son wanted to communicate to "Pharisee types" who felt that God was holy and moral and had to be bought off with good behavior, and to "publican types" who felt that God was so holy and moral that there was no possibility of a relationship with the "Holy One of Israel." To these people Jesus proclaimed the good news that God is for us and that we do not have to earn his favor.

C. *The Anointed One also proclaimed "the year of the Lord's favor," which was begun in the person and work of Jesus.* All that Jesus has proclaimed is based on the fact that it is the year of the Lord's favor. Inferiors are given significance, prisoners are released, and blind sinners see what God is really like, because it is the year of the Lord's favor. God is for us. He is on our side. That is good news indeed!

III. What the incarnation means today.

What does all of this ancient history have to do with us today?

A. *The incarnation means, first, that humankind is guilty.* The presupposition of the movement of God to man is that there is a gulf between God and man because of our sin. Therefore, God comes. Sin is taken seriously. The mighty gulf of estrangement, alienation, fear, resentment, and guilt that exists between God and humankind can be dealt with in only one way: the incarnation of the Word. Our guilt made incarnation necessary, and incarnation makes our guilt obvious.

B. *Incarnation means, second, that humankind needs God, that people cannot move to God or attain the majesty of God on their own.* The self-movement of God to humans is needed because people at their own initiative will never move toward God. But God did not wait for people to seek him. God moves to people first; he seeks rather than is sought.

C. *Incarnation further means that humankind is loved by God.* God's love is constant, not conditional. Witness his love for the rebellious children of Israel. Remember Romans 5:8: "But God demonstrates his own love for us in this: While we were still sinners, Christ died for us" (NIV).

D. *Incarnation means that humankind is summoned to return.* The "coming" of God to humans always involves the summons of a person to return to God. God did not become flesh for thrills or kicks, to masquerade or to play a game. He came to redeem, and thus he demands a response.

Conclusion

So Christmas answers the question "What is God like?" Christmas did not happen *how* we would have expected—a baby; nor *why* we would have expected—to proclaim God's favor. With notes loud and clear, the manger proclaims that God is on our side! Hallelujah!

Sunday Evening, December 7

Title: Is God on Your Christmas List?

Text: "When they were come into the house, they saw the young child with Mary his mother, and fell down, and worshipped him: and when they had opened their treasures, they presented unto him gifts; gold, and frankincense and myrrh" **(Matt. 2:11)**.
Scripture Reading: Matthew 2:7–12

Introduction

The Magi were Greek wise men who followed the signs of the Messiah. One evening while studying the stars, they discovered the sign of the coming of Jesus. They went to Jesus, and they brought him gifts. Should we do any less?

I. We know he will be present.

The visitors had seen the star in the east. They did not have a map, but the light guided them. We may not have every detail of life worked out, but we have a guiding light and a goal. The light of Jesus Christ draws us. As Isaiah prophesied, "Nations will come to your light, and kings to the brightness of your dawn" (60:3 NIV).

Jesus has come. What should be our response?

II. We should present him with our gifts.

The wise men experienced exuberant gladness. They were delighted. When they fell down, it was not so much a bow as it was an attempt to be on the level of the Child. They wished to experience Jesus. They had prepared to worship him. Look at the symbolism of their gifts.

A. *Gold.* In the ancient world no one could approach a king without a genuine gift. Gold was a gift for a king. Jesus is our King.
B. *Frankincense.* This aromatic gum distilled from a tree was a gift for the priest. Jesus Christ is our Great High Priest, who has bridged the gap between God and humankind.
C. *Myrrh.* This was a gift for one facing death. It was used to embalm. Jesus Christ as our supreme Savior was born to die that we might live.

Conclusion

The visit of the wise men explains the breadth of the universality of the grace of God. He comes to everyone, not just to an exclusive group.

The story is told of a church building in New York that had been damaged by an Atlantic storm some years before. An auction was held to raise funds to repair the building. An old embroidered tablecloth had been donated for the auction, but no one bid on it, so the pastor finally bought it to cover a hole left in the plaster by the storm.

The day before Christmas the pastor observed an elderly woman standing on the corner waiting for a bus. Since the bus ran every hour, he went out and invited her to come in out of the cold. When she saw the tablecloth, she wept. In broken English she said, "This is mine. My husband bought it for me in Vienna before the Nazis ran us out. We haven't seen each other since before the concentration camp." The pastor offered her the tablecloth, but she refused to take it. She left on the next bus.

Later that day in a Christmas Eve service, an elderly man visited the church. He too noticed the beautiful tablecloth. He came to the pastor after the service and observed that the cloth looked like one he had given his wife in Vienna before the Nazis had run them out. He shared exactly the same story the elderly woman had shared with the pastor earlier that day.

The pastor went to work. In his conversation with the woman, the pastor had discovered that she was interviewing for a cleaning job. He called all the ads in the newspaper for a housekeeper. One call uncovered a family who had interviewed a woman that day. They had not hired her because of her broken English, but they had her address. On Christmas morning the pastor and the old man journeyed to the home of the elderly woman. After many years, each thinking the other dead, they were brought together in the miracle of Christmas—centered around a storm, a hole in a church wall, a tablecloth nobody wanted, a lonely woman waiting for a bus, and a lonely man.

Christmas means giving and discovering. What will you give Christ for Christmas?

Wednesday Evening, December 10

Title: Confidence for Each Day
Text: "Give us this day our daily bread" **(Matt. 6:11)**.
Scripture Reading: Matthew 6:19–34

Introduction

To be hungry or to lack other vital necessities such as shelter, clothing, or health care is a terrible thing.

I. We need to acknowledge our needs.

Jesus spoke of our "daily bread." It is a necessity, and he acknowledged it. Sometimes we confront persons whose irresponsibility is so great that they spend their wages on unnecessary things, forgetting that food must be bought or that rent must be paid. Certainly we must be aware of our daily needs.

However, too much concern may bring about as much destruction as a lack of concern. Worry and anxiety can create all sorts of health problems. They can ruin one's personality, take away one's sense of humor, and even make one selfish and offensive. They can destroy character, prompting one to lie and cheat in business dealings. Some may even resort to stealing because of their fears when they are in need. Worry and anxiety can deprive them and their families of the enjoyment and meaningful use of their substance. They can remove charity from one's heart, destroying the evidence that there is any Spirit of God within. A well-filled pantry or bank account does not remove excessive concern, for we know all that we hoard can be destroyed by "moths and rust" and "thieves who break through and steal."

II. The practice that leads to daily peace and confidence.

Our text begins, "Give us . . ." Jesus leads us to express our faith in God as the source of our necessities. We look to him. Our daily spiritual exercises frequently need to dwell on passages that testify to God's faithfulness to provide for us. Psalm 23 and others bless us because of their promises. Our daily spiritual meditations should focus often on such passages.

Note that in our text "Give us" is plural and it acknowledges a state of dependency. Having shared our needs with members of the faith, we can be sure that persons who have the Spirit and spiritual nature of God will care and share.

Conclusion

We believe that this is God's world and that he cares for us. We can gladly and confidently submit ourselves to his care. Let us take a moment to:

- personally note the necessities that bring anxiety, then acknowledge these to ourselves and to God
- share together about our needs and abundance
- give to God the anxiety of each day's bread
- walk in hope and confidence and sharing

SUNDAY MORNING, DECEMBER 14

Title: God with Us

Text: "'She will give birth to a son, and you are to give him the name Jesus, because he will save his people from their sins.'

"All this took place to fulfill what the Lord had said through the prophet: 'The virgin will be with child and will give birth to a son, and they will call him Immanuel'—which means, 'God with us'" **(Matt. 1:21–23 NIV)**.

Scripture Reading: Isaiah 7:14; Matthew 1:18–25

Hymns: "Joyful, Joyful, We Adore Thee," Van Dyke

"We Have Heard the Joyful Sound," Owens

"Joy to the World! The Lord Is Come," Watts

Offertory Prayer: Holy Father, we walk through many valleys—valleys of death, despair, disillusionment, and darkness. Sometimes we cannot find our way through—and then you come. Thank you for the gift of your Son with us. May we now give so that the proclamation of "Immanuel, God with us" will be broadcast with notes loud and clear. In Jesus our Savior's name. Amen.

Introduction

How do you expect God to help you? In our text this morning, Matthew proclaimed the purpose of God's mission on earth by showing that the name *Jesus* means "Savior." Thus the purpose of Jesus' birth is to save, but how will that take place? How do you expect God to help you?

The Jewish religious establishment had some ideas about how God could help his people. God could give military liberation and kingly rule. The Messiah would destroy a hostile world, lead the people of Israel to power, and rule them brilliantly. Or the messianic reign would mean a time of economic prosperity. God could give them peace—a time when Israel was neither oppressed nor at war.

How will God help us? How will he save us? Both biblical texts we read this morning proclaim the same truth, namely, that "presence" is the way of God's salvation—"Immanuel, God with us." The passage from Isaiah 7 is referring directly to the birth of Christ; but it makes the same point that Christ's birth would make more than seven hundred years later. The only promise that God would make to Ahaz was the sign of his abiding presence. And this is the only promise God ever makes to his followers. We will never walk alone. The promise of God's presence with his people is ultimately and uniquely fulfilled in the advent of Jesus. His birth is heralded as "Immanuel, God with us." The birth of this Child brings the presence of God near to us. Presence is the way of God's salvation.

How does God help us? "Immanuel, God with us"! Let us look briefly at three ways God ministers to us through the gift of presence.

I. God's presence establishes communication between God and humankind.

God desired to redeem humankind, to restore relationship, to open the lines of communication, but how? He wanted to communicate to humankind that he loves us, that he has our best interests at heart, that he can deal with our fears, pain, and feelings of meaninglessness, estrangement, and alienation. People feel an inability to communicate with a God who is distant, abstract, only holy. But we can relate to a person. We can share with a person our struggles and successes, pains and problems, heartaches and hopes. We can talk to a person—to Immanuel, God with us.

II. God's presence gives meaning to human existence.

Often life does not seem fair or right. Innocent people suffer. Six million Jews are executed ruthlessly at the whim of a sick and sadistic man. A youth bound for seminary is run over by a drunken driver. Two husbands and fathers shoot and kill each other in a senseless fight over who has rights to the CB airways. A prized daughter dies in her youth after an eighteen-month bout with leukemia. The direction of a country is changed as a result of a pistol shot at the back of the president's head in Ford Theater or a rifle fired at another president's head in Dallas. Sixty youth on a church-sponsored trip die in a bus crash. What, you ask, does all of this have to do with Christmas? Why speak of this insanity now? Why tell of these awful things at this happy time? Because they are the reason Christ came, and his coming gives meaning and purpose to it all. He took it! He took the best punch Satan had to give. He declared that life was worth living by coming to live himself. Immanuel, God with us! As Dorothy Sayers so aptly put it: "For whatever reason God chose to make man as he is—limited and suffering and subject to sorrows and death—he had the honesty and the courage to take his own medicine." Immanuel, God with us.

III. God's presence provides redemption.

Matthew wrote that the birth of God's Son would be as Savior—Jesus—and that God's Son would be Savior through his presence—Immanuel. By his presence he becomes the map to find one's way to ultimate reality. By his presence he is the model of what it is to be human and what it is to be God. He comes to us to be the guide to take us to God. Many could not be saved by a distant Savior. Good News not only had to be heralded but also had to be brought. Jesus both proclaims the Good News and is the Good News—Jesus, Savior, Immanuel, God with us.

Conclusion

How do you expect God to help you? A seminary professor had a poster on his office wall that showed hills of sand with a set of human footprints. The poem on the poster contained a conversation between a man and God. The man complained that God had promised never to leave or forsake him; yet when he looked back on his life, he noticed that during the tough and difficult times, there was only one set of tracks rather than the customary two. The man wanted to know why God chose the difficult times to leave him. God responded that during the tough times, when there was only one set of prints, it was then that God had shouldered the burden and carried him.

Immanuel, God with us. Isn't that something!

Sunday Evening, December 14

Title: The Changeless Character of Christmas

Text: But when the fulness of the time was come, God sent forth his Son, made of a woman, made under the law, to redeem them that were under the law, that we might receive the adoption of sons" **(Gal. 4:4–5)**.

Scripture Reading: Galatians 4:4–5

Introduction

Our world is rapidly changing. Even Christmas customs change. Many families no longer cut down a Christmas tree or buy one from a lot; instead, they use an artificial tree. And we have gone from using candles, to electric lightbulbs, to fiber-optic lights on our Christmas trees. In a changing world with changing customs, it is good to know that there are some things that do not change. One thing that never changes is the character of Christmas.

I. God provides Christmas at the right time.

Paul wrote about Jesus arriving on earth at just the right time. God sent his Son by divine appointment in the fullness of time. It was the right time politically. The transportation system of Rome allowed a marvelous opportunity for the gospel to spread rapidly in the ancient world. There was economic unrest and poverty. People were ready for a change. The morals of the Roman Empire had degenerated to paganism. They needed reform. Linguistically, the technical precision of the Greek language made the writing of the New Testament possible in a universal language of the culture. It was the right time. Christmas always comes at the right time if we will let it.

II. God sends his Son.

A. *The deity of Christ.* God's sending his Son implies the preexistence of Christ. By his divine authority, he was sent on a mission to die that we might have life. Jesus said in John 8:58, "Before Abraham was, I am."

B. *The humanity of Christ.* Paul noted that Jesus was born of a woman under the law. Christ submitted himself to the law in order to redeem those enslaved by it. Jesus was born of a virgin. He was fully human in his birth and growth.

Why did God send his Son?

III. God offers redemption by adoption.

Paul noted that Jesus came to redeem that we might receive adoption. Redemption means that we have been set free. The concept comes from the setting free of slaves in the ancient world.

In addition, being under the law meant a child possessed nothing until he or she came of age. A child made no legal decisions and had little freedom. We are like helpless children without Christ. God has adopted us into his family so that we might be restored and have fellowship with him.

Conclusion

Several years ago a wealthy bachelor passed away without leaving a will. The courts discovered seven heirs. All except one were found. For years the courts searched to find his heir. He was located living in the streets of Chicago. After he received his inheritance, he returned to the streets of Chicago to live the same life of loneliness he had known. He had been given a great gift, but he did not know how to use it.

At Christmas we receive the greatest gift of all—Jesus Christ. What do we do with him? How do we claim our inheritance? Some things change in our world. Some things do not. The changeless character of Christmas remains. We are confronted with Christ. What will we do with him?

Wednesday Evening, December 17

Title: Overcoming through Forgiveness
Text: "And forgive us our debts, as we forgive our debtors" **(Matt. 6:12)**.
Scripture Reading: Matthew 6:14–15; Psalms 32:1–5; 51; 103; Jeremiah 31:34

Introduction

There are two things about people that must always be remembered. First, they are created in the image of God for eternal life to be a blessing to one another. Humans are truly of great worth. Second, they fall short of all standards and goals. This results in a state of condemnation in which guilt and uncleanness compel them to perform all kinds of religious rituals and self-defending actions. A great amount of the energy that compels people to both service and competition is generated by their embarrassing shortcomings. The tragedy is that neither services rendered nor competitors defeated truly give people a sense of cleanness or peace. Only the forgiveness of their faults by God can do that.

How can we humans dare confess our faults to an almighty God?

I. First, we must meet the forgiving nature of God.

There are many warnings from God about the results of rebellion against him; however, the basis of human victory is not in the warnings but in the promises on which we are to build our lives. Warnings and punishments cannot save; they only serve to get one's attention. Salvation and life are derived from a faith relationship with God.

Psalm 103 provides us with one of the richest statements about God's attitudes and actions toward human shortcomings. God does not deal with people according to their sins but according to his mercy (vv. 11, 13, 17). "God's kindness is meant to lead you to repentance" (Rom. 2:4 RSV).

Let us note passages such as Psalms 32, 51, and 103, and meditate on God's forgiveness until we meet the forgiving God.

II. We must acknowledge our shortcomings to receive God's forgiveness.

As noted above (Rom. 2:4), the kindness of God is meant to lead us to repentance. Acknowledging our shortcomings is necessary for a full experience of forgiveness and cleansing.

A. *All of us have certain flagrant sins we may prefer to forget; however, we must fully confront them in the presence of God.* When we acknowledge them in the confidence of his forgiveness, we will experience cleanness and strength for victories. Remember 1 John 1:9.

B. *Most of us need to pause and evaluate habits of minor or major excesses, such as eating, talking, buying, recreating, and the like.* By confessing them one by one, we focus our efforts and God's grace on our weaknesses.

C. *Finally, we Christians need to measure our character by the fruit of the Spirit that we bear: love, joy, peace, patience, kindness, goodness, faithfulness, gentleness, and self-control (Gal. 5:22–23).* Such a comparison will illuminate shortcomings that are too often overlooked. These can be confessed so that forgiveness and grace can bring victories.

Let us pause to identify

1. our great sins
2. our excesses
3. our spiritual fruit

III. Personal forgiveness results in forgiveness toward one another.

". . . as we forgive our debtors." When faced with a "debtor," one who has received full and eternal forgiveness will have compassion and the desire to heal personal relations by forgiving. To deal with persons outside the church with the attitude of forgiveness may be difficult, but it can be a witness for our God who forgives.

Within the church fellowship, forgiveness provides an atmosphere for spiritual growth. It can lead to trust and to sharing of human frailties. It can lead to mutual help by finding encouragement and strength in the victorious experiences of others.

Conclusion

God has given us three sources of strength for victory over sin—ourselves, his grace, and the church. To receive from each of these resources, we must first admit that we have needs. When our energies, God's help, and the encouraging help of the church are marshaled, surely we can experience many more victories. Are you humble enough to seek help from the resources provided?

Sunday Morning, December 21

Title: God over Us

Text: "In the beginning was the Word, and the Word was with God, and the Word was God. He was with God in the beginning. . . . The Word became flesh and made his dwelling among us. We have seen his glory, the glory of the One and Only, who came from the Father, full of grace and truth" **(John 1:1–2, 14 NIV)**.

Scripture Reading: Genesis 1:1–31; John 1:1–14

Hymns: "A Mighty Fortress Is Our God," Luther

"Hark! the Herald Angels Sing," Wesley
"God of Our Fathers, Whose Almighty Hand," Roberts

Offertory Prayer: O Lord, our Redeemer and Creator, we are yours—our lives, our all. Now we give you an offering, a small token of our allegiance to you as citizens of your kingdom. In the name of Jesus, our Lord, Savior, and King. Amen.

Introduction

It is the twenty-first day of December, 2025, "the year of our Lord." How did that tiny, dependent baby, who grew up and lived an earthly life just like us, get to be so important that the calendar was changed to mark his birth? History is marked by everything happening either before or after this event, which we celebrate at this time of the year every year. How in the world?

One begins to get the impression that there is more here than meets the eye. We have seen the Baby; we have heard his cry. We have seen him learn to walk after many stumbles, falls, and tries. We have seen the young man attend the synagogue to learn from the rabbis, and we have seen him nailed to the cross. Yet it is 2025, "the year of our Lord." How in the world? There must be more to it.

And there is. This Son is no normal man's son. His Father is Yahweh, Jehovah, the Lord God Almighty, the Maker of heaven and earth. Jesus shows us not only that God is for us and with us but also that God is over us.

I. A look back.

A renowned theologian of the twentieth century would say that these sermons have been preached in the wrong order. He would contend, "Before we knew that God was for us and with us, he was God over us."

And Karl Barth is correct. God over us, in point of fact, was first. (There is a reason for the chosen order.) God over us is first, and thus Christmas points us back. This Baby, who grew up to be the King of the only eternal kingdom of civilization's history, reveals the God who is Almighty, Creator, Redeemer, and Sovereign Lord.

God is the one who addresses humans and makes himself known to us. God is the personality who speaks. We are addressed by God and demanded to respond to his call. He meets us as the absolute Lord who claims us unconditionally for himself. God reveals himself as the one who has an absolute right to lay his claim on us.

God has now spoken through his Son, and the demand for obedience is undeniable and inescapable. His coming makes our responsibility unconditional. We must say yes or no. We are summoned to carry out his will and his demands. He is "God over us."

Thus the birth of Jesus points back to the God who laid the foundation of the world, who is Almighty, Creator, Redeemer, and Sovereign Lord. That Baby in the manger is no less than "God over us."

II. A look forward.

The birth, life, ministry, and death of Jesus inaugurated the kingdom of God. The dominant concept of Jesus' messages is the reign of God. Jesus proclaims its immediately impending eruption. Everything is swallowed up in the single thought that God will rule.

Because God is King, Jesus calls for radical obedience. He makes a demand for decision. Now is the last hour. Now it can be only "either-or." Now the question is whether a person really desires God and his reign or the world and its goods; and the decision must be made. "No one who puts his hand to the plow and looks back is fit for service in the kingdom of God" (Luke 9:62 NIV). "Follow me, and let the dead bury their own dead" (Matt. 8:22 NIV). "Anyone who does not carry his cross and follow me cannot be my disciple" (Luke 14:27 NIV). "If anyone comes to me and does not hate his father and mother, his wife and children, his brothers and sisters—yes, even his own life—he cannot be my disciple" (v. 26 NIV). Thus Jesus calls for radical obedience to God's will.

The birth of Jesus brings in the reign of God. In the birth of Jesus, "God over us" takes on new form. Jesus calls each person to radical obedience to a love that has no boundaries and needs no instructions.

Conclusion

So Christmas points us forward, and again we encounter God Almighty: the one who created and calls; the one who redeems, rules, and reigns; the one to whom we respond with obedience because he is "God over us."

Sunday Evening, December 21

Title: Have We Outgrown Christmas?
Text: "And the child grew, and waxed strong in spirit, filled with wisdom: and the grace of God was upon him" **(Luke 2:40)**.
Scripture Reading: Luke 2:40

Introduction

A young couple, proud to bring their firstborn child home from the hospital, placed the boy in a beautiful wooden cradle. Over the months he grew. The cradle that had once swallowed him could no longer contain him. He began to look like a giant in a baby bed. His parents kept the cradle as a symbol of the child's birth, but the boy could not stay in the cradle forever. He outgrew it.

One cannot have Christmas without the cradle. But Jesus did not stay in the manger long. We too must outgrow the cradle.

I. We spend most of our lives outside the cradle.

Jesus' growth was natural and normal. As a child, he grew in wisdom and stature. The Bible does not indicate that Jesus had any adult capacities as an infant or a child. He could have, but we have no such biblical authentication. Apparently, he went through the natural growth stages of child development.

Like Jesus, we too must be willing to grow. We should allow the church to nurture us. The Bible samples for us the voice of God as a correcting and stabilizing force. The lordship of Christ encourages us to focus our attention on Jesus. Knowing Christ allows us to come into a closer relationship with him. Yes, one spends most of life outside the cradle.

II. Survival outside the cradle requires strength.

When Luke recorded that Jesus became strong, he indicated that such strength was given to him. In the same way, we must receive faith, courage, and strength from God. Look at the strength demonstrated by Christ.

Jesus exercised the power of his will and self-restraint. He measured the strength of a man by the power of his feelings he subdued, not by the power of those who subdued him. Jesus' strength was not unbridled. It was directed and controlled by the will of God. In the same fashion, our lives should be controlled by God's hand. We must achieve a balance.

III. Strength must be complemented with wisdom.

Jesus grew in wisdom. The New Testament teaches us that Christ was fully God and fully man. He grew in wisdom as a man. He did not simply acquire facts or obtain information. Paul warned young Timothy not to substitute mere facts for wisdom, "ever learning, and never able to come to the knowledge of the truth" (2 Tim. 3:7).

The student who studies only the night before an exam to earn a grade may pass but does not learn. In a world where random data passes for wisdom, we must learn that Jesus came to apply knowledge. People desperately need his wisdom today. "To get wisdom is better than gold; to get understanding is to be chosen rather than silver" (Prov. 16:16 RSV). The world needs wisdom, not just information! We need today a sound wisdom for life built on the Judeo-Christian concept that God, not man, is the center of our universe.

IV. God's grace extends beyond the cradle.

God's gift came to Bethlehem two thousand years ago. God's grace comes to our community also. We must grow beyond our simple views of life.

The late George Buttrick shared a story about his grandmother who was visiting the United States from Czechoslovakia. She tried to cross against a traffic light in New York City, and someone pulled her away from the path of an oncoming bus. After he composed himself, Buttrick rebuked her, "Do not walk against the light!" She responded, "But this is a free country!"

That is the problem with too many people today. People feel they can do anything they want and get away with it. They cannot.

Conclusion

Have you outgrown the cradle? You should have by now. Move beyond the ABCs of Christianity. Do not neglect the cradle, but let it become a beginning point for a new year to grow, become strong, be filled with wisdom, and accept God's grace. Outgrow the cradle. Jesus did. You can too.

WEDNESDAY EVENING, DECEMBER 24

Title: Sharing the Purposes of God
Text: "Thy kingdom come, thy will be done, on earth as it is in heaven. . . . Lead us not into temptation, but deliver us from evil" **(Matt. 6:10, 13 RSV).**
Scripture Reading: Galatians 3:1–9; 1 Peter 1:14–15; 2:1, 11, 16; 2 Peter 3:17–18; 1 John 1:7–10; 2:15–17

Introduction

God intends that believers walk with him in his care and purpose, escaping the evils of the temptations that confront our frail humanity.

I. God purposes that man live first in his care and then in his nature.

"Thy kingdom come, thy will be done, on earth as it is in heaven." God's kingdom is primarily his personal care for us, which we realize by faith in him. In it he gives us security, provides for our daily needs, forgives our shortcomings, gives us his nature and Spirit, and directs us by his will. In short, it is all that the Lord's Prayer is about. It is not surprising that Jesus began this model prayer by praising God for his goodness and then asking that God's kingdom be experienced on the earth.

God's purposes for us can be seen at three levels, which should best occur in order: first, that we walk by faith in his care; then that we love one another (John 3:34–35), bearing the fruit of his Spirit (Gal. 5:22–23); and finally, that we lead others to faith in his care and purpose (Matt. 28:20).

II. We are tempted to abandon his care and his nature.

"Lead us not into temptation." This passage directs us as individuals and as a body of believers to admit that we can be tempted. Our temptations are mainly of two kinds: (1) to turn from God's grace to personal works and (2) to slip into loose, sinful living. As Christians we must know that pride and passion remain at work in us, and each of us can be tempted.

The major temptation that confronted the early church—a concern of the books of Galatians, Hebrews, and 2 Peter—was that of turning from the pure gospel of grace back to a religion of works and rituals. This sin took away the peace and security of depending on God and replaced it with the religious pride of having met a set of requirements. This, in turn, produced scorn instead of compassion toward those who failed their religious duties.

Present-day cults tempt us to accept their baptisms, spirit-fillings, and rituals, which they claim make them secure by their own actions. Let us not be tempted by these proud people to share in their arrogance of presumed superior insight and standing. Rather, let us treasure God's grace and confess our dependence.

Grace is intended to free us *from* sin, not free us *to* sin, to indulge ourselves in greed and lust. Wrongdoing must not be taken lightly, for it has ways of destroying body and spirit.

III. We are delivered by dependence.

"Deliver us from evil." We must have God's help to avoid temptations and escape the evil havoc that will follow yielding to them. "Deliver us" is an expression of need and of faith. Realizing our needs, we are to take them to God in faith. Let us talk regularly to God about our temptations.

We also need the help of our fellow Christians. Jesus' use of the pronoun *us* would suggest that the confession was meant to be made together where people acknowledged their need of one another. When one shares the fact of a temptation and of the difficulties resulting from it, we are all made more aware of how close to us trouble can be.

Conclusion

How are we to have faith sufficient to enjoy the kingdom and avoid the evils of temptations?

- by growing in knowledge of and faith in God
- by growing in the awareness of daily needs and temptations
- by growing together in trustworthiness and gentleness that we may share our needs together

"Our Father who art in heaven, hallowed be thy name. Thy kingdom come."

Sunday Morning, December 28

Title: God in and through Us

Text: "God was reconciling the world to himself in Christ, not counting men's sins against them. And he has committed to us the message of reconciliation. We are therefore Christ's ambassadors, as though God were making his appeal through us. We implore you on Christ's behalf: Be reconciled to God" **(2 Cor. 5:19–20 NIV)**.

Scripture Reading: Luke 2:1–20

Hymns: "Angels We Have Heard on High," Traditional
"Hail, Thou Long-expected Jesus," Wesley
"We'll Work Till Jesus Comes," Mills

Offertory Prayer: Loving Father, you have given us the gift of life—natural, abundant, and eternal. You have given us yourself. May we give you ourselves. Please accept these gifts as we become partners with you in gospel proclamation. In the name of the one who came and who comes. Amen.

Introduction

Christmas is such a happy time: Santa Claus and Christmas trees, grandmothers and turkey dinners, football games and fun, a Baby in a manger long ago. What does the Baby in the manger have to do with Santa Claus and Christmas trees, grandmothers and turkey dinners, football games and fun?

I. Centuries ago God was localized.

God became flesh and bone, blood and water. He was localized and visualized in one person—a male child. In that event of God becoming flesh, we humans begin to see what God is like.

He is like a shepherd who loses a sheep, but rather than forgetting the one and focusing on the ninety-nine he still has, the shepherd values the one enough to go on a long, lonely search. And when he finds that scared, scrawny sheep, he calls and comforts it. He is like a woman who does not have many coins—only ten—and when she loses one, she sweeps the entire house until her prize is found. He is like a father who has two sons, each of whom is lost—one because of arrogance and one because of irresponsibility. Yet the father deals with each independently, personally, graciously, and lovingly to bring about reconciliation. God has become localized and visualized, and we can see who he is and what he is.

God showed himself to be *on humanity's side.* He came preaching "the year of the Lord's favor."

God also showed himself to be *at humanity's side.* God ministers through nearness and warmth, closeness and comfort, touching and holding. His name is Immanuel, God with us. He would go through life with us—knowing our concerns and interests, our pains and problems, our trials and tribulations.

Further, he showed himself as *God over us*—the one who addresses humankind and demands obedience. He is King. Yes, it is good news that Jesus came, that God was localized and visualized.

II. How can God be localized today?

But all of that is history, more than two thousand years of history. How about now? Does God become localized and visualized in our time, in our place? How will the citizens of our community see what God is like?

It will take an incarnation. That is the way God works. But how? Will Jesus of Nazareth have to be born again? Will another virgin need to be found? It will take an incarnation, but it will be an incarnation in us—within you and me. As Christ came to proclaim the Good News, he commissions us to proclaim the message that he lived and died (John 20:21).

The purpose of that first incarnation in Bethlehem was to facilitate future incarnations in our community and in our church. God becomes flesh in us. He is localized and visualized in us. To some we are the only picture of God they will ever see.

As we provide for sick and elderly persons, God provides for the sick and the elderly. As we visit nursing homes and hospitals, God ministers in those places. As we proclaim the good news of the forgiveness of sins, we do so for God as his representatives. God is in us, and he does his mission in the world through us.

This fulfills the point of the Christian message. We become redeemers. The redeemed redeem. Christmas defines whose we are, who we are, and what we are. We are Christ's ambassadors.

Humans are the agents of God's business in the world. And that is the way one would expect it, since it is the way God does things. He became a man. Since humankind could not relate to a God who was distant and abstract, God became a man. Incarnation is the way God works, the way he redeems and reconciles. He works "in flesh" through persons—humans telling other humans about redemption, meaning, integrity, life, light, and love. God lives *in* us and works *through* us.

III. Incarnation calls all persons to reconciliation.

One more word must be heard by all this Christmas season. Not only does Christ come to save, and not only does he commission all Christians to be his ambassadors or agents, but he also calls all persons to reconciliation. No more do you have to see God as an adversary, enemy, or foe. You too can be reconciled. You can join in this ministry of proclaiming reconciliation to all. God can be in you, and he can work through you.

Conclusion

As we have journeyed to Christmas this Advent season, we have heard many sounds—the good news that God is for us, that he is with us, and that he is over us. And now we have heard another joyful sound—God lives *in* us and works *through* us! God and humans are partners. Would you ever have dared think that the God you thought was against you is really for you? That this God is King and summons you? And that he wants to live in you and work through you? God in you, depending on you? That is GOOD NEWS in capital letters. That is an offer you can't refuse.

SUNDAY EVENING, DECEMBER 28

Title: What Would You Like in 2026?
Text: "You have made known to me the path of life; you will fill me with joy in your presence, with eternal pleasures at your right hand" **(Ps. 16:11 NIV)**.
Scripture Reading: Psalm 16:8–11

Introduction

What would you like in 2026?

One may want any of a number of external things to happen in 2026—new job, marriage, college, higher profits, weight loss, etc. But the psalmist points to inward changes. He looks in his heart at the basic needs of life. His insight has been admired for centuries.

Psalm 16 was popular with the apostles. Peter used this psalm in his sermon at Pentecost (Acts 2:25–31). We also find these verses cited by Paul in the book of Acts (13:35). Why was it such a popular psalm for the New Testament writers? Simply stated, it addresses the deepest inner needs of humankind. What would you like in 2026? Listen to the psalmist.

I. Would you like the stability that God offers (v. 8)?

Two phrases in this verse merit our attention. First, note "I have set." It literally means to make level or even. The psalmist testified that he was working at making level his relationship with God. Growing as a Christian takes time. It is a delicate balance.

Have you ever tried to level something? A family received a surprise gift of a grandfather clock. They read the instructions to discover, "You must level the clock before it will run." It took them three months to level it perfectly!

It takes time to balance out our Christian lives. Allow the Word of God to bring you into a position of evenness in your commitment.

In addition to leveling, the psalmist wrote, "I will not be shaken." He understands his responsibility to God. We too must be open to God's leadership. We should be flexible as he leads us, for we need stability and flexibility. Too many people make superficial commitments in life. They try to anchor themselves in the shallow beds of the ocean. Then when problems and crises arise, the waves of life crush them. God wants us to understand that he will stabilize us and give us flexibility. Based on this assumption, Paul could write to the church at Corinth in 2 Corinthians 12:9 that the grace of God is sufficient for everything in life. After we have accepted God's stability, the psalmist asks us another question.

II. Would you enjoy inner peace (v. 9)?

Would you enjoy the inner peace that only God can give? If so, note three words: *heart, glory,* and *flesh* (KJV). The language of the Old Testament could be translated "spirit," "soul," and "body." Your spirit differentiates you from all other living creatures on this planet. It separates you from the animal world in a distinct way—you have an awareness of God's presence. Your soul contains your mind, will, and emotions; and your body is the organism through which your soul expresses itself.

A tragedy of our society is that we have reversed the biblical order for God's peace. Usually we begin with physical thoughts, not spiritual. For example, young people, in your dating relationships, where do you begin?

Normally we begin with the outward appearance. That is, we usually take note of such things as a person's grooming, clothing, and car before we stop to consider his or her soul and spirit. The Bible teaches us to look beyond the physical and to get to know people. Find out what others are thinking. Discover their emotions. Talk about spiritual matters.

We try to impress people in man's order: body, soul and spirit. Note that the Bible does not say that the flesh is wrong nor that the soul is wrong. It says that these areas have been corrupted by the fall of humankind. These areas need to be reborn through the filling of God's Spirit in our lives. The problem is that we have reversed the priorities.

First Thessalonians 5:23 says, "May your whole spirit, soul and body be kept blameless" (NIV). See the priority? Do you desire inner peace in 2026? Concentrate on the spiritual first.

III. Would you appreciate God's companionship (v. 10)?

Psalm 16:10 says, "You will not abandon me to the grave, nor will you let your Holy One see decay" (NIV). God will be your constant companion in 2026. Are you looking for a friend and confidant, a friend who knows your faults and yet loves you in spite of them? God loves you unconditionally, and he loves you forever.

Psalm 16 is like a rosebud not yet unfolded. The Old Testament gives hope for eternal life even though the doctrine of the resurrection of the body had not yet been revealed at that time. Now we have a fuller understanding through the New Testament because of Jesus Christ.

IV. If so, embrace his purpose for your life (v. 11).

Embrace God's purpose for your life. The psalmist's "path of life" literally means a way of coming into new existence. It was used in the Old Testament for the changing of the seasons and the coming of spring.

Suppose you were given $86,400 with the stipulation that you must spend all of it today. Any money left over must be given back. You could not save it or earn interest on it. How would you spend it?

God gives you 86,400 seconds in a day to live. How will you spend these precious seconds? If you have a purpose in your life and have discovered the path God has set for you, you will not waste life. You will invest yourself in his kingdom. You will have purpose. His purpose will transcend whatever obstacles might come your way.

Conclusion

Today as you look into 2026, commit your life to God. You may not know the specific avenues of his will for your journey; but if you are committed to his ultimate purpose, he will lead you and guide you. He will direct your path.

Wednesday Evening, December 31

Title: Looking Backward and Looking Forward
Text: "Grace and peace be multiplied unto you through the knowledge of God, and of Jesus our Lord" **(2 Peter 1:2)**.
Scripture Reading: 2 Peter 1:1–11

Introduction

As we come to the end of one year and approach the beginning of a new year, it would be profitable to take a look backward and count our blessings and then take a look forward and make our plans to cooperate with the Lord.

The first few verses of Peter's second epistle provide us with an opportunity to look at some of the blessings God has bestowed on us in the past. It also provides us with some words of instruction and encouragement to live a life in which we are growing spiritually and serving significantly.

Peter addressed his message "to them that have obtained like precious faith with us through the righteousness of God and our Saviour Jesus Christ" (1:1). He wrote from the perspective of an aged pastor who was living on the edge of eternity. He spoke of his body as a tabernacle, or tent, from which he would soon depart. He referred to his approaching death as his "exodus," or departure—the word used for the departure of the children of Israel from Egypt.

I. The blessings of the past (2 Peter 1:3–4).

The apostle called to the attention of his readers the exceeding great and precious gifts from God to them through Jesus Christ. These two verses are a spiritual treasure chest that reveal the blessings that God has bestowed on believers through Jesus Christ. The generosity of God's provisions for his children is magnified and emphasized.

A. *"All things that pertain unto life and godliness."* In Christ Jesus, believers have received everything necessary for experiencing the abundant life. It is unnecessary for them to turn to any other teacher or discipline in order to be all God would have them to be.
B. *"Through the knowledge of him that hath called us to glory and virtue."* Through the beauty and the glory of the life and character of Jesus Christ, God calls all people to himself. The initiative belongs with God. Salvation is of the Lord. The human response to the gospel is a voluntary commitment of faith that makes possible the bestowal of these divine gifts.
C. *"The exceeding great and precious promises."* The Bible is a record of God's promises to his people. The Old Testament contains a continuing

series of promises concerning the Messiah who was to come. Peter had witnessed the fulfillment of these exceeding great and precious promises in the person and life of Jesus Christ.

Jesus made many promises to his disciples. We will greatly enrich our spiritual life and deepen our faith if we will discover these promises, claim them for our own, and move forward depending on the Lord to keep his promises as people of faith have done in the past.

D. *"That by these ye might be partakers of the divine nature."* Faith in the promises of God makes possible the new birth. The new birth does not produce a divinity in people, but it does mean that the divine character, the divine nature, has been imparted in embryonic form. This new nature provides the believer with the possibility of experiencing and demonstrating the holiness, the tenderness, the gentleness, and the power of God.

By every means at our command, we should cooperate with the Holy Spirit as he seeks to develop the new nature that came to us in the miracle of the new birth.

E. *"Having escaped the corruption that is in the world through lust."* Through their experience with Jesus Christ, believers receive the potential for complete deliverance from the powerful evil forces that work in the world. Christ has granted forgiveness from sin. He provides spiritual power to overcome the contaminating presence of evil in the world. Through faith in him and through obedience to him, we can be victorious over the assaults of thc devil.

II. The opportunity of the future (2 Peter 1:5–7).

The gift of new life has been given to those who had put faith in the promises of God. This new life is like a divine seed that needs to be developed by earnest care. Spiritual growth will not take place automatically or accidentally. Peter encouraged his readers to hasten with all diligence to cooperate with the Spirit of God in developing the beautiful graces that are associated with spiritual maturity.

As we enter a new year, we should give careful consideration to these words of encouragement from the apostle Peter.

A. *"Giving all diligence, add to your faith."* Faith is the human response to God's grace that makes possible the gift of new life. Faith is the basic foundation for all spiritual growth and service.

Peter challenged his readers to supplement their faith with the Christian graces that are needed for fruitful Christian living. Seemingly, each of the graces mentioned grows out of the preceding grace. The word translated "add" probably would be more correctly translated by the word "supply." This word was used by the Greeks to describe the actions of those who provided financial resources for the production of the great plays and dramas. It was also used for the action of furnishing the provisions and supplies for an army. Peter declared that Christians are to supplement their faith with these virtues, which are actually the pieces of equipment needed for the living of a genuine Christian life.

The apostle gives us a blueprint for spiritual progress.

B. *In your faith supply virtue.* Faith makes possible the power by which virtue is to be developed. The word *virtue* means courage, moral excellence, noble character. It is not tame and passive; it is active, aggressive, and on the march.

C. *To virtue supply knowledge.* In the practice of virtue an effort is put forth to gain knowledge, which is practical skill in choosing the right and refusing the wrong. To secure this knowledge, one must make a diligent study of God's Word.

D. *To knowledge supply temperance or self-control.* Self-restraint enables a person to curb his evil impulses and resist the lures of sin in the world that surrounds him. Each person must be in command of his own moods and impulses, or his life will end in ruin.

E. *To temperance supply patience.* The grace needed is endurance, steadfastness, fortitude, perseverance. Patience is that attitude of determination that enables a person to stay under the load until the victory is won.

F. *And to patience add godliness.* Godliness is that trait that characterizes the life of a person who lives continually "as seeing him who is invisible." Perhaps this grace refers to the growth of the divine nature received in the new birth.

G. *To godliness supply brotherly kindness.* The life of reverence for God is issued in brotherly kindness. The genuine worship of God will affect one's attitude toward fellow human beings (1 John 4:20).

H. *To brotherly kindness supply love.* The crown of Christian graces is love. Paul affirmed that love is the chief gift of the Holy Spirit (1 Cor. 13:13). It was concerning Peter's love that the Lord had inquired (John 21:15–17). Peter recognized and commended the believer's love for Christ (1 Peter 1:8) and encouraged love within the Christian brotherhood (1 Peter 1:22).

Conclusion

The apostle Peter was concerned that his readers experience the benefits that flow from spiritual maturity. He was eager that they escape the tragic results of persistent immaturity (1 Peter 2:8–9).

By adding Christian graces, believers will be assured that they can avoid both idleness and unfruitfulness in their experience of salvation through Christ. Peter declared that he who does not put forth a sincere effort to grow toward Christlikeness is blind. This term most likely refers to a state of mind that is alienated from spiritual reality. The phrase "cannot see afar off" refers to a condition of shortsightedness. The picture is that of a man who is squinting his eyes because of the light. Consequently, he is greatly limited in forming a true perspective concerning the things that really matter. In contrast to these conditions, it is inferred that the believer who strives for growth will experience meaningful activity, fruitful productivity, and spiritual insight into the meaning of life.

We are approaching the end of another year in the journey of life. The past is gone. Nothing can be done concerning the past except to admit and to confess past failures. The future is before us. With God's help, let each of us respond to the apostle's challenge for the future.

MISCELLANEOUS HELPS

MESSAGES ON THE LORD'S SUPPER

Title: The Savior and His Supper
Text: "He took some bread, and after a blessing He broke it, and gave it to them, and said, 'Take it; this is My body.' And when He had taken a cup and given thanks, He gave it to them, and they all drank from it. And He said to them, 'This is My blood of the covenant, which is poured out for many'" **(Mark 14:22–24 NASB)**.
Scripture Reading: Mark 14:1–31

Introduction

It was the last week of Jesus' ministry, Passion Week, which would climax with his death and resurrection. Sunday was the day of manifestation; Monday, the day of authority; Tuesday, the day of controversy; Wednesday, the day of silence; and Thursday, the day of preparation. On Thursday Jesus observed the Passover and instituted the Lord's Supper. Three things will help to bring these events into focus.

I. We are inspired by beautiful devotion (Mark 14:1–9).

When the story in Mark is compared with the gospel of John (chap. 12), some names identify the persons of the story. The woman was Mary, sister of Martha and Lazarus. The indignant disciples focused on Judas Iscariot, who created quite a scene. We do not know who Simon the leper was, but probably he was one whom Jesus healed. Another important person there was Lazarus, whom Jesus had raised from the dead. This could very well have been an "appreciation dinner" for Jesus, because Martha was also there serving the meal.

A. *Mary's deed was the climax of the evening.* She anointed Jesus' head with an alabaster vaseful of pure nard valued at about three hundred days' wages. It was a gift fit for a king!
B. *Judas's discord was openly expressed so that the other disciples began to talk about it. Judas called Mary's gift a waste; Jesus called it wonderful!* Of course, Judas's true spirit was veiled from human eyes but not from the Savior's.
C. *Jesus defended Mary.* He told the complainers to leave her alone, for she had done a beautiful thing. Her deed was both a prophetic act and an act of pure devotion.

D. *Mary's dedication was beautiful.* Jesus said, "She has done what she could" (v. 8 NASB). She publicly demonstrated her love for the Master. What are our motives in our relationships with Christ? What are we doing to demonstrate our devotion?

II. We are warned by a treacherous deed (14:1–2, 10–11).

The attitudes and activities of Judas have intrigued people for centuries. Why would he do such a treacherous deed?

Luke says that "Satan entered into Judas" (22:3 NASB). Matthew says that greed was the cause of betrayal (26:14–15). The point is that Judas had a secret desire, a selfish goal in his heart that gave Satan a handle to enter his life. Even so, we have to recognize that behind it all was the will of God at work, allowing this treacherous deed to transpire.

Any of us can commit the sin of claiming to be a Christian but secretly living an ungodly life! Woe to the person who betrays the Lord Jesus Christ!

III. We are challenged by a memorable dedication.

On that night the Lord Jesus Christ was dedicated to the eternal purpose of God his Father. Two suppers were joined that night.

A. *The Passover (Mark 14:12–21).* This was one of the most sacred of the Jewish feasts. It had been observed by the nation ever since the night the death angel passed over Israel in Egypt. It was indeed a celebration.
   1. The purpose of the Passover was to remember God's mercy and miracles in their deliverance from death.
   2. The preparation of the Passover had to be done with great care. The room had to be cleansed of anything that had leaven. The meal called for bitter herbs, because the Egyptian taskmasters had made their lives bitter through oppression. A year-old unblemished male lamb was slaughtered at the temple and then roasted. It was to be eaten on the night of the Passover. So while the Passover lamb was being slain at the temple, Jesus was symbolically offering his life's blood to the disciples in the upper room.

   During the celebration Psalms 113 and 114 were sung. At the end Psalms 115 through 118 were sung. Certain words from Psalm 118:21–24 filled their hearts with joy and hope. God was giving them a new song, Jesus Christ the Headstone! Now Christ has become our Passover Lamb (1 Cor. 5:7).

B. *The Lord's Supper (vv. 22–26).* During the course of the Passover meal, "Jesus took bread," unleavened flat cakes that were on the table, and "gave thanks"; that is, he blessed the bread. He "broke" it for distribution and said, "Take, eat: this is my body," or "This represents my body."

Then he took the cup and, when he again had given thanks, he gave it to them, and they all drank of it. He identified it as "my blood of the new testament, which is shed for many."

The fact of Christ's blood being "poured out" speaks of both the violent nature and the vicarious nature of his death. The preposition "for" reveals that it was a substitutionary death. He died for us all in order to settle the sin problem of humankind once and for all.

Conclusion

The Lord's Supper, in light of Jesus' resurrection, enables us to look back to Jesus' life, look forward to his coming again, and look upward to his lordship.

Title: Questions about Spiritual Examination

Text: "Now when evening came, Jesus was reclining at the table with the twelve disciples. As they were eating, He said, 'Truly I say to you that one of you will betray Me.' Being deeply grieved, they each one began to say to Him, 'Surely not I, Lord?' And He answered, 'He who dipped his hand with Me in the bowl is the one who will betray Me. The Son of Man is to go, just as it is written of Him; but woe to that man by whom the Son of Man is betrayed! It would have been good for that man if he had not been born.' And Judas, who was betraying Him, said, 'Surely it is not I, Rabbi?' Jesus said to him, 'You have said it yourself.'" **(Matt. 26:20–25 NASB)**.

Scripture Reading: Psalm 51

Introduction

Matthew 26:20–25 and Psalm 51 indicate that something important needs to happen in this service as we observe the Lord's Supper.

Let us read 1 Corinthians 11:17–32 to see if the spirit of these passages is found there. Yes, it is found there, because verse 28 says, "But a man must examine himself, and in so doing he is to eat of the bread and drink of the cup" (NASb).

In Psalm 51 David, the psalmist-king, is spiritually examining himself. He prays, "Create in me a clean heart, O God, and renew a steadfast spirit within me" (v. 10 NASB).

At the institution of the first Lord's Supper, a spiritual examination took place. The disciples asked, "Lord, is it I?"

In 1 Corinthians 11 the apostle Paul tells us that the observance of the Lord's Supper is so serious that we must spiritually examine ourselves for any unconfessed sin in our lives. Verse 27 says, "Therefore whoever eats the bread or drinks the cup of the Lord in an unworthy manner, shall be guilty of the body and the blood of the Lord" (NASB). In "an unworthy manner" may be considered as "without proper reverence or due thought" or "with unconfessed sin."

Let us ask two questions about this spiritual examination.

I. Why is spiritual examination so serious?

The answer is because of the judgment of God on unconfessed sins against the body and blood of the Lord (1 Cor. 11:27). God's judgment comes in three forms, as seen in 1 Corinthians 11:30.

A. *Weakness.* This is a lack of physical strength, which is the result of spiritual laxity.
B. *Sickness.* The word refers to feebleness and illness. Many times physical problems are the result of spiritual needs left untended. It is God's way of bringing judgment on us.
C. *Sleep.* This refers to death. Some had committed the "sin unto death." The verb *sleep,* when referring to death, always refers to the death of believers. These Christians had not lost their salvation but the privilege of service on earth.

These problems are serious enough to demand that we permit the Holy Spirit to do some deep spiritual searching.

II. How do we examine ourselves spiritually?

A. *By submitting ourselves to the heart searching of the Holy Spirit and the Word of God.*
B. *By asking the Lord to search us.* Psalm 139 says, "Search me, O God, and know my heart: try me, and know my thoughts: and see if there be any wicked way in me, and lead me in the way everlasting" (vv. 23–24).
C. *By yielding ourselves to the light of God's presence.* "But if we walk in the light, as he is in the light, we have fellowship one with another, and the blood of Jesus Christ his Son cleanseth us from all sin" (1 John 1:7).
D. *By subjecting every relationship of our lives to examination.* Are our priorities out of order? Is there any area in our lives where Christ is not Lord? Is there any failure to seek first the kingdom of God and his righteousness? Is there any wrong use of our bodies, which are temples of the Holy Spirit? Any wrong relationship to others? Any wrong relationship to the church, our spiritual family? Any broken family relationships that need correcting? Any squeezing of our lives into the world's mold? Questions like these are not optional; they are essential!
E. *By confessing sin.* We must transfer our sins to the cross of Christ and forsake them.
   1. If the sin is against God, we must confess it to him alone.
   2. If the sin is against God and another person, we must confess it both to God and to the other person to make things right.
   3. If the sin is against God and a group of people, we must confess it to God and to the group to make things right for his glory.

   As wide as the sin, so wide should the confession be.

   Thus will we be cleansed from all sin. "If we confess our sins, he is faithful and just to forgive us our sins, and to cleanse us from all unrighteousness" (1 John 1:9).

Conclusion

What blessings come upon sincere spiritual examination. We are free in our spirits. We are clean. We are free to worship.

Title: Lest We Forget
Text: "Do not slay them, lest my people forget. . . ." **(Ps. 59:11 NKJV)**.
Scripture Reading: Psalm 59:1–11

Introduction

Many years ago the English poet Rudyard Kipling wrote a poem entitled "Recessional." In it are two familiar lines of refrain:

Lord God of Hosts, be with us yet,
Lest we forget, lest we forget!

The Bible speaks of the danger of God's people forgetting him. And Psalm 59:11 reveals that God will go to great lengths to prick the memory of his people. This verse says that God raised up enemies against his people to make them remember him.

God gives some strong scriptural warnings about forgetting him (Deut. 4:9; 6:10–12; Ps. 106:13, 21). Just as Israel forgot God, so do we. So what are we to do? In Deuteronomy 6 three challenges come to us through Moses' message to Israel, three things we ought never forget.

I. Remember your redemption.

"Then watch yourself, that you do not forget the Lord who brought you from the land of Egypt, out of the house of slavery" (v. 12 NASB). Your Redeemer is the Lord, and your redemption is from the house of slavery.

Israel was a slave in Egypt, having lived there for four hundred years. In the Bible Egypt represents sin and its bondage. Israel was delivered from this bondage by means of the Passover lamb. When its life was given, its blood shed, and its blood marked on the doorposts, the death angel passed over.

Jesus Christ is our Passover Lamb (1 Cor. 5:7), the Lamb of God, and his blood was shed. We are redeemed by his blood and forgiven of our sins (Eph. 1:7). We ought never to forget this!

II. Remember your resources.

"Then it shall come about when the Lord your God brings you into the land . . . to give you . . . splendid cities . . . houses full of all good things . . .

hewn cisterns . . . vineyards and olive trees . . . and you eat and are satisfied" (Deut. 6:10–11 NASB).

Just as God gave to the Israelites and was their Source, so he gives to us and is our Source. Everything we have we have received (1 Cor. 4:7). We own nothing of our own; it has all been given to us. But we forget that so easily. We become attached to the things of life, thinking they are ours. But we are only stewards, trustees, caretakers of all we have.

Psalm 24:1 says, "The earth is the LORD's, and the fulness thereof." Romans 8:32 says, "He who did not spare His own Son, but delivered Him over for us all, how will He not also with Him freely give us all things?" (NASB). First Timothy 6:17 says, "God . . . richly supplies us with all things to enjoy" (NASB).

III. Remember your requirements.

God's requirements, the Ten Commandments, are referred to in Deuteronomy 6:4–9. They are God's moral principles for our personal lives, our families, and our nation. They are also requirements for the future. As we follow the Lord, blessings come; when we forget him, judgment follows (vv. 14–15).

How do we remember these requirements so that we can keep them?

A. *Hear the Lord (v. 4).* Listen! There is power in listening.
B. *Love the Lord (v. 5).*
C. *Instruct the family (vv. 6–7).* Make the Word of God a part of your home, the center of conversation, your daily meditation. The home—not the church or the school system—is the center of teaching. Also, we must memorize Scripture.
D. *Apply the Word (vv. 8–9).* Build reminders of Scripture into your life. "Bind" and "write"—that is, do something to make it stick in your heart. Writing down Scripture helps to make it sure. Physical reminders can help us just as the children of Israel had reminders for themselves.

Conclusion

We need reminders today of the Lord Jesus Christ! This is what the Lord's Supper is all about. It is a living reminder of the Savior—who he is, what he has done, how he did it, and why we are his followers.

Remember him! Lest we forget!

MESSAGES FOR CHILDREN AND YOUNG PEOPLE

Title: The Greatest Truth in the World

The greatest truth in the world is found in John 3:16. These are the twenty-five most powerful words in all of literature: "For God so loved the world, that he gave his only begotten Son, that whosoever believeth in him should not perish, but have everlasting life."

Simply put, God loves you! Have you ever thought about the fact that God loves you? He is the great God, who made the world, the mountains, the seas, and the stars. The strong, powerful, true, holy God loves you!

John 3:16 says:

I. God loves you personally.

God loves each of us. He "so loved the world." This does not mean the sun, moon, and stars, nor the trees, flowers, and animals. God loves people like you and me. He knows you and loves you.

God loves you even when you have done wrong. A wicked man like Saul of Tarsus, who persecuted Christians, said, "[Christ] loved me, and gave himself for me" (Gal. 2:20). What great love that is!

II. God loves you openly.

"God so loved the world, that he gave . . ."

God did not hide his love for us, and he does not hide his love from you. He loved us all in his Son, Jesus Christ, who came into the world and showed us how to live.

But the most important thing Jesus did was to die on the cross. He was betrayed by one of his disciples and arrested. He was tried falsely. He suffered pain and finally died on a cross. He hadn't done anything wrong, so why did he die? Because of God's love!

Jesus was buried in a tomb, but God raised him from the dead. He lives today! And through his Spirit he is telling you that it was love that made him die for you. God loves you openly!

III. God loves you to help you.

". . . whosoever believeth in him should not perish . . ." To perish means to die and be separated from God forever.

Everybody needs help. We have all kinds of needs—food to eat, clothes to wear, and homes in which to live. But our greatest need is in our hearts. We need help spiritually.

What does the Bible say? It says the heart is evil and makes us think evil thoughts, say wrong things, and do bad things. It makes us steal, lie, and cheat. "All have sinned, and come short of the glory of God" (Rom. 3:23). It also says we die for our sin: "The wages of sin is death" (Rom. 6:23). This is what it means to perish. But God doesn't want you to perish, because:

IV. God loves you to give you life.

"Everlasting life" and "only begotten Son" go together. "Life" is God's gift. He alone can give forgiveness of our sins and peace and hope and joy. This is the new life God gives in his Son.

How do you receive this life? John 3:16 says, "Whosoever believeth in him." You must believe in Jesus Christ. To believe in him is to trust him. To believe in Jesus Christ is to receive him. John 1:12 says, "As many as received him, to them gave he power to become the sons of God, even to them that believe on his name." And to believe in him is to open the door of your heart to Jesus. The Bible says, "Behold, I stand at the door, and knock: if any man hear my voice, and open the door, I will come in to him" (Rev. 3:20).

Conclusion

John 3:16 is the greatest truth in the world. Do you believe it? I ask you to give your heart to Christ. Open your heart's door to Jesus. He will give you everlasting life.

Title: What to Do in Your Problems

Do things ever go wrong for you? Do you ever get discouraged? I'm sure you do, because there are times when all of us have problems.

We need to be prepared for these times. Different people react in different ways. Some get bitter toward God while some turn to him. The Bible tells a story about a young man whom God loved greatly. In fact, his name is mentioned more often than the name of any other person in the Bible. Do you know his name? It's David.

David learned how to be cheerful even through the problems he faced. Once when he returned home from a battle with the six hundred men who were with him, he discovered that their city had been burned. Their homes had been burned, and there was nothing left. Some enemy soldiers had attacked while they were gone, taken their wives and children captive, stolen their possessions, and burned their houses.

David and his men sat down and wept. Then something unusual happened. The men became angry and began to blame their leader. They even began to talk about stoning David. From being accepted and praised by the nation, now David was being rejected by the very ones he was serving. He was about to flee since he had no family or faithful friends left. In that moment of despair, he did something that brought a new spirit into him, and he began to have new courage and hope.

What did he do? The Bible tells us that "David encouraged himself in the Lord his God" (1 Sam. 30:6). He received such strength that he knew he would be victorious. So he led his six hundred men to pursue the enemy. They surprised them and defeated them and rescued those who had been taken captive. It was a victorious time in David's life.

The Lord wants us to learn how to be joyful and cheerful when all seems to be hopeless. How is this possible? By doing the same thing David did—by encouraging ourselves in the Lord.

If things don't go well with you, you might get angry with the Lord and your parents or friends. Elijah sat down under a juniper tree and wanted to die (1 Kings 19:4), and Jonah said that it was better to die than to live (Jonah 4:8). But David encouraged himself in the Lord his God!

What would you do? David knew the Lord. Do you know him too? The Lord was David's God. Is he yours? If he is yours, you can encourage yourself in him. This means that every battle in your life, whatever it is, can be won! Your life can be full of joy.

When you are having a difficult time with yourself and others, watch out for the Devil's best tool! According to one story, the Devil was going out of business and was offering to sell his tools. At the time of the sale, all the tools were on display—hate, jealousy, anger, and many others. Apart from the rest lay a harmless-looking tool, much worn and priced higher than any of the others.

Someone asked the Devil what it was. "That's discouragement" was the reply. "And it is priced so high because it is more useful to me than any of the others. It is well worn because I use it with nearly everybody, as very few people yet know it belongs to me."

The price for discouragement was so high that it was never sold. The Devil still owns it and uses it.

Don't become discouraged! Encourage yourself in the Lord your God! Read and know his Word, and pray to him. He will encourage your heart!

Title: Jesus Can Help You

Have you ever been sick? I have, and it's no fun!

One day Jesus saw a man who had been sick for thirty-eight years and couldn't get well. Jesus asked him if he wanted to get well, and the man said he had no one to help him. Then something wonderful happened: Jesus helped him, and immediately the man became well. All of us are like that man in other ways—in our hearts. We need to be made well in our hearts.

Let me tell you a story about a girl named Ida who has a new face. She was born with her face out of shape. Her eyes were farther apart than normal. She didn't realize there was anything wrong until her first day of prekindergarten. That day she realized she was different, and she went home to her room and stayed alone. Ida didn't have peace in her heart. You may be like Ida—not in your face—but in your heart. You need a new heart because you have something wrong inside. You are not like God wants you to be. You don't have peace!

The Bible tells us that we have sin in our hearts and that we need to be forgiven. It says that "all have sinned, and come short of the glory of God" (Rom. 3:23).

For Ida, change looked hopeless. There was nothing she could do. For us, it is the same. There is nothing we can do to make our hearts right.

Then there came to Ida the possibility for a new face. A school counselor told her of a medical center where she might get help. It meant that a surgeon who knew what he was doing would be needed. Also it would be costly, and it would require about ten hours of surgery. She might even lose her senses of taste and smell. But there was hope!

That is the way it is for you in your heart. There is only one person who can give you a new heart. That person is Jesus! He has the power to do this because he loves you. He died on the cross and was raised again from the dead for you. He promises to help.

Ida's decision time came. She said she wanted help and was willing to have the surgery. She responded with a willing yes. She just wanted to know "when." She trusted herself to her doctor. And now Ida has a new face!

Jesus asked the man who had been sick for thirty-eight years, "Do you want help?" And when the man saw that Jesus could help him, he was willing. He trusted Jesus, and immediately Jesus made him well.

Let me ask you a question: Do you want help to be made well in your heart? Do you want Jesus to forgive your sins? Do you want him to come into your heart?

Then be willing to trust him to help you. Invite him into your heart today. He promises to come in as you do. He says, "Behold, I stand at the door, and knock: if any man hear my voice, and open the door, I will come in" (Rev. 3:20). Christ will give you a new heart!

FUNERAL MEDITATIONS

Title: The Comfort God Gives

Text: "Blessed be the God and Father of our Lord Jesus Christ, the Father of mercies and God of all comfort, who comforts us in all our affliction, so that we may be able to comfort those who are in any affliction, with the comfort with which we ourselves are comforted by God" **(2 Cor. 1:3–4 RSV)**.

Introduction

Numerous times the Bible speaks about the comfort God gives. The Living Bible paraphrases our Scripture text this way: "What a wonderful God we have—he is the Father of our Lord Jesus Christ, the source of every mercy, and the one who so wonderfully comforts and strengthens us in our hardships and trials. And why does he do this? So that when others are troubled, needing our sympathy and encouragement, we can pass on to them this same help and comfort God has given us."

Psalm 23 says, "Thy rod and thy staff they comfort me" (v. 4).

Isaiah 40:1 proclaims the reality of comfort in the words, "Comfort, comfort, my people, says your God" (NIV).

Second Corinthians 1:3 says that God is the God of all comfort. He comforts us in all our trouble; and the comfort he gives is not merely the patching up of a broken heart; he comforts us from the inside out! The word *comfort* is related to *courage*. He gives courage to face trouble of the future and decisions that have to be made.

How does he comfort when death comes?

I. He comforts by his presence.

As Jesus went to the home of Mary and Martha at the death of Lazarus, so he comes to us. He delayed his arrival there not because of insensitivity, but because of a greater glory. He spoke words of power and hope, announcing, "I am the resurrection, and the life" (John 11:25). But it was his presence that transformed this scene of sorrow into one of victory.

We often think that if Jesus were here, things would be different. Well, he is here—by his Spirit! He promised in John 14:16–18 the presence of the Holy Spirit: "And I will pray the Father, and he shall give you another Comforter, that he may abide with you for ever; even the Spirit of truth; whom the world cannot receive, because it seeth him not, neither knoweth him: but ye know him; for he dwelleth with you, and shall be in you. I will not leave you comfortless: I will come to you." He comforts by his presence!

II. He comforts by his Word.

Romans 15:4 says, "For whatsoever things were written aforetime were written for our learning, that we through patience and comfort of the scriptures might have hope."

The Word of God has power to encourage your heart. Words from beautiful poetry and prose could be read but would not last. Isaiah 40:8 says, "The grass withereth, the flower fadeth: but the word of our God shall stand for ever." God's Word is unique and eternal and deeply inspirational.

> Word of God, across the age
> Comes Thy message to our life;
> Source of hope forever present
> In our toil and fears and strife;
> Constant witness to God's mercy,
> Still our grace whate'er befall,
> Guide unfailing, strength eternal,
> Offered freely to us all.

The psalmist drew hope and comfort from God's words: "Remember thy word unto thy servant, upon which thou hast caused me to hope. This is my comfort in my affliction: for thy word hath quickened me" (Ps. 119:49–50).

III. He comforts by his hope.

First Thessalonians 4:13–18 proclaims this hope: "But we do not want you to be uninformed, brethren, about those who are asleep, so that you will not grieve as do the rest who have no hope. For if we believe that Jesus died and rose again, even so God will bring with Him those who have fallen asleep in Jesus. For this we say to you by the word of the Lord, that we who are alive and remain until the coming of the Lord, will not precede those who have fallen asleep. For the Lord Himself will descend from heaven with a shout, with the voice of the archangel and with the trumpet of God, and the dead in Christ will rise first. Then we who are alive and remain will be caught up together with them in the clouds to meet the Lord in the air, and so we shall always be with the Lord. Therefore comfort one another with these words." (NASB).

The purpose of these words is comfort! The future for a believer is not defeat. Death does not mean that the end has come, because God's hope lives on! This is not loss; this is gain!

Conclusion

"Blessed be God" who gives us comfort. As we bless him, he releases his comfort to us.

Title: God Cares for You

Text: "Therefore, humble yourselves under the mighty hand of God, that He may exalt you at the proper time, casting all your anxiety on Him, because He cares for you" **(1 Peter 5:6–7 NASB)**.

Scripture Reading: Psalm 23; John 14:1–6

Introduction

The Living Bible paraphrases 1 Peter 5:7 with these words: "Let him have all your worries and cares, for he is always thinking about you and watching everything that concerns you."

The distinctive truth of the Bible is found in the four simple words "He cares for you." This is the sweep of the message of the entire Bible. In countless ways we discover that God does care. Evidence of his care is reflected in Psalm 23:1, "The Lord is my shepherd, I shall not want." Jesus Christ is the most revealing evidence that God cares. Everything he said or did was living proof of God's care. How does he care for us in a time like this?

I. God cares in our time of need.

Matthew 6:31–32 says, "Do not worry then, saying, 'What will we eat?' or 'What will we drink?' or 'What will we wear for clothing?' For the Gentiles eagerly seek all these things; for your heavenly Father knows that you need all these things." (NASB). God has promised to meet our needs. Our part is to trust him. We especially need to trust him when death comes to a family member.

II. God cares in time of sorrow.

This is expressed in Jesus' ministry to Mary and Martha at Lazarus's death. When Jesus arrived at their home, Lazarus had already been laid in the tomb four days. Many friends had come to console Martha and Mary, but it was Jesus' arrival that let them know how truly God cared (John 11:17–19).

Jesus still enters into our times of grief with us. He was a man of sorrows and acquainted with grief. "What a friend we have in Jesus, all our sins and griefs to bear!"

III. God cares in time of storm.

As Jesus was crossing the Sea of Galilee with his disciples after a full day of teaching, he fell asleep in the boat. A fierce storm blew across the sea, breaking the waves over the boat. It looked as if the boat would fill up and sink. The disciples were afraid, so they awoke Jesus and said to him, "Teacher, do You not care that we are perishing?" (Mark 4:38 NASB).

Jesus took charge. He rebuked the wind and commanded the sea to be still. The sea became perfectly calm. Jesus asked his disciples, "Why are you afraid? Do you still have no faith?" (v. 40 NASB).

This story is talking about two types of storms. One storm was on the sea, and the other was in the disciples' hearts. Jesus cared and brought peace to the storm-tossed experience.

God cares for you in your storm!

IV. God cares in time eternal.

Nothing will ever separate us from God's loving care. Romans 8:35–39 clearly states this and concludes with this statement: ". . . nor any other created thing, will be able to separate us from the love of God, which is in Christ Jesus our Lord" (NASB).

This is eternal, loving care!

Conclusion

An old song says how much God cares for us.

> Be not dismayed whate'er betide,
> God will take care of you;
> Beneath his wings of love abide,
> God will take care of you.
>
> Through days of toil when heart doth fail,
> God will take care of you;
> When dangers fierce your path assail,
> God will take care of you.
>
> All you may need He will provide,
> God will take care of you;
> Nothing you ask will be denied,
> God will take care of you.

No matter what may be the test,
God will take care of you;
Lean, weary one, upon His breast,
God will take care of you.

—*C. D. Martin*

Title: "How Great Thou Art!"

Text: "Thine, O Lord, is the greatness, and the power, and the glory, and the victory, and the majesty: for all that is in the heaven and in the earth is thine; thine is the kingdom, O Lord, and thou art exalted as head above all." **(1 Chron. 29:11)**.

Scripture Reading: Psalm 46; 1 Chronicles 29:11–13

[This is an example of how you can create a personalized service using favorite stories, songs, poems, and Scripture passages of the deceased.]

Introduction

Several weeks ago a friend I will call Roy asked me to visit him. We talked primarily about his funeral and how he wanted it conducted. We talked about life and death and assurance. He asked me to read him the story "The Greater Fool." I'll share that with you now.

> A potentate of ancient Asia presented his court jester with a beautifully wrought wand, and said, "Keep this until you find a greater fool than yourself."
>
> The jester good-naturedly accepted the emblem of magic and flourished it on special occasions. Some years later the ruler was dying and asked to see the jester, of whom he had grown fond.
>
> "I wanted to say good-bye; I am going away on a long journey."
>
> "Where are you going?"
>
> "I have no idea."
>
> "How long will you be gone?"
>
> "That I can tell you—it is forever. I know nothing more about this journey I am about to take."
>
> "What have you done about providing for your well-being on this great trip?" asked the jester.
>
> "Nothing whatever," replied the king. "There is nothing to be done."
>
> "Since that is the way you feel," said the jester, "Take this wand. You are the one to whom I should give it."

Roy, however, was prepared to die. He knew where he was going, and he had the assurance that should fill the heart of a Christian.

Three thoughts make this service a special occasion.

I. God's greatness.

Roy's heart was filled with the thoughts of the greatness of God. His desire was that we recognize the truth.

God's Word proclaims it. The text of the service affirms it. A portion of Psalm 145 declares God's greatness: "Great is the LORD, and greatly to be praised; and his greatness is unsearchable" (v. 3).

"How Great Thou Art" was Roy's favorite hymn:

> O Lord my God! When I in awesome wonder
> Consider all the worlds Thy hands have made,
> I see the stars, I hear the rolling thunder,
> Thy pow'r throughout the universe displayed,
> Then sings my soul, my Savior God to Thee.
> How great Thou art! How great Thou art!
>
> —*Carl Boberg*

II. God's presence.

Roy wanted us to know a special secret that many people do not know—the secret of meeting God daily. "I Met God in the Morning" is a poem he shared with many others.

> I met God in the morning
> when my day was at its best,
> and His presence came like sunrise
> and a glory filled my breast.
>
> All day long His presence lingered,
> all day long He stayed with me,
> and we sailed in perfect calmness
> over a very troubled sea.
>
> Other ships were blown and battered,
> other ships were sore distressed,
> but the wind that seemed to drive them
> brought to me a peace and rest.
>
> Then I thought of other mornings
> with a keen remorse of mind
> when I too had loosed the mooring
> with His presence left behind.
>
> So I think I know the secret
> learned from many a troubled way.

You must seek Him in the morning
if you want Him through the day.

—*Ralph Cushman*

III. God's hope.

We are here in hope. The circle will not be broken. We have the hope of a heavenly home. "In My Father's house are many dwelling places; if it were not so, I would have told you; for I go to prepare a place for you" (John 14:2 NASB).

We also have the hope of a heavenly reunion. "And the dead in Christ shall rise first. Then we who are alive and remain will be caught up together with them in the clouds to meet the Lord in the air, and so we will always be with the Lord" (1 Thess. 4:16–17 NASB).

Conclusion

Roy helped write his own funeral service and could so conclusively say:

I know not where His islands lift
Their fronded palms in air;
I only know I cannot drift
Beyond His love and care.

—*John Greenleaf Whittier*

WEDDINGS

Title: A Simple Ceremony

Prelude

Seating of mothers

Solo

Processional

Scripture Reading: Mark 10:6–9; 1 Corinthians 13:7; Ephesians 5:33

Meditation: In light of these words, it is one of life's most hallowed moments to observe love made ready for marriage.

It also is a joyful moment when a new home is established. Yet with all of its happiness, there is the sense of sacredness and humility that makes the marriage altar a time of solemnity. Such a time is approached when two hearts are devoted to one another in love and committed to one another for life.

The teachings of Jesus tell us the true importance of marriage. He reminds us that God institutes marriage now even as he performed the first marriage ceremony ages ago. The secret of a beautiful marriage, then, is the fact that God unites two persons into one relationship. The God who made marriage possible as an institution is the same one who makes possible your marriage today.

We earnestly hope that you are dedicated to God and to one another in all that you are and for all you ever hope to be in the years to come.

Giving away the bride

The vows

Bride and Groom repeat the following vow:

I promise to love and cherish you,
to honor and sustain you,
in sickness as in health,
in poverty as in wealth,
in the bad that may darken our days,
in the good that may lighten our ways,
and to be true to you in all things
until death alone shall part us.

Ring ceremony

Dedication prayer

Pronouncement of marriage

Solo: "The Lord's Prayer"

Bride and groom kiss

Recessional

Title: An Informal Ceremony

Prelude

Seating of mothers

Special music

Processional

Meditation: Jesus spoke these words concerning marriage: "From the beginning of creation, 'God made them male and female.' 'For this reason a man shall leave his father and mother and be joined to his wife, and the two shall become one.' . . . What therefore God has joined together, let not man put asunder" (Mark 10:6–9 RSV).

I remind all of us today of the intense importance of marriage, that it is not just a human arrangement but a divine ordinance.

The Bible describes marriage as a covenant relationship rather than a mere contract. Although legally it may be broken, in God's eyes it is a lasting relationship. It is both a "leaving" and a "cleaving" experience. It is a covenant of unconditional love, acceptance, and availability. It is a covenant of honesty, sensitivity, and accountability. It is a covenant to a oneness of spirit and prayer.

The Message paraphrases 1 Corinthians 13:4–8 like this:

Love never gives up.
Love cares more for others than for self.
Love doesn't want what it doesn't have.
Love doesn't strut,
Doesn't have a swelled head,
Doesn't force itself on others,
Isn't always "me first,"
Doesn't fly off the handle,
Doesn't keep score of the sins of others,
Doesn't revel when others grovel,
Takes pleasure in the flowering of truth,
Puts up with anything,
Trusts God always,
Always looks for the best,
Never looks back,
But keeps going to the end.
Love never dies.

This is God's holy covenant. May it ever remain sacred to you.

Giving away the bride

Vows

(Groom to bride) I, ______, covenant with you, ______, to submit myself to God and to love you as Christ loved the church and gave himself for it; to nourish you and cherish you, even as the Lord does the church. I covenant to lead you, to provide for you, and to protect you in the power of the Holy Spirit.

(Bride to groom) I, ______, covenant with you, ______, to submit myself to God and to you as my husband as God's head for my life. I covenant to abide under your authority and your protection. I covenant to honor and respect you as my husband, in the power of the Holy Spirit.

Ring ceremony

Prayer

Pronouncement of marriage

Prayer

Bride and groom kiss

Recessional

Title: A Formal Church Ceremony

Prelude

Seating of grandparents

Seating of parents

Solo

Processional

Solo

Parents' permission: The Scripture says, "For this reason a man will leave his father and mother and be united to his wife, and the two will become one flesh" (Matt. 19:5 NIV). *(Groom's parents),* do you release *(groom)* to marry *(bride),* and will you receive her as his wife? (Parents respond: *We do.*)

(Bride's parents), when the servant found Rebekah for Isaac and requested her release to become Isaac's wife, her father said, "Behold, Rebekah is before you, take her and go, and let her be the wife of your master's son, as the LORD has spoken" (Gen. 24:51 RSV). So do you release *(bride)* to be *(groom's)* wife, and will you receive *(groom)* as her husband? (Parents respond: *We do.*)

Lighting of unity candles by parents

Meditation: This is a joyful and victorious experience, so let us worship in that spirit. As Psalm 100 says:

> Make a joyful noise unto the LORD, all ye lands.
> Serve the LORD with gladness: come before his presence with singing.
> Know ye that the LORD he is God: it is he that hath made us, and not we ourselves; we are his people, and the sheep of his pasture.
> Enter into his gates with thanksgiving, and into his courts with praise: be thankful unto him, and bless his name.
> For the LORD is good; his mercy is everlasting; and his truth endureth to all generations.

Proverbs 18:22 is an appropriate verse for this occasion: "He who finds a wife finds a good thing and obtains favor from the LORD" (NASB).

Marriage is a divine institution, which when rightly entered into, is blessed of God. Marriage is a companionship that involves mutual commitment and responsibility. So I encourage you together to dedicate your home to the Lord Jesus Christ.

Take the Bible, God's Word, for your guide. Talk with your heavenly Father every day in prayer. Give loyal devotion to his church, and live your lives as the Lord's willing servants. As you do, genuine joy will be yours, now and forever.

______ and ______, the Lord has uniquely prepared you for this time. Both of you are believers in Christ; both of you are spiritually grown Christians; and both of you have waited for God's special timing for your marriage.

In conclusion, I have a special challenge for you related to your names. ______, your name literally means ______ and suggests the spiritual quality of ______. May your life be a living extension of the meaning of your name. (Share the meaning of both names.)

Giving away the bride: Who gives this one to be wed in holy matrimony?

Father's reply: I do.

Vows: In God's sight vows are very important. You may join your right hands and repeat after me the vows of your covenant.

Groom to bride: I, ______, take you, ______, to be my wedded wife in the sight of God and these guests. I vow to love you as Christ loved his church, to honor and cherish you, and to always seek the Lord's direction for our lives.

I vow to lead you spiritually and to make Christ the center of our home.

I commit myself to serve your needs and to protect you.

I vow to submit myself to Jesus Christ and you in this act of marriage, until Jesus comes again or until death takes us to our heavenly home.

Bride to groom: I, ______, take you, ______, to be my wedded husband in the sight of God and these guests. I vow to submit to you as to the Lord. I acknowledge you as the head of our home, just as Christ is the head of the church.

I will love you, honor you, and reverence you.

Believing that God has joined us together, I will never leave you. In the name of our Lord and Savior Jesus Christ, I give myself to you to be your wife.

Ring Ceremony

(Exchange of rings by bride and groom answering the questions: Do you give this ring as a token of your love for ______?)

Prayer

Pronouncement: Having pledged your faith in and love to each other, and having sealed your solemn marital vows by the giving and receiving of rings; acting in the authority vested in me by the laws of this state, and looking to heaven for divine sanction, I do now pronounce you husband and wife in the presence of God and these assembled guests.

Solo

Unity Candle

Benediction

Bride and groom kiss

Announcement: Dear friends, I am happy to present to you Mr. and Mrs. ______.

Recessional

Sentence Sermonettes

Never put a question mark where God puts a period.

Your problems are never too great for God's grace.

Death can make you either rich or poor.

If life is to be a song, then love is the music.

Everybody wins in a contest of kindness.

Prayer should be our first resource, not our last resort.

You may give out but never give up.

It is always too soon to quit.

When doubt comes in the door, trust goes out the window.

The safety zone for the child of God is the center of God's will.

The best way to break a bad habit is to drop it.

Children have more need of models than of critics.

A day hemmed with prayer seldom unravels.

Reputation is what men and women think of us. Character is what God and angels know of us.

Bibles that are falling apart usually belong to people who aren't.

There is no lovelier way to thank God for your sight than by giving a helping hand to someone in the dark.

Every time the clock ticks, it says now . . . now . . . now.

Christmas: Christ is the reason for the season.

Happiness is a rainbow in your heart.

There is no greater joy than giving and no greater gift than love.

We always have time for the things we put first.

A kind word may be incomplete without action.

Compromise is the language of the devil.

If you have time to pray, God has time to listen.

The future is as bright as the promises of God. —William Carey

God is as near as a whispered prayer.

God will speak loudly enough for a willing soul to hear.

People brought up in Sunday school are seldom brought up in court.

God's work can only be done by God's people with God's power.

A willing helper does not wait until he or she is asked.

A pessimist is one who is always blowing out the light to see how dark it is.

Love is a gift to be used every day, not to be smothered and hidden away. —Edgar A. Guest

Many who plan to repent at the eleventh hour die at ten-thirty.

Nothing makes marriage rust like distrust.

Anytime is a perfect time for making someone happy.

The Lord never panics.

Love forgets mistakes!

God listens to prayer, not advice.

A small leak will sink a great ship.

No one plans to waste one's life; it just happens.

Life is too short to waste in idleness or empty pursuits.

Time that is past never returns.

God listens to our hearts rather than to our lips.

The day that starts without a plan will end in chaos.

Anyone can count the seeds in an apple, but only God can tell how many apples are in a seed.

Faith is the eyesight of the soul.

Everybody needs everybody.

Each day is a gift from God wrapped in his love.

Subject Index

Index of Scripture Texts

Acts

1 Corinthians

2 Corinthians

Galatians

Ephesians

Colossians